MEXICAN-AMERICANS IN THE UNITED STATES:

A Reader

MEXICAN-AMERICANS IN THE UNITED STATES:

A Reader

BY

JOHN H. BURMA

Schenkman Publishing Company, Inc.

Distributed by Canfield Press,
A Department of Harper & Row, Publishers

For information, address
Harper & Row, Publishers
49 East 33rd Street, New York, N. Y. 10016

TABLE OF CONTENTS

ACKNOWLEDGEMENT

The author expresses herewith his great debt to all those whose support has made this volume possible, and especially to Dorothy, Susan, Marcia, Lorie, and Mary Kay, without whose very active assistance it would never have been completed.

PREFACE

Among the large minority groups in the United States, unquestionably the least has been written about the Mexican Americans. Articles about Blacks in the United States have been published, in the last twenty years, at such a rate and in such a variety of sources as almost to overwhelm the bibliographer. This is not so for the Mexican Americans. On the contrary, until the last five years it was very difficult to secure information on this important ethnic group. Articles, scholarly studies, and essays not only were few but often were in obscure sources. For most Anglo Americans the Mexican American is a relatively little known group. It is no coincidence that Samora's book bears the title *La Raza: Forgotten Americans;* Heller's study, *Mexican American Youth: Forgotten at the Crossroads;* Sanchez's major work is titled *Forgotten People;* and the N.E.A.'s Tucson study "The Invisible Minority."

The major purpose of this book is to make available in compact form a number of worthwhile and up-to-date studies concerning Mexican Americans. Purposely the authors chosen are both Anglos and Mexican Americans. They include sociologists, anthropologists, historians, attorneys and judges, doctors, economists, public administrators, social workers, educators, and journalists, among others. The book represents no narrow approach, special theory, or selected view, except as expressed in a particular study or essay. It does not attempt to prove or disprove a particular point of view or action program. The author's aim is to present a multiplicity of aspects and a multiplicity of points of view, trusting to the judgment of the reader to recognize and evaluate each differing approach.

INTRODUCTION

There presently live in the United States of America approximately five million persons of Spanish-Mexican descent. This is to be compared with some 22 million Blacks, almost six million Jews, and over a million mainland Puerto Ricans. No exact numbers are available, because the United States does not make an accurate count. Decennial censuses, official samples, and state censuses sometimes have counted persons "of Spanish mother tongue" or "of Latin American surname" but there is no accurate measure of the number of Mexican Americans. Currently a movement is on to pressure the United States Bureau of the Census to count Mexican Americans in the 1970 census, but preliminary evidence indicates this will not occur.

Despite a lack of an exact counting, enough information exists to prove that Texas historically has had the largest percentage of the Mexican American population. The proportion in California, however, has increased rapidly so that at the present time the two states are about tied and between them contain approximately three-quarters of all Mexican Americans. Arizona, Colorado, and New Mexico account for the location of a majority of the remainder. Although only about one-tenth of all Mexican Americans now live outside the Southwest, that proportion is increasing steadily. Chicago, for example, has a large Mexican American population.

The literature dealing with the group whom the author — and most others writing on the topic — call Mexican Americans is by no means uniform in its terminology. This group, as a point of fact, is quite heterogeneous, little unified, and is described and evaluated differently by differing segments of the Anglo population. At the same time the sense of nationalism always present in this group has increased and diversified in recent years, as is true of American Blacks.

To clarify the author's own terminology, and to state for the uninitiated what little consensus exists, the following terms are presented. In Texas, the preferred term is "Latin American," or "Latin"; outside Texas or areas where Texans of Mexican descent settled, "Latin American" is more commonly used to designate persons from Central or South America. In most states "Mexican" most properly refers to a recent immigrant or a person from Mexico who expects to remain here temporarily. "Spanish American," as used in New Mexico and southern Colorado, refers to persons of mixed Spanish-Indian origin whose ancestors have lived in the area for 300 years (the word *hispano* is also used). Elsewhere this term is sometimes used, especially by Anglo Americans, to indicate any Mexican American who is at least upper middle class or to whom an Anglo wishes to be polite or flattering. Both within and outside the group itself, however, the most commonly recognized term is Mexican American. This is especially true in California. The use of a hyphen is grammatically inconsequential, but since the sizeable number of persons who consider themselves Americans of Mexican ancestry usually prefer not to use the hyphen, this author does not do so. Recently the term *Chicano* has gained reasonably wide acceptance, as has *la raza,*. A few militant nationalists have tried to popularize "brown," without apparent success. Numerous disrespectful terms are applied — cholo, spik, Mex, beaner, pachuco, greaser, and the like — and these terms should be shunned.

The ancestors of the Mexican Americans came voluntarily to the United States, some as long as 300 years ago, and one needs only to look at the names of older towns and cities in the Southwest to realize their widespread settlement. Much of the territory was grazing land, however, and the thousands of square miles of land were not matched by a population of equal size. The events by which the northern provinces of Mexico became the Southwestern United States do not provide a highly moral story, but become part of the United States they did, piece by piece. Only a small proportion of the ancestors of the present Mexican American population were on the land at that time; most came later as immigrants from Mexico.

No restriction was placed on immigration from the United States of Mexico to the United States of America until the immigration legislation which went into effect in 1968. Before World War I, however, few immigrants arrived. When World War I cut off the huge wave of immigration from Europe, and induced Southerners, black and white, to move to Northern industrial centers, a sizeable number of Mexican immigrants began to arrive, but few of them moved outside the Southwest. This tide continued through the prosperous 1920's; it was stopped and then reversed (both voluntarily and involuntarily) during the depression. When the extreme need for manpower arose during World War II, literally hundreds of thousands of Mexican nationals came to work in the fields and the industries of North America. Generally speaking, this immigration was welcomed, but welcomed as a source of cheap labor, probably temporary. In order to regularize this rapid flow, and to protect both the employer and the employee, the governments of Mexico and the United States entered into a mutual agreement whereby large numbers of selected workers, later called *braceros,* were recruited in Mexico and brought under contract to the United States, primarily to work as migratory agricultural laborers. Technically, though not in actuality, all the *bracero* returned to Mexico. But so successful was the program from the standpoint of factory-in-the-field employers that *braceros* continued to be imported into the 1960's, to the pleasure and utility of the employers and to the dismay, displacement, and harm of the native Mexican Americans and other migratory laborers who felt strongly that "foreigners" were taking jobs which should be theirs.

All during the 1940's, 1950's, and 1960's the stream of Mexican immigrants continued, although in some years considerably diminished. The present immigration law will not markedly affect this number, for up to 120,000 a year, plus wives and children of citizens, may still enter. The tremendous industrial increase in Mexico is yet insufficient to furnish adequate jobs for the fruits of its even more tremendous population increase, so undoubtedly a continued sizeable immigration will occur in the foreseeable future.

Throughout the long history of Mexican Americans, poverty has been their crucial problem. Mostly functionally illiterate (in English at least), often untrained in a skill saleable in the United States for more than a minimum wage, unable to function to full capacity in an alien culture, frequently expecting to return to Mexico some day, and hence forced by these conditions into the poorest jobs, the Mexican male in only a small proportion of cases was able to care for his usually large family above the level of poverty. Lack of American citizenship, or inability to meet the state residence requirements, or stubborn pride, or ignorance of proper procedures kept him from receiving the advantages of the welfare system to the same extent as Anglo and Black Americans in the same economic situation. In part by historic accident, a number of Mexican Americans from the 1940's to the mid 1960's found themselves engaged in migratory agricultural labor, and ranged in pursuit of such employment from the southernmost portions of Texas and California to the Canadian border and from coast to coast. Most such workers left the migratory streams as soon as they found better employment; many never made it. The minimum wage, employee compensation, NLRB protection, and unionization typically have been unavailable to migratory agricultural workers. These factors, among others, are the cause of *la huelga,* the much publicized strike and boycott against grape growers, which at this writing is about three years old.

It was not meant to leave the impression that the majority of Mexican Americans are migratory agricultural workers. They do make up the largest single segment of this occupational group, however, and others who are not migratory are engaged in local agriculture, but increasingly second, third and more generation *Chicanos* are finding industrial employment. Although such jobs may not be culturally appealing to some immigrants, their children and grandchildren have acculturated sufficiently to seek and hold such positions successfully. In every community with a sizeable number of Mexican Americans there are sales personnel, managers, and business owners, teachers, doctors, lawyers and dentists, and others in occupations ranging from college professor and judge to professional athlete and policeman. Slowly but clearly, the economic and occupational structure of the larger Mexican American community, the *barrio*, is changing.

For any immigrant group a chief source of acculturation, of upward mobility, and of personal adjustment has been the public schools. This is true also for Mexican Americans. For example, all second generation *Chicanos* speak some English, and some fourth generation *Chicanos* cannot converse in Spanish, but the American educational system functions far from perfectly in the instance of this ethnic group. Faced with a serious language handicap, a high proportion of *Chicano* children fall further and further behind each year in school, until for many of them dropping out becomes a reasonable and natural consequence. For three decades attempts have been made to solve this problem. While for some children the success is phenomenal, the great majority are subjected to exactly the same program as English-speaking, middle class Anglo children, with a wholly predictable lack of success. Sociologically speaking, many Mexican Americans now are marginal men; they partake partly of two cultures and wholly of neither. Only a very few are sufficiently familiar with both cultures to seek for themselves the best of each. The most advanced educational programs use the Spanish language and Mexican culture as strengths upon which to build a successful educational life for the Mexican American child. Not all are very successful, and even including the most successful programs, only a small proportion of Mexican American youth are exposed to anything other than the "normal" American educational pattern. The large number of children of migratory workers are a special case; at worst they grow up illiterate; at best they are retarded well beyond their potentialities and aspirations. That the average reading ability of students in the Mexican American *barrio* in East Los Angeles is slightly worse than in the Black ghetto of Watts is not surprising. What is surprising is the number of *Chicano* youngsters who are academically superior.

Throughout their history Mexican Americans have been subjected to prejudice and discrimination: in jobs, housing, voting, education, civil rights, organizations, and social activities. Traditionally, Mexican Americans are ranked close to the bottom on studies of social distance. Yet despite all this, prejudice is rarely the blinding, traumatic force it has often been for Blacks. Anglos are always more or less willing to make exceptions. But if a Mexican American makes only a few strides toward acculturation, if he is dark in color, poor, uneducated and unskilled, and lives in a *barrio* and these things are obvious, he can expect prejudice and discrimination. If he is acculturated or assimilated, light in color, well-to-do, educated, engaged in a "status" occupation, and lives outside the *barrio* he will receive little if any overt discrimination. For the latter type person and his children, the rate of intermarriage with Anglos is relatively high.

Religiously, Mexican Americans tend overwhelmingly to be Catholics. This does not indicate any greater or any less interest in religion than is true of Protestants or Jews. Like many Protestants, many Catholic Mexican American males "have their religion in their wife's name." For a number of decades the major Protestant denominations have maintained mission churches among Mexican Americans, with slow but observable results. Recently the pentacostal type of denominations can claim increasing success in their proselytizing activities. In response, the Catholic Church achieved what might be considered a rebirth of interest in and concern for the religious, civil, and economic well-being of their Mexican American constituency.

In the *Chicano* community the family is recognized as a major and basic institution. This concern is honored verbally more in the breach than in the practice. As a broad generalization one might say that the stated cultural norms of the Mexican American subculture are "higher" than in the case of the Anglo cultural norms but the divergence between the "ideal" norm and the actual behavior is greater than in the Anglo society. For most *Chicanos*, the family is considered very important, children are desired, and there are differentiated male and female marital roles. There is still a tendency to "watch" girls more closely, but to grant greater freedom to boys, as compared with the Anglo norm. Where possible, the extended family pattern is retained, and interaction which the Anglo has with his neighbors is more likely among Mexican Americans to occur within the kinship group. The strengths of the Mexican American family may well be coveted by Anglo society and culture.

During most of the history of Spanish-speaking people in the United States they have been a politically impotent group. A variety of factors contributed to this condition, including a high proportion of lower class members, an expectation of returning to Mexico, a feeling of "What's the use?," discrimination and violation of civil rights, small populations except in a few localities, internecine quarrels, and a distrust of government as a solution for problems. Consequently, outside of New Mexico, few Spanish-speaking people achieved positions of leadership or even sought them. After World War II the Spanish-speaking veterans asserted the new values and attitudes they brought home with them, and Mexican American political organizations began to bear fruit in the form of a few elected Spanish-speaking officials. The League of United Latin American Citizens, the G.I. Forum, and other groups became prominent, although no widely based, grass roots, nationwide organization exists. During the 1960's, the rise of nationalistic attitudes among Blacks is paralleled, at a lower level, by the rise of nationalistic attitudes among urban Mexican Americans. They, too, developed militants, semi-militants, and ethnically oriented liberals. Boycotts, marches, sit-ins, and riots occur, but with far less frequency, far less effect, and involve a lower proportion of the *Chicanos* than is true of the Black population. A resurgence of pride in *la raza* and in things Mexican, coupled with a decline in interest in assimilation and a desire for cultural pluralism is resulting in a new force, a new strength, and a new unity in the *barrios*. Full unity seems unlikely to be achieved in the near future, but one cannot but believe that the new concept of "Today, not mañana" will bring greater strength to *la raza* and a better life to many of its people.

GENERAL CHARACTERISTICS

GENERAL CHARACTERISTICS

As was stated in the Introduction, demographic data on the Mexican American group are scarce because most government data sources do not distinguish between Mexican Americans and Anglos or only gather and report information on specific locations. Were such raw data available, to present a "national" statistical profile would be highly misleading without good comparative data for other groups as well, and this data is also inadequate.

Suppose one did try to summarize such data, for instance, for America as a whole. What would happen to the "beautiful people" of the Jet Set, the Black Panthers, and the Montana cowboys? Each of these groups, and a myriad others, which contribute to the uniqueness that is America, would lose their individuality and be swallowed up into an amorphous whole like that reported by the public opinion polls.

Mexican Americans, too, differ greatly among themselves, and what is true of one subgroup may be false for another. The "Latins" of South Texas are largely rural, close to the Mexican culture in many ways, and their single largest occupation is agricultural labor. The "Mexican Americans" of East Los Angeles are highly urban, close to the Anglo culture, and agricultural labor is wholly insignificant as an occupation for them. The Spanish Americans of New Mexico and southern Colorado are different from either. Although increasingly urbanized, their heritage is heavily rural, and they have had relatively little contact with Mexico since 1800. They have a much higher proportion of owners of agricultural land than either of the other groups. At least on the county level they hold a large number of political offices, probably a higher raw number than the California or the Texas group, although outnumbered fifteen to one by either of them.

To make generalizations lumping together the above three groups is dangerous, but this is not the only type of division observable. Scholarly studies show considerable inter-generational differences within the Mexican American group; the experiences of a young man now 21 years old are far different than were those of his 45 year old father, and these differences — with their concurrent attitudes, values, and behavior patterns — appear to be increasing. Compounding these variations are those engendered by virtue of some persons being immigrants from Mexico (20% in Los Angeles County), some second generation, some third generation, and so on. There is evidence that the direction of the generational change is toward greater assimilation. Third generation Mexican Americans in Los Angeles, for example, are more likely to marry Anglos than to marry immigrants from Mexico.

A large number of Mexican American children still are unable to handle English well enough to compete equally with Anglo children in an Anglo school, but this proportion is decreasing. The number of Mexican American students in institutions of higher education is proportionately even less, in California for example, than for Blacks or any other minority. California now has a state-wide program aimed at alleviating this problem, and Mexican American Studies programs are ı ow the rule rather than the exception at California colleges and universities. In Texas the situation is especially serious. The average number of years of school completed for Anglos is 10.8 years, for nonwhites 8.1 years, but only 4.7 years for persons of Spanish surname from Spanish-speaking homes. Increased use of Spanish as a medium of instruction in the primary grades and increased recruiting of Spanish-speaking teachers permit a prognosis of some lessening of this problem in the fairly near future. Other potentially significant programs include teaching both English and Spanish in the primary grades to all children, instruction in Mexican history and culture, preschool classes, adult education programs for parents of bilingual children, special courses for dropouts or potential dropouts, and special trade, vocational, or technical programs.

One of the keenest problems of Mexican Americans everywhere is their low income and poor occupational status. Although rapidly leaving or being driven from the migratory agricultural labor which was so common an occupation for them a generation ago, *Chicanos* everywhere tend to be concentrated in the lowest paying occupations and to suffer from unemployment at a significantly higher rate than Anglos. A recent and yet unpublished research report by Burma, Cretser, and Seacrest compares intermarriages and intramarriages for Anglos and the larger minority groups in Los Angeles County. The twenty-eight numerically largest types of intramarriage and intermarriage were compared by mean occupational level as reported on marriage license applications. Persons of Spanish surname who married other persons of Spanish surname had the lowest mean occupational ranking of all, 28th out of 28 possibilities. On the other hand persons of Spanish surname, who traditionally have ranked very low on social distance scales, were found to rank high in composite social acceptance; i.e., they intermarried with all groups, and at a rate considerably greater than the norm.

The selection "Mexican-Americans: A Handbook for Educators," by Jack D. Forbes, is an example of the need to present at least a minimum of information to teachers about the cultural background and Mexican heritage of the Mexican American children whom they teach. The Far West Laboratory for Educational Research and Development at first intended to make this summary available to all teachers who wished it, but the demand was so great and so immediate that they were financially unable to continue, so that its distribution had to be taken over by the federal government through the Superintendent of Documents.

In "A Comparison of the Mexican American Subculture with the Oscar Lewis Culture of Poverty Model," John H. Burma presents in summary form the chief characteristics of the Mexican American subculture, showing that it is presently a blend of the Mexican and the American-Anglo cultures. These characteristics are then compared with a model of the culture of poverty proposed by Oscar Lewis, who is the outstanding anthropological proponent of the theory of a subculture of poverty. The comparison shows and the reader will recognize both likenesses and uniquenesses in these two subcultures, which clearly are not equivalent or synonymous.

Dr. Horacio Ulibarri, a native Spanish American, interviewed in depth samples of Spanish Americans, Mexican Americans, and Mexican Nationals in order to ascertain certain of their social and attitudinal characteristics. In "Social and Attitudinal Characteristics of Spanish-speaking Migrant and Exmigrant Workers in the Southwest," he reports that no basic differences were found between the three groups. Each had a strong present-time orientation and a strong present-time self-projection. Each group showed a strong dissatisfaction and bitterness in their inability to earn a better living, and expressed an overwhelming fear of want. Their destitution basically dominated all their orientations toward life, resulting in negative attitudes and disorientation. They indicated little motivation toward helping themselves, and their existence was one of fatalism and anomie. The family emerged as the strongest area of life activity and the one which provided the greatest satisfactions.

In the selection "The Changing Mexican-American in Southern California," Fernando Penalosa, a professional sociologist, presents his view of the modern Mexican American. He find the view of the Mexican American as a foreign, unskilled agricultural worker to be anachronistic. At least in southern California this group is 80% native-born and 85% urban and over half are semi-skilled, skilled, or white collar workers. The Anglo-Mexican semi-caste system broke down during World War II, he reports, and trained professionals and political activists of Mexican descent are working energetically to promote the educational, economic, and social advancement of the group.

MEXICAN-AMERICANS*

JACK D. FORBES

Approximately five million persons of Mexican ancestry reside in the United States. Most live in the states of California, Arizona, New Mexico, Texas, and Colorado, but a large number have made homes in the greater Chicago area and in other industrial centers. In many sections of the Southwest, particularly along the border from San Diego, California, to Brownsville, Texas, Mexican-Americans are the majority population, and their language and culture serve to provide the entire region with much of its charm and distinctiveness.

Modern-day Mexican-Americans play a vital role in the industrial, agricultural, artistic, intellectual, and political life of the Southwest but the significance of this group cannot be measured solely in terms of present-day accomplishments. It is certain that the Southwest as we know it would not exist without the Mexican-Spanish heritage. That which sets New Mexico off from Oklahoma, and California off from Oregon is in large measure the result of the activities of the ancestors of our fellow citizens of Mexican descent. Our way of life has been and is being immeasurably enriched by their presence north of the present-day international boundary.

Prior to 1821 (when the modern Mexican nation won its independence from Spain), a Mexican was usually a person who spoke the Mexican or Aztec language (Náhuatl). In fact, the early Spaniards almost always referred to the Aztec people as Mexicans. This practice has continued in modern Mexico where the Náhuatl language is called "Mexicano" by the common people and where writers usually speak of the Mexican Empire rather than the Aztec Empire. The modern people of Mexico, who are said by scholars to be about 80% native Indian in their ancestry, are proud of their descent from the ancient Mexicans and trace the history of their people back to the builders of the magnificent cities of Teotihuacán, Monte Albán, and Chichén Itzà.

The Mexican heritage of the United States commences long before the time of Christ. About the year 4000 B.C. Indians living in southern New Mexico learned how to raise corn as a result of contacts with

*Abridged from *Mexican-Americans: A Handbook for Educators*, Far West Laboratory for Educational Research and Development, Berkeley, California.

Mexico (where that remarkable plant was first domesticated). Other crops, including squash and beans, were subsequently borrowed and still later (about 500 A.D.) Southwestern Indians began to develop the Pueblo Indian Civilization. This advanced way of life, which still flourishes in Arizona and New Mexico, was largely based upon Mexican influences in architecture, pottery-making, clothing, religion and government.

In about 1000 A.D. a people known as the Hohokam moved from northern Mexico into what is now southern Arizona. They brought many advanced traits with them, including the construction of monumental irrigation systems, stone etching techniques, and, very possibly, new political concepts. The Hohokams constructed a large center at Snaketown, Arizona and spread their influence widely, apparently establishing a colony at Flagstaff and trading their pottery as far as the San Fernando Valley in California. During the same general period Mexican influences seem to have reached the Mississippi Valley and advanced cultures developed there. The Indians of the southern United States developed a Mexican-style religious and political orientation and constructed small pyramid-temples while the Ohio River Indians built fanciful effigy mounds, sometimes in the shape of serpents.

The ancient Mexicans excelled as artists, craftsmen, architects, city planners, engineers, astronomers, statesmen, and warriors. They also developed centers of higher education, wrote excellent poetry, and produced many historical and religious works. One philosopher-king, Nezahualcóyotl, put forth the view that there was only one Creator-God, while Maya scientists developed a calendar which is more accurate than the one we use today.

In the 1520's the Spaniards commenced their conquest of Mexico. Although the Aztecs were conquered quickly, in spite of a noble defense of Tenochtitlán led by Cuauhtémoc (the present-day national hero of Mexico), the rest of what is now Mexico was subdued only very gradually. In fact, many Indian groups in northern Mexico and in the jungles of Yucatan-Guatemala were never conquered. Also, many of the Mexicans who were subdued never lost their identity and this explains why at least one-tenth of the people of modern Mexico speak native languages, often in addition to Mexico Spanish.

The Spanish invasion did not bring an end to the vitality of the Mexican, as churches, aqueducts, and palaces of the colonial period are essentially the result of native labor and craftsmanship. Educated

Mexicans helped to record the history of ancient Mexico and for a brief period a Mexican university, Santa Cruz del Tlaltelolco, flourished, training many persons of native ancestry. The conquering Spaniards, if of high rank, often married native noblewomen and the common Spaniards married ordinary Indian women, in both cases contributing to the mixture of the Spanish and native Mexican races.

The number of Spaniards who came to Mexico was always very small and the growth and expansion of the Spanish Empire depended upon the use of native and mixed-blood (mestizo) servants, settlers, craftsmen, miners, and soldiers. The conquest of the north would have been impossible without Mexicans and every major settlement, from Santa Fe, New Mexico, to Saltillo, Coahuila, had its Mexican district *(barrio* or *colonia)*. Many of the settlers taken by Diego de Vargas to northern New Mexico in the 1690's were called "Españoles Mexicanos," that is, "Aztec-Spaniards"; and Juan de Oñate, was the second governor of that province. Every major expedition, including those of Coronado and De Soto, utilized Mexicans, and eight Mexican soldiers were stationed at San Diego, California in 1769 by Gaspar de Portolá. The northward movement of Spain into the southwestern United States was, therefore, a Spanish-Mexican affair. It was Spanish-led but depended for its success upon Mexicans and mixed-bloods. In California, for example, well over half of the Spanish-speaking settlers were of Indian or mixed ancestry and the forty-six founders of Los Angeles in 1781 included only two persons called Spaniards, and their wives were Indian.

Gradually the way of life brought to America by the Europeans became mixed with native Mexican influences, until the life of the common people became a blend of Spanish-Arabic and Indian traits, much as the culture of England after 1066 became a blend of French-Latin and Anglo-Celtic traditions. The Spaniards used the Mexican language for governmental, scholarly, and religious purposes for several generations and many Mexican words, such as *coyote, elote, jicara, tamal, chile, chocolate, jacal, ocelote,* and hundreds of others, became part of Spanish as spoken in Mexico. Roman Catholic religious practice was modified by many Indian customs and devotion to the Virgin of Guadalupe has had a lasting impact upon the Catholic faith.

Meanwhile, the Mexican people intermixed with diverse tribes and eventually began to absorb both the non-Mexican Indian and the Spaniard himself. This process of migration and mixture made possible the creation of the independent Mexican republic in 1821, after a ten-year struggle for freedom.

Independent Mexico was to have a lasting impact upon the southwestern United States. Many Mexican leaders were imbued with new republican and equalitarian ideals and they sought to implement these reforms. Legislatures and elected local councils were established in California and elsewhere, the Indians and mixed-bloods were granted complete legal equality and full citizenship, and foreigners were encouraged to take up a new life as Mexicans. On the other hand, many persons found it hard to break with the authoritarian legacy of Spain, and republican reforms were often subverted. Foreign settlers did not always choose to become good Mexican citizens, as for example the Anglo-Texans who refused to set their slaves free or to obey Mexican land-title and tariff regulations.

The early Mexican governments were often beset by financial difficulties and progress was difficult in the face of widespread illiteracy and an unequal distribution of wealth and power. Gradually, however, these negative conditions were overcome and the Mexican people advanced along the road of democracy, albeit with backward steps from time to time.

In what is now the United States, Mexicans were active in the development of new mining regions (gold was discovered in California in 1842, for example), opening up new routes for travelers (as from Santa Fe to Los Angeles via Las Vegas, Nevada), founding schools (some twenty-two teachers were brought to California in the 1830's and a seminary was established at Santa Ynez), establishing new towns (Sonoma, California is an example), and setting up printing presses (as in California in 1835). The north was a frontier region and was, therefore, not in the forefront of Mexican cultural progress, but it did benefit from developments originating further south.

Commencing in the 1830's Mexican settlers began moving north once again. Some 200 craftsmen, artisans, and skilled laborers sailed to California in that decade, and soon overland immigrants from Sonora were joining them. Thereafter a steady stream of Sonorans reached California, only to be turned into a flood by the discovery of gold in the Sierra Nevada foothills in 1848. The Sonorans were often experienced miners and their techniques dominated the California Gold Rush until steam-powered machinery took over at a later date. Chihuahuans and other Mexicans also "rushed" to California by sea and by land and they too exercised an impact upon mining as well as upon commerce.

The United States-Mexican War of 1846-1848 did not immediately alter the character of the Southwest greatly, except in eastern Texas and northern California. The Gold Rush changed the language of central California after 1852 (when Mexican miners were largely expelled from the Sierra Nevada mines), but Mexicans continued to dominate the life of the region from San Luis Obispo, California, to San Antonio, Texas. Southern California, for example, remained a Spanish-speaking region until the 1870's with Spanish-language and bi-lingual public schools, Spanish-language newspapers, and Spanish-speaking judges, elected officials, and community leaders. The first Constitution of the State of California, created in part by persons of Mexican background, established California as a bi-lingual state and it remained as such until 1878. Similar conditions prevailed in other southwestern regions.

Gradually, however, Anglo-Americans from the east who were unsympathetic toward Mexican culture came to dominate the Southwest. Having no roots in the native soil and being unwilling to become assimilated to the region, these newcomers gradually transformed the schools into English- language institutions where no Spanish was taught, constructed buildings with an "eastern" character, pushed Mexican leaders into the background, and generally caused the Mexican-American, as he has come to be termed, to become a forgotten citizen.

By the 1890's, on the other hand, tourists and writers began to rediscover the "Spanish" heritage and "landmark" clubs commenced the process of restoring the decaying missions of the Southwest. A "Spanish" cultural revival was thus initiated, and soon it began to influence architectural styles as well as the kind of pageantry which has typified much of the Southwest ever since. Unfortunately, the Mexican-Indian aspect of the region's heritage was at first overlooked and the Mexican-American people benefited but little from the emphasis upon things Spanish.

In the early 1900's a new group of Mexican immigrants began to enter the United States, attracted by job offers from agricultural developers who wished to open up virgin lands in southern California, Colorado, Arizona, and south Texas. During World War I and the 1920's this movement became a flood, a flood which largely overwhelmed the older group of Mexican-Americans (except in northern New Mexico and southern Colorado) and became ancestral to much of the contemporary Spanish-speaking population in the Southwest.

These hundreds of thousands of new Mexican-Americans had to overcome many obstacles as they attempted to improve their life patterns. Anglo-Americans were prejudiced against people who were largely of native American, brown-skinned origin, who were poor, who of necessity lived in substandard or self-constructed homes, who could not speak English, and who were not familiar with the workings of a highly competitive and acquisitive society. Gradually, and in spite of the trauma of the Great Depression (when all sorts of pressures were used to deport Mexican-Americans to Mexico), *los de la raza,* as Mexicans in the United States frequently refer to themselves, climbed the economic ladder and established stable, secure communities in the Southwest.

The Mexican-American community was not simply a passive force during this long period of transition. Everywhere mutual benefit societies, patriotic Mexicanist organizations, newspapers, social clubs, small stores and restaurants were founded, and artisans began to supply Anglo-American homes with pottery and other art objects.

Mexican-American mutual benefit organizations soon commenced the task of helping to upgrade the status of agricultural and industrial workers by seeking better wages and conditions of employment. During the 1920's and 1930's Mexican-American labor organizers, with little formal education and less money, traveled from region to region, helping in the unionization process. Ever since, labor leaders have played an important role in Mexican-American affairs and Spanish speaking union officers are a significant element in the structure of organized labor in the Southwest. Current efforts directed toward the unionization of agricultural workers and obtaining a minimum wage for agricultural laborers, from California to south Texas, are being led by organizers of Mexican ancestry.

During the past twenty years the cultural and political life of Mexican-Americans has advanced remarkably. Today, fine Spanish-language newspapers blanket the Southwest and Far West, some of which are daily periodicals with the latest dispatches from Europe and Mexico. Magazines, including bi-lingual ones, issue forth with slick paper and exciting photographs. Spanish-language radio and television stations reach much of the Southwest, and theatrical-musical productions of a folk or modern nature are frequently staged for the benefit of both *los de la raza* and Anglos.

Mexican-American civic, business and political leaders are now prominent in many regions, and they include within their ranks members of Congress, mayors, and all types of professional people. The image of the Mexican heritage has vastly improved due not only to the activities of individual Mexican-Americans, but also due to the cultural renaissance occurring in Mexico itself concurrent with the incredible richness of the Mexican past revealed by contemporary archaeological discoveries. Anglo-Americans have ceased emphasizing the Spanish legacy at the expense of the Mexican, and a more healthy climate of mutual understanding has evolved.

Educationally, Mexican-American progress has been striking in individual cases but has been slow over-all. Generally speaking, whenever Anglo-Americans gained control over a particular state or region in the Southwest they chose to import the kinds of public schools developed in the Middle West or East. Hispano-Mexican and bi-lingual schools were replaced by English-language, Anglo-oriented schools from which Mexican-American children were sometimes excluded. After the turn of the century greater numbers of Spanish-speaking youth began to attend schools, but the latter were either irrelevant to the background, language, and interests of the pupils (as in New Mexico) or were segregated, marginal elementary schools (as in much of California and Texas). Normally, secondary-level education was not available to Mexican-American pupils except in an alien Anglo-dominated school (and even that opportunity was often not present in many rural counties in Texas and elsewhere).

During the post-World War II period segregated schools for Mexican-Americans largely disappeared, except where residential segregation operated to preserve the ethnic school. Greater numbers of Mexican-Americans entered high school and enrollment in college also increased, although slowly. Nevertheless, drop-out rates remain high, even today; and it is also true that the typical school serving Mexican-Americans makes little, if any, concession to the Mexican heritage, the Spanish language, or to the desires of the Mexican-American community.

In summary, the Mexican heritage of the United States is very great indeed. For at least 6,000 years Mexico has been a center for the dissemination of cultural influences in all directions, and this process continues today. Although the modern United States has outstripped Mexico in technological innovation, the Mexican people's marked ability in the visual arts, music, architecture, and political affairs makes them a constant contributor to the heritage of all of North America. The Mexican-American people of the United States serve as a bridge for the diffusion northward of valuable Mexican traits, serve as a reservoir for the preservation of the ancient Hispano-Mexican heritage of the Southwest, and participate directly in the daily life of the modern culture of the United States.

The United States' five million citizens of Mexican origin do not form a homogeneous group with identical values, customs, and aspirations. One can divide the Mexican-American community along class (economic) lines, from the affluent rancher, businessman, or public official to the migrant farm worker or isolated self-sufficient farmer in the mountains of New Mexico. One can also divide the Mexican-American community on the basis of the degree to which the individual has become Anglicized and integrated into the larger society. One can further classify Mexican-Americans according to the degree of Caucasian ancestry which they possess, or according to whether or not they object to being called "Mexicans" and prefer to be called "Spanish-American." But whichever type of classification system one uses, it is clear that there is no single way of life possessed by our Mexican-American people.

Nonetheless, it is possible for purposes of generalization to ignore those individuals who are non-typical and to concentrate upon the large majority of Mexican-Americans who have many things in common.

First, the Mexican-American community is basically proud of being of Mexican background and sees much of value in the Mexican heritage. By means of folk-level educational agencies, such as benevolent societies, patriotic organizations, and the extended family, many Mexican traits are kept alive, either as functioning parts of the individual's personal life or at least as items with which he feels some degree of familiarity. Mexican arts and crafts, music, dances, cooking, family structure, concepts of the community, the Spanish language, and other characteristics, are maintained in this manner. Spanish-language radio and television stations, newspapers, and magazines, and Mexican-American political organizations, help to carry on this process as well as to bring in new cultural influences from Mexico. In short, the Mexican-American community possesses many internal agencies which serve to maintain a sense of belonging to *la raza* and which also serve to carry foward aspects of the Mexican heritage.

In many rural areas of the Southwest, as well as in some wholly Mexican urban districts, most adults can be described as belonging primarily to the culture of northern Mexico. The Spanish language is universally favored over English and the bilateral extended family provides a satisfying and strong social background for the individual. In other urban districts, as well as in suburban regions and on the fringes of Mexican neighborhoods in rural areas, one finds numerous Mexican-Americans who are completely bi-lingual, or who in some cases favor English over Spanish. These people have not become "Anglos," but their Mexican cultural heritage has become blended with Anglo-American traits.

Unfortunately, many younger Mexican-Americans, educated in Anglo-oriented schools, have not been able to relate in a positive manner toward either the north Mexican or Mexican-Anglo mixed cultures, primarily because their parents have been unable to effectively transmit the Spanish language and Mexican heritage to them. At the same time the public schools have either attacked or completely ignored that heritage and have attempted to substitute an often watered-down Anglo heritage. The youth subjected to this pressure have not ordinarily become Anglos, though, because of a feeling of being rejected by the dominant society (because of frequently experienced prejudice and discrimination) and by the schools (because the curriculum is so totally negative as regards their own personal and cultural background). These young people have frequently developed a mixed Anglo-Mexican subculture of their own, based upon a dialect of Spanish heavily modified by an ingenious incorporation of English words and new expressions and upon a "gang" style of social organization.

Another important factor which retards the complete absorption of partially Anglicized Mexican-Americans into the larger society is the fact that more than 95% of Mexicans are part-Indian, 40% are full-blood Indians, and most of the mixed-bloods have more Indian than non-Indian ancestry. Mexican-Americans are, therefore, a racial as well as a cultural minority and the racial differences which set them apart from Anglos cannot be made to "disappear" by any "Americanization" process carried on in the schools.

The larger Mexican-American community is in a process of rapid cultural transition, wherein most individuals are acquiring a mixed Anglo-Mexican culture, while smaller numbers are marrying into or otherwise being absorbed into the dominant Anglo society. An unfortunate aspect of this process is that extremely valuable Mexican traits, such as the strong extended family, the tendency toward mutual aid, the Spanish language, artistic and musical traditions, folk dances, fine cooking, and such personality characteristics as placing more emphasis upon warm interpersonal relationships than upon wealth acquisition tend to be replaced by what many critics might suggest are the lowest common denominator of materialistic, acquisitive, conformist traits, typical of some elements within the Anglo-American population. That this is occurring is largely a result of the fact that many Mexican-American graduates of the public schools feel ambivalent about their own self-identity and about cultural values. They have been deprived of a chance to learn about the best of the Mexican heritage and, at the same time, have been, in effect, told to become Anglicized. They tend, therefore, to drift into the dominant society without being able to make sound value judgments based upon cross-cultural sophistication.

On the other hand, the Mexican-American community considered in its entirety is a vital, functioning societal unit with considerable ability to determine its own future course of development. It may well succeed in developing a reasonably stable bicultural and bi-lingual tradition which will provide a healthy atmosphere for future generations and which may prove attractive to many Anglos. In any case it is clear that the proximity of Mexico will insure a continual flow of Mexican cultural influences across the border and the Mexican-American community, as a bicultural population, will not soon disappear.

A COMPARISON OF THE MEXICAN AMERICAN SUBCULTURE
WITH THE OSCAR LEWIS CULTURE OF POVERTY MODEL

JOHN H. BURMA

The concept of subculture is an increasingly used and useful one in modern sociology and anthropology. Borrowing from the anthropologists, sociologists now study such disparate subcultures as those of prisoners, adolescents, Mexican Americans, Amish, homosexuals, Chinese Americans, hippies, juvenile delinquents, Negro Americans, and persons living in poverty. The concept of a subculture must be defended or condemned on the same grounds as any proper concept; i.e., is it a theoretical tool which produces greater clarity and hence aids theoretical understanding.

Milton Gordon, in his *Assimilation in American Life,*[1] points out that culture as a concept is used to refer to the social heritage or way of life of a particular society at a particular time. Thus one speaks of culture, and subculture, in terms of time, and location, and group. Gordon also points out that in any large, complex, multigroup nation, cultural uniformity is impossible and should not be expected. When any sizeable segment of a multi-group society has developed a rather unique way of life, from which members receive status and recognition, norms, sources of support and identification, and meaningful reference groups, it is proper to call that way of life a subculture. Members of a subculture are at least partially aware of the parent, conventional culture and its norms, and they can and usually do behave, on occasion, in terms of the larger culture.

At the present stage of theory building or concept construction relating to subcultures there is no sharp, consensual definition, no "right" or unique definition or usage. James Coleman speaks of adolescent youth culture, and Earl Bell uses the concept of college subculture; Schrag, Sykes, Clemmer, and others make free use of the term prison subculture, and Cohen, Cloward, Ohlin, Miller, Bloch and

17

others write about delinquent subcultures. Liebow describes the subculture of Negro street-corner men. Schnur uses the concept of the subculture of the dope addict, and so in a somewhat different way does Finestone. Killmorgan's study of the Amish subculture handles the concept differently than Cohen does in his description of homosexual subculture, and my own attempts to describe as a subculture the way of life of the permanent migratory agricultural laborer differ from both.

It is somewhat of a theoretical oversimplification, but a useful one, to think of a subculture as a group adaptation system to a situation, which situation and which adaptation are largely shared by members of a sizeable group. This adaptation system, this subculture, is transmitted by socialization, either generationally or by peers.

One properly may study many aspects of a subculture; its sources, its pervasiveness and limits, its traits, its relation to the parent culture or cultures, or its relation to other subcultures; or one may bend one's efforts toward an exact description of the structure, functions and traits of a subculture. This paper chooses to consider two somewhat related subcultures, and to attempt synoptically to analyze how these cultures compare with each other and with the parent cultures. Thus it deals with the concept "subculture of poverty," especially as described by Oscar Lewis, and also with that more well-known amalgam of the Mexican and American cultures which is properly called the Mexican American subculture.

That the concept "subculture" is a useful and proper one does not prove that every set of traits or behaviors one discovers can properly be called a subculture. It is well agreed that it is proper to apply this concept to the subculture of Mexican Americans; there is less agreement, but considerable evidence, that the subculture of poverty also is a reality.

There is one point of view which holds that no subculture of poverty exists. The "subcultural" uniformities observed among the poor are seen as resulting from strictly limited choices, not subcultural imperatives. Thus the repetitive behavior among delinquent groups is seen as logical and predictable responses to certain conditions, rather than as subcultural patterns. Liebow, in *Tally's Corner,* illustrates this point of view excellently in regard to the observed "serial monogamy" of the lower class urban Negro.[2] His interpretation is that one may look at the succession of mates as being a cultural referent, and by so doing use it as an illustration of subcultural behavior. Leibow believes a more correct appraisal, however, is that this is not a subcultural difference, but rather is to be seen as a series of marriages, each of which it was hoped would follow the pattern of the larger culture, but each of which failed, and was then followed by another which failed, and so on. The succession of mates pattern, using this approach, is seen as seeking the cultural model of the larger society, but being a series of failures to achieve it. Purported subcultural generation similarities in behavior need not result from cultural transmission, but may result instead from failure in both generations to achieve the behavioral patterns of the larger society.

This paper recognizes but does not address itself to the above conflict of opinion. The underlying assumptions presented here are only that a Mexican American subculture does exist, and that a hypothetical model of a subculture of poverty has been presented by Oscar Lewis. Regardless of what is found about the eventual validity of the Lewis model, it can be compared to the Mexican American actuality. Conversely, one legitimately could compare either with Liebow's "failure model" if he wished.

Oscar Lewis, in his *Five Families* says, "Poverty in modern nations . . . becomes a dynamic factor which . . . creates a subculture of its own. One can speak of the culture of the poor, for it has its own modalities and distinctive social and psychological consequences for its members . . . The culture of poverty cuts across regional, rural-urban and even national boundaries. I am impressed . . . by the remarkable similarities in family structure, the nature of kinship ties, the quality of husband-wife and parent-child relations, time orientation, spending patterns, value systems, and the sense of community found in lower class settlements in London, in Puerto Rico, in Mexico City slums, in Mexican villages, and among lower class Negroes in the United States."[3]

Michael Harrington seems correct in *The Other America*[4] when he suggests that what he calls the "old poor" were part of the parent culture, albeit a disadvantaged part; but that many persons in those groups he calls the "new poor" are so alienated from the parent culture that they now possess a separate culture of their own, the subculture of poverty. One of Oscar Lewis' contributions in his book *La Vida* is that a distinction must always be made between poverty, which is financial, and the subculture of poverty, which is a way of life shared by some poverty-striken people.[5] He repeats this in an article in the *Scientific*

American,[6] and hypothesizes that in some societies, especially either primitive or socialistic ones, there is no subculture of poverty; on the other hand, in rapidly developing but not as yet fully developed countries, the great majority of the urban poor participate in the subculture of poverty. He estimates that possibly 20% of poverty-striken people in the United States participate in the subculture of poverty. The highlander from Appalachia, for example, may be very poor, but he has his own subculture, which in many ways differs from the subculture of poverty. A considerably higher proportion of the Spanish speaking people in the United States partake of the Mexican American subculture. With this as a background, let us first partially describe and analyze the Mexican American subculture.

The parent Mexican culture, which is itself something of an amalgam, has been introduced into the United States by immigrants each year for many decades. Those persons entering our borders from Mexico tend to find themselves in a different situation requiring new adaptations for success. In actual practice the immigrant and his children retain, or retain in modified character, some of the old Mexican culture traits. Also they accept and use, either directly or in modified character, some of the new Anglo culture traits. The result is a mixture, a reasonably fluid one, of the parent cultures, a mixture which quite properly may be considered a Mexican American subculture, with traits and characteristics which stem from both cultures, but whose configuration is unique, and whose amalgamation certainly is different from either of the parent cultures. Because of its dynamic nature, this hybrid culture is shifting, changing in time and place, and Mexican Americans do not all partake of it to the same degree. A number of studies show that there is a significant correlation between generation and culture. There are marked exceptions, but as a broad generalization the first generation is the most Mexican in culture patterns and the third and fourth generations are nearest the Anglo culture. Celia Heller, in her *Mexican American Youth*[7] says, "Both in the rate and the degree of acculturation and assimilation Mexican Americans are among the least 'Americanized' of all the ethnic groups in the United States." It is only a mild digression to report regarding intermarriage that Burma's studies in southern California and those made by Gary Cretser at California Polytechnic and those by Dr. Joan Moore at U.C.L.A. show that intermarriage of Anglos and Mexican Americans definitely increases by generation and by assimilation out of the Mexican American subculture.

Now, a direct application of this theoretical construct to actual life: in any subculture the family is a major aspect, and it is an excellent example for the comparative analysis we are making. In the subculture of poverty anywhere, the family tends to be matrifocal. In the Negro subculture the tendency is toward a matrifocal, matriarchal family. Frazier, Johnson, Price, and Moynihan have amply described this matriarchy. In the Puerto Rican subculture of poverty described by Lewis, the tendency is toward a matrifocal but patriarchal family; however, in the Mexican American subculture there is a tendency toward a matrifocal family with a mixture of patriarchal and equalitarian authority; considerably more equalitarian than in the case of the parent Mexican culture, for example.

In both the subculture of poverty and the Mexican American subculture the family is not a very stable unit. In each, sexual experimentation begins soon and early pregnancies are common, both in and out of either legal or consensual marriage. The legitimacy of children is likely to be in terms of whether they are recognized or supported by the father. If the family separates, the children in most cases will remain with the mother or her family, which contributes to the aforementioned matrifocal character of the family in the subculture of poverty. In each subculture there is the phenomenon Oscar Lewis [8] calls "the syndrome of the absent father," in which children may grow up either physically or psychically without a real paternal model. Each characteristic above is less true in the Mexican American subculture than in the subculture of poverty, but the differences are of degree, not of kind.

A major difference does exist, however, because in the stable Mexican American home there is a likelihood that the children will receive some training in respectful conduct, and obedience. This carries over into adulthood, and Mexican American men commonly are more polite to each other than an Anglo man is to an Anglo woman. Good manners stand high in the list of desirable attributes. A Mexican American who tried the lower class Negro subcultural behavior called "playing the dozens" would find himself involved in immediate physical violence.

Unlike the subculture of poverty pattern, Mexican American marriage is at least supposed to arise from a deep romantic attachment, and ideally is expected to be permanent. The father and mother are both expected to love the children. The mother ideally will be affectionate, pampering, self-sacrificing; she will minister both to the creature comforts and the psyches of the children and father; she plays a "love" role and is a love symbol. The father, according to the Mexican American subculture, provides for his family, defends them, and wields authority by virtue of his position as husband and father. A man who does not fulfill these expectations loses status in his own eyes as well as those of his community. While these ideal patterns are never fully followed in practice, the existence of the ideal provides a major family difference in the Mexican American subculture and the general subculture of poverty.[9]

A culture trait which illustrates well the overlapping which sometimes occurs between subcultures is that of time and tempo. In the parent American culture one rushes about; wasting time is evil; we say, "time is money." This does not make sense either from the standpoint of the Mexican American subculture or the subculture of poverty. The organization of one's day into short, sharply defined, significant units fits the affluent American parent culture where time is a valuable commodity, but it is not part of either of the subcultures. "Busyness" is a virtue in the American culture; it is an affliction in both subcultures.

Common to both subcultures is an orientation toward the present, with little practical concern for the future or the "deferred gratification pattern." In each subculture this is closely related to what the parent Anglo culture calls fatalism, the feeling that one's destiny is not in one's own hands, so that ambition is not particularly useful because it is so rarely fulfilled.[10] This attitude, which is evaluated negatively by the parent culture, nevertheless has a real subcultural value in helping persons whose upward mobility is blocked, to accept their inability to rise without ego damage to themselves.

Still another trait shared, but differentially shared, is what Weber called the Protestant Ethic. Oversimplified this is the idea that God wants you to work hard, to be thrifty, to be honest, to get ahead financially; and the proof of God's blessing was that one did prosper financially by ambition, hard work, thrift, etc. A typical proverb was "The devil finds work for idle hands to do." All this has been reasonably well incorporated into the parent Anglo culture; in fact, for many Anglos it is a pivotal element of their culture, but it is not a pivotal element of either Mexican or Mexican American cultures. To most Mexican Americans work is a necessary evil; they work because they have to; they may work very hard, but not because they want to; they work to get the things they need and want; and when these needs are satisfied, they are usually willing to stop work. Moreover, the Mexican American is not as materialistic in his values and goals as the Anglo; the Mexican American values, class for class, cover a broader spectrum, and hence material elements are a smaller proportion of the total than is true for the parent Anglo culture.

The same general situation exists for each subculture vis-a-vis education. Both believe that education ought to be pragmatic, that it usually is not, and that anything beyond grade school is of little use except as it helps get a better job. Although there is a considerable verbalized favoring of education by parents in both subcultures, children are allowed to do poorly, to attend irregularly, and to drop out early.[11] The whole problem is exacerbated by the Mexican American's language difficulty, which usually results in his being bilingual, but one to three years retarded in achievement. This problem is doubly accentuated for the children of migratory agricultural workers.

In studies of the subculture of poverty one of the commonly remarked upon traits is the feeling of inferiority, of helplessness, of dependence and of a lack of individual pride and dignity. Social workers and community organizers often give considerable priority to attempts to instill feelings of pride and self-worth in their clients. To the extent this is true, we have a major difference in the two subcultures being compared. In the Mexican American subculture pride, *dignidad,* is very important. It results in an unwillingness to push oneself where one is not wanted, and a desire always to appear at one's best. Sometimes the personal pride which a semi-literate, poverty stricken Mexican American demonstrates seems quite unreasonable by the standards of middle class culture. Many a Mexican American teenage male has dropped out of school, or been kicked out, because of an attitude which he considered necessary pride, but Anglo teachers interpreted incorrectly as insubordination or insolence.

In both subcultures there is the pride of the male in his maleness. In the Mexican American culture, where it is particularly strong, it is called *machismo.* The term does not translate well; it connotes virility, pride, and a self-concept of personal worth in one's own eyes as well as those of his peers. *Machismo* may be demonstrated differently by different persons — for some it means physical violence, the necessity to defend all slights to one's "honor" by fists or knife; for other men it may mean the sexual conquest of many women, and especially being "irresistible" to women. For others it may mean what to an Anglo is reckless disregard for money, through gambling, by buying unneeded articles, or using up one's paycheck setting up drinks for one's friends. Because real or claimed male sexual prowess is always a part of *machismo*, sexual promiscuity is likely to be considered a sort of necessary evil for males, and to some degree for females as well, although there is no question but that there is a very real double standard both in theory and in practice. When an outsider counts the large number of women whom it is claimed have submitted to the overwhelming sexuality of a group of Mexican American males, and then counts the virtuous wives and the virginal sisters and daughters, the total may be about 200% of the actual female population of a Mexican American community!

It is of practical significance that an acceptance by the Mexican American community of *machismo* leads to a differential attitude toward male juvenile delinquency. Mixed with what both Mexican Americans and Anglos consider delinquent acts is other behavior which the Mexican American community sees primarily as a young male proving his manhood, reaching for adulthood, sowing his wild oats, or "getting it out of his system." Whatever you wish to call it, to the Mexican American community this boy is not doing anything which will interfere seriously with his later becoming a good husband and father and provider. The middle class Anglo community, which makes the laws and enforces them, may see the same behavior as clear delinquency, leading, unless punished and stopped, to a life of crime, degradation, and worthlessness. This also illustrates the frequent difficulty of communication and understanding between a subculture and a parent culture.

Walter Miller has suggested that lower class young people live in a world where "trouble" of some sort is an ever present probability.[12] This expectation of "trouble" plays four roles: (1) a self-fulfilling prophecy which helps bring about trouble or at least prevents significant efforts to avoid it; (2) a pre-acceptance of failure, and a consequent bolstering of the ego by other (subcultural) means in order to avoid ego damage; (3) a behavior syndrome (not staying in school or vocational training, not trying for a better job, not really expecting a stable, happy marriage) based on an expectation of failure; (4) a willingness to engage in acts of deviancy, delinquency, or crime which are known to be likely to lead to trouble, because trouble is likely to come, anyway.

In the important characteristic of social interaction, both subcultures seem to have much in common. In each case there is a tendency for narrow social horizons and relatively few formal, organized social relationships. Interaction is with the family, the gang, the corner clique, and in the case of the Mexican American possibly also with the *palomilla* or with the variant of the god-parent pattern called *compadrazco*. In neither subculture is there likely to be much close interaction with neighbors, fellow workers, or groups like the P.T.A. Comparatively, social relationships are few but deep, and possibly quite emotional. Liebow found that the "friendship webs" among his Negro corner men were likely to be based largely on propinquity, to be supported somewhat by friendship behavior but much more by verbalized protestations, to be more fluid than stable, more shallow than deep (despite vows to the contrary), and "as if friendship is . . . a private agreement between two people to act 'as if,' rather than a real relationship between persons."[13] In the middle class parent culture friendship relations are more numerous, more formal, rarely verbalized, and often organization oriented. Related to this trait is the often-noted tendency of many Mexican Americans to tear down rather than support indigenous leaders who arise. Mexican Americans possess many close-knit, small groups, but they have difficulty in achieving lasting, large scale organizations. In fact, it has been said that one of the proofs of the increasing Anglization of Mexican Americans is that they are beginning to set up Anglo-type organizations, with accepted pragmatic priorities and pragmatic, planned means to achieve perceived goals.

Social interaction in the Mexican American subculture, however, has a qualitative difference as well, with a greater stress on politeness, pleasantness, and mutual agreeability. Conversation should be pleasant, and unless the topic is one on which the person feels emotionally, in the Mexican American subculture far more than in the general subculture of poverty, one is likely to agree to someone else's statement, observation or conversational gambit. In the Mexican American subculture one is more likely to say "yes" when he really means "maybe" or even "no." This degree of pleasant agreement, of keeping one's temper, of not reacting aggressively, is not found to the same degree in the subculture of poverty. This quality is not hypocrisy, but it does make for greater superficiality. There is also at least one psychiatric interpretation that because of this characteristic Mexican Americans are "better able to endure stress passively."[14]

The final trait of both subcultures which will be analyzed is that of language and communication; that is, language *differences* between the subcultures and the parent culture. The difference is three-fold: first, there are different connotations for the same concepts or mind symbols. If X speaks certain concepts to Y and thereby evokes the same symbols in Y's mind which are in X's mind, then successful and accurate communication has taken place. However, if using the same word or concept evokes different mind symbols, or no mind symbol, then only confusion can result. This is crucial because it is exactly this level at which communication often breaks down between a social worker and a client, between members of an O.E.O. committee from different sides of the tracks, or between an interviewer and a subcultural interviewee. There are important subcultural differences in words and symbols as compared to the parent culture. Secondly, the subculture of poverty furnishes its members with a paucity of word symbols compared to the number in the parent culture. Again and again there are reports from Headstart and similar programs that children from the subculture of poverty cannot converse on many subjects because they simply do not know the words. When they do learn the words, they communicate adequately. Third, the language of the subculture of poverty tends to be stark, realistic, simple, crude, coarse, concrete and is likely to be limited in expressiveness in that it lacks richness of adjectives, adverbs, nouns and verbs, and does not readily express nuances, subtleties, or shades of meaning. Subcultural language is one of the most definitive criteria for drawing boundaries between subcultures and their parent cultures. Even the more transitory types of subcultures such as the adolescent subculture, the homosexual subculture, or the prison subculture have markedly different languages or argots which have been collected and analyzed. One of the best illustrations that there is a true Mexican American subculture is the very real mixture of Spanish and English words in the same sentence, or even the mixture of Spanish and English within the same word: *Que pasa con el* pick-up? *No se. Parece el* timing *o el* carburetor, *o los esparke ploges; y tiene un* flat.

To conclude, one might pause and try to answer the question, "What are the futures of these two subcultures in the United States?" First, it appears that both subcultures do exist. It is true that when a phenomenon first comes under special study, the fact of learning more about it may give the false impression that the phenomenon is increasing when it is really knowledge and identification of the phenomenon which are increasing. Both subcultures seem realities, rather than abstract figments of sociological theory.

Like any pattern of generational socialization, or like any vicious circle, subcultures tend to perpetuate themselves until some outside force breaks in upon them. For analytical purposes one can view social work and community organization as normative attempts to assimilate persons into the middle-class-oriented culture. This analysis views social work as essentially a matter of norms, attitudes, values, and behavior. Then, from this assimilation point of view, it is accurate to say there has been only limited success in such assimilation. In the case of the subculture of poverty, for example, there seems to be an increasing proportion of welfare recipients who are the children of welfare recipients. We have no presently successful way of keeping a flow of people moving out of the inner city ghettoes which are the strongholds of the subculture of poverty. This is an index, possibly, of the strength of socialization into the subculture of poverty, and the difficulty of assimilating people out of that subculture into the parent culture. As an oversimplification, and still viewing social work primarily as a normative process, it would seem that we are successful in preventing from entering the subculture of poverty a sizeable proportion of what the social workers call "single problem" families, but that we are very unsuccessful in assimilating out of the subculture of poverty any appreciable number of those "multiple problem" families who are the hard core of the subculture of poverty. Certainly the findings of the National Advisory Commission on Civil Disorders, the so-called Kerner Report, point toward an increase rather than a decrease of the significance of subcultural differences and divergences.

In the case of the Mexican American subculture, the future seems somewhat different. First, the number of bearers of the Mexican parent culture entering the United States in the future is likely to be somewhat lessened as the new immigration legislation is enforced. This is important because for many persons the Mexican American culture has been a temporary adjustment on the way to a relatively full assimilation into the Anglo parent culture. Contrarywise, numerous aspects of the Mexican American culture are in areas of indifference to or mesh well with the middle class Anglo culture and hence are subject to no normative stress. Fourth, what limited commitment America has to the concept of cultural pluralism and culture diversity applies much better to the Mexican American subculture than to the subculture of poverty, with the result that there is less concern about securing conformity from the members of the Mexican American subculture. Finally, in it much more than in the subculture of poverty, participants reject assimilation on grounds of self-identity, self-realization, and the "equal value" of the subculture. When to this is added the strong belief of many Mexican Americans that one can and even should choose for himself the best elements from the subculture and both parent cultures, no viable conclusion seems to exist except that the Mexican American subculture will continue into the foreseeable future.

FOOTNOTES

1. Gordon, Milton, *Assimilation in American Life,* New York, Oxford University Press, 1964, pp. 33-34.
2. Liebow, Elliott, *Tally's Corner,* Boston, Little, Brown, and Co., 1967, pp. 219-223.
3. Lewis, Oscar, *Five Families,* New York, New American Library, 1959, p. 16.
4. Harrington, Michael, *The Other America,* New York, The Macmillan Co., 1963.
5. Lewis, Oscar, *La Vida,* New York, Random House, 1965, p. xlviii.
6. Lewis, Oscar, "The Culture of Poverty," *Scientific American,* Oct. 1966, pp. 19-25.
7. Heller, Celia, *Mexican American Youth,* New York, Random House, 1966, p. 4.
8. Lewis, Oscar, *La Vida, op. cit.,* p. 18.
9. Liebow, on the basis of his study of Negro street corner men, might deny the validity of this statement on the grounds that the poverty stricken Negro male is aware of this role and ideally would prefer to play it. In practice, he is so sure he will fail, however, that his efforts are so weak as to set in motion a self-fulfilling prophecy. G.D. Suttles, although he does not address himself directly to the subculture of poverty concept in *The Social Order of the Slum,* does propose that the dimensions of the life style of the poor are determined primarily by the struggle for social and economic security as a bulwark against the ravages of economic insecurity, rather than being determined by ethnic subcultural patterns per se.
10. Liebow interprets present time orientation not as being part of any subculture, but rather as a situation-specific phenomenon present when persons are in distress. Whatever its origin, this present time orientation is very common among persons participating in the subculture of poverty or the lower class Negro subculture.
11. In all fairness, when children in fact are falling more seriously behind each year, or are not equipped to do the work expected, e.g., a boy who still reads at the third grade level although he has been "passed" to the tenth grade, dropping out may not be irrational.
12. Miller, Walter B. "Lower Class Culture as a Generating Milieu of Gang Delinquency," *Journal of Social Issues,* XIV, No. 3 (1958), pp. 5-19.
13. Liebow, *op. cit.,* p. 207.
14. Unpublished document from the Filfillon Clinic, Los Angeles, 1967.

SOCIAL AND ATTITUDINAL CHARACTERISTICS OF SPANISH-SPEAKING MIGRANT AND EX-MIGRANT WORKERS IN THE SOUTHWEST*

HORACIO ULIBARRI

A study of the educational needs relating to the adult migrant workers was jointly conducted by agencies in Arizona, Colorado, New Mexico, and Texas. The study was divided into two parts, namely, demographic and sociopsychological. This report is concerned with the sociopsychological characteristics of the migrant and agrarian culture oriented workers in the four-state area.

In order to analyze the social and attitudinal orientations of the migrant and ex-migrant workers, a series of depth open-end interviews was conducted. The interviews attempted to draw out the individual's attitudinal characteristics by delving in depth into his life history, his level of educational attainment, and his work history. The interviews were conducted in the vernacular, tape recorded, transcribed, and translated. A total of sixty-five persons was interviewed. All subjects were Spanish-speaking. They comprised a comparable number of Spanish-Americans, Mexican-Americans, and Mexican Nationals.

A model for interpretation of the data was developed from the attitudinal patterns that emerged from the interviews. These patterns were present time orientation, submissiveness, passivity, dissatisfaction, a sense of failure, fear, apathy, particularism, familism, ethnocentrism, and a sense of being objects of discrimination. A seven-point scale for each pattern was developed. The scale ranged from an abnormal extreme on one side to the opposite abnormal extreme on the other. For example, the scale for reward expectation has the following range:

Reward Expectations
1. All rewards will come in the future.
2. Long-range, well-planned rewards are expected.
3. Medium to short-range in expectation of future rewards.

*This article is a condensation of a report prepared for Southwestern States Development Project Relating to Educational Needs of Adult Agricultural Migrants and submitted to Cooperative Research, United States Office of Education, Washington, D.C. Published in *Sociology and Social Research*, Vol. 50, No. 3, April 1966, pp. 361-370.

4. Immediate reward expectation.
5. Immediate reward expectations, but wishing to be able to get rewards available in the past.
6. Present rewards less worthy than past ones.
7. Rejection of present rewards; not capable of accepting rewards after they have been earned.

These scales, when applied to the institutional life activities afforded a quantification of the patterns emerging from each interview. Besides this type of quantification, a simple numerical count regarding the number of times an individual referred to a given activity in a specific manner was made to determine salience. For example, the most salient characteristic of the sample group was concern, bordering on fear, for earning a living.

The data were analyzed in terms of the range and mode. While other more sophisticated statistical designs were possible, this one gave a good general picture of the attitudinal characteristics as related to the institutional areas for the same sample group. The data were appropriately ordered by such technique. Even though the modality for the sample was thus clearly seen, no normality for the total population could be assumed.

A group of judges, to whom the model had been thoroughly explained, was asked to read the interviews and then independently classify the subject, using the scales in relation to the variable and institutional area. Most of the time, agreement existed among the judges as to the classification of a subject in each area. Wherever disagreement was encountered, the judges and the investigator discussed the problem and resolved it.

The Findings and Analysis of the Findings

The analysis of the findings was made by applying the several attitudinal orientations to the institutional areas. A summary was made by applying each attitudinal characteristic across the institutional area. No significant *basic* differences were found among the three Spanish-speaking groups. Whatever differences existed were factors of social mobility rather than cultural differences.

Religion. The area of religion did not emerge as a strong factor in the lives of these people. These people did not seem to have the preoccupation with religion that was characteristic of the traditional Spanish-speaking cultures. One may conclude that the sample generally showed an attitude of detachment and irregularity in their religious practices even though they did not express an a-religious or anti-religious feeling.

Most studies dealing with the cultures of the Spanish-speaking people have generally indicated an almost blind submission toward the clergy on the part of the people. The sample did not indicate this orientation. Rather a complacent contentment toward religion, where involvement in religious affairs was minimal, seemed to prevail among the migrant and ex-migrant workers in the sample.

The Family. The family tended to emerge as one of the strongest areas of life activity in this study. The migrant's nuclear family tended to be a closely knit unit, where all members seemed to enjoy great status and esteem. The indications were that the concept of the extended family has been lost among these people. The only expression of extended familism was a feeble uneasiness for distant relatives and some concern for married brothers and sisters. When asked if they would help their relatives when in distress the usual answer was, "I don't think that we can afford it."

The nuclear family seemed to be rather strongly oriented to the present. They were content with the fact that they were together at the moment. As a family unit they seemed to be rather passive about taking any action to ameliorate their problems. An atmosphere of contentment seemed to prevail within the family's activities. When relating other areas of life to family living, dissatisfaction was expressed as to their living conditions, the fact that they could not provide adequately for their children, that they could not provide such things as clothing for themselves, and that they could not better their lot in life. Their anxiety was often summed up in these words, "I wish I could do more, but what can I do?"

Despite their passivity some expressed a sense of shame at not being able to do better for their children. Yet from a broad perspective, perhaps the most successful involvement of the migrant and ex-migrant worker in all his life's endeavors was with his family. The migrant and ex-migrant's nuclear family exhibited itself as a well-organized unit where all members enjoyed wholesome status and prestige and where there was mutual concern for each other.

Education—Adult. In general, disassociation seemed to be prevalent among the adults in the sample as to education for themselves. They saw no reward resulting from further education and, therefore, did not project themselves into any possibility for improvement through education. For example, when asked "What do you think that you could do to better your lot in life?," the answer never was that they wanted more formal education.

The only ones who expressed any enthusiasm for education were the Mexican nationals who could not speak English. They desired literacy training in English. With the exception of two young migrants none expressed any traumatic experience in separating themselves from school. Either they had just drifted away or there were no educational opportunities available to them in their youth. It seemed that the vast majority of the people in the sample had experienced so much failure in life they seriously doubted their potential for further learning. Most of them replied to a question of whether they would attend tuition-free adult education classes if they were established, "Yes, but we are too old to learn anymore." Some answered, "I am too stupid to learn." Others replied, "I am so far behind that I don't think that I can learn anymore."

Education—Children. At first glance, the sample seemed to feel a ray of hope that perhaps through education their children might be able to enjoy a better life than they had experienced. When these people were asked what their hopes for their children were, most of them expressed desires such as wanting their children to become lawyers, doctors, or "at least teachers." Further probing into the attitudinal characteristic indicated a blind faith for education summarized thus: "I want my children to get an education, so that they will not have to work as hard as I have." Furthermore, the majority in the sample were doubtful that their children would finish high school. More important still, the children expressed the same attitude, and neither parent nor child was concerned about the problem.

There was minimal participation on the part of the migrant and ex-migrant in school affairs. This lack of articulation with the school rendered this class victims of inequality of educational opportunities for their children.[1] Because of ignorance regarding the nature of education, complacency seemed to prevail regarding the schools. Hostility toward the schools was minimal. When dissatisfaction was expressed, it revolved around some minute particular of the total school situation. For example, one mother condemned the total high school from which her child had dropped the year before because they made the students wear gym suits for physical education classes.

In such a life space, academic achievement can hardly be expected. This was very true of the people in the sample. The average level of educational achievement for the adults was fifth grade level. The children, who with rare exceptions were not achieving in school at a high level, were dropping out about three to four grades above where their parents had dropped out of school. There seemed total lack of concern for the bleak future that they would undoubtedly face because of lack of educational achievement. Their impoverished condition apparently placed earning a living above getting an education, and, therefore, both parents and children seemed to be totally apathetic regarding progress in education.

Health. The area of health, initially, did not seem to be of particular concern to the sample group. Statements regarding health were only interspersed through the interview, but when these statements were isolated, it became evident that a high degree of importance was relegated to health by these people.

For the most part, these people expressed happiness at enjoying their present good health. They seemed to take their present state of good health for granted. Paradoxically, they were extremely concerned about becoming ill. Yet aside from a few minor activities, there seemed to be no directed efforts at promoting and preserving good health. The only preventive efforts seemed to be the kind imposed on them, e.g., vaccination.

Schulman found that among the Spanish-Americans, unless pain or other disfunctioning factors of life's activities were present, sickness was not recognized.[2] The same tendency seemed to exist in the sample group. Thus, because they did not seem to understand the true nature of health and illness, whenever illness struck often they failed to see the causal factors. Therefore, unless the cause was readily evident, sickness was thought to be a complete matter of destiny. During protracted illness, some in the group thought that little could be done to help the person recover. What needed to be done by all concerned was to resign themselves to the problem rather than to become anxious over it.

The most important attitude regarding health was a very strong apprehension, bordering on fear, about being sick. When they were asked, "What is the saddest thing in life for you?" invariably the response was, "Being sick." No one was able to explain rationally this fear of illness. Most attempted an explanation with, "When you are sick you have nothing." Some gave a vague indication that sickness prevented them from earning a living. This attitude had family-wide dimensions. Regardless of who was sick, all said that illness caused everybody in the family to be sad. Some said that it was sadder to have small children sick than to have adults ill.

Economics. The most obvious and intense concern of the total group was in the area of earning a living. Usually, the greater part of the interview was related to the problems of earning a living and the difficulties encountered in providing adequately for their families.

Most of the individuals in the sample felt that they were not earning enough money to sustain their families. They believed that the government should develop projects to provide them with job opportunities. Despite their impoverished conditions these migrants and ex-migrants did not seem to have internalized what may loosely be called the "welfare complex." They expressed a necessity to have their earnings supplemented by the free commodity distribution or food stamp programs, but none expressed a desire to become public welfare clients.

Most in the sample group had not attempted in the recent past to qualify themselves for a better type of job. Those, yet in the stream, realized that they were not actually improving themselves. Those no longer migrating seemed to have given up hope of trying to improve themselves. In either case, the idea of getting training for other types of better paying jobs had apparently not entered into their thinking.

The spending patterns also indicated a strong present-time orientation. Of course, most of the income, since it was so low, was spent for basic necessities. There was, however, strong evidence of much impulsive buying. Rather expensive items, such as encyclopedias and television sets, were noted about the house. Useless buying was also noticed. All stated that they spent their money as they earned it. None had any money in the bank; none had any savings.

The whole family was affected seriously by the amount of, and the manner in which, earnings were made available to them through the year. During the working season, the typical seasonal worker in the sample worked as much as sixty hours a week and earned up to seventy dollars a week. During the off-season, however, he worked sporadically, and his earnings seldom amounted to more than twenty-five dollars a week. One of the most evident results of this low income was the impoverished conditions under which these people lived. All the homes visited, with the notable exception of two crew-leaders, were run down or dilapidated, over-crowded, and poorly furnished. Similarly, their poverty was noticed in their dress and in their nutrition.

Because of their low educational attainment level, relatively few jobs were open to the migrant and ex-migrant. Some stated that they had tried looking for other types of jobs, but had been unsuccessful. The factor of not possessing saleable skills in an era of technology, coupled with the factor of discrimination, apparently reinforced their depressed state of mind. Most seemed to have resigned themselves to the problem of poverty instead of trying to fight it any longer. A typical saying among the Mexican-Americans was, "You are Mexican; you have to pick cotton." This fatalistic attitude, however, did not make them aggressive in a socially unacceptable manner. Rather much timidity was noticed both in job-seeking and the toleration of the conditions under which they worked, for example, housing, hours worked, and wages earned.

Dissatisfaction in the area of economics ranged from mild to very strong coupled with bitterness. In most cases the dissatisfaction centered around the working conditions, the housing conditions, and having to exist in a state of fear of want. This fear of want was projected mostly in the form of providing the basic necessities such as food and clothing for their children. The total group considered themselves failures in the area of steady employment. Their typical statement was, "There are no more jobs available; I don't know what we are going to do."

In regard to the nuclear family, this extreme poverty was a blessing in disguise. It seemed to have produced a strong cohesiveness in the nuclear family. This poverty is also probably responsible for the disintegration of the extended family among this group. No evidence was found that the parents seriously considered helping or asking for help from their brothers and sisters. The married sons and daughters were not expected to contribute to the support of the parental family. The explanation was, "They have obligations of their own." When the unmarried sons and daughters were working, they contributed as much as one-half of their earnings to the support of the ñuclear family. Similarly, the total family shared in poverty during the off-season period of unemployment.

Government. The majority of the sample seemed to have disassociated themselves almost completely from the government. In general, they seemed to be ignorant of the governmental structure. By their manner of referring to the government, they seemed to think of the government as a personality.

In general, most of the people in the sample seemed oblivious to the types of help available from governmental agencies. Neither did they involve themselves in politics or in any other form of activity where conscious responsibility as American citizens was exhibited. Rather, the ignorance about government seemed to be so great and the apathy so enervating that one could almost conclude that these people, even though living in the United States, functionally are not citizens of the United States.

Recreation. Recreation among the sample group was confined almost entirely to the nuclear family. The forms of recreation in which they participated were watching television, playing cards, visiting, going to the movies, and dancing. None belonged to social or fraternal organizations. In general, the total amount of recreational activities was either confined to the nuclear family or to the ethnic group to which they belonged.

Ethnocentrism and Discrimination. Relatively little contact existed between the Spanish-speaking and the Anglo-American in the sample. About the only contact evident existed in the relationship of boss to worker or foreman to farm hand. All said that they had very little social relations with the Anglo. None stated that he had any close Anglo friends. Rather, whatever contact existed seemed to be of the negative type, that is, in the form of discrimination. Very little contact seemed to have existed among the three Spanish-speaking groups, namely, the Spanish-Americans, the Mexican-Americans, and the Mexican Nationals, although no animosity among the three groups was detected.

Regarding discrimination, the Spanish-Americans from northern New Mexico and the Mexican Nationals were not conscious of being objects of discrimination. The Spanish-Americans from Colorado, especially the San Luis Valley, were very conscious of being discriminated against by the Anglo. Similarly, the Mexican-Americans from

Texas felt intense, and sometimes vicious, discrimination directed against them.

To interpret these phenomena one must go beyond the data acquired for this study. The Spanish-Americans from northern New Mexico have had minimal contact with the Anglo and are just one step above the social ladder from the agrarian Spanish-American.[3] The Mexican National has been virtually insulated from the Anglo world because of the language barrier. A further mental insulation was provided by the "comparison factor," where the Mexican National is forever comparing the conditions under which he is presently living with those that prevail in Mexico. Thus, when these people move out of their "cultural island" they are almost totally unaware of being discriminated against even when discrimination is very obvious.

The problems of discrimination in Colorado and Texas seemed to be almost identical in nature. One form of discrimination was in the working conditions — long hours of work and low wages prevailing. The other type of discrimination was that brought about by fear, especially in the area of economic competition, by Anglo Americans who were in the same social class or just one step above the Spanish-speaking.[4] The only important difference between the two situations is that Texas, being the gateway for the Mexicans entering the United States, has a consistent stream of immigrants from Mexico.[5] These newly arrived groups cannot participate widely in the general milieu of American life because of their foreign language and foreign culture. This consistent group of new arrivals helps to keep alive the stereotypes relegated to the Spanish-speaking even though there is constant horizontal and vertical mobility within the group as they progress in the process of acculturation.

Conclusions

No basic differences in social and attitudinal characteristics were found among the Spanish-American, Mexican-American, and Mexican Nationals. Whatever dissimiliarities existed tended to be factors of total sample and showed the following social and attitudinal characteristics:

1. Strong present-time orientation in reward expectation in all areas and strong present-time orientation in self-projection in all areas.
2. The sample showed timidity in action and a tendency to avoid

facing the situation in the area of education by having their children drop out of school. They showed great passivity in the area of health. They tended to be timid in trying to improve themselves in the area of economics. By default, they were escaping the situation in the area of involvement in government. They were passive in the area of recreation, confining their recreational activities to the nuclear family or to their ethnic group.

3. The sample showed strong satisfaction in the area of the family life; complacent satisfaction in the areas of religion and government, and in education as it related to education for the children; and strong dissatisfaction and bitterness at their inability to earn a better living and to provide more adequately for their families.

4. The sample group felt that they were achieving to their utmost capacities in the area of the family; that they had exhausted their own potential for education for themselves, and financially they were futilitarian about the education of their children; that they were exhausting their potential in the area of economics.

5. The sample was not concerned with the dominance-subordinance factor in the area of the family; they were submissive by default in the area of education for their children and thought that their own lack of education was only lack of educational opportunity. They thought that health was mostly a matter of one's destiny. They showed tendencies of resignation to poverty in the area of economics.

6. The sample showed concern about the area of education for their children. They showed some fear of not finding a job and of not being able to provide for their families. They showed fear of ill health, although they were not directing any activities toward preserving or promoting their good health.

7. The sample felt successful involvement with the nuclear family. They were apathetic about education for themselves. They were apathetic, meeting slight success, in the area of economics. They showed almost complete disassociation with government. They felt complacent about recreation and religion.

8. The sample showed an overall particularistic attitude in all areas except the nuclear family, where they gave equal importance to particulars and universals — namely, they thought that the family existed because of the members, to whom they relegated great status and esteem.

9. The sample indicated that the limits of their familism was the nuclear family, and this orientation extended into education, health, economics, and recreation.

10. The sample showed definite ethnocentric tendencies where few contacts were made with anyone outside their ethnic group. Contact was generally maintained only with primary groups of the same ethnic stock.

11. The group in the sample from northern New Mexico showed little awareness toward discrimination, except in work relations; the Mexicans seemed to be unaware of discrimination; the Spanish-Americans from Colorado indicated strong awareness of discrimination; and the Mexican-Americans were similarly aware.

FOOTNOTES

1. Robert J. Havighurst, *et al., Society and Education* (Boston: Allyn and Bacon, 1962, 2nd ed.), 237-42; 284-85.

2. Sam Schulman, *et al.,* "The Concept of 'Health' Among Spanish-speaking Villagers of New Mexico and Colorado," *Journal of Health and Human Behavior,* 4 (Winter, 1963), 226-34.

3. John H. Burma, *et al., An Economic, Social, and Educational Survey of Rio Arriba and Taos Counties* (Mimeographed, 1962).

4. O.C. Cox, *Caste, Class, and Race: A Study in Social Dynamics* (New York: Doubleday and Co., 1948), 215-16.

5. William Madsen, *Mexican-Americans of South Texas* (New York: Holt and Co., 1964).

THE CHANGING MEXICAN-AMERICAN IN SOUTHERN CALIFORNIA*

FERNANDO PENALOSA

One of the hazards of any empirical science such as sociology is the constant temptation to reify what is essentially a statistical concept or a theoretical construct of the researcher. When such a model is essentially homologous with empirical reality, little theoretical or practical harm may come from reification. But when the model is essentially static, while the empirical reality with which the model is putatively homologous is in fact in a process of dynamic change, either the theoretical or the practical consequences, or both, may be unfortunate. It may safely be asserted that the concept or construct "Mexican-American population" as ordinarily found in the sociological literature frequently manifests a significant gap with empirical reality.

The most often used, and undoubtedly the best, approximation to the parameters of this population relies on a count of the Spanish-surname population, particularly in the states of the Southwest. But while the term "Spanish-surname population" is operationally definable, the terms "Mexican-American population" or "Mexican-American community" are not so easily controlled. Existentially there is no Mexican-American community as such, nor is there such a "thing" as Mexican-American culture. The group is fragmentized socially, culturally, ideologically, and organizationally. It is characterized by extremely important social-class, regional, and rural-urban differences. Partially because of the great regional variations of this ethnic group, this paper will be concerned primarily with southern California, one of the areas of greatest concentration of this population in the Southwest.

Despite or perhaps because of its extreme fragmentation, there is significant evidence of increased self-consciousness of the group as it struggles through a crisis for self-identity. A perennial topic of discussion in Mexican organizations, as well as in talks given by Mexican-American leaders before Anglo groups is, "What shall we call ourselves?" In southern California the most prevalent term used is

*From *Sociology and Social Research*, July 1967, Vol. 51, No. 4, pp. 405-17.

"Mexican-American." This term, however, has little currency outside of southern California, and even in the latter areas there is some dissatisfaction with the term. In recent years there has been an increase in use of the expression "Americans of Mexican descent" at the expense of the term "Mexican-American." Yet these terms are not in any strict sense synonymous, but realistically represent two quite different segments of the population under discussion. Persons of Mexican descent who were not at one time enculturated into the subculture of some Mexican-American neighborhood are best labelled "Americans of Mexican descent" rather than "Mexican-Americans." The former do not constitute an ethnic minority group as do the latter. Another recent trend is that the attempt to disguise Mexican ethnic origin by self-identification as "Spanish" appears to be on the wane.

At the present time, in southern California as in the Southwest as a whole, the Mexican-American population is increasing more rapidly than the white population as a whole and only slightly less rapidly than the Negro population. In southern California the Spanish surname population increased 92.3 per cent between 1950 and 1960, but more than 100 per cent in Los Angeles (100.5) and nearby Orange (122.0) counties. The result is that the Mexican-American continues to be the largest minority group in southern California. In 1960 there were 870,600 Mexican-Americans in the eight southern California counties. It is probably now well over 1,000,000. This population is 78.8 per cent native-born. The fact that immigrants from Mexico during 1955-60 accounted for 5.1 per cent of California's Spanish surname population five years and over in 1960 indicates that natural increase is not the only significant factor contributing to the population's growth. Since 78.0 per cent of the Mexican-Americans in southern California in 1960 were under the age of 35, this young population has a very high growth potential. Undoubtedly this fast growing segment of California's population will become numerically and proportionally even more important in the future.

The standard accounts of Mexican-Americans stress their relatively high degree of cultural conservatism. This population is partially indigenous to the region, since it was largely responsible for settling the Southwest before its acquisition by the United States from Mexico in 1848. The continuing waves of immigrants, largely rural lower-class in background, from Mexico have been of much larger dimensions than the flow of acculturated individuals into the mainstream of

American life. Thus it has been that persons of Mexican descent have resided in southern California for almost two hundred years and many have largely retained their language and culture over this long span of time.

The primary reasons would seem to be the nearness of the country of emigration and the failure of the public school system to teach an adequate command of the English language and the other skills necessary for successful entry into the occupational world. As a result Mexican-Americans have had to compete economically with a continuous incoming supply of cheap Mexican national labor. The latest waves of the latter were those of the braceros and of the hundreds of thousands of "wetbacks" who have played their part in the continuing low average economic status of the Mexican-American population.

Despite great obstacles, this population as a whole is clearly moving further away from lower-class Mexican traditional culture and toward Anglo-American middle-class culture, so that both its cultural status and its social-class status are changing. It is true that immigrants in many ways reinforce the traditional patterns locally, but they are coming from a changing Mexico much more urbanized and industrialized than the Mexico known to the immigrant of two, three, or four decades ago. The latest waves of immigration have come from socioeconomically higher, more urbanized strata of Mexican society. Mexican-American migrants also come in important numbers from other states of the Southwest, particularly from Texas and New Mexico. The communities from which they have come are generally more traditionally oriented than southern California Mexican-American communities. On the other hand, in the latter, particularly the urban ones, intermarriage and normal social relations among the various subtypes of Mexican-Americans are promoting their merger into a more homogeneous population.

There have been no recent major published studies specifically concerning southern California Mexican-Americans, but the tacit assumption of general works or of studies of communities in other areas is that their conclusions apply with equal force to the former. Many reports have either concentrated or limited aspects of the group, or used source materials two or more decades old, or both.

The most competent documentations of traditional Mexican folk culture in both Mexico and in the United States often make the assumption that understanding this culture is somehow the key to understanding Mexican-American culture. The latter is frequently dealt with as if it were a variety of Mexican folk culture. The rejection of such an oversimplification does not imply, of course, that there is no value in understanding this "folk" or "preindustrial" culture with its close ties to the land, its different sense of time, its lack of emphasis on formal education, and a social structure based primarily on personal rather than impersonal relationships. At the same time, such concepts should not constitute a perceptual screen with which to view the current situation. It is important to note in this connection that in recent years Mexican-Americans in southern California have been categorized along with a number of other ethnic groups and social strata as "culturally deprived" or "economically disadvantaged." It is patent that the nature of the "cultural deprivation" or "economic disadvantage" of this ethnic group is primarily a handicap of class and not of culture, unless we specify lower-class culture. The middle-class Mexican immigrant and his descendants have not been ordinarily "culturally deprived" or "economically disadvantaged," unless they gravitate to a Mexican-American *barrio* with its particular culture. If they move into a predominantly Anglo neighborhood, as they usually do, their problems are normally no greater than those of middle class immigrants from other countries. Mexican middle class persons are more like American middle class persons in their general way of life and basic outlook than they are like lower class persons from their own country.

There is a reaction among educated Mexican-Americans and among some informed social scientists against the characterizations of Mexican-American culture to be found in authoritative books and articles on the subject. They feel that these sources tend to create stereotypes by which even well-trained and well-meaning Anglos will tend to perceive the group, not taking account of individual differences and achievements. Pride and sensitivity about the collective image remain important traits even among the most highly acculturated Mexican-Americans.

The type of characterization which is most unsatisfactory revolves about concepts of the Mexican-American population as largely engaged in migratory agricultural labor. Such broad generalizations as those quoted tend to blur the lines of distinction among the various social classes among Mexican-Americans. They further fail to differentiate clearly among a number of interrelated factors: the lower class, rural origins of the immigrants; the low average occupational status of Mexican-Americans at the present time; and the ways in which their present day problems are shared by the members of lower class groups, ethnic or otherwise. They further fail to take into consideration the broad rural-urban, class, occupational, educational, and regional differences of the Mexican-American population. A homogeneity is postulated or inferred where none exists. Even if we confine our attention to one broad geographical area, such as southern California, and examine the culture and social structure of this population, the homogeneity fails to appear.

The Mexican-American subculture in its most common variant is probably best regarded and understood as a variant of American working-lower class culture. This culture is, of course, affected by all the limitations of lower status in a predominantly middle-class society. The group's way of life is further conditioned by the effects of the reaction of the group to discrimination. If we accept the concept of Mexican-American culture, at least in its southern California variety, as a variant of the United States working class subculture, but influenced to a lesser or stronger degree by traditional Mexican folk culture, it follows that these people should be regarded as partially Mexicanized Americans rather than as partially Americanized Mexicans. No one who has carefully observed the way of life of rural and of urban lower-class people in Mexico, which would represent the original roots of most Mexican-Americans, would make the mistake of considering them the reverse.

The forces of acculturation and assimilation working over a period of three or more generations have brought about the present situation. Most of the change has been slow and barely perceptible to many of the most-quoted authors in the field. Nevertheless, there was a major breakthrough during World War II of forces promoting change and the solution of problems confronting the Mexican-American community. At this time there was a great flow of people out of the *barrio* or Mexican-American neighborhood. Young Mexican-Americans took industrial jobs in increasing numbers, went off to war, traveled around the world, and were treated as individuals, some for the first time. During World War II Mexican-Americans volunteered in greater numbers and won more Congressional Medals of Honor per capita than any other ethnic group. Veterans especially returned to find themselves dissatisfied with the old ways, and many went to college under the provisions of the G.I. Bill. Occupational skills were upgraded because of wartime industrial experience, and because of the additional educational opportunities made available to younger members of the group.

Social change involves of course not only a realignment of individual perceptions, attitudes and actions, but also a reorganization of structural relationships within the community. It is important to note that the types of American communities, both rural and urban, into which Mexican immigrants and interstate migrants of yesterday and today have moved form a most heterogeneous congeries. Some of the differences found from one Mexican-American community to another are undoubtedly due to the varying natures of the several Anglo-American matrices in which the Mexican-American communities are imbedded. The rate of sociocultural change therefore varies widely from one southern California community to another.

Before World War II the Mexican-American population in the Southwest was largely rural, but by 1950 it was two-thirds urban, and by 1960 it was four-fifths urban. In southern California this population was 83.7 per cent urban in 1960. With the tremendous rate of urbanization and metropolitanization of the region many communities that were rural towns or semiisolated suburbs have now become thoroughly urbanized, with a consequent further urbanization of the resident Mexican-American populations.

One significant phenomenon occurring in these newly urbanized areas has been an attenuation of formerly very rigid interethnic lines of stratification. The older studies characterized Mexican-Anglo relations in southern California as of a caste or semicaste nature, with virtually separate Anglo-American and Mexican-American castes in the communities studied. The World War II and postwar periods promoted occupational and geographical mobility to such an extent that rigid caste barriers against intermarriage and equality of employment and housing opportunities have all but disappeared, particularly in urban areas.

Changes in the employment pattern in the Mexican-American work force appear to lie at the very confluence of forces promoting changes in this population. Closely related to the fact of increasing urbanization has been the shift from rural to urban occupations and the shift from unskilled to skilled jobs. These shifts have affected primarily the younger generation. Just over a decade ago Broom and Shevky had phrased the problem of studying Mexican-American social differentiation as one of determining to what extent people had left migratory labor and become occupationally differentiated. But California as a whole no longer has a Mexican-American population which to any significant extent engages in migratory agricultural labor. Only 14.9 per cent of the Mexican-American labor force is engaged in agriculture, forestry, or fisheries, and only 12.2 per cent are employed as farm laborers or foremen. Mexican-American field hands were largely displaced during the World War II and postwar periods by the huge influx of contract laborers from Mexico, the *braceros.* Having been displaced from agriculture, Mexican-Americans are not likely to return to this type of employment in large numbers now that the *bracero* program has almost completely been suspended.

From a preponderance of unskilled employment, Mexican-Americans in California have since World War II been concentrated primarily in blue-collar work of a semiskilled or skilled nature (46.3 per cent) as compared to the total number of unskilled (farm laborers and foremen, other laborers, and private household workers: 23.4 per cent). A significant proportion for the first time are now found also in entrepreneurial, professional, and other white-collar occupations (22.2 per cent). Especially important has been the entry of Mexican-Americans into types of professional employment where they are in a position to assist in the efforts to solve the manifold problems confronting Mexican-Americans in southern California urban centers. Because to assert that Mexican-Americans have largely left behind the problems associated with migratory agricultural labor is not to say that they have no problems. It is rather that now their problems have become those of an underprivileged urban minority group.

The most serious problem undoubtedly lies within the area of education. In this connection it is important to recognize that Mexican-American children are not necessarily any more "culturally deprived" than are children of other low-income families. School authorities in southern California generally consider "bilingualism" as a handicap. Some teachers and administrators consider it as virtually tantamount to mental retardation. This is, of course, a misreading of the true meaning of bilingualism, which is equal fluency in two languages. The problem is obviously a lack of command of English, and not the ability to speak Spanish. Yet all poor and underprivileged people speak poorly and with an accent because they have not enough contact with the majority. True bilingualism, a potential asset in an increasingly international world, is actually discouraged, or at least is not fostered, by the public schools.

Educational progress of the group as a whole has been relatively slow. Between the last two censuses of 1950 and 1960 the average number of years of schooling of the Mexican-American population in California increased by a little over one year (from 7.6 and 8.0 to 8.9 and 9.2 for males and females respectively). It is only in long range perspective that any impressive educational progress can be seen, e.g., the percentage of Mexican-Americans in Los Angeles who were completing junior college in 1957 was as large as the percentage of those completing the eighth grade in 1927.

Another focus for change among southern California Mexican-Americans lies in family structure. In urban areas of southern California at least, the traditional extended family group including siblings and their children is no longer found to any significant extent. The *compadrazgo* or ritual coparenthood relation no longer has any significance as a fictive kinship relation. Related to the increased emphasis or individualism is the move away from traditional Mexican values and toward the Anglo-American values of achievement, activity, efficiency, and emphasis on the future.

The breakdown of traditional Mexican family structure appears to be related to a relatively high incidence of juvenile delinquency for the group. At the same time, Mexican-Americans delinquency is on the downgrade because many of the neighborhoods which contributed to such conditions are slowly disappearing as a result of urban renewal and freeway construction. As a proportion of total state commitments, Mexican-Americans delinquents dropped from 25 per cent in 1959 to 17 per cent in 1965.

Housing discrimination has eased considerably in southern California urban areas and Mexican-Americans can now purchase or rent housing in many desirable areas formerly closed to them. This is not to deny that widespread discrimination still exists. It is ironic, therefore, that analysis of voting results in precincts with high proportions of Spanish surname individuals showed that in the November 1964 state election Mexican-Americans voted heavily in favor of the controversial Proposition 14. The latter, when passed, (although recently ruled unconstitutional by the California Supreme Court) put a provision into the state constitution outlawing antidiscrimination legislation in the housing field. Mexican-Americans apparently failed to realize that the measure was directed against them as well as against the Negro. Their political leaders had simply assumed that Mexican-Americans would vote against a measure which was self-evidently against their own interests. They had failed to reckon with the Mexican-American fear of Negro competition for housing, and the latent hostility between the two groups in some residential areas.

Some Mexican-American neighborhoods have disappeared through forced urban renewal, that is, without the consent of the persons displaced. Some Mexican-Americans have come to refer cynically to urban renewal as "Mexican removal," since for the families concerned no problems are solved by urban renewal. In a number of southern California communities in the past two or three years, Mexican-American leaders (notably in Pico-Rivera in 1964) have been able to muster enough political power, with the assistance of sympathetic outsiders, to prevent urban renewal programs from uprooting them from their homes to higher priced housing elsewhere. It is now unlikely that a situation, such as that of Chavez Ravine, will be repeated. The latter was taken over several years ago by the city of Los Angeles for a housing project, but sold for $1.00 to the Los Angeles Dodgers for a baseball stadium. The highly publicized forcible removal of several Mexican-American families from the ravine left an indelible impression on the public, Mexican and Anglo alike.

Anglo professionals tend to perceive Mexican-American problems as connected with various forms of social disorganization. Mexican-Americans, on the other hand, perceive their problems primarily in terms of the blocking of their aspirations. While biculturalism and bilingualism are viewed by most Anglos as problems, they are not so viewed by most Mexican-Americans. On the other hand, these two characteristics do in fact lead to problems in a society ostensibly committed to cultural pluralism but in reality sustaining the melting pot ideology. There have always been cleavages and factionalism in Mexican-American communities, but never before has the issue of whether to assimilate or not to assimilate been so clearly placed before Mexican-American public opinion.

The major goal now presented to the Mexican-American community by its leaders is no longer simply the abolition of discrimination as it was in the nineteen-thirties and nineteen-forties, but rather of allowing the Mexican-American to make the best use of his abilities including the opportunity to capitalize on his bilingualism. Formerly the community was drained of talent as trained, professional people left the ethnic enclave and became integrated into the dominant society. Now they are finding that by moving professionally back into the *barrio* and working on Mexican-American problems they can advance their own careers and become recognized as community leaders. The community is therefore no longer losing its potential leadership as it once did. The old conservative Mexico-oriented leadership has been giving way to a new leadership of college educated professionals who are thoroughly at home in the Anglo world, but who have retained their ethnic roots.

Current changes appear to indicate a metamorphosis of the group from a lower ethnic caste to a minority group resembling a European immigrant group of a generation or two ago such as, for example, the Italian-Americans in New York, Boston, or San Francisco. Thus, for the first time since the 1850's Mexicans in southern California were appointed to public policy-making positions during the recent adminis-tration of Governor Edmund G. Brown. These political appointees in state and local government have been in a position to help open up employment opportunities to other Mexican-Americans and have also provided for better communication between various state agencies and the people. Similarly, Mexican-Americans now have their own political organizations such as The Mexican-American Political Association (MAPA) and have emerged as a political force in their own right. At election time the Anglo-American power structure has become increas-ingly cognizant of this new political force. Mexican-Americans for their part have learned that if they want such benefits as streets paved and kept in good repair, street lighting, adequate schools, Mexican-Americans on teaching staffs and on the police force, they have to make their power felt at the polls. As a result, a significant number of officials have been elected. There are at latest count 15 mayors, 56 city councilmen and 20 school board members of Mexican-American origin throughout the state, the great majority in southern California.

Another indication of increasing Mexican-American political strength was the recent defeat of the *bracero* program, for which Mexican-Americans are taking a great deal of the credit. Their leaders had long fought this program which they felt had undermined efforts to establish minimum wages, adequate housing, and schooling for farm workers and their families.

On the national level, one result of the 1960 and 1964 campaigns was that numerous political patronage opportunities were opened up to professional Mexican-Americans in the Peace Corps, the Alliance for Progress, AID, and in the War on Poverty. Mexican-American leaders are increasingly becoming concerned not only by what they can do for their own ethnic group but also for their country as a whole. They are especially eager to utilize their unique abilities and skills in promoting United States goals in Latin America, to which area they will no doubt continue to be sent in increasing numbers. Southern California, where the largest urban concentration of Mexican-Americans in the country is found, has produced and no doubt will continue to produce more than its share of such leaders, as this population as a whole moves even closer to the mainstream of American life.

PREJUDICE

PREJUDICE

We now know that, along with capitalism, industrialization, urbanization, and individualism, prejudice and discrimination are basic and deep-rooted elements in the ethos of American culture, and no ethnic group has entirely escaped their evils. For all minorities there is always the unanswerable question, "Where would we be now if we had not been held back?" Of much more current importance are the questions, "How much are we being handicapped now?" and "What can be done about it?" While the latter two questions may not have sufficient "hard data" evidence available to offer scientifically complete answers, adequate information can be found to give a reasonably clear picture of the first question and to permit rational prediction on the second.

With numerous individual exceptions, Mexican Americans have been subjected to personal prejudice in social situations and in stereotyping and to discrimination in occupations, housing, education, and political activity. As a generalization, the discrimination against Mexican Americans was never as deep or as pervasive as against black Americans, but neither has it been as shallow and sporadic as for German Americans. Without question, however, it has been very serious for the Mexican American community as a whole and continues to hamper many Mexican Americans. Some individuals seem fully to have overcome this handicap, others to have been fully overcome by it. It is clear that the Mexican American community as a whole, *la raza,* no longer will accept such treatment with humility and good will.

The four selections in this section are quite different in content and approach. In the first, "Mexican Americans, Prejudice and Discrimination: An Application of the Simpson and Yinger Model," Dr. John H. Burma briefly presents certain aspects of theory concerning prejudice and discrimination, and then applies those theories to the present situation of Mexican Americans. In "Interminority Relations," Leonel J. Castillo, an officer in the Neighborhood Centers Association in Houston, Texas, addresses himself to some of the problems shared by blacks and Mexican Americans. He describes some of the civil rights tactics which can be used to ameliorate these problems, what each group can learn from the other, how minority groups can and should engage in joint endeavors for their mutual benefit, the serious problems of marginality, and how marginal men can live full, meaningful lives. In "Prejudice toward Mexican and Negro Americans: A Comparison," Dr. Alonzo Pinckney, a sociologist and anthropologist, reports on a scientific study of attitudes held by "native white American adults" toward specific, locally significant civil rights issues and toward civil rights for Mexican Americans and for blacks. He not only states the differences he found, but gives some indications as to why these variations exist. James De Anda, a Texas attorney, presents an excellent factual report specifically dealing with discrimination against Mexican Americans in the three areas of jury service, voting eligibility, and school enrollment. He concludes by calling for an immediate rectification of these disabilities.

MEXICAN AMERICANS, PREJUDICE AND DISCRIMINATION: AN APPLICATION OF THE SIMPSON-YINGER MODEL*

JOHN H. BURMA

The fact that prejudice and discrimination today are constantly used words does not mean that they have uniformly agreed-upon definitions. In fact, their wide usage in recent years has distorted each concept into such a varied set of meanings that, like "racism" and "democracy" and "law and order," their use can no longer be depended upon to transfer a clear thought-symbol from one mind to another. The following analysis is one attempt to clarify this current conceptual confusion, and to apply the terms to Mexican Americans.

Prejudice is best used to describe an attitude, a feeling, and as such is covert. Discrimination is best used to describe an act, and hence is overt. The terms are not synonymous, and although prejudice commonly results in discrimination, it need not and often does not. Discrimination usually is the result of prejudice, but it may have other sources, as for example simple self-interest.

One of the sources from which prejudice arises is the emotional and psychological needs of an individual. Possibly the person is frustrated in his attempt to achieve goals — a common condition — and feels a desire to aggress against what he considers the blocking agency. In some cases this agency is not subject to aggression; e.g., it may be world conditions; it may be an act which has already occurred and cannot be recalled; it may be a force against which he cannot aggress because it would seriously and successfully retaliate against him; or it may be the person does not even know the source of the frustration. In such circumstances this frustration may lead to feelings of anger which

*In *Racial and Cultural Minorities,* Harper and Row, 1965, George E. Simpson and J. Milton Yinger present a seven chapter analysis of the causes and consequences of prejudice and discrimination. The following selection uses portions of their work as a model to clarify and analyze the causes and consequences of prejudice, with particular application to Mexican Americans.

are relatively undirected, and are called "free-floating hostility." This hostility, this frustration, may seek a subject, even though this subject is not the cause, against whom to aggress with reasonable safety: a wife, an institution, or a minority group. The above is a simplified version of what has been called the frustration-aggression theory of prejudice and discrimination. It does explain the source of some prejudice and discrimination. It does not explain why some persons who are frustrated aggress against others, and why some persons do not, for everyone is frustrated in his goals to a greater or lesser degree. It does not explain why one minority group is chosen as a subject rather than another, or why no minority group at all is chosen. The frustration-aggression theory is a useful explanation of why Mr. A. or Mr. B. or Mr. C. have attitudes of prejudice, but it is inadequate to explain why Mr. A. holds this prejudice completely covertly; why Mr. B. is prejudiced only against Indians, and why Mr. C. not only is prejudiced against whites but participates in rioting, sniping, and looting. If Mexican Americans are subjected to this type of prejudice or discrimination the factors involved are largely adventitious and opportunistic — almost accidental — and such behavior is neither very predictable nor preventable.

Another source, this one more of discrimination (behavior) than prejudice (attitude), is the fact that for most desirable things in any culture, the supply is inadequate to meet the demand: wealth, power, status, material goods, position, friendship, organizational membership, good housing, and the like. In some cases discriminatory behavior does "pay off" in terms of securing cheap labor, segregated housing areas, political power through disfranchisement of a part of the potential electorate, or additional income achieved through unethical business practice. The involvement of psychological factors may be negligible. The subjection of Mexican Americans to discrimination from this type of source is much more predictable. If there is a desire for cheap labor, and if *Chicanos* are available as a labor force, and if the employers can and do manage through discrimination to exploit them economically, one need seek no deep-rooted, psycho-analytic explanation. If there are not enough tax resources to furnish good schooling for all children in a district, if the Anglos control the school system and wish their children to get as good an education as possible, the naked self-interest which results in an unequal division of resources between the "Anglo" school and the "Mexican" school is obvious and practical, and from a short-term, narrowly focused point of view, it pays off for the discriminators. Often in such cases of selfish discrimination the rationalizations are given that "they don't need a good education;" "they would only waste the money from better wages;" or "they don't want better housing, they're happy where they are." If illiterate parents fail to see the full usefulness of a good education for their children, it proves nothing more than the operation of a vicious circle, or the "self-fulfilling prophecy."

One other source of prejudice and discrimination against any group, including Mexican Americans, is the traditional, historical source which is part of the cultural heritage. Many attitudes and behavior patterns exist today primarily because they have been passed down through the social heritage, not because they are currently true, or any longer exploitatively useful. Children receive most of their attitudes through the process of socialization into their particular culture or subculture. More specifically, there exists today much prejudice by and against Mexican Americans because such attitudes were held by the previous generation or by someone else participating in the socializing process, and the children absorbed it as uncritically as they absorbed the other aspects of the social heritage being passed on to them. Such prejudice may or may not be deep; the point is that it exists regardless of the fact that it no longer serves any purpose for anyone.

The person subjected to prejudice and discrimination suffers in a variety of ways. He receives psychic wounds which, to use a crude analogy, may be constantly open sores, very frequently re-irritated and re-inflamed, never able to heal, and resulting in constant pain; or they may be wounds which partially heal, whose pain diminishes or temporarily disappears only periodically to be ripped open again for the whole process to be repeated; even if the wounds do heal, they may leave psychic scars which are permanently disfiguring or distorting.

When a society prevents an individual from achieving his fullest growth and making his greatest contribution, not only is that person harmed, but so is his family, his community and his nation. If ten million persons are prevented, on the average, from achieving 10% of their potential, this is equal to losing the intellectual and productive potential of a million individuals. If, as is more nearly correct, ten million persons are prevented from achieving a half of their original potential, the unintended, latent consequences to our society are almost unbelievable, and certainly greater than any nation can afford.

Where the prejudice and discrimination are directed against cultural differences in a minority, the results for the majority can only be a narrowing of its cultural potential. Any culture is a set of adaptations which a society has worked out that successfully meet its basic needs. Only the most arrant ethnocentrism could hold that "our" culture (in actuality one of the greatest amalgams in history) has not benefited and could not continue to benefit from the inclusion of selected culture traits from all our minorities. For those who have lived or vacationed in the Southwest it is redundant to mention the wide variety of culture traits and practices which have been so usefully borrowed from the Spanish and Mexican American cultures, and to repeat how much culturally poorer the area would be without them.

It is possible to indicate a number of "type" responses to prejudice and discrimination from within the Mexican American community:

1. Withdrawal from the *Chicano* community; moving into an Anglo neighborhood, seeking one's friends from within the Anglo community, and in general disassociating oneself from the Mexican American subculture and community; possibly intermarriage.

2. Withdrawal deeply into the *Chicano* community; avoiding all possible contact with Anglos, and to as great an extent as possible ignoring the existence of the Anglo community.

3. Using discrimination as an excuse for not trying to achieve, for dropping out, for being a failure by the standards of both communities, but protecting one's ego by saying it is all "their" fault.

4. Participating aggressively in organizations seeking to extoll, advance or strengthen *la raza* or some element of its cultural heritage.

5. Exaggerated pride in the achievements of persons from the *barrio,* especially if their success is in competition with Anglos.

6. Physical reaction, non-violent or violent; boycotts, demonstrations, sit-ins, personal physical violence, riots, looting, selective vandalism.

7. Accepting a certain amount of prejudice and discrimination as inevitable, but ignoring it, and participating in both communities with as much ease and freedom as possible; being cautious about one's behavior, selecting it in terms of the group with

which one is at the time to be as acceptable and successful as possible in both groups.

8. Ignoring possible prejudice and discriminatio and actively seeking for oneself the best elements of both cultures; practicing the cultural pluralism approach, which holds that a culture consists of ways of adapting to one's physical and social environment, and trying rationally to choose the best adaptations.

9. In connection with any of the above reactions, holding prejudice against the Mexican American group (self-hatred), against Anglos, against Jews or Blacks, or any other minority and by so doing transferring one's frustration and aggression to a scapegoat.

INTER-MINORITY RELATIONS*

LEONEL J. CASTILLO

Probably one of the least discussed problems of poverty in the Southwest is that of inter-minority relations.

The problem shows itself in the scramble for the limited number of jobs, programs and even in the essentials of subsistence. In those urban areas where there exist sizeable populations of both groups the problem will boil down to a specific: "Would it be better to hire a Mexican or a Negro for this job?" or it could become: "Which neighborhoods will be the recipients of this federal program?" or "Which neighborhoods should be dropped from the 'target areas'."

The problem manifests itself in the struggle to fill the jobs on the lower end of the economic totem pole.

The problem manifests itself in the public debates about the percentage of minority group members serving in Vietnam.

The problem manifests itself in the Anglo's hesitancy in either placing the Mexican American on a par with the Negro, or on an equal level with himself, the Anglo.

The problem will become even more pronounced if the Anglos continue to flee the inner city leaving the Mexican Americans and Negroes who continue to multiply as fast as they have, and who continue to move from the farm to the city. In 1950, 66.4% of the Spanish-speaking were in urban centers. But in 1960 the U.S. census found 79.1% were city folk. Comparable figures exist for the Negro population.

In every one of the Southwestern States the potential political power of a coalition of Mexican Americans and Negroes is sharply coming into focus. As of 1960 in Texas, together with the Negro, Mexican Americans comprised 27.1% of the total population; in New Mexico 36.4%; in Colorado 12.1%; in California 17.1%; and in Arizona 25.1%. The 1970 population will show much higher figures.

*The Mexican American: A New Focus on Opportunity, Inter-Agency Committee on Mexican American Affairs, U.S. Govt. Printing Office, Washington, D.C., 1967, pages 203-208.

Cultural Background

Although it is the purpose of this paper to consider some approaches toward developing better inter-minority relationships, some cultural background information is necessary before any rational solutions can be presented.

If one could make a list which described the "typical" Mexican American and then compared it with a list which described the "typical" Negro, he would find that they both differ sharply from the "typical" Anglo.

He would, for example, have to consider several different definitions of the term "my family." For the Mexican American *familia* means an extended group of individuals related by blood, by kinship ties, by ritual. For a Negro, "family" all too often refers to groups in a household not necessarily bound by blood. The lack of strong, male father images has been cited by many persons, from Frazier thru Moynihan.

But the textbook Anglo family given us in school shows a father, a mother, Dick, Jane and Spot. Sociologists call this a nuclear, conjugal family.

This is a real and vital question. The definition of family which is used determines who will be included in a federal program.

If the nuclear, conjugal defintion is used, the "typical" Mexican American family with its assortment of uncles, aunts, grandfathers, compadres and cousins is likely to be excluded.

There are other strong cultural forces that distinguish the two groups from each other and from the Anglo. The Mexican American is Roman Catholic, the Negro is Baptist Protestant. The Mexican American has deep roots in the Southwest; the Negro is a more recent arrival; the Mexican American woman is supposed to concern herself only with domestic and Church affairs; the Negro and Anglo women have more freedom to participate in civic affairs. The Mexican American has strong kinship ties to his relatives (both near and far); the Negro does not. The Mexican American places high value on his "machismo"; the Negro does not. There are many operational implications that can be drawn from these facts.

Of course, the most common bond between the two minorities are those which Oscar Lewis described as characteristic of the Culture of Poverty in his famous *Children of Sanchez*. In the Southwest the Negro and the Mexican American share the problems of bad housing, poor health, discrimination, low educational achievement, low incomes — as well as all the other commonly accepted measures of urban and rural social health.

Using Civil Rights Tactics

It is a truism, commonly held and universally ignored, that the two minorities have much to learn from one another. May I suggest some civil rights tactics which could be extremely useful to the Mexican American in his fight for equal opportunity.

First, as a counterpart of the Freedom School concept Mexican Americans must press hard for the bilingual school system. They have a proud heritage and the Spanish language is an essential ingredient of that heritage. Indeed it can truthfully be said that "A people without a history, is like a tree without roots." Without ancestral ties they lose their identity.

Second, they should support the Urban League, the NAACP, the local Councils of Human Relations and the other groups which are trying to promote harmony among the different races. As much as possible they should try to see that the Councils of Human Relations concern themselves with the problems of the Mexican American as much as they concern themselves with the problems of the Negro.

In cooperation with such groups they should begin to sponsor workshops with local civil rights groups on such subjects as:

Organizing and conducting economic boycotts.

Organizing and conducting negotiations with companies and with governmental agencies which exclude minority group members.

Using the mass media.

Techniques for reaching the hard core.

Ways of conducting anti-slumlord campaigns.

Election of sympathetic politicians.

The list could be extended indefinitely.

Along with Negro groups Mexican Americans will then be able to develop effective coalitions which can insist on stronger representation on OEO executive boards, City Councils, School Boards and other elective and appointive positions.

It seems that the Office of Economic Opportunity would be well advised to convene a series of workshops or institutes to give deep consideration toward the development of better inter-minority relations.

The Office of Economic Opportunity could also be influential in helping other governmental agencies such as the Department of Labor modify some of their operational definitions and methods so as to be more compatible with the cultural values of minority group members. OEO community development workers could, for example, assist local citizens groups in having police departments lower the height requirements, and thereby allow more citizens an opportunity to join the force.

What Can the Negro Learn From the Mexican American?

Just as there is much that the Mexican American can learn from the Negro and from the civil rights movement, there is also much that the Negro can learn from the Mexican American.

From them the Negro can learn more about the strength and beauty of family ties. From them he can gain insights into the vast continent that is South America. From them he can learn about the true value of having two languages. From them he can learn a humane way of caring for the elderly by keeping them at home; rather than putting them in miserable Homes for the Aged. In short, from them he can learn about a way of approaching life that is different from the WASP worldview.

How can they help the Negro to learn about the Mexican American?

First they must arrange for meetings between the Catholic priests in their barrios and the Protestant ministers in the Negro slums.

Then, they must open the little doors. They can invite Negro church choirs to sing at Mexican American functions. They can invite Negro civil rights officers to go with them on trips into Mexico. They can conduct youth leadership-training conferences for participants from both minorities.

Another way in which the relationships between the minority groups could be improved would be by the providing of stronger, public and private support to persons who elect to marry cross-culturally. This same kind of support should be given to couples who adopt children from ethnic backgrounds different than their own. The people who enter into such racially mixed situations need all the support they can get. Perhaps it is time for the organizations represented here to take an active interest in this matter.

Joint Urban Planning

The Model Cities Act offers a good example of the type of planning process which could be used to develop effective inter-minority structures and communications patterns in urban centers. Under the Model Cities concept, the minorities can work together in the development of concrete ways of converting slums into viable, beautiful communities. Together they can, and should, and must, insist on the use of some of this country's vast engineering and industrial genius in rebuilding the ghettoes.

Mexican Americans could, if they but had the will and the vision, insist that those areas of cities which are now used for residential-industrial purposes, be rebuilt with the emphasis on the resident and not on the industrialist. Let them insist that cement factories, lumberyards, brickyards, etc., all be required to relocate underground, and be required to stop polluting the air, and be required to use underground passageways for the movement of dangerous and bulky cargoes. After all, it is their children who have to walk through polluted air, across railroad tracks, and around massive truck trailers . . . to inadequate schools.

They must insist that the American city be built for *people*—and not for the car or for the industrialists.

The task of redesigning urban governments and of recreating cities is as much that of minority group leaders as it is that of white America.

New Towns

On a wider scale Mexican Americans should join with the other minority groups in planning for the development of completely new communities. These communities could be planned as multi-cultural, multi-lingual, centers. They could be built as satellite towns of some of the existing larger metropolises, or they could be planned in some of the wide, open spaces of the Southwest. Into the organizational structure of these communities they could build democratic mechanisms which would allow for full participation by minorities in government.

This is not a frivolous idea. The present population birth trends and the continuous migration of people to the cities require a viable alternative to continuous urban sprawl. Satellite towns in the Southwest represent one such alternative.

Furthermore, such cities could be planned so as to foster a healthy relationship between modern technology and human cultural factors.

Urban Index of Social Health

One difficulty in determining which area or which individuals are to receive priority in the allocation of the limited federal funds to fight poverty is the lack of a clear-cut index of social health. How indeed does one decide who is poverty-stricken and who is not?

It is difficult to define poverty or social deprivation without going into philosophical distinctions. One has to discuss potential, opportunity, freedom of movement and other crucial issues.

At present this is not possible, and many of us feel that programs go to the cities with the best proposal writers and not the greatest need.

How does one decide what to use as a proper measure of poverty?

I would suggest that the OEO commit itself to a project of several years duration which would be charged with the development of an index of social health. This index would include cultural factors, discrimination patterns, quality of housing, feasibility of movement, quality of education, general economic levels, mental health, and as many other variables as are relevant and feasible.

The general aim of such an index would be the development of a measure roughly similar to the Gross National Product, which is used to indicate the economic health of the nation.

These measures would be a great aid in reducing the possibility of friction among minority groups. Decisions to allocate limited resources would not seem so arbitrary or be so subject to political forces.

Marginal Americans

The problems of marginality are best exemplified by the young Mexican American or Negro who goes away to school, earns some advanced degrees, and then finds it impossible to return to the place from which he came. This person no longer talks the same. He wears a different mental outlook. He, however, has retained enough of the old so that he is not completely comfortable in his suburban dwelling. While he may be regarded as a "success" by the general public, most can only call him a failure.

Less dramatic, perhaps, but nonetheless as real, are the problems faced by the Negro or Mexican American high schooler who is outstanding in his studies. He is always being reminded to refrain from abandoning his group. Even joining the Honor Society will mean spending a great deal of time among the Anglos. The marginality of these youngsters is increased by the low self-image which their ethnic group has. Once in school they are not allowed to speak their native language. They are subtly but surely taught that a little band of Anglos can whip a big band of Mexicans through such things as the Alamo and the battle of San Jacinto. The awful thing is, of course, that they learn these lessons all too well. Mexican Americans complete high school with very little fluency in either Spanish or English. Negroes complete high school several class-years behind their Anglo fellow students. They are thereby unable to relate completely to either culture.

While we should allow for every man to live his life according to the dictates of his own conscience, we should still try to ingrain a sense of heritage and of responsibility to one's own. We might begin to do this by accepting and giving fewer scholarships, from any source. We might begin to do this by insisting on the development of a National Service Corps, which would insure a free college education to every American, in return for a year of service to his country. For the Mexican American and Negro, tours of duty could be arranged which would bring them into the barrios and ghettoes on community development missions.

In a sense all Mexican Americans are marginal men. It is much easier for them to assimilate into the total American culture than it is for Negroes. It is now possible for Mexican Americans to marry Anglos without being ostracized by the community. Some of them, because of their fair features, have no difficulty at all in passing as a "typical American."

The Negro cannot escape his color. He is black. This identity, while denying him some of the assimilation afforded the Mexican American, serves as a very tangible link with his brothers. For Mexican Americans the links are in the language and in the cultural values.

The young Mexican American college student experiences, as does his Negro counterpart, some severe identity problems. The youth wants to believe that he can have the best of two worlds. He wants to plant a foot in each culture's camp. For too many the end result is an unfortunate isolation from both cultures.

How can Mexican Americans help these marginal men to live full, meaningful lives?

1. Together with the Negro they should explore the possibility of developing more cooperative dormitories, such as those at the University of Texas, which could be used to house students from diverse racial and ethnic backgrounds. These cooperative dormitories, run at minimal cost to the students, could be financed by any of the many nonprofit corporations interested in this type of project. The cost to the sponsoring organization would be small, as the students themselves would be responsible for the maintenance, and operation of the dormitory.

There is no reason why a neighborhood council in a poverty area could not secure a charter as a nonprofit corporation for the purpose of building and sponsoring such cooperative dormitories.

The students living together in these facilities would have the opportunity to live with persons of other backgrounds; they would present to the total community a living proof of the possibilities of interracial living.

2. They should encourage these students to serve as Volunteer tutors to high school students of similar ethnic origin.

3. They should encourage minority youth to use programs such as VISTA, SDS, Accion and Peace Corps for the benefit of their people.

4. They should periodically invite them to attend their meetings, even after they have returned to live in a beautiful suburban home on the other side of the tracks.

5. They should hold special conferences, retreats, seminars and meetings to brief these students on the problems they and other minority members face.

6. They should make vigorous efforts to have the voting age in the Southwest lowered to 18. This would allow minority youths to participate fully in the solution of minority group problems. (It would also increase the political power of both minorities since both have median ages which are below that of the Anglo.) Such a step would also allow the Mexican American and Negro youth with an opportunity to exercise his voice on public matters.

7. The OEO, should with the cooperation of the LULAC's and the GI Forum and other groups, undertake a campaign to involve scholarship winners in community action efforts.

There can be no question but that some new ways of communicating the notion of interracial harmony are needed. By and large the educational institutions they have are inadequate for this task.

They have to design different types of schools. They have to create schools which are equipped to teach for life as it is. They have to insist, along with their Negro brothers, on the introduction of courses on minority groups in the curriculums followed by prospective teachers. They have to educate local interracial study groups.

A few friends of mine and I are working on the development of Spanish-language comics which portray interracial situations as normal and healthy. I see no reason why the same thing can't be done with other forms of communications media. Why not, for example, invite some of the Latin-American, Negro baseball players to speak to groups in Mexican American barrios during the off-season?

Utilizing Cultural Strengths for International Purposes

There has been so much emphasis in the past on the problems of alienation, apathy, disease and poverty of the minorities, that only rarely are we able to do more than cast supercilious glances at the strengths of these minorities.

This country and the world could profit greatly from the development of projects and programs which would allow for participation of Mexican Americans and Negroes in the international training and educational programs.

The American Southwest is a perfect location for the numerous training and study programs which are sponsored by the Peace Corps, the Agency for International Development, the State Department, the United Nations, the military, and by private industry. Here we have a blend and mixture of races and cultures struggling with the problems of urban development. Here we have a climate and architecture similar to that of many underdeveloped countries.

But where are such programs now being conducted? They are held at Harvard, Yale, Rutgers, Radcliffe, or in Washington, D.C., or in other places which are considered better only because they have more "experts" on their faculties and more books in their libraries. And who benefits from these programs? The "deprived" communities of Harvard, Yale, etc., benefit from these programs.

Texas, Arizona, New Mexico, Colorado, and California where Mexican Americans could obtain many bilingual staff members, albeit not with college degrees, is where the programs are needed.

There are many institutions and corporations which have the competence and the capability to administer such programs. There are numerous resources available. In Houston, for example, there is a large community of Spanish speaking professionals who would be invaluable in training Americans for service abroad. Yet, just the other day I spoke with a Cuban lawyer who is working as a bus boy, and with a Mexican professor who can't find a job because he doesn't speak English.

It would seem only reasonable that the Government should make strong efforts to relocate some of its international programs, particularly those dealing with Latin American and Africa in the Southwest. It would seem only reasonable that some of the many jobs which these programs generate should go to Spanish-speaking individuals.

If you wanted to train technicians or workers for Latin-America, Mexican Americans could furnish you with Spanish-speaking cooks, with Spanish-speaking janitors, with native speakers of Spanish to serve as informants, with Spanish language movies, with Spanish language comics, with Spanish language television stations, and with Spanish language newspapers. Trainees could be housed in communities or *barrios* where Spanish was the medium of communication.

It could even furnish urban and rural slums which are as debasing to their residents — American citizens — as any slums anywhere in the world.

The use of the Southwest as a training ground for the Western Hemisphere would result in better jobs for local residents, in a better appreciation by the public of cultural values, and in better-prepared Americans abroad. In fact, the programs could be structured so that the language informants also learned the technical skills that the trainees did. It would also result in better international relations with our Latin-American neighbors.

More important than all the preceding, is the logical progression such programs would represent in efforts to develop a World Community based on humanism and on respect for the dignity of the individual. These would be positive steps to alleviate the national blight of poverty and to assist other countries where the degree of human misery is so much greater.

This would also be a logical and natural way in which to introduce modern technological innovations to the "other world," of Poverty.

PREJUDICE TOWARD MEXICAN AND NEGRO AMERICANS: A COMPARISON*

ALPHONSO PINKNEY

THE PRESENCE of numerous racial and cultural minorities in the United States has stimulated much empirical research, which has subsequently led to many well-established generalizations in sociology. However, the presence of one minority — Mexican Americans — has led to little or no quantitative research, either in terms of its attitudes toward the dominant group or the attitudes of members of the dominant group toward it. Carey McWilliams has said:

> No effort whatever has been made, on a national scale, to assist these immigrants in their adjustment to a radically different environment. Culturally, racially, linguistically, Mexican immigrants are sharply set apart from the general population. Instead of assisting in a process of gradual acculturation, we have abandoned the people to chance and circumstance.

In terms of research, sociologists, like others, have virtually forgotten about the Mexican Americans in our midst.

The largest of America's racial minorities — the Negro — on the other hand, frequently has been the subject of investigation, both in terms of his attitudes and of the attitudes of others toward him. The aim of this paper is to compare the attitudes of native white Americans, in one city, toward Mexican and Negro Americans, in an attempt to determine if there are differences in extent and nature of prejudice expressed toward the members of these two social categories.

The city in which these data were collected had an approximate population of 100,000. Located in the West, it had a wide diversity of racial and cultural minorities; present in the population were Chinese, Filipino, Japanese, Jewish, Mexican, and Negro Americans. The two largest minorities were Mexican and Negro Americans, both of which accounted for roughly 8 percent of the population during the greater part of the year. The Mexican Americans were employed mainly as unskilled laborers in agriculture and the oil industry, usually working only with other Mexican Americans. Few of them held either skilled or

*Phylon, Winter, 1963, pages 353-359.

professional jobs, and as a community they lived in segregated areas, either by themselves or in areas which they shared with Negroes. In education, while they attended schools with non-Mexicans, one school was reserved for Mexican American grade school pupils.

The Negro residents of this community were mainly recent arrivals from the South, and their general situation was similar to that of the Mexican Americans, with minor exceptions. They were mainly working class, and employment in this category was relegated mainly to the cotton industry and other low-status occupations. While Negro skilled and professional workers were rare, there were more Negro Americans in these types of jobs than Mexican Americans. Like the Mexican Americans, most of the Negro grade school pupils attended one all-Negro school.

Both Negro and Mexican Americans were relegated to the lowest possible status in the community. But the status of Mexican Americans was somewhat more rigid, since, because of the language barrier, they were relegated to a caste-like position in the occupational structure. This study was accomplished before the advent of state laws barring discrimination in places of public accommodation and employment, and such practices were widespread in the city.

These data were collected by means of interview schedules with a random sample of 319 native white American adults. In this paper concern will be focused mainly on (1) the responses of members of the dominant group to what may be called attitudes toward local policy in regard to the rights of both Negro and Mexican Americans, and (2) attitudes toward rights in general for individuals in these two social categories. Judging from the responses, these sets of questions appear to be valid indicators of prejudice. This is further indicated by a comparison of these replies to other indicators of this attitude.

The items concerned with local policy regard attitudes toward both Negro and Mexican Americans: (1) living in integrated neighborhoods, (2) joining integrated social clubs, (3) using unsegregated barber and beauty shops, (4) staying in local hotels, (5) being served in local restaurants, and (6) being hired as clerks in local department stores. The questions were asked in regard to the local situation, i.e., the community in which they lived.

In the category of general rights, each of the 319 respondents was asked four questions about the approval of rights for individuals in these two minorities with regard to: (1) integrated neighborhoods, (2) social mixing, (3) membership in integrated organizations, and (4) equality in employment. In both cases the respondent was simply asked a straightforward question which required a "yes" or "no" answer, or given a statement to which he was to express either agreement or disagreement.

When the respondents were asked to express opinions in regard to what local policy they approved of insofar as the relations between members of the dominant group and Mexican and Negro Americans were concerned, on the whole they approved of greater integration of Mexican Americans than of Negroes into the life of the community. The order in which they were willing to approve of the policy items for the two social categories of individuals is the same: greatest disapproval of integrated housing, and greatest approval of integration in employment in department stores. However, the difference in proportion approving in each case is striking. For example, twice as many people indicated that they would not object to living in neighborhoods with Mexican Americans as those who said they would consider integrated neighborhoods with Negro Americans acceptable (see Table 1). For each of the items the differences in response are significantly more in favor of integration with Mexican than with Negro Americans. The range of difference is from 22 percent on the question of integrated neighborhoods to 28 percent on the question of service in local restaurants.

These differences in attitudes may be attributed, in part, to the general feeling among Americans that race is a function of skin color and that the closer a minority approaches the dominant group on this trait, the more acceptable its members. That is, these attitudes may be part of a feeling of racism. That is not to say that Mexican Americans are in any way exempted from this feeling. They are not, but there is greater tolerance of them than of Negro Americans. In his early study of race attitudes, Bogardus found that in terms of social distance, both Negro and Mexican Americans were ranked toward the bottom of the list of the forty different social categories used. Mexicans, placing thirty-second, ranked higher than Negroes, who ranked thirty-fifth. Between these two were Japanese and Filipinos, and following them were Turks, Chinese, mulattoes, Koreans, and Hindus, in that order. It is not surprising, then, that in the present study, attitudes toward Mexican Americans are more favorable than attitudes toward Negro Americans. That is to say, this community mirrors the larger society.

TABLE 1

Percentage of Respondents Expressing Tolerance In
Local Policy Toward Mexican and Negro Americans

| | Percentage Approving* | | Range of |
	Mexicans	Negroes	Difference
I wonder if you would tell me whether you approve of the following for Mexicans and Negroes:			
living in mixed neighborhoods with other Americans (*i.e.*, whites)	45	23	22
joining social clubs with other Americans	48	25	23
using integrated barber and beauty shops	61	34	27
staying in integrated hotels	61	38	23
being served in integrated restaurants	74	46	28
being hired as department store sales clerks	76	52	24

*Those who expressed disapproval and those who refused to answer are omitted. However, in no case did more than 3 percent of the respondents in the sample fail to respond.

The ranking of these items forms a definite hierarchy, i.e., the items form a scale pattern; but there does not seem to be any single principle running through the ordering of the practices as to acceptability. There appears to be no direct relation between acceptability and impersonality, or public character, of the type of activity characterizing the various situations. While it is true that being a member of the same social club may involve a greater possibility of interpersonal relations than being served by a Negro or Mexican American sales clerk in a department store, to have a member of one of these minorities as a neighbor does not necessarily imply interpersonal association.

One possible explanation for the ordering of the items is that they imply to the respondent certain degrees of social equality. That is, it is possible that an individual perceives of residence in the same neighborhood as indicative of greater social equality than being served in the same restaurant, and so on. This may be the case regardless of the degree of physical proximity involved. It is also likely that these situations indicate the degrees of association which members of the dominant group have come to regard as "appropriate" or "normal" for members of minorities. For example, it is entirely possible that if serving members of a minority in restaurants has been taken for granted over the years in a particular location, and staying in hotels has not, the residents would be more likely to approve of the former than the latter. Field observations in this community indicate that there is greater acceptance of Mexican Americans in places of public accommodation than Negro Americans; hence, greater approval of integration with Mexican Americans as a matter of local policy.

It is true that in the South Negro Americans have been preparing food and serving as nursemaids for families in the dominant group for centuries. Both of these activities involve intimate (although not equal status) association, yet the same people who permit or even expect this type of association are unwilling to patronize a drive-in restaurant where Negroes are served in the privacy of their automobiles where no association is likely. In the one case the behavior is "appropriate;" in the other it is not.

These two explanations, of course, are not necessarily separate; they may be part of the same pattern. An individual may perceive of the existing local situation as one which has become "appropriate" or "normal" because it protects his position of social superiority.

Many of the residents of this city felt that minorities should be deprived of the rights they themselves enjoy. In each case, as was the situation with the local policy items, the members of the dominant group were willing to accord greater rights to Mexican than to Negro Americans. The range of difference varies from 11 percent on the item concerning social mixing to 22 percent on the item pertaining to membership in the same organizations. That is, in the first case, 11 percent more of the respondents were willing to grant this as a right to Mexican than to Negro Americans, and in the latter case, 22 percent more were willing to grant Mexican Americans this right than Negro Americans.

The order in which members of the dominant group were willing to accord these as rights to individuals in these two social categories is not unlike the ordering of the social policy items. A majority of the respondents felt that both should have the right to equal employment, while few felt that they should have the right to equality in housing (see Table 2). Again, in the case of these items, if one knows how many of these rights are acceptable, one can predict with reasonable assurance which they are. A respondent who is willing to grant individuals in these two social categories the right to live in an integrated neighborhood is also likely to approve of social mixing,

TABLE 2

*Percentage of Respondents Expressing Approval of
Equal Rights for Mexican and Negro Americans*

	Percentage Approving*		Range of Difference
	Mexicans	Negroes	
Should Mexicans and Negroes have the right to:			
live with other Americans	36	22	14
mix socially with other Americans	46	52	21
join the same organizations as other Americans	53	31	22
work side-by-side on the same jobs as other Americans	83	66	17

* Negative responses and instances where individuals refused to respond are not included. In no case did the latter exceed 4 percent.

integration in organizations and integrated employment. There is a slight difference in the attitudes of individuals in the dominant group toward minority rights in general as against what rights should be granted to minorities as a matter of local policy. There appears to be a greater willingness to grant rights as a matter of local policy than to accept them as something to which minorities might be entitled on a national scale. To take the case of integrated neighborhoods, 45 percent of the respondents said they would approve of this as local policy for Mexican Americans, but only 36 percent felt they should have this as a general right. There are slight differences on other comparable items, but these are not as great. Apparently these people feel that to put these questions in terms of rights is to accord to these minorities more than they are entitled to expect and that social and economic equality for minorities is more a privilege than a right.

The difference in degree of prejudice expressed toward Negro and Mexican Americans is, in part, a function of the nature of the two communities. In this city Mexican Americans as a community were less well-organized than the Negro Americans, and there was less pressure from the former for equal rights than from the latter. For example, the respondents were asked: "As you see it, are Negro Americans today demanding more than they have a right to or not?" One-third of them thought they were, while only 9 percent responded similarly regarding Mexican Americans when asked the same question about them. Greater pressure for equality on the part of Negro Americans, then, may have resulted in greater antipathy toward them. The greater prejudice toward Negro Americans is also probably partially a result of economic competition. In this community both Negro and Mexican Americans are engaged in primarily unskilled occupations; however, Mexican Americans generally are limited to occupations with other Mexican Americans, while Negro Americans tend to compete with unskilled members of the dominant group for work. Hence the latter may be more likely to perceive of Negro Americans as greater economic threats than Mexican Americans. The caste-like occupational status of Mexican Americans in the labor force in this community is characteristic of the status of Mexican Americans in other cities in the United States.

In the United States as a whole the Mexican American community has been without leadership and without organized political action groups. This is due partially to their lack of intergenerational social mobility. First and second generation Mexican Americans alike engage in the same low-status occupations. In general, they have been relegated to the lowest paid jobs in agriculture and industry. Many of them are seasonal agricultural workers. In this city alone, an additional 2,000 appear during the peak crop season. The long-time residents of Mexican descent are often resentful of their migratory fellow-country-men and endeavor to have the members of the dominant community perceive of them as "different." Finally, the Mexican American community is made up to a large extent of people who speak only Spanish. Rarely does the highly literate, English-speaking Mexican immigrate to the United States.

The pattern of prejudice toward Negro and Mexican Americans in this community is essentially the same. The differences which exist are in the degree to which the respondents expressed prejudice toward these two minorities. In this regard the differences are often great. Insofar as attitudes are concerned then, there is considerably less prejudice expressed toward Mexican than toward Negro Americans. In addition to the series of responses discussed above, the respondents were asked the rather direct question: "On the whole would you say you like or dislike Mexican people?" They were then asked the same question about Negroes. The first question elicited a "dislike" reply from only 6 percent of the respondents while the latter drew this response from 21 percent. These responses are not unlike those to the two sets of questions concerning local policy and rights insofar as the differences in attitudes toward these two minorities are concerned. Nevertheless, the status of the two minorities in practice is not significantly different. While it must be admitted that attitudes and behavior are not always correlated, it seems likely that in this community the possibility for improving the status of Mexican Americans is greater than for Negro Americans. While the former have language as an additional major barrier, they have potentially fewer handicaps than the latter.

CIVIL RIGHTS—NEED FOR EXECUTIVE BRANCH TO TAKE POSITIVE STEPS TO RECTIFY DISCRIMINATION IN JURY SELECTION, VOTING ELIGIBILITY AND SCHOOL ENROLLMENT*

JAMES DE ANDA

This paper discusses the problems of discrimination against Mexican Americans in jury service, voting eligibility and school enrollment, and the role of the Executive Branch in ending this discrimination.

When we speak of remedies for the denial of constitutional rights as they pertain to schools, voting and jury service, we are in the domain of the lawyer. So we must look not only at the Mexican American, the injured party, but to the private practitioner as well.

First, what of the party on whom the harm is inflicted? What kind of complainant does he make? Does he have a "damn the torpedoes, full speed ahead" approach? Unfortunately, no. There appears to be a uniformly fatalistic tolerance to the intolerable on the part of those whose rights are denied. Fear of reprisals, fear of failure, and ignorance of those rights are calculated to make a reluctant litigant. These factors are magnified in smaller communities where economic necessity requires a subservience to those who control the purse strings. In these areas, oftentimes the persons who make unlawful school board policies are the employers of the parents of children who are being discriminated against. Suing your boss, when a job is not easy to come by, is a very unhappy event calling for almost unnatural courage. The usual situation requires that a stimulus be provided to precipitate action by the injured parties to protect these cherished rights.

Can the individual lawyer provide this needed impetus? And will he? To date, the answer, with rare exception is "no." The traditional role of the lawyer, the canons and mores of the legal community, oppose the instigation or fomentation of lawsuits. Apart from this philosophi-

*The Mexican American: A New Focus on Opportunity, Inter-Agency Committee on Mexican American Affairs, U.S. Govt. Printing Office, Washington, D.C., 1967, pages 217-221.

cal barrier, there are practical considerations which make it difficult to find an advocate. The lack of funds for legal expenses is a detriment. Furthermore, identification with civil rights causes of this nature is calculated neither to enhance a lawyer's social status in his community nor his acceptance by the established economic interest. Again, these factors weigh most heavily in rural areas and in smaller urban centers.

How can this void be filled? How can these problems be exposed and corrections be made? One possible remedy would be for the administration to recommend legislation to provide for attorney's fees in school, jury and voting cases as is now provided under the equal employment provisions of the statutes. But this would not relieve the community pressures, economic reprisals and social stigma involved. The solution lies in executive action through investigators whose responsibility would be to ferret out violations, to consult and negotiate with school officials and to recommend court proceedings to the Attorney General in appropriate cases. This approach has been successfully used in practically all areas of government concern and regulation. The Equal Employment Commission is very active and openly solicits complaints and follows through on those complaints. The Labor Department is most active in enforcing minimum wage provisions. The accomplishments of these agencies in a relatively short time, illustrates the good that can flow through an aggressive agency, competently staffed.

Jury Discrimination

Other than the field of criminal law, where the defendant claims violation of his constitutional rights, little has been done to insure cross-section participation of the community on jury panels. Criminal lawyers are never hesitant to raise defenses based on violations of constitutional rights, and the protective court decisions touching on jury discrimination have been almost exclusively in this area where cases have been reversed because of illegalities in the jury selection process. These same illegalities occur in civil cases. An example of this was exposed in Corpus Christi, Texas, where I live. A study was made of civil juries and it was found that although forty-five percent of the people of Nueces County were of Mexican extraction, that only about five percent of the jury panels were Mexican Americans. This was attributed to disqualifications of jurors due to language handicap, absenteeism and a general group reluctance to serve on juries. However, a study made by a group of lawyers disclosed that residents of certain precincts, comprised almost exclusively of Mexican Americans and Negroes, were never called for jury service. The evidence was damning and overwhelming. The local bar association reviewed the facts presented by the study and consultations were had with the officials involved in jury selection. Unofficially the reason given for the situation was that "these jurors would never appear for jury service anyway and the county would lose money." "That these people were not qualified for jury service." The official reason given was that the jury wheel was too small and that the name cards did not properly mix. Solution — get a larger jury wheel. This was done and amazingly enough the following year the number of Mexican American names appearing on jury rolls increased to as much as forty percent of the total persons selected. The composition of the juries changed and so did the results of jury trials. A jury system is fair only if the jury selection is fair and only if the jury truly reflects a cross-section of the people. When this fails, then the miscarriages of justice that we are witnessing and have witnessed in the deep South in criminal cases results. What people do not understand is that their civil rights, their economic rights are affected just as are their personal privileges and liberty. Insurance companies are aware of this and there is a reluctance on the part of many insurance companies to issue liability insurance to minority groups simply because they think that a member of the minority group, when he goes to the courthouse, has two strikes against him; first, law enforcement prejudice, and second, juror and judicial prejudice. "An injured or dead Mexican isn't worth as much as an injured or dead Anglo" — I have had insurance company adjusters and lawyers blatantly make this statement to me in settlement negotiations and I have recognized the accuracy of what they say. Only a year ago one of my associates participated in a trial that resulted in a hung jury because one of the jurors believed and stated her position "that no Mexican was worth ten thousand dollars." Token representation on jury panels is not enough because under our system of pre-emptory challenges, the attorneys for each side have the right to strike a certain number of jurors without stated cause or reason. I do not criticize my adversaries for taking advantage of the situation. These are advocates whose duty is to do anything legal to win their case. I can and should criticize officials who permit this situation to exist. One other example might serve to illustrate the importance which all attorneys attach to the make-up of the jury. Court records in my county revealed that for a long period of time the prosecutors in criminal cases without exception struck from the jury list all Mexican American names in cases where a Mexican American was the defendant. One prosecutor had the habit of numbering his strikes in the order in which he made them. Invariably, the first names he struck were the Mexican American names. Again, I want to emphasize that this is not a criticism of the lawyer whose business it is to try to obtain the most favorable possible jury from the panel for his side of the case. My purpose in relating this story is to point out the need for more than token representation on juries of a particular ethnic group. Jury selection in federal courts has also been discriminatory and in many areas it has been accepted practice to use service club lists and personal knowledge to make up a jury list. In many areas federal juries have a reputation of being "blue ribbon juries." Voter registration lists have not been used but should be to get a true cross-section representation. The excuse that there will be inconvenience due to disqualified jurors may have some validity, but it does not override the necessity of an impartial jury of one's peers to pass judgment on a case.

School Enrollment

A steady stream of federal court decisions have made what we refer to as "de jure" segregation, old hat. Insofar as the Mexican American is concerned, "de jure" segregation (that is, segregation under color of law or policy — intentional segregation), while once widespread and accepted as much as the segregation laws directed toward the Negro, is past history. Occasional exceptions to this statement occur. But practicing segregationists, like other unlawful elements in our community, have moved "uptown." The segregationists and their methods have become more sophisticated and when backed to the wall by legislative enactments and court decisions, their ingenuity rises to the occasion. Therefore, we still have segregation, and be it "de jure" or "de facto," it is as harmful to its child victims.

Our neighborhood school concept has brought about substantial de facto (that is, unintended) segregation. This unfortunate result of neighborhood schools has been augmented by occasional de jure acts in creating school boundaries, broad exceptions to strict compliance with boundaries, and connivance with the real estate industry. While discrimination in housing is not within the gambit of my discussion, it bears a relationship to our school discrimination which cannot be ignored. The neighborhood school policy has made school segregation and housing segregation bedfellows. The housing segregationists, just as the school segregationists, have grown sly with the years. We seldom find deeds with racial covenants and restrictions. The provision that "No Mexicans, Spaniards, Spanish-speaking, Mexican Americans, Americans of Mexican origin" can own land or live in a particular area except as "groundkeepers, chauffeurs, maids and/or cooks" has been replaced by unwritten agreements on the part of developers, builders, real estate salesmen, and even financial institutions. Loans are not approved, houses are sold to others by "mistake," delays are encountered, appointments are not kept. Combinations of these things or all of them occur to prevent the sale of a house to an undesirable. Yet we have the tools to prevent the occurrence of these injustices. There are FHA and VA regulations promulgated to prevent discrimination. Unfortunately, there has been very little effort that I have observed on the part of these agencies to enforce these rules. These agencies and their inspectors are quick to point out any deficiency or inadequacy in a home or any failure to comply with building requirements. But these same staff people ignore violations of racial discrimination, and if they are doing anything about it, they have been most discreet. If these agencies would mend their ways and require compliance with their rules, there would be at least slight relief to our current de facto segregation. I want to emphasize the word "slight" because our minority group has other serious hurdles to clear apart from the housing practices mentioned.

The low economic state of many Mexican Americans would keep most out of the more desirable residential areas. What of the children who are kept in the slum areas and in the ghettos by the low economic state of their parents? These children must depend wholly on the school system for their academic betterment. They can get little or no help with their homework or advice on school matters from parents who never attended a day of school. These children should have the very best that a school system can give them to substitute for that which is expected of more fortunate parents. Yet the opposite is true. These children usually attend school in old and dilapidated buildings;

their curriculum is "toned down" partly because school officials don't expect them to know much anyway and partly because their teachers are usually the most inferior that the system has. These schools are overcrowded and school supplies and teaching aids are scarce and rundown. As pointed out by one recent federal court opinion, we cannot ignore the constitutional mandate of "equal education" despite the demise of the "separate but equal" doctrine. De facto segregation is a burden of the poor. Be the child, "white trash, mexican or nigger," it is his poorness that makes him the object of discrimination.

What can be done? Unequal schools, unequal facilities, overcrowding and ill-prepared teachers are obvious to anyone who will but look. And when such a situation is known to exist, the policy of "deliberate speed" has no place. It should be replaced by a policy of "immediate change." Such can be accomplished by an aggressive agency, prompt to seek judicial relief and prompt to take administrative steps such as the suspension of funds, accreditations, purchase of government equipment and other steps, when cooperation is not immediately forthcoming.

In the administration of housing policies, such as rent supplement housing, care should be taken not to authorize projects where they will result in creating slums and ghetto areas. As an example of this, I again point to Corpus Christi. A recently approved housing development is to be constructed which will be used exclusively by Mexican Americans for it will be in a Mexican American neighborhood and no one else will want to live there. The schools in this area are already overly congested and inferior to the system as a whole. Yet the problems of this area will now be magnified and increased and left to some future generation to try to solve. Inadequate planning, well meaning though it be, is still inadequate.

Voting Discrimination

It is a statistical reality that the Mexican American group falls far behind other ethnic groups in its participation at the polls. This applies both to persons registered to vote and to those who vote after being registered. In Texas the reasons for this state of affairs have been a poll tax now abolished; an unreasonable and unfair deadline for registering to vote (January 31 of each year); rigid and unrealistic interpretation by our state officials of our registration laws; and setting general elections on a weekday.

We must acknowledge with some embarrassment that our voter partcipation is less than just about any country in the world which holds free elections. In Vietnam we have been told that approximately seventy-five percent of the electorate went to the polls in the recent elections. Texas could seldom top or equal this figure. The precincts of the wealthy, of the controlling interests, of the well-to-do, invariably vote much more heavily than do the precincts of the minorities. Indifference plays a part, but like the jury wheel situation I discussed earlier, it is not the answer. I do not know how much effort has been made to change our general election day from a Tuesday to a Saturday but I do not hesitate to make this recommendation, or as an alternative, to declare election day a national holiday. Although our election laws provide that the polls shall be opened from 7 a.m. until 7 p.m., for all practical purposes, the poor working man can vote only late in the afternoon and early evening. Job requirements, not infrequently artificial, may deprive a person of his right to vote.

The legality of unnecessary and unreasonable voter registration procedures should be challenged at every turn by the Attorney General. Only a few days ago, the Attorney General of the State of Texas, issued an opinion (in direct contradiction to a previous opinion issued by another attorney general) that persons who send in their registration applications by mail, must send those applications in individual envelopes, and that voting registrars could not accept applications mailed in bulk, nor presented in bulk by civic organizations or others. The stated reason for this interpretation was that "it would prevent fraud." Our Attorney General has never stated why mailing applications separately rather than together makes for a more honest registration. In view of the fact that it is the duty of the registrar in each county to mail the registration certificate only to the applicant at the applicant's residence, I have been unable to find anything beneficial in the interpretation. It does make it most difficult for civic organizations and volunteer public spirited citizens to hold registration drives and register voters. It would appear to me that such an interpretation should be challenged in the courts but to date, nothing has been done. In Texas, voting instructions can be given only in the English language. Such a rule has no valid purpose in areas where representatives of all interests are bilingual.

Conclusions. Despite the real or fancied impediments to immediate, effective administrative action, the Executive Branch and its agencies must recognize that we can no longer afford to wait, to make studies, to gather statistics and then shake our head in anguish. The problems demand immediate solutions. Those agencies that have exercised diligence and sincerity have been rewarded for their work. Our draft boards have not had the same difficulty in finding qualified people as have our jury commissioners. In Nueces County, over 75% of the men killed in Vietnam bear Mexican American names. I do not mention this boastfully for I have no reason to brag of the heroism and sacrifice of others. I simply use this illustration to point out that where an agency wants minority group participation, this is accomplished quickly and in full measure — protests, language handicap, lack of training and all else, notwithstanding.

EDUCATION

EDUCATION

The chief means by which a culture reproduces itself are agencies through which the cultural heritage is transmitted from one generation to the next. In primitive societies this is done largely through the extended family, by imitation, and by practice. When cultures are highly complex, as is that of the United States, formal institutions arise which are entrusted with much of this socialization process. Young people cannot function to their full potential if this educational, socialization process is poor or partial. It is not only a truism but also a demonstrable, scientific fact that for the majority of children the school is a chief source of occupational success and social and economic status. In modern American society there are few niches left for the functionally illiterate.

Acquiring a satisfactory amount of the current cultural heritage is easy for children who enter the educational system without handicaps. If they do have handicaps, their problems are serious, and most Mexican American youths do have at least two handicaps. On the average they possess, on entering school, less of the "American" cultural heritage; e.g., are "culturally disadvantaged," as compared to the average Anglo child. Second, instruction is in English, and the fluency in English of a majority of Mexican American children from the *barrio* is considerably below that of their Anglo peers. Although they have equal intelligence, their progress through the middle class, Anglo-oriented school is significantly less. If the motivation for education which the average *Chicano* child receives from home and from his peers is also less than the Anglo average, his progress is even more slow and uncertain.

It is estimated that approximately 45% of the Spanish speaking residents of the five southwestern states have less than five years of schooling. This is even more serious than appears on the surface, because many Mexican American parents cannot pass on to their children the attitudes, skills, and culture traits which are necessary for a successful adjustment to the dominant Anglo culture. This places the larger portion of the burden for such training on the schools, and if the child is unsuccessful in school and does not remain long, he loses this important potential as well as the more routine educational benefits. The problem is particularly acute for the children of *Chicano* migratory workers, although the federal Migrant Children Educational Assistance Act of 1960 provides some financial assistance for states which make special efforts to give the migrant children a successful educational experience. Even if no hard data are available, it is probable that Mexican American children from the *barrio* rank lower educationally than other groups in the United States except the American Indians and blacks in specific areas of the Deep South.

In "Statement of Philosophy and Policy as They Pertain to the Acculturation and Education of the Mexican American," Marcos de León, a professional educator from California, indicates some of the principles which should underlie education in the United States, and he makes a series of specific recommendations as to how these principles should be implemented, especially in the education of Mexican American youth. In "Adult Illiteracy," A. R. Ramirez, a professional educator in the Rio Grande Valley of Texas, formulates the causes of illiteracy among Mexican Americans, the typical life cycle of an illiterate, and gives strong recommendations for action to prevent the continuation of this condition. "The Invisible Minority" selection, a portion of a pamphlet (subtitle: *"Pero no vencibles"*), reports a study made by the National Education Association in Tucson, Arizona, on the teaching of Spanish to Spanish-speaking children. This study reports the problems, shows examples of concrete programs which cope with those problems, and makes specific recommendations for future programs. In "School Bells for Migrants," Mr. Blubaugh, a California journalist, reports on the recent educational programs for the children of migratory agricultural workers in California. Julian Nava, a professional historian, an elected member of the Los Angeles City Board of Education, is one of the top twenty-five Mexican Americans holding elective office in the United States. In "Cultural Backgrounds and Barriers that Affect Learning by Spanish-Speaking Children," Dr. Nava focuses particularly on the role of language in public education, and how it affects learning by Mexican American children. For some such children English language instruction causes a serious trauma, damaging their ego and self-image, and resulting in under-achievement. Difficulty with English, says Nava, is at the bottom of the entire complex of problems the child faces. Lack of understanding by teachers makes the situation worse, and "the teaching schedule must go on." A speaking accent is an immediate and usually continuing handicap. Among the major differences which set the Mexican American group apart are: (1) they do not fit the European immigrant model; (2) they are of widely varying types; (3) they exemplify a conquered people; (4) they have a reluctance to assimilate; (5) their being of Mexican descent is a special handicap; (6) the proximity of Mexico causes a constant reinforcement of Mexican culture. Mr. A. R. Rodriguez, chief of the Office of Education's Mexican American Affairs Unit, authors "Speak up, *Chicano*," a brief narrative report of a recent official visit to the "Mexican" schools in five states.

STATEMENT OF PHILOSOPHY AND POLICY AS THEY PERTAIN TO THE ACCULTURATION AND EDUCATION OF THE MEXICAN-AMERICAN*

MARCOS DE LEON

I. PRINCIPLES:
1. The purposes of Education in American Democracy, as defined by the Educational Policies Commission specifying the function of the school are to be implemented as basic principles.

II. CONCEPTS:
1. To strengthen the underpinnings of these principles and make the acculturative process a smoother and more stable process, the following concepts are offered as imperatives.
   (a) Accept the reality of the Anglo Saxon and Hispanic ethic as they exist in the Western Hemisphere, meeting and throwing circles of influence over one another in the Southwest, creating a permanent and perpetual historical cultural continuum through the movement of peoples.
   (b) This cultural buffer area forms the framework for the process of acculturation affecting both groups, from which emanates two subconcepts; the culture within a culture concept and the function of the school having to become twofold, i.e., perpetuating the core of values of the cultures of which the school is a functional part.
   (c) Within this framework any "long or short term goal" educational program to be effected has to be based on the values, cultural potential and educational needs of both communities, together with the needs of all individuals, including ages, abilities, interests, cultural differences and socioeconomic status. This is the motivation, the "glue" that will hold it together.

---

*Unpublished manuscript, 1964.

(d) Embrace a functional theory of culture and its relation to the growth of human personality and how such a person adjusts to a maximum to the demands of the two cultures: bilingual in the true sense, and the proud inheritor of both the Anglo Saxon and Hispanic traditions, thus permitting greater social mobility, participation and acceptance as a useful citizen to his community and the nation. This entails a broader acceptance of the acculturation process as an educational precept.

III. RECOMMENDATIONS:

1. The school-community idea be given greater depth in meaning, better purpose in implementation. These two entities have long been geometrical parallel lines: Never meeting to explore and exploit their potential.

   (a) The creation of a core of counselors to serve as liaison workers between school and community, establish and supervise programs in which the leadership of both school personnel and community are to be utilized to a maximum. Wherever possible these counselors should be bilingual, especially, where the demand for Spanish exists as the spoken vernacular.

2. To Strengthen Cultural Awareness and Self-image:

   (a) Spanish should be taught as early as possible on the Elementary level and coordinated with the English Program and made a "must" or a strong elective for non-academic students in the Junior and Senior High Schools;

   (b) Units on History, Literature, Art, Music, regional dress and foods concerning Spain, Mexico and other Latin-American Countries be developed in the present courses in Social Studies, Home Economics and Art, not only for the purpose expressed above, but also to create a more informed general citizenry.

3. Establish a definite and specific program for compensatory education with the objective of supplementing the normal education effort and preparing the Mexican-American child to compete and achieve within the existing education program:

(a) Such programs whether in the Elementary, Junior High or Senior High School should have continuity as determined by (1) "C" under Concepts; (2) stipulations made by Federal and State Authorities.

(b) These programs can be extensive and costly as the "Higher Horizon Program" in New York City, or smaller target areas can be selected involving the community, curriculum, guidance, counseling, attendance, and tutorial areas as specific projects.

(c) While it is recommendable that such programs be made available for the Elementary, Junior High and Senior High Schools, it is strongly recommended that a great deal of concentrated effort be placed within pre-school, the Elementary and Junior High Schools.

4. The total concept of education as to philosophy and program can certainly be extended and implemented in the area of Adult Education.

5. It is strongly recommended that the potential leadership in the various schools as well as the community be utilized to effect any program within the District.

(a) In-service training for teachers and community leaders is recommended, preferably in small groups with the technique of the workshop at its best.

(b) Utilize panels, speakers, and seminars for this purpose, correlating any effort with compiled materials in a Kit containing historical, sociological, and statistical materials, and recommendations as to philosophy and programs.

6. Develop continuing flexible programs of testing, guidance and counseling which will permit the discovery as early as possible of the potential and creativeness of each child, the identification and development of the academically able student, the so-called "slow gifted" and the culturally different child, motivating him toward definite educational goals, thus preventing him from becoming misplaced within the school as to ability and interest and thus becoming a drop-out.

7. Expanding and modernizing the vocational program of the comprehensive high school so as to give adequate adaptability to a technological changing community.

8. In reference to community relations and communications it is urged that bulletins be developed which are more meaningful to the general public and more interesting in format especially when they are intended to be sent home, and that Spanish be used in the appropriate areas.

9. Recruit, hire, and place bilingual teachers, counselors and administrators *who have understanding of the Mexican-American child and his community.*

10. Consultants should be utilized to the fullest extent to (1) aid school personnel set-up projects; (2) act as consultant for such, for teachers' in-service training, and in-service training for community leaders.

ADULT ILLITERACY*

A. R. RAMIREZ
Assistant Director, Valley Association for Superior Education,
Edinburg, Texas

The rate of illiteracy among Americans of Mexican ancestry is unusually high as a result of one or a combination of the following factors:

1. Immigration laws which permit a constant flow of new citizens unable to speak, read or write the English language;

2. Inadequate instruction of non-English speaking school children due to untrained teachers, inappropriate methods and materials, and sometimes, to discriminatory practices;

3. Limited educational aspirations of this population which are often a result of frustration brought about by repeated failures at impossible tasks imposed by the school;

4. Limited opportunities for adults to get a second chance to achieve literacy.

A change in immigration laws may not be in the national interest, and in any case, this in itself would not help raise the educational level of individuals already residing in this country. Any permanent solution lies in the improvement of educational opportunities for both children and adults rather than in the control of the growth of this population group.

The typical life cycle of the undereducated Mexican American develops in the manner:

1. He is reared in an humble home, in a large family. Spanish is the only language spoken and it is seldom read or written in the home.

2. He lives in a Spanish speaking neighborhood and at age 6 attends a neighborhood school where all of the pupils come from Spanish-speaking homes. His daily schedule, his books, his tests, his entire

---

*The Mexican American: A New Focus on Opportunity, Inter-Agency Committee on Mexican American Affairs, U.S. Govt. Printing Office, Washington, D.C., 1967, pages 119-120.

school life is patterned after that of his English-speaking counterparts in the school across town. Academic failure — the repeating of grades or retentions — and eventual dropout constitutes the school record of at least 75% of these youngsters. The school has not helped him achieve literacy in his native language and has insisted that he learn to read English before he speaks it well. At best, he leaves school without marketable skills and with only a slight knowledge of English.

3. He marries a fellow dropout at an early age. They have several children and the cycle begins anew for each of his children.

This cycle can be broken in the public schools. Better still, it can be broken through a comprehensive program of family education in combination with improvements in public education.

First, the agency with the responsibility for the education of citizens beyond the public school age must be determined. School districts are reluctant to assume responsibility. Institutions of higher education do not indicate willingness to accept the assignment. If neither local nor state educational agencies willingly provide the funds, organization, and leadership required, perhaps a federal system is needed. We have federal law enforcement, federal employment assistance, federal mail service, federal agricultural assistance, federal housing assistance—why not a federal educational system for needs not being met by local and state governments?

Probably the most desirable arrangement is one of a cooperative endeavor involving the three levels of government, but there are local authorities all across the Southwest who are not ready to accept this challenge. If all local districts had met their obligations in the past, we would have no need for federal aid. No blanket indictment is intended by these general statements. There is ample evidence that many of our school boards are committed to quality education for all citizens.

In referring to the life patterns of the non-English speaking individual, the question of adequacy of instruction was mentioned. Regardless of the sponsorship of adult schools, this problem of instructional methods will still have to be resolved. Materials and methods currently employed in literacy classes in my state are those developed for illiterate English speakers. There are no guides for teachers, no adequate training of teachers, no texts for teaching English as a second language — hardly any consideration given to the special needs of the Spanish-speaking adult student. This is exactly the same deficiency noted in our public schools. How can we convince our educators of the fundamental premise that no meaningful instruction in reading and writing can take place until the learner has mastered orally the material he is expected to read and write? Until this gets across we are going to be stumbling around and creating unnecessary confusion and discouragement. We need to give these learners a series of successful experiences and we cannot do it with the methods and materials we have been using.

We should consider the possibility of providing Spanish literacy instruction as part of the adult program. For beginning students, part of the evening would be devoted to reading and writing Spanish and the rest of the time, perhaps three-fourths, to oral English instruction. By the time the students are ready to begin reading English they will have acquired skills that will enable them to read *Life, Popular Mechanics, Readers Digest,* and other English language periodicals translated into Spanish, as well as newspapers and books also readily available along the Mexican border. Furthermore, most of the mysteries of the reading process will have been cleared up, and the pattern of failures reversed.

While he is achieving literacy in Spanish, the adult learner is taught the sound system and the grammar of English through example and through extensive practice. Teachers need special training in this type of instruction. They need guides, illustrations, and tapes — both for Spanish literacy classes and for the oral English instruction.

Odd as it may seem, the United States government has done more to help citizens of other countries learn English in their own lands than it has done for non-English-speaking American citizens in this country. We know that there are texts and tapes and teacher training programs available through the State Department for overseas use. Why can't these materials be made available to our teachers and students of English?

Above all, we need a planned program that will be adequately financed for several years and that will be broad enough to take into consideration the factors working against us. Evening classes are inevitable, but, in a way, desirable. Classrooms and teachers are easier to contract for night classes. All members of the family are available for instruction at that time of the day.

It would be possible to have child care and kindergarten activities for the children below school age, study and enrichment activities (perhaps Spanish literacy classes) for those of school age, and a full adult education program for the parents. The enthusiasm that can be generated for learning under such a schedule can be of inestimable value in changing the levels of aspiration of our under-educated citizens.

Several teachers of Mexican American adult basic education classes were asked to make recommendations and suggestions for presentation at these hearings. There was unanimous concern about materials, both for students and teachers. One group of teachers asked for research findings on the suitability of various instructional materials for classes of Spanish-speaking adults and for the selection of materials on this basis. They also suggested that the number of class hours, now set at 120, be increased in order to progress more rapidly.

Now for a final suggestion. In order to limit the chances of failure, let us have the materials on hand, the teachers trained, the funds assured, the facilities contracted, and the maximum enrollment determined BEFORE we seek students. Then let us establish enforceable policies concerning age, family size, residence, attendance, etc., that the father will accept for himself and his dependents. Then let us enroll families, teach them, and keep teaching them until they achieve independence as literate bilinguals and as self-sufficient participating citizens.

THE INVISIBLE MINORITY*

While a majority of the Spanish-speaking people in the Southwest were born in this country and are citizens of the United States, they tend to be regarded both by themselves and others as Mexicans. The term Mexican-American would be more nearly accurate. More important than technicalities, however, is how they feel . . . how they regard themselves.

Me

To begin with, I am a Mexican. That sentence has a scent of bitterness as it is written. I feel that if it weren't for my nationality I would accomplish more. My being a Mexican has brought about my lack of initiative. No matter what I attempt to do, my dark skin always makes me feel that I will fail.

Another thing that "gripes" me is that I am such a coward. I absolutely will not fight for something even if I know I'm right. I do not have the vocabulary that it would take to express myself strongly enough.

Many people, including most of my teachers, have tried to tell me I'm a leader. Well, I know better! Just because I may get better grades than most of my fellow Mexicans doesn't mean a thing. I could no more get an original idea in my head than be President of the United States. I don't know how to think for myself.

I want to go to college, sure, but what do I want to be? Even worse, where do I want to go? These questions are only a few that trouble me. I'd like to prove to my parents that I can do something. Just because I don't have the gumption to go out and get a job doesn't mean that I can't become something they'll be proud of. But if I find that I can't bring myself to go to college, I'll get married and they'll still get rid of me.

After reading this, you'll probably be surprised. This is the way I feel about myself, and nobody can change me. Believe me, many have tried and failed. If God wants me to reach all my goals, I will. No parents, teachers, or priest will change the course that my life is to follow. Don't try.

This was a paper turned in by a 13-year old girl for an English assignment in the eighth grade of a school in one of the Southwestern

*The Invisible Minority. Report of the NEA-Tucson Survey on the Teaching of Spanish to the Spanish Speaking; Department of Rural Education, National Education Association, 1201 Sixteenth Street, N.W., Washington, D.C. 20036, 1966.

states. The assignment was to write about "Me." The melancholy tone of the essay would suggest that the youngster was a "loner" — obscure, unattractive, not very popular. But no. She was attractive, articulate, an honor student, member of the band, outstanding in girls' athletics, popular among her fellow students, admired by her teachers. "She never *seemed* to be a child with a problem," remarked one of the teachers, in some puzzlement, after reading "Me."

The problem can be stated plainly and simply: The young girl who wrote that essay was Mexican-American. If she, with all her advantages, felt that her lot inevitably would be failure, how must thousands of other Mexican-American children — many of them less endowed physically and intellectually — view their own prospects?

357 Years of History

To understand the problem fully, we must understand how it came about. The first white people to migrate into what is now the American Southwest were Spanish-speaking. They came by way of Mexico during the period of Spain's colonial expansion and settled portions of the Southwest even before the founding of the Plymouth Colony. Plymouth was established in 1620, but the first Spaniards settled at Santa Fe, New Mexico, a full 11 years before that — in 1609. By 1680 there were some 2,500 Spanish-speaking settlers in what we now call New Mexico. By 1790 there were an estimated 23,000 Spanish-speaking people in the five Southwestern states covered by this study area. Indeed, the white population of the Southwest — what there was of it — was practically all Spanish. New Mexico had the largest concentration.

But soon after the 13 colonies gained their independence from England, the migration of English-speaking Americans into the Southwest began. Mexico, its own independence newly-one from Spain, encouraged such migration. This vast Southwestern area, stretching from the western border of Louisiana to the Pacific, belonged to Mexico. She was anxious to see it settled and developed, and few Mexican colonists were moving there. So the government of Mexico granted large blocks of land to contractors who would bring in colonists. The response was large and prompt. By 1835 there were 25,000 to 35,000 American farmers, planters and traders in Texas, and more were on the way.

The deluge dismayed Mexico, and she tried to check it. Land grants were cancelled. The Texans became irked, and in 1836 they revolted against Mexican over-lordship and won their independence. Shortly afterward Texas was admitted to the Union. A dispute broke out between the U.S. and Mexico over the southwestern boundary of Texas. The result was the Mexican War and the loss by Mexico of nearly all that remained of her Northernmost empire. To the U.S. were ceded much of New Mexico, most of Arizona, the future states of California, Nevada and Utah, and parts of Colorado and Wyoming. Five years later the Gadsden Purchase added a strip of land between the Gila River and the present southern boundary of Arizona and New Mexico, completing the American acquisition of what is now the Southwest.

Alien and Alienated

Thus, by one of history's ironies, the majority became a minority. Spanish-speaking people who had been the first whites to settle the Southwest became, if not an alien group, an alienated group. They were Americans, yes, but with a language and culture different from the language and culture of the region in which they found themselves. On both sides feelings had been exacerbated by the way.

Nationalistic passions have long since cooled. Mexico and the United States live side by side in peace. But in the Southwest a cultural and linguistic gulf still exists between Mexican-Americans — the "invisible minority," as they have been called — and Anglo-Americans. "Unlike the immigrant from Europe," says John M. Sharp, Professor of Modern Languages at Texas Western College, El Paso, "(the Mexican-American) is by no means willing to abandon his ancient cultural and linguistic heritage, in which he takes — however inarticulately — traditional pride, to accept the cultural pattern common to native speakers of English in our nation. His position may, perhaps, be compared to that of the Greeks in Sicily, who, though citizens of a Latin-speaking area, have maintained their language and mores for some 23 centuries." Thus the strong assimilationist impulses of other immigrant groups — Jewish, Irish, Italian, etc. — are not so conspicuous among the Mexican-Americans. Nor are all Mexican-Americans possessed of the strong materialistic drive — the "individual success psychology," as one authority has put it — of so many Anglo-Americans.

The Legacy of Poverty

There is another factor which makes the gulf difficult to bridge — which to a considerable extent keeps the Mexican-American an "outsider" in his own land. It is the fact that so many immigrants from Mexico were well down on the economic scale when they came to this country. They were, in the main, unskilled and semi-skilled laborers, dissatisfied with conditions in Mexico, hoping that in the North they would be able to improve their lot. And, as is so often the case, first-generation immigrants tended to bequeath their poverty to the generations that come after them.

Thus we find poverty far more prevalent among Mexican-Americans than among Anglo-Americans. In all five Southwestern states, the average income of white people with Spanish surnames is well below that of the general population, as the following table illustrates:

TABLE 1

*Frequency of Low and High Family Incomes in the Southwest
(Census of 1960)*

	Families with Incomes under $1000		Families with Incomes under $3000		Families with Incomes of $10,000 or more	
	General Population	White Spanish Surname Population	General Population	White-Spanish Surname Population	General Population	White-Spanish Surname Population
Arizona	5.9%	7.2%	21.3%	30.8%	14.4%	4.6%
California	3.3	4.5	14.1	19.1	21.8	10.8
Colorado	3.5	6.4	18.3	35.0	14.6	4.8
New Mexico	6.9	11.3	24.4	41.5	14.3	4.5
Texas	7.6	13.6	32.5	51.6	11.8	2.7
Southwest	4.9	8.8	21.0	34.8	17.6	6.6

Low Achievers . . . Dropouts

An almost inevitable concomitant of poverty is low educational achievement. Herschel T. Manuel, in his definitive book, *Spanish-Speaking Children of the Southwest: Their Education and the Public Welfare (University of Texas Press, Austin, Texas)*, reports that one-sixth of the school-age population of the five Southwestern states is Spanish-speaking. Yet, he notes, the proportion of school dropouts among the Spanish-speaking is far higher than one-sixth. California made a study of the educational disparity between the Mexican-American and his fellow citizens as of 1960. It found that the level of education reached by that part of the population bearing Spanish surnames was well below the level of the total population and even below that of the non-white population. More than half of the males and nearly half of the females 14 years old and over had not gone beyond the eighth grade. By contrast, only 27.9 percent of the males and 25 percent of the females over 14 in the total population had not gone beyond the eighth grade. A little over 72 percent of the males in the total population and 75 percent of the females had completed one or more years of high school, but only 48.5 percent of the males and 52 percent of the females of Spanish surnames had done so. In the total population, 23.4 percent of the males and 19.4 percent of the females had completed one or more years of college. But no more than 8.8 percent of the Spanish-surnamed males and 6.2 percent of the females had reached that educational eminence.

Why does the Mexican-American youngster drop out of school in such large numbers? For an answer, we need to look at his performance while he is still in school. Again California supplies us with some vital clues. An analysis of achievement tests was made in the Lindsay Unified School District of Lindsay, California, a city of 5,500 located about midway between Fresno and Bakersfield. It is an agricultural community with a high proportion of Mexican-Americans. The analysis showed that in all the educational fundamentals — reading, arithmetic and language — Mexican-American children lagged far behind the Anglo-Americans, as measured by the California Achievement Tests. In reading, 63.9 percent of the Mexican-American children were below grade level compared to 27.3 percent of the Anglo-Americans. In arithmetic, 38.7 percent of the Mexican-Americans were below grade level, compared to 20.8 percent of the Anglo-Americans. In language, the comparative percentages were 55.5 and 30.6. Total battery: 53.4 percent of the Mexican-Americans below grade level; 28.1 percent of the others.

Said the Lindsay report: " . . . These children (Mexican-Americans) start school with a decided handicap, fall behind their classmates in the first grade, and each passing year finds them farther behind.

They are conditioned to failure in the early years of their schooling and each passing year only serves to reinforce their feelings of failure and frustration. Is it any wonder that as soon as they are 16 or can pass for 16, they begin dropping out of school?"

That question having been asked, we need then to ask another and more significant question: Is there something inherent in our system of public schooling that impedes the education of the Mexican-American child — that, indeed, drives him to drop out? And the answer, unhappily, must be yes. " . . . The greatest barrier to the Mexican-American child's scholastic achievement . . . is that the schools, reflecting the dominant view of the dominant culture, want that child to grow up as another Anglo. This he cannot do except by denying himself and his family and his forebears. Dr. Manuel puts it another way: "Ironically the child who enters school with a language deficiency and the cultural deprivation of long-continued poverty is often made unbearably aware of his disadvantages. School is supposed to help him solve these problems; instead it convinces him that they are beyond solution."

The Spanish-Speaking Home

Let us see what happens to the average Mexican-American child when he starts school. He comes to school speaking Spanish. He knows some English but has used it infrequently. The language of his home, the language of his childhood, his first years, is Spanish. His environment, his experiences, his very personality have been shaped by it.

To understand how totally Spanish the background of such a child may be, consider the results of a study made in 1965 in San Antonio, Texas, and reported to the El Paso conference of foreign language teachers. Six hundred Mexican-American adults were interviewed in San Antonio, and it was found that 71 percent of husbands and wives spoke only Spanish to each other. Among the grandparents, 94 percent spoke only Spanish to their children and 89 percent spoke only Spanish to their grandchildren.

Understandably, therefore, the child from this Spanish-saturated environment, once embarked on his school career, finds himself in a strange and even threatening situation. The language of instruction is English. Yet English, as John M. Sharp expressed it at the El Paso conference, may be "no less a foreign language to him that it would be to a child from Argentina or Columbia. He suddenly finds himself not only with the pressing need to master an (to him) alien tongue, but, also at the same time, to make immediate use of it in order to function as a pupil. His parents, to whom he has always looked for protection and aid, can be of no help at all to him in his perplexity. Moreover, as a result of cultural and economic differences between the English-speaking and Spanish-speaking segments of his community, many of the objects, social relationships and cultural attitudes presented to him in his lessons, though perfectly familiar to an Anglo youngster, lie without the Latin American's home experience. Accordingly, the problem of learning English is, for him, enormously increased by his unfamiliarity with what objects and situations the no less unfamiliar words and phrases stand for."

Barriers and Bastions

Even in schools with an almost totally Spanish-American enrollment — schools which are for all practical purposes *de facto* segregated — textbooks and curricula used are often the same as in schools with a large Anglo-American majority. As Professor Sharp tells us: "The three R's are taught in English from the first grade up, and *no classes specifically with English as a foreign language are offered.* Operating under such unrealistic conditions (which appear to have been devised by people who seemed to believe that if they paid no attention to the problem it would go away), conscientious teachers and administrators have done the best they could for their students. Subject matter is watered down and used as a means to teach English. During the two or three years of primary school while the pupil is acquiring a minimal knowledge of English, he falls seriously behind his English-speaking contemporaries in other phases of the curriculum. This loss in subject-knowledge is seldom made up by the time he enters high school, where he finds himself unable to compete scholastically with his Anglo-American schoolmates."

The Mexican-American child encounters not only linguistic barriers but psychological barriers. One of the working committee reports developed at the El Paso conference described them in these words: " . . . A sudden immersion in English at six years of age, especially in an environment which lacks the plasticity and warmth of human relationships found in the home, occurring at the same time that new demands of work and discipline are made, may create psychological barriers almost instantaneously which will not disappear in a lifetime.

The teacher may sense the presence of these barriers and may react by putting up barriers of his own, unconsciously attempting to compensate thereby for his sense of inadequacy in dealing with the child. The result may be that the Spanish language becomes a refuge into which the child retreats at every opportunity, and the Spanish-speaking community a bastion of defense against the outside world."

The Laws of the Anglos

In most states, the schools are actually mandated by law to make English the language of instruction. An appropriate comment on this type of law was forthcoming recently from Charles Olstad, Assistant Professor of Romance Languages at the University of Arizona: "I had always thought such a law archaic, a carry-over from early days of benighted ethnocentrism, a distorted form of super-patriotism which saw anything non-English as a threat to the nation." In some schools the speaking of Spanish is forbidden both in classrooms and on the playground, except, of course, in classes where Spanish is taught. Not infrequently students have been punished for lapsing into Spanish. This has even extended to corporal punishment. A member of our Survey team tells of one school at which such punishment was dealt out to children who lapsed into Spanish despite the fact that 99 percent of the school's enrollment was Mexican-American! The obvious theory is that a child will learn English if he is required to speak English and nothing but English, at least during those hours of the day when he is in school. "If you want to be American, speak American," he is admonished over and over again.

Fitting the Stereotype

Nor is it only a different language that the newly-arrived Mexican-American child encounters. He also encounters a strange and different set of cultural patterns, an accelerated tempo of living and, more often than not, teachers who, though sympathetic and sincere, have little understanding of the Spanish-speaking people, their customs, beliefs and sensitivities. He is given an intelligence test in which language and cultural and socio-economic background are depressing factors. He may have fully as much intellectual potential as his Anglo-American classmates, but he shows up on the test as a "low achiever." He tends thus to become stereotyped in the eyes of the adults whose lives impinge on his. All of them — teachers, administrators, even parents —

expect little of him, and he usually measures up (or down) to their expectations.

If he knows little or no English, he may be placed in a special class with other non-English-speaking children for a year and then "promoted" to the first grade the following year. But that means he must go through school a year behind other children of his age, and this embarrasses him.

Even if he speaks both English and Spanish, he may be only nominally bilingual - not truly so. He may have, as he often does, a low level of literacy in both languages. He watches television at home, as do his Anglo-American schoolmates. He listens to the radio. Soon he is speaking a language which is neither Spanish nor English but a mixture of the two — a kind of linguistic hybrid. He doesn't speak English correctly and he doesn't speak Spanish correctly.

There is something sadly paradoxical about the schools' well-meaning effort to make the Mexican-American child "talk American" — to eradicate his Spanish. For they are at the same time working strenuously to teach Spanish to the Anglo-American student, acclaiming the advantages of being able to communicate fluently in a language other than one's own. The National Defense Education Act is providing funds to schools to strengthen the teaching of modern foreign languages as well as mathematics, science, and other subjects. And so, while they strive to make the monolingual student bilingual, they are making — or trying to make the bilingual student monolingual.

Compulsion Breeds Withdrawal

The prohibition against speaking Spanish leads to some curious situations. For one thing, the school cannot enforce it. Or, rather it cannot accomplish what the rule is intended to accomplish, which is the universal speaking of English. "Obviously," says James Burton, who teaches English and speech to Mexican-American students at Jefferson High School in El Paso, Texas, "it is impossible to make a person speak a language. Any teacher in control of his classroom can prevent his students from speaking Spanish, but the result is likely to be a thundering silence; it is certainly no guarantee that fluent, idiomatic English will gush forth like the water from the biblical rock. Arrogance or even thoughtlessness in enforcing such a regulation is easily self-defeating. If the student is somehow left with the feeling that the person doing the enforcing is belittling him in an alien language for his normal use of his own language, bitter resentment is sure to ensue. Punitive measures in this case are only too likely to prove ineffectual under most circumstances. After all, few students speak Spanish as a deliberate act of defiance."

John M. Sharp of Texas Western remarks, too, on the absurdity of a dictum that says a teacher facing a class of Spanish-speaking youngsters may never use an occasional word of Spanish to clarify a point. Yet it may be perfectly clear, he observes, "that the point being made is not 'getting across' in English." And he adds, "It should be noted here, to the credit of teachers, that conscientious instructors frequently violate this prohibition."

The Damaged Self-Image

The harm done the Mexican-American child linguistically'is paralleled — perhaps even exceeded — by the harm done to him as a person. In telling him that he must not speak his native language, we are saying to him by implication that Spanish and the culture which it represents are of no worth. Therefore (it follows) the people who speak Spanish are of no worth. Therefore (it follows again) this particular child is of no worth. It should come as no surprise to us, then, that he develops a negative self-concept — an inferiority complex. If he is no good, how can he succeed? And if he can't succeed, why try? Suddenly the full import of the essay about "Me" — the poignant outcry of the Mexican-American girl who "never *seemed* to be a child with a problem" — becomes crystal clear.

"Somewhere along the way," says Marcos de León, School-Community Coordinator of the Los Angeles Public Schools and member of the board of the Latin-American Civic Association and the board of the Council for Mexican Affairs of Los Angeles, "the Mexican-American must make a stand and recognize the fact that if there is to be progress against those barriers which prevent and obstruct a more functional citizenship, he must above all things retrieve his dignity and worth as a person with a specific ethnic heritage, possessing a positive contribution to civilization. No man can find a true expression for living, or much less think right, who is ashamed of himself or his people."

At a Mexican-American seminar held in Phoenix in 1963, Daniel Schreiber, then Director of the NEA's Project Dropout, spoke of the need of young people to "achieve confident self-identity." "The youngster," he said, "whose school experience begins and ends in failure — and those of minority children too often do — having discovered that he is good *at* nothing, stands a strong chance of becoming good *for* nothing. And far too many young lives, with all the potentials and real talents and capabilities they embody, are being wasted and crushed. The challenge is to redeem them, through inventiveness and energy and dedication."

This is the challenge that the public schools face in the education of tens of thousands of Mexican-American children in the five Southwestern states. It is a challenge which, with an appropriate approach and sound techniques, can be fully and triumphantly met. We believe these techniques are at hand.

WHAT IS BEING DONE: SOME SPECIFICS

Encouraging and exciting programs directed specifically to a more appropriate educational accommodation of children in bi-cultural communities have been developed in some places. The following reports are illustrative of the wide variety of innovative practice the NEA-Tucson Survey Committee observed in the schools selected for visitation.

Laredo, Texas

Laredo is a Texas border community of some 65,000 population, located on the Rio Grande, just opposite its Mexican counterpart, Neuvo Laredo. Its economic sustenance derives in good part from the pursuits of agriculture and a busy Air Force base.

Two school districts serve the metropolitan area of Laredo. The larger of the two in population is the Laredo Independent School District, serving the city of Laredo proper. Far larger in area is the United Consolidated Independent School District. It is larger, in fact, than Rhode Island, taking in no less than 2440 square miles and entirely surrounding the Laredo Independent School District on three sides, with the Rio Grande constituting the fourth side. Located within the far-flung boundaries of the United Consolidated Independent School District are the suburban homes of some of Laredo's Air Force families and ranches and farms where many Mexican-American families live.

The district operates three elementary schools and a unique high school, much of which has been built underground. This school was built underground to provide fallout protection in case of a nuclear attack on Laredo Air Force Base, to shut out the disrupting screams of jet planes, and for economy's sake. An underground school uses less land, is more economical to air condition, requires no shades or blinds or window cleaning and offers no tempting midnight target for vandals with air rifles.

The educational program of United Consolidated Independent School District has one strong common denominator: Bilingualism. Students, Anglo-American as well as Mexican-American, are encouraged to become truly bilingual — speaking, reading and writing fluently in both English and Spanish. English instruction and Spanish instruction go side by side.

One Year At a Time

Federal funds had not yet become available for the Laredo "biliteracy" program (as they were subsequently to become available under the Elementary-Secondary Education Act of 1965.) The United Consolidated Independent School District had to finance the program itself. And so it started the first year with only the first grade. The next year it expanded to the second grade. It was bilingualism not merely for the Mexican-American child but for both Mexican-American and Anglo-American — for all children.

Eventually bilingualism will extend through all the grades, including high school. Yet even now the high school reflects the beneficial effects of the bilingual-bicultural revolution taking place. Picturesquely displayed at the high school's main entrance, on equal terms, are the proud symbols of the two neighbor nations — the American eagle and the Mexican eagle. They are vividly colored, stylized cutouts made by students and suspended from wire supports. Student art work is displayed all through the school, and there is stress throughout on the worthiness of each of the two cultures. An unmistakable *esprit de corps* prevails among the students. They walk proudly. They dress neatly — all of them.

Bilingualism: A Valid Objective

The Laredo program and other similar programs that we observed in our Survey — plus our own experiences and independent studies —

have persuaded us beyond any doubt of the validity of bilingualism. Unhappily a large majority of Southwestern school districts have no bilingual programs. In a few instances, such programs exist but they are conducted inadequately. Most school districts have yet to discover that bilingualism can be a tool. It can be a tool — indeed the most important tool — with which to educate and motivate the Mexican-American child. It can be the means by which he achieves an affirmative self-concept — by which he comes to know who and what he is, takes pride in his heritage and culture, and develops a sense of his own worth. It can be an invaluable asset to him as an adult, economically, intellectually and socially.

One of the proofs of the validity of this approach, it seems to us, is the fact that children born and receiving their early schooling in Mexico or some other Spanish-speaking country generally do better in our schools than Mexican-Americans born here.

Recommendations for Desirable Programs

This, then, might be the time to make some recommendations that the NEA-Tucson Survey Committee believes to be basic in the education of native speakers of Spanish:

1. Instruction in pre-school and throughout the early grades should be in both Spanish and English.
2. English should be taught as a second language.
3. Contemporaneously there should be emphasis on the reading, writing and speaking of good Spanish, since Mexican-American children are so often illiterate in it.
4. A well-articulated program of instruction in the mother tongue should be continued from pre-school through the high school years.
5. All possible measures should be taken to help Mexican-American children gain a pride in their ancestral culture and language.
6. Schools should recruit Spanish-speaking teachers and teachers' aides. Beyond that, a special effort should be made to encourage promising young Mexican-Americans in high school and college to consider education as a career.
7. Schools, colleges and universities should conduct research in bilingual education, train or retrain bilingual teachers, create appropriate materials and, in general, establish a strong tradition of bilingual education. (For this suggestion we are indebted

To Theodore Andersson of the University of Texas who incorporated it into a memorandum directed to the Office of Economic
Opportunity in Washington, D.C.)

8. School districts desiring to develop good bilingual programs but
   lacking funds should look to the possibility of financing them
   under new federal programs and in some cases state compensatory education programs.
9. State laws which specify English as the language of instruction
   and thus, by implication at least, outlaw the speaking of Spanish
   except in Spanish classes should be repealed.

We might set forth a tenth recommendation—that no two programs
of Spanish for the Spanish-speaking need to be, nor are they likely to
be, alike. Each school district has its own special problems. Each
requires its own unique solution. The Laredo program is one approach.
There are others, and what follows is a series of capsule reports on
some of them, as seen by members of our Survey team in their
investigatory travels through the five Southwestern states. We are
intentionally omitting descriptions of other good programs in order to
achieve brevity and avoid repetition. We have selected for description
those programs which we consider to be representative — programs
which, by their example may offer ideas and inspiration to schools
contemplating entry into the area of Spanish-for-the-Spanish-speaking.

Tucson, Arizona

The Spanish roots of Tucson, this one-time walled pueblo, go very
deep. Having been a bit of Spain even before it became an outpost of
Mexico, Tucson traces it Spanish beginnings as far back as 1700, when
Father Kino began building the historic mission of San Xavier del Bac.
Appropriately, therefore, modern-day Tucson counts a substantially
higher proportion of Mexican-Americans among its population than
Phoenix. This accounts for the fact that fully 48 percent of the student
body of one of Tucson's high schools — Pueblo High which serves the
southwest part of the city — is Mexican-American.

Pueblo High's program of Spanish for the Spanish-speaking began
in 1959. The faculty and administration realized that the Spanish-
speaking students were bored with the Spanish classes and materials to
which they then were being exposed. It was understandable. The
program had been designed for beginning students without previous

experience with the language. Much of the content seemed elementary. Yet at the same time, in what must have seemed a paradox to some, a number of native speakers were receiving failing grades in Spanish.

And so an experimental program was developed. At first it was made available only to students fluent in Spanish and highly motivated. Admission to the class was considered an honor. Along with the linguistic content, the course included emphasis on the cultural heritage of Spain and Mexico to help students develop a positive sense of identity.

At the end of the first year the students petitioned for a continuation of the program. Their interest was met and during the second year they were introduced to Mexican and Spanish literature. Compositions which they wrote were based primarily on literary works read in and out of class. There was also a unit of commercial correspondence.

At the end of the second year, the students again asked for more. In the third year, they explored Spanish and Mexican literature more deeply and read several of the masterpieces such as the Spanish play *Don Juan Tenorio* by José Zorrilla.

Meanwhile, the enthusiasm of the pilot group spread through the student body. New classes were organized, including some for students whose ability was average and even below-average. Today the program at Pueblo High includes eight first-year classes, three second-year classes, two in the third year and one in the fourth year. Over this four-year span, attention is given to the basic skills of speaking, reading and writing. Equal if not even greater emphasis is given to helping the student develop a more positive self-concept through the study of his rich Spanish and Mexican cultural heritage.

Students at Pueblo High who enroll in the native speakers' classes are required to pay a $3.50 fee per year. This money has been used to buy class sets of literary pieces.

The program has generated enthusiasm among all concerned — students, faculty, administration and parents. And it was a major factor in the designation of Pueblo High in 1965 as a "Pacemaker School" — one of 45 nationwide — by the NEA and *Parade* magazine. In the near future, Pueblo plans to enlarge the program with a commercial Spanish course at the third and or fourth-year level for terminal students.

A program of Spanish for the Spanish-speaking also has been instituted at Sunnyside High School, in a separate school district serving the southernmost area of Tucson and an area beyond the city limits. Nearly 45 percent of that student body is Spanish-speaking. A special Spanish class was organized in 1961, and the program has expanded to two first-year classes and one each for the second, third and fourth years. During the first and second years, emphasis is given to correcting common grammatical mistakes.

The instructor at Sunnyside, L. Louis Labiaux, has traveled extensively in Spanish-speaking countries. Dissatisfied with available materials for the first year students, he has developed materials that he considers more appropriate. *Gramatica espanola de repaso* by Francisco Ugarte is used in the second year. The third year stresses Spanish-American history and culture, the basic text being *Historia de México* by Wigberto Jiménez Moreno, José Miranda and María Teresa Fernàndez. The fourth year's work revolves around the history and culture of Spain, for which the basic textbook is *Panoramà de la civilización española* by Francisco Ugarte.

Anxious to build more parental interest, Mr. Labiaux has appeared on local TV to explain the program. He also has worked to interest other groups in the problems of the Spanish-speaking at Sunnyside High School.

SCHOOL BELLS FOR MIGRANTS
California's Schools Welcome the 78,000 Children of its
Crop-following Families into the New Master Plan*

RONALD BLUBAUGH

For nearly two months Alicia Rodriguez worked on her English in
Virginia Phillips' special reading class at the Esparto Elementary
School near Sacramento, Calif. Then, one morning in late October,
Alicia was gone. Mrs. Phillips was not surprised. It was part of a
familiar cycle.

When the crop is harvested from nearby tomato fields, the students
leave with their parents. Most likely, Alicia would return to Texas for
the winter. Most likely, Mrs. Phillips would see her again next fall.

There are 78,000 youngsters like Alicia who either lived in or passed
through California in 1967. They are the children of migrant farmworkers and their education has become a major concern to the State
of California, as well as to teachers like Mrs. Phillips.

Prior to 1966, only sporadic attention had been given to the
problems of migrant children in California's schools.

Impetus for the new interest in migrants has come from the
"Migrant Amendment" to title I of the Elementary and Secondary
Education Act. This amendment channels Federal money for compensatory education into programs for migrant children. With the extra
financial help, schools now are willing and able to do something for
the youngsters of the workers who help make agriculture California's
leading industry.

In 1966, during the first months of the new effort, the Federal
Government supplied $1.4 million to California for the education of
migrant children. This year, the amount is $6.2 million, still not enough
to help all of the State's migrants.

Ramiro Reyes, assistant chief of the Bureau of Community Services
and Migrant Education, explains the massiveness of the problem: "By
my calculation, we would have needed $10 million in 1966 to provide
some assistance to each of the 78,000 children. With $1.4 million we
were able to help only 10,000 of them."

*American Education, March 1968.

119

Forty-three of California's 58 counties have migrant children some time during the year. Since the $6.2 million in Federal help is not enough to aid every child, the State has directed the funds to the 27 counties that have the largest number of migrants rather than spread the money thinly over all.

An early result of Federal aid was a dramatic increase in the number of migrants in summer programs. Prior to the new financing almost no migrant children enrolled in the summer school offerings of local schools. Last summer, 5,412 migrant children participated in summer programs.

Summer programs also have been started for preschool children in various farm labor camps in California. Financed with Economic Opportunity Act funds, these preschool centers help children with their English while ensuring that they get proper food and rest. However, in places where preschool centers have not been opened, parents still face the choice of leaving their young ones unattended at home, locked in a hot car, or letting them run loose in the fields.

When the regular school year began, Esparto authorities visited the nearby Madison farm labor camp many times to encourage parents to send their children to school. Children who went to school received continued instruction in English.

A much larger migrant program is that conducted jointly by 14 school districts in the San Joaquin Valley counties of Merced, San Joaquin, and Stanislaus. State authorities consider the three-county effort to be a demonstration project, an example to other districts with similar problems.

The 1,575 children involved in the plan receive such services as:

1.   Individualized instruction from bilingual teacher's aides and language specialists.
2.   Special textbooks aimed at the problems and deficiencies of the migrant child.
3.   Field trips.
4.   Intensified instruction in English with programs to teach some children English as a second language and Spanish as a first.
5.   Evening tutoring and the use of a library in the migrant housing camps.
6.   Summer classes.

The program also provides night adult education classes in the camps for the parents of enrolled youngsters.

Teachers who work with the migrant children frequently report changes in the attitudes of the participating youngsters. Pat Lowrey, a kindergarten teacher in the Winters School District near Sacramento, explained: "One outstanding improvement noted by other school personnel was in the active participation of the student in regular classroom work. It was also noted that the children played more often with their classmates than was the case at the beginning of the program. A certain pride in their cultural background was also evidenced when they pointed out objects in the language room which were of Mexican origin."

Mrs. Lowrey's remarks also show another key aspect of the California migrant program: integration. It is the basic philosophy of the California approach that migrant children should be placed in classrooms with regular students The State board of education policy forbids the operation of separate schools for migrants.

In addition to its efforts for students, the California migrant program last summer included a pilot project to help prepare potential teachers for future classes of migrants. Because only 14 teachers-to-be were enrolled in the initial effort, the name "mini-corps" was given to the project.

Modeled on the Teacher Corps program, the mini-corps drew its recruits from young people with junior college backgrounds and a desire to teach migrants. They worked alongside experienced teachers and also went into the State migrant camps where they each lived for a month. Representative of the reaction of the participants was that of the girl who had seen migrants on her father's ranch all her life. No longer, she said, would she consider migrants as "inferior."

The San Joaquin Valley districts of Cutler-Orosi Unified and Woodlake Union High School have made a particular effort in drawing money from a variety of national, State, and local sources. There were 333 youngsters in their program last year, all attending grades seven through 12. The students received instruction in basic subjects as well as some vocational education and on-the-job training. During the summer, they worked 32 hours a week and were paid $1.40 an hour. They also went to classes for five hours a week and spent three hours either in recreation or counseling.

Federal funds for this effort were drawn through the Elementary and Secondary Education Act, the Neighborhood Youth Corps, and the local Office of Economic Opportunity. County agencies also contributed. Among these were the Tulare County welfare and health departments and the county office of education.

"This is an effort to get all of the existing agencies to focus on the needs of migrants," explained Cutler-Orosi superintendent Laurence Elrod. "We tried to get all the agencies to supplement each other. We had to get them to bend a little and work together to solve the problem."

In addition to its efforts at the local level, the California Master Plan for Migrant Children also calls for more interdistrict cooperation. Under the plan, the State is establishing a central records repository in Sacramento for migrants. Within a central records center, a teacher who gets a new student will be able to determine his educational background.

Many migrants travel solely through California, Texas, Arizona, Oregon, and Washington. Carrying the idea to these other States, California has agreed to a records transfer with them. A teacher in Fresno will now know the title of a textbook a student was using and the page he was on when he left Texas.

Although the migrant plan has been a major step toward helping the State's wandering children, some problems have developed. There is, for example, a serious shortage in California of bilingual teachers. It is estimated that not more than 50 of the 257 teachers employed in the various projects speak both English and Spanish.

Planning must be done in advance. State officials complain they never know the amount of Federal money that will be available to local schools until it is almost too late for the schools to take action. In its last session, the U.S. Congress made provisions to eliminate this uncertainty.

Wilson C. Riles, State director of compensatory education, also complains that the Federal money which went into the migrant program was removed from other compensatory education efforts. "The Federal Government has not given more money to the States to operate this program," he said. "It has simply earmarked money which formerly was going to other compensatory education projects. This means you have to dilute other programs. We welcome an attack on this problem, but it tends to jeopardize other activities which are underfinanced."

Xavier Del Buono, a consultant with the California State Department of Education, warns that the educational problems of the migrant child must either be solved now or they will haunt the cities later. "We already can see that there are not going to be migrant jobs forever," he says. "As the need for migrant farm laborers is reduced, it does not eliminate the problem. The same educational needs will be there. Studies have shown that these people will move to the large urban centers. If we don't help now, we will just add to the problems of the large central cities."

Forward-looking educators in California, with fiscal assistance from the Federal Government, State and local agencies, are now bending to the task of sparing the cities this additional burden.

CULTURAL BACKGROUNDS AND BARRIERS
THAT AFFECT LEARNING BY
SPANISH-SPEAKING CHILDREN*

JULIAN NAVA

America is a fascinating society of such size and complexity that no sooner is something firm or true but conditions change and call for a new evaluation. As important as other elements in our history are, nothing is more significant than the people that have formed our United States.

Among the many different peoples that have come to this land at various times, the group which I represent is difficult to understand for many because few historians have given it proper attention. However, it exemplifies both the problems and prospects our country has faced as it endeavors to "Americanize" the many races, cultures and peoples in a new set of conditions that no country has ever faced before.

All educators are concerned with evaluating their teaching in terms of certain goals. In light of this, it is important to point out that the Mexican-American students — taken as a group — have not responded to public education as most educators assumed they would. Generally, these young people have not reached the goals we have set for them and pose questions for which educators do not have sufficient answers. A good look at the effects of public education upon Mexican-Americans will show that this ethnic group poses serious problems which cannot be ignored any longer. The resulting costs to our society are too great to assume that the trouble lies alone with the individual student.

The general methods and educational values we have maintained produce puzzling effects when applied to this group. In an effort to shed some light on the educational problems of Mexican-American students, I would like to focus my attention on the role of language in public education, and how it affects learning by these children.

*Mimeographed article, 1966.

The teaching of English in public schools has certain social and psychological consequences that many instructors and administrators may not fully realize. Guided by the melting pot theory, it has been an assumption among educators that instruction was for a basically homogeneous student population which was already English speaking.

This is not the case in most of the Southwest, where perhaps about 4 million people have Spanish as a native language. For these people English is a second language. The objectives of schools and teachers are very difficult for Spanish-speaking people to achieve because of their bilingual situation. From kindergarten on, the encounter with education spoken in an alien tongue (English), produces in the Spanish-speaking child various profound impressions which are often destructive. For many children the encounter with English language instruction causes greater shock than the child can cope with. A negative pattern is established which helps explain the general failure of most of this ethnic group to develop as our educational institutions desire.

The net effect of English language instruction is often destructive of the self-image and very ego of many Spanish-speaking children. Their individual needs have been submerged or suppressed in favor of a uniform curriculum established to make everyone speak and act like a typical American. Efforts to suppress certain ethnic backgrounds cause long-lasting wounds and these result in social maladjustment and under-achievement. These outward manifestations frustrate teachers. Moreover these negative results cause the loss to society of many thousands of potentially highly productive individuals. There is no grand design to bring this about. Our educational institutions find it necessary to deal with general standards or molds into which raw material must fit or suffer the consequences. We have taken little time to study the reactions of Mexican-Americans to an experience which is so alien to our own. Thus we find it hard to accept that millions of young and sensitive minds believe that public education suppresses a major part of their personality and looks down upon them. A sophisticated person would say that public schools damage the self-image they bring to school.

These general observations stem from both professional sources and my personal experience. I have lived through all of this, first as a simple child that tried to cope with all the frightening forces to which school experiences put me as a bilingual child. As an adult, I have looked back in a rational manner to see what happened to me, and what is still happening to countless others.

To focus more sharply, let me confine myself to the group we call the "Mexican-American." Although there are other labels for the group, this combines clarity of meaning and brevity. The Mexican-American constitutes the vast majority of Spanish-speaking people in the Southwest and the country at large. Although recent immigration, such as the Puerto Rican and Cuban, has altered the composition of Spanish speaking population figures, the situation of the Mexican-American is distinct from that of other Latin American peoples in our country. As long as Mexico and the U.S. share a border there will be unique aspects of U.S.-Mexican relations. Mexican-Americans will be in the middle of powerful and complex forces that are not well enough understood.

Most teachers of English are so subject-oriented that they find little time to show concern for the negative effect that English teaching has on many of their bilingual students. After all, English teaching is judged by the extent to which students acquire certain skills that will help them fit the pattern we have set for our American public school graduate. We leave to over-loaded counselors the tasks of dealing with personal problems related to school experiences. Crowded schools only aggravate the situation.

We tend to assume that something is wrong with the boy if he cannot do well in school. It is easy to assume that he is either deficient in intelligence or not properly motivated. In either case, there is little we do beyond keep the class in order, get a minimum amount of subject matter across (maybe some ideas), and survive another day. We are not paid to change society or play God. Many teachers assume that learning involves pain as well as pleasure, anyway. Others feel that curiosity, enthusiasm and pleasure are more creative forces.

Teachers who are aware of after-school situations are perplexed by the Mexican-American school children. The confusion among educators arises in great part from the misapplication of sociological data. Mexican-American low educational achievement has been explained by over-simplifications that stem from our experience with European minorities and the Negro. The failure of simple explanations for low educational achievement of Mexican-Americans has in turn perpetuated critical stereotypes of this group. In many cases, low educational achievement of Mexican-Americans is used as support for prejudice.

So many of these children remain aloof from the mainstream and withdraw into a shell that educators despair of helping them — and so do their parents. Many teachers will write-off a Mexican-American student by remarks such as, "well, he is better off going to work anyway!"

The Mexican-American in our society finds that difficulty with English is at the bottom of the entire complex of problems he faces in gaining acceptance and equal opportunity. The learning ability of all children is vitally affected by socio-psychological factors. The training of teachers in the psychological foundations of education may vary across the country, but most teachers know that for the child in school, feelings of personal security, knowledge of acceptance by the peer group and native curiosity about knowledge are all very fragile blossoms that must be cared for tenderly. All of these elements in the personality are hurt by a hostile environment, sometimes permanently.

For Mexican-American children all the general problems are aggravated and compounded by the language gap. Their lack of communication skills ties their hands and gags them. Their response to learning situations may well be positive and creative, but they cannot express themselves well in English. Teachers find it difficult to wait for them to catch up in English because the teaching schedule must go on. To visualize what happens one must imagine that the situation is reversed, that all teaching were in Spanish and that a minority of the students speak only English learned at home and their neighborhood. For both national interests and their own, teachers must force the English-speaking minority to speak only Spanish. Of course, many of these will cling together for mutual assistance, reassurance and for a relief from the foreign language. The same teacher would very likely scold or punish the offenders for their poor manners, lack of interest . . . and so on. In many cases, teachers imply disdain for the minority culture. Switching back to the Mexican-American vantage point, such classroom experiences constitute a painful ordeal for many Mexican-American children. Few teachers know or guess what is going on behind those dark eyes in class.

An accent is one of the most immediate handicaps a Mexican-American creates by the way in which he speaks English. An accent has always helped identify certain classes or groups, such as immigrants and minorities. In our country, traditionally bent on making its citizens fit the White-Anglo-Saxon-Protestant (WASP) New England model, an accent other than some accepted ones has usually brought ridicule or disdain. Thus an English accent has been generally an asset of at least snob appeal. A Jewish or Italian accent has been a mixed blessing. And so it is true of Mexican or Spanish accent when speaking American English.

Mexican-Americans are the largest single ethnic minority group in the Southwest and one of the least understood in the nation. We can read a legion of specialists on European immigration. And Negroes are the object of a frontal assault by scholarly circles now. But very few have studied the movement north from Mexico. The collision of the two major cultures is often ignored. I have heard even major authorities on American immigration ignore the Hispanic Southwest from their survey of American development. Most authorities lump the peculiar development of this region with later European immigration to the East coast. This uncritical identification has led some to observe: "the Irish and Jews have made it. What's wrong with the Mexicans?"

Mexican-American school children pose a great problem to public education. Their level of education achieved, as measured by the average school years completed (8), is lower than any other minority group, including the Negro. Trouble in school starts with the first experiences in kindergarten. Most Mexican-American children attend schools that are segregated to various degrees. Since their parents tend to live in pockets, which they call *colonias* or *barrios* (which academicians call ghettos or slums), it is not difficult to draw school lines so as to put problem children into certain schools. Like craters on the moon, "Mexican schools" dot the Southwest. In larger cities where most Mexican-Americans now live, segregation is less effective, and much of it is self-imposed. Even where they constitute the numerical majority of students, language and personal problems are still serious. A young child is suddenly forced to socialize with and compete in school with other children who speak a foreign tongue. Many of his classmates will soon regard him negatively because he cannot speak English well, if at all. This child falls behind from the start, and tends to stay behind till he drops out voluntarily. He is pushed out in effect, in some indifferent, hostile or over-loaded schools.

School problems often mirror those of society in general. Thus we find that among adults there is a schizophrenia toward Mexican-Americans. Most people like things "Spanish," such as the missions, the dances and music, the old padres and the myths about Old

California days, but most look differently at the Mexican of today. This is hardly surprising in view of the critical tone of most written sources on the Mexican. It seems like the "Black Legend" of colonial times, whereby northern European writers painted the deeds and culture of Iberian peoples in dark tones, has carried over to their descendants in America. These have inherited the legacy of Northern European hostility to Catholic Spain and its culture on the one hand, and to the Indian on the other. But Mexicans combine the mixed blessings of being both Spanish and Indian. Mexicans are different than Spaniards, and Mexican-Americans are different from Mexicans (in Mexico). These differences exist for reasons that are not generally understood by the American public. And yet, our society is affected by these realities just the same. Teachers are among the first to see these effects, but they do not, as a group, understand them.

What makes Mexican-Americans different from other minority groups? Ultimately all peoples have some unique qualities, or manifest universal characteristics in different manners. It is a delicate matter to apply labels to national characteristics because personal feelings run high over these questions. Irish, German, Scotch or French are no different in this. Nothing will arouse such heated debate among Mexican-Americans at any level, as the very use of such a term to describe them. Self-analysis goes on at an increased tempo among "Americans of Mexican descent." and so it is understandable that the majority of Americans (whom this group calls "anglos") is confused. Among the major differences that set this group aside from other minorities, we could suggest that:

1.   Although many Mexican-Americans are literally immigrants or second generation Americans, the group does not fit neatly into the pattern of European immigration. Its role in U.S. history cannot be fully understood if we use the European immigration model.

2.   Mexican-Americans are of widely varying physical, racial and social types. The group is what I call "indoafrohispanic." Although the vast majority of Mexicans are *mestizos* (Indian and Spanish to varying degrees), many are mulattoes and *zambos* (Indian and Negro). And there are also great numbers of pure Spanish blood Mexicans, Indians (about 50 dialects) and Negroes.

3.   Most Mexican-Americans exemplify a "conquered people." They carry the burden of Spain's conquest over their Mexican Indian forefathers. In the United States they are not allowed to "forget the Alamo." Socially and politically, they carry the burden of the outcome

of the Mexican War. Only American Indians have lived an experience that approximates that of the Mexican-American. However, since the Revolution of 1910 in Mexico, a new pride has been forming around being Mexican, and this has carried over to the U.S.

4.   Most Mexican-Americans are not assimilated into American society after a hundred years of U.S. control over this region. In certain respects, Spanish-speaking Americans are not immigrants at all, for the stamp of Hispano-Mexican culture has been present in the Southwest for 300 years. Some of the reluctance to assimilate stems from the view of Mexican-Americans that many of their values and attitudes are superior to those of the general U.S. population.

5.   Although most Mexicans are Caucasians, they are not always so considered. Even when they are, it is more of a handicap to be of Mexican descent than it is to be Irish or German-American. Many individuals who rise in status by virtue of achievement or recognition try to pass off their name as being Spanish, rather than Mexican. Shame for Mexican identification will bring others to say they are from old Californian or New Mexico Spanish families. This aside, the reception of a Spanish surname does vary greatly. Among some circles it can be an asset, and where there are no problems connected with large numbers of them, Mexican-Americans can be truly free as individuals. The rise of Mexico as a leader in Latin America and its notable progress as a producer of ideas, art and social progress has altered the traditional picture most Americans have of both Mexico and its people. These changes have brought some benefits to Mexican-Americans.

6.   The proximity of Mexico is a constant reinforcement of stereotypes held about the Mexican-American. Within the group, the proximity of Mexico complicates acculturation and assimilation to the U.S. No other U.S. minority group encounters such a situation.

These suggestions as to how Mexican-Americans differ from other minority groups are not all inclusive. But they should help explain why the usual formulas for social betterment do not seem to work as well with this group as they do with others.

How many people are we talking about? In the U.S. there are about 4 million Mexican-Americans. Some estimates take the number up to 5 million. Most are in the Southwest, chiefly in Texas and California.

California's share is steadily increasing at the expense of Texas. Recent data reveal the population of school-age children in California as follows for July, 1966:

White Spanish surname	660,000
Non-Whites	546,000
Other Whites	3,493,000

For our purposes, it will suffice to point out that Mexican-Americans outnumber Negroes in this state 2 to 1. Moreover, they are found everywhere in the state. Contrary to accepted impressions, they are mostly urban dwellers, although they comprise 60% of the field hands in California agriculture.

Most of these Spanish-speaking children have experienced some of the following situations in school:

1. Bilingual children have been forced to suppress their mother tongue in favor of wholly English school learning.

2. There is commonly a connotation of inferiority to Spanish as against other foreign languages. Besides, "Mexicans don't really speak true Castillian Spanish," you will often hear.

3. The suppression of Spanish in school has made most Mexican-Americans feel that something is wrong not only with Spanish, but everything they associate with it. They soon feel ashamed of speaking Spanish and being "Mexican." An inferiority complex often results in a defeatist attitude from an early age.

4. Most Mexican-Americans have poor English language skills that hamper all educational and social experiences in school.

The magnitude of the problem can be summarized by reminding ourselves that no other racial or ethnic minority group of any consequence produces fewer High School graduates. Millions of Americans of Spanish-speaking extraction have been conditioned to accept second class status. Many educators believe that our society has higher spiritual values and greater interests than to permit such conditions to continue. Others believe Mexican-Americans deserve what they are willing to settle for; this is a common attitude.

What can you do to help the Mexican-American student?

1. Find out more about the group and how it affects your community.

2. Help children feel pride in their native language and culture.

3. Learn Spanish yourself and use it in class as a resource.

4. Give Hispano-Mexican history its fair share of attention.

5. Make it clear that all minority groups have enriched our country.

There seems to be a new movement among educators which bodes well for the future. They are starting to deal face to face with many problems which have been ignored. In California, for example, the requirement for some Spanish instruction in Elementary and Junior High is the beginning of a new and creative era in public education which will benefit all students. This new program will soften the effect whereby English language has served as a form of cultural oppression for Americans of Mexican descent. Much remains to be done, however, in order to enrich our American society through positive and fruitful diversity. Hispano-Mexican peoples do still have much to offer our society. Whether they do depends upon teachers in great part.

SPEAK UP, *CHICANO*

The Mexican-American Fights for Educational Equality*

ARMANDO M. RODRIGUEZ

I sat quietly and listened as 15 Mexican-American citizens who had gathered in a crumbling adobe community center in San Antonio's oldest slum talked about their schools. As director of the U.S. Office of Education's Mexican-American Affairs Unit, I was there to learn what the local citizens and school people felt were their most pressing educational needs.

"We ought to be consulted more about what goes on in our schools," the president of the Mexican-American Community Club said heatedly. "Our high school needs a Mexican-American on the counseling staff. But the school people say the can't find a qualified one to hire. Over 60 percent of the kids are Mexican-Americans and most of them have trouble speaking English. Yet we have only five Spanish-speaking teachers, and not a single person in the school office speaks Spanish. Is it any wonder the kids drop out like flies? The hell with the requirements. Let's take care of these kids' needs, and one of the first is to get somebody who can talk to them."

"Now wait just a minute," interrupted the school district's assistant superintendent. "We have to follow State regulations, you know. You can't put just anybody in the counseling office. You tell us where to find a qualified Mexican-American teacher or counselor and we'll be delighted to hire him."

"At least you could have Mexican-Americans in the school as aides, couldn't you?" asked a neighborhood representative on the community action program board. "But you folks downtown made the requirements so high that none of our people could get a job. Why?"

"We have to have qualified people to work with the youngsters," answered the director of instruction.

"Qualified?" the president broke in. "What could be better qualifications than speaking the language and understanding the kids?"

"Well, we haven't seen much show of interest from the parents," countered a schoolman. "We can't get them out to PTA meetings, can't

American Education, May 1968.

135

even get many of them to come to parent's night. We hired a Mexican-American school-community coordinator for some of our schools, but she's finding it an uphill battle getting the parents to take an interest in school matters."

And so it went at meeting after meeting that I attended with Lupe Anguiano and Dean Bistline, my coworkers in the Mexican-American Affairs Unit. We visited 17 communities on our three-week tour of Arizona, California, Colorado, New Mexico, and Texas. Both Mexican-American community leaders and school people — some 1,700 altogether — poured out their frustrations, and we learned a great deal about what the people want and need and in what priority.

In those five States alone, there are more than 5.5 million people of Spanish surname. Eight out of 10 live in California or Texas. Their numbers are constantly reinforced by a stream of immigrants from Mexico. Add the 1.5 million other Spanish-speaking people — Cuban, Puerto Rican, Central and South American, and Spanish — who live in Florida and the Northeast and Midwestern industrial cities, and it becomes apparent that the United States has a substantial second minority group. They are a minority whose historical, cultural, and linguistic characteristics set them apart from the Anglo community as dramatically as the Negro's skin sets him apart. Few people outside the Southwest realize the degree of discrimination this difference has brought about.

For me the introduction to discrimination began 37 years ago when my father brought the family to California from Durango, Mexico. I was nine years old when we settled in San Diego in an extremely poor but well integrated community of Mexican-Americans, Negroes, and poor Anglos. The trouble was in school. I knew only a dozen words of English, so I just sat around the first few weeks not understanding a thing. I was not allowed to speak Spanish in class. But after school each day I played with neighborhood kids, so I soon picked up enough English to hold my own on the playground. Then I made this smattering of English do in class.

It didn't occur to me or my family to protest. In those days people didn't talk much about ethnic differences or civil rights. The *chicanos* (our favorite nickname for fellow Mexican-Americans) pretty much stayed "in their place," working as domestics and laborers in the cities or as wetback stoop laborers in the fields and orchards. Only a few became professionals or businessmen.

I remember being advised by my high school counselor to forget my dreams of going to college and becoming a teacher. "They don't hire Mexican-Americans," he said. Then World War II came along, and when I got out of the Army in 1944 the G.I. Bill of Rights saw me through San Diego College. I got a teaching job and eventually became a junior high school principal in San Diego. But my experience was a rare one for the times.

Since the conditions have changed a good deal. There is spirit in the Mexican-American community now. On my recent trip I saw a pride in the young people that was not so evident when I was growing up. The *chicano* today is proud of his role as an American. Many parents, even those who are illiterate, as were mine, are determined that their children will not be like them. And they see education as the means. But along with their determination has come a new impatience. Gone is the meek, long-suffering separateness of the *chicanos*. They are beginning to stand up and make their voices heard.

"Head Start is great," said a parent-businessman at one of our meetings. "But is isn't enough. Some of the programs are only for the summer and our kids need a whole year if they are to have a chance to start out even with the Anglo kids."

"Many of our kids go to school hungry," another complained. "Why can't the schools use more of their Government money for food and health services?"

As we listened to their grievances, I realized that our most valuable role at these meetings was as a bouncing board for their ideas. With us present, both school and community leaders found themselves saying things to each other they had heretofore said only within their own group. Inevitably, though, they looked to us, the spokesmen for the Government, to "do something." Of course, that was not our role. We were there to help them establish lines of communication and to explain to them the ways in which the U.S. Office of Education can support their efforts. But we had to make clear that it is they, the State and local school people and the community, who must design the programs and carry them out.

Nationally there is a growing amount of concern about Mexican-American affairs that has generated much real help. In evidence is the recent series of conferences at Tucson, Pueblo, and El Paso sponsored by the National Education Association. Also, the Federal Government created three new agencies with specific responsibilities to the

Mexican-American. The Inter-Agency Committee on Mexican-American Affairs assists in development of services that cover the wide range of Government activities. The United States-Mexico Commission on Border Development and Friendship is charged with creating programs to improve cooperation on both sides of the border. And the U.S. Office of Education's Mexican-American Affairs Unit seeks to bring some expertise to bear on the education of the bilingual-bicultural citizen and to develop a focus on the effort. This unit is now supported by a newly created Advisory Committee on Mexican-American Education. Still another evidence of concern and help is the passage by Congress last December of the Bilingual Education Act (title VII of the Elementary and Secondary Education Act). It authorizes funds and support for schools to develop programs in which both English and the native language of the student can be used as teaching tools until a mastery of English has been achieved.

These are a healthy start, as is the rising involvement of the Mexican-American community itself in directing attention to educational issues. Still, some major obstacles remain in the way of the Mexican-American's progress toward educational equality. Of prime consideration is the shortage of teachers qualified to cope with the Mexican-American's particular situation. There are only 2,000 bilingual teachers in the elementary and secondary schools today. Equally distressing is the lack of teachers who are even aware of the *chicano's* cultural background and recognize his language as an asset. It is a striking contradiction that we spend millions of dollars to encourage schoolchildren to learn a foreign language and, at the same time, frown upon Mexican-American children speaking Spanish in school. The impression they receive is that there must be something inherently bad about their language. This, of course, leads to self-depreciation. To make the situation even more ridiculous, they are often asked to take Spanish as a foreign language later in school.

Only bilingual teachers can correct this situation — teachers who can treat the *chicano's* Spanish as an asset while the student is learning English. And that will require a tremendous effort in teacher education. As a starter, the Teacher Corps, cooperating with the Mexican-American Affairs Unit, has set up a high intensity language training component for a group of interns teaching in schools with a number of Spanish-speaking students. This program lasts six weeks and gives considerable attention to cross cultural values as well as to language instruction.

A second obstacle to a comprehensive education for the *chicano* is the lack of well-integrated curricula. As I toured the Southwest, I saw good programs here and there for preschool youngsters, some good adult basic education going on in one place, a good program to educate the whole migrant family in another. But in no single place did I see a school district whose curriculum and instructional program correlated with the needs of the Mexican-Americans from kindergarten through high school. There were glimpses of hope, though.

In San Antonio, Texas, I was impressed with a program developed by the Southwest Educational Development Laboratory of Austin that used linguistic techniques to improve the fluency of Mexican-American youngsters in oral language as a foundation for reading. Intensive instruction is given in English as a second language, and an identical program of instruction is given in Spanish. The program was started two years ago in nine schools and is in formal operation in the first two grades in San Antonio with plans for continuation in grades three and four. The first group of youngsters in the program are now equaling national norms in reading and some are even achieving the fifth-grade level. Traditionally Mexican-American boys and girls in southern Texas have lagged at least a year behind the national norms.

San Diego, California, has developed a demonstration center for English as a second language to help school districts create specialized educational programs for students who initially learned a language other than English. One of its bright features has been the large number of parents who worked with the professional staff in designing these programs for non-English-speaking parents and youngsters alike.

The Foreign Language Innovative Curricula Studies at Ann Arbor, Michigan, used funds from title III of the Elementary and Secondary Education Act to develop a bilingual curriculum program with materials for language arts instruction. The program has been aimed at the Spanish-speaking youngster — both migrant and permanent resident — whose linguistic handicaps severely limit his educational achievement. It is for the primary grades and stresses the development of materials which are exciting to all youngsters and are suitable for use by teachers with a minimum of specialized training.

By sharing their experiences in these innovative programs, school districts can help one another. And a wealth of good ideas are emerging from conferences such as the one sponsored by the Advisory Committee on Mexican-American Education and the Mexican-American Affairs Unit in Austin, Texas, last month. Here at the Office of

Education we have a special task force that works closely with the eight bureaus in considering funding proposals for projects aimed at improving educational opportunities for the Mexican-American.

A third obstacle to the young *chicano's* educational success is a lack of models — "heroes," if you will. The school needs to put before him successful Mexican-Americans whom he can emulate as he sets his educational goals. A teacher, a counselor, a principal who is Mexican-American can do the trick. Discrimination in past generations has, unfortunately, limited the number of such persons. In many heavily Mexican-American schools, there is not a single Mexican-American teacher, let alone a counselor or administrator. Now, however, with the *chicano's* education improving and discrimination diminishing, I am hopeful that more and more of today's children will have the career models before them that they need.

If my impression of all this activity and promise is correct, the Mexican-American is about to see the dawning of a new era. He will become a far more productive member of society. His cultural and linguistic heritage will be turned to good use.

Although the *chicano* has suffered and lost much in the last 100 years, he now intends to do what is necessary to win his fight for educational equality. And he will do it today. Mañana is too late.

ECONOMICS

ECONOMICS

Scholars who make scientific studies of social problems report that poverty is a major root cause of a host of other problems. That is, being without sufficient food, clothing, and shelter can breed such aspects of social disorganization as higher rates of crime, sickness, mental illness, family disintegration, illigitimacy, suicide, and alcoholism. The psychic and social scars of poverty are as serious as the economics ones.

The vast majority of Mexican immigrants were and are poverty-stricken individuals. They brought with them little in the way of high-priced skills, so that in order to improve economically, they had to lift themselves by their own boot-straps. Common labor was all they could achieve, and often that was only temporary. Their children, however, sometimes were able to move up a notch occupationally, and their grandchildren were even more likely to be able to do so.

Most Mexican immigrants settled in the Southwest. Desirable though this area is in some ways, with a few exceptions it is an agricultural section and has limited industrial opportunities. Agricultural labor never has been a well-paid occupation, and the constant stream of new immigrants without jobs kept the pool of available labor overflowing. The benefits of union membership were rarely available. Only as the *Chicanos* moved into the urban areas of San Antonio, El Paso, Los Angeles, Denver, Omaha, Chicago, and the smaller industrial cities of the Southwest, did improved economic opportunity begin to appear, and then rarely for the first generation immigrant.

The largest single occupation of Mexican Americans has been migratory agricultural labor. The eastern seaboard migratory stream has few Spanish-speaking members except some Puerto Ricans and Cubans. But the great central stream, arising in South Texas and spreading over all of the Midwest up to the Canadian border, is heavily Mexican and Mexican American in character. The western stream, originating along the Mexico-California border, also has been predominantly Mexican and Mexican American. Low wages, intermittent work, transportation difficulties, badly substandard housing and sanitary facilities, an almost insurmountable problem of a good education for the children, and the general disorganization which comes with "rootlessness" are epidemic among the migrants. Inability to meet residence requirements is a most serious handicap in a welfare society based on legal residence as well as need.

Aggravating the entire situation, from the standpoint of the laborers, was the *"bracero* problem." During World War II hundreds of thousands of Mexican males were imported on a contract basis for "temporary work." They proved popular with the operators of large farms for harvesting vegetables, fruit, cotton, sugar beets, and other crops with a "peak" season. From the standpoint of the native migrants, the *braceros* continued to be imported long after the labor shortage disappeared. As late as 1960 over 400,000 *braceros* were imported, plus possibly half as many illegal entrants. The legal contract program now has all but ceased, with less than 8,000 entrants (to "crisis" situation) in 1967. As some selections in this section point out, the rapid increase in mechanization makes the need for migratory laborers less and less each year. In 1968 well over 300,000 illegal entrants entered the United States from Mexico, about half of whom were apprehended by the Border Patrol. At the present time these "wetbacks," when caught, are deported, but the persons who employ them are not penalized.

Paul Bullock is a professional economist from the Institute of Industrial Relations at the University of California at Los Angeles. In the selection "Employment Problems of the Mexican-American" he characterizes the role of the Mexican American in the labor market and the influences of culture on the success of Mexican Americans in the economic aspects of American society. He presents a statistical profile of the Mexican American worker, describes discrimination in employment, the problems of education and training of Mexican Americans, and concludes, somewhat pessimistically, that the Mexican American and the Negro will continue to share serious economic handicaps in the foreseeable future. In "Discrimination Against Mexican Americans in Private Employment," attorney Albert Armendariz, a former president of the League of United Latin American Citizens, defines discrimination and then proposes a series of solutions, stating a sound rationale for each step in the program and concluding with recommendations concerning action by such federal agencies as the O.E.O.

Judge Alfred J. Hernandez, another past president of the League of United Latin American Citizens, in "Civil Service and the Mexican American" documents discrimination in the supposedly bias-free Federal Civil Service Commission and the Departments of Labor, Health, Education and Welfare, Housing and Urban Development, Agriculture, Justice, Defense, Commerce, Interior, and even such agencies as the O.E.O. and the Equal Employment Opportunity Commission. He makes four specific recommendations for the improvement of the conditions he cites. Dr. Salvador Ramirez, professionally engaged in youth work, in "Employment Problems of Mexican American Youth" describes the employment situation of Mexican American youth and outlines in detail the specific programs needed to alleviate the more pressing of their occupational problems. Dr. Ernesto Galarza, one of the most prominent Mexican Americans in the State of California, describes in general but discerning terms the economic situation of the Mexican Americans today and speculates concerning the future. The selection he authored, "*La mula no nació arisca . . .* " is part of an old Mexican saying which translates "The mule was not born stubborn." Dr. Galarza says Mexican Americans are not apathetic, but because of the hostility with which they have been met, they have become unresponsive as a form of self-protection. In "How Much Longer . . . The Long Road," Armando Rendon, who is with the federal Civil Rights Commission, presents probably the best brief description of the situation of migratory agricultural workers that can be found in any source.

EMPLOYMENT PROBLEMS OF THE MEXICAN-AMERICAN*

PAUL BULLOCK

The appearance of this article in a symposium on minorities and employment is perhaps symbolic of the changing and expanding role of the Mexican-American in our society. It is unlikely that, even as late as a decade ago, a journal editor would have considered the Mexican-American worthy of such attention. An appalling and almost universal indifference to the problems of this group has been reinforced, until recently, by the general inaccessiblity of data on employment, educational, and cultural patterns of Americans of Mexican descent. Only in 1950 did the Bureau of the Census initiate a consistent series of reports on the "Spanish surname" population, a category which only approximates the Mexican-American totals for the five southwestern states. The few researchers toiling in this area have been lonely and isolated.

The lack of knowledge and information concerning the Mexican-American population is all the more remarkable in view of its size. In California, Mexican-Americans outnumber other "minority" groups (including Negroes and Orientals) by a substantial margin. A total of 1,426,538 white persons of Spanish surname lived in this state in 1960, compared with 880,486 Negroes and 159,545 Japanese. The pattern within the Los Angeles metropolitan area is essentially the same, with Mexican-Americans outnumbering Negroes by about a 3 to 2 margin. Negroes in Texas numbered 1,185,476 while the Spanish surname population totaled 1,417,810. Yet this vast group seemed obscure or at least remote to most Anglos until recent events forced a degree of recognition (Table 1).

The reasons for this neglect are not always clear. It is likely, however, that forces within both the Anglo and Mexican-American communities are responsible. Many Anglos, and many Mexican-Americans, have never regarded the urbanized Mexican-American as being "disadvantaged" in any significant way, though most would concede that the lot of migratory farm workers is less than ideal. In

*Reprinted from *Industrial Relations,* Vol. 3, No. 3, May 1964.

Southern California particularly, an aura of sentiment, history, and romance has often surrounded the Mexican-American population, effectively obscuring the realities.

Urban Mexican-Americans with the lowest levels of income and education and the highest rates of unemployment are usually concentrated in ghettos (barrios) where they are hidden from the sight of their more prosperous Anglo and Latin compatriots. Financially successful Mexican-Americans situated in other parts of the community and well integrated into the larger culture, do not identify with the disadvantaged and evince, at best, only a token concern with their problems.

Perhaps a critical reason for community insensitivity to Mexican-American problems lies in the traditional inability of the Mexican-Americans to organize into effective political and economic groups. Many other minorities have secured a redress of their grievances

TABLE I

Distribution and Growth, Spanish Surname and Negro Population,
Five Southwestern States, 1950 and 1960

State	1950		1960	
	Spanish surname	Negroes	Spanish surname	Negroes
Arizona	128,318	26,298	194,356	43,585
California	760,453	462,576	1,426,538	880,486
Colorado	118,131	20,198	157,173	39,827
New Mexico	248,880	8,423	269,122	17,109
Texas	1,033,768	977,458	1,417,810	1,185,476
Totals	2,289,550	1,494,953	3,464,999	2,166,483

Sources: *Persons of Spanish Surname,* U.S. Census of Population: 1960, Final Report PC(2)-1B; and *Nonwhite Population by Race,* U.S. Census of Population: 1960, Final Report PC(2)-1C.

through a skillful use of votes and economic strength, but cultural factors, among other things, have heretofore prevented the Mexican-Americans from achieving the unity required for organizational effectiveness. Individualism and distrust of organizations (even of government itself) are characteristic of the Latin community.

Even the relative advantages enjoyed by this minority — for example, less intensive housing discrimination — have conspired to weaken its political cohesiveness, since the absence of overt repression and the greater dispersal of the population reduce the possibility of bloc voting which could command respect for the group's demands. Growing political awareness, however, is one of the most striking changes now in process throughout the Mexican-American communities of the Southwest.

It is impossible to describe the role of the Mexican-American in the labor market without giving attention to some of the cultural forces which influence him. The Mexican-American, especially the youngster, is in a sense a person between cultures, neither fully a Mexican nor fully an "American." He is asked by many of his Anglo associates to reject the cultural heritage of his family, a demand which places overwhelming (and, in the author's judgment, unnecessary) psychological pressures upon him. The predominant values of Anglo society come into conflict with many of those which characterize the Mexican culture.

Economists have rarely focused on the relationship of cultural values to employment patterns, probably because most regard this as a sociological problem and therefore out of their jurisdiction, but it is certain that the model of a coldly rational income-maximizing worker, so familiar in economic theory, bears little resemblance to reality. Values and motivations differ from one person to another and, a fortiori, from one culture to another. In the case of the Mexican-American, traditional values have been strongly influenced by a folk or rural culture in which organized and continuous striving for future monetary gains plays little part. Satisfaction of present wishes and needs tends to take precedence over long-range planning which requires immediate sacrifices.

This pattern of living, particularly among the poor, involves a mixture of individualism and family unity which leaves little room for an interest in the community. Youngsters have a primary obligation to the family and its welfare, which often requires them to leave school early and contribute to the family's support. Little concern is expressed for those large and impersonal factors which are of critical importance to the urbanized Anglo: law, government, politics, social organization.

If ever in the native culture there is frequent suspicion of hostility toward social institutions such as government, the police, and the schools, and if there is a deep conviction that those institutions "belong" essentially to other persons and other classes, those feelings will be exacerbated in an alien culture. The overt and subtle discriminations against Mexican-Americans, the expressed antagonism to Mexican culture, the prohibitions in schools and elsewhere against the speaking of Spanish, the assignment of Mexican-Americans to low-level jobs, and the callous exploitation of the unskilled and the uneducated to serve the economic interests of particular employers have only served to heighten the alienation of the Mexican-American.

In addition, the male has traditionally played the dominant role in the Mexican family. Machismo — the expression of masculinity and male dominance — can lead to an emphasis on physical strength and a suspicion of an interest in education as unmasculine. Occupations requiring muscular prowess may have greater appeal than those associated with intellectual effort. Women are actively discouraged from participating in community activities or taking jobs usually identified as male jobs. All major decisions are left to the male members of the family.

However strong these influences may have been in the past, there is evidence that an acculturation process is now taking place which is infusing the Mexican-American family structure with many "Anglo" characteristics and is, in turn, increasing the awareness by Anglos of the needs and contributions of the Mexican-Americans. The role of the Mexican-American woman may be changing. Available statistics suggest that more and more Mexican-American women are employed in traditionally male occupations, that the emphasis on education is increasing drastically, and that women are assuming a more active role in both family and community affairs.

Perhaps of greatest significance, there is a growing willingness to form and join organizations, though the Mexican-Americans still lag far behind the Anglos and the Negroes in this respect. Several unions, notably those in the garment trades and unskilled construction work, have high percentages of Mexican-American membership. New community organizations have sprung up in recent years, one of which succeeded (with the help of the Teamsters Union) in winning full control of municipal government in Crystal City, Texas. Mexican-American Congressmen now represent constituencies in California, Texas, and New Mexico. Ad hoc Mexican-American committees on employment and education, under the aegis of the Los Angeles County Commission on Human Relations, are presently active in the Los Angeles area. Political awareness has increased enormously, and government agencies and legislative bodies are responding more sensitively to the needs and demands of the Mexican-American community.

Among the interstate or interregional Mexican-American organizations which have received particular attention are the League of United Latin American Citizens (LULAC), the GI Forum, and the Community Service Organization (CSO). Local Mexican-American groups throughout the five states are too numerous to list.

Contrary to some impressions, Mexican-Americans in Arizona, California, Colorado, New Mexico, and Texas are concentrated overwhelmingly in the cities and towns. About 80 per cent of all white persons of Spanish surname in these five states are urban dwellers. Furthermore, almost 85 per cent are natives of the United States, and 55 per cent have native-born parents (see Table 2). Even in California, which has the lowest percentage of natives, 80 per cent of all residents of Spanish surname are native-born.

There is evidence of considerable migration from one area to another, particularly to California and more specifically to Los Angeles County, but the available statistical data provide little insight into precise patterns. The increase of Mexican-American population in the Los Angeles area has been especially striking: the Spanish surname total for the metropolitan area doubled between 1950 and 1960 and made up almost 10 per cent of the total population in the latter year. The combined Mexican-American and Negro populations now equal close to one-fifth of the total. In all probability, close to two-thirds of the 318,000 increase resulted from in-migration. The birth rate for Mexican-American families exceeds the average for Anglos, further stimulating population growth.

Like the Negroes, the Mexican-Americans are heavily concentrated in the blue-collar job categories and have made comparatively little headway in the managerial, professional, clerical, and sales occupations. Over 76 per cent of all males with Spanish surnames were

TABLE 2

Nativity of Spanish Surname Population, Urban and Rural,
Five Southwestern States, 1960

	Total	Per cent	Urban	Per cent	Rural nonfarm	Per cent	Rural farm	Per cent
Total	3,464,999	100.00	2,740,950	100.00	541,659	100.00	182,390	100.00
Native-born	2,930,185	84.6	2,309,852	84.3	476,235	92.2	144,098	79.0
Native parentage	1,899,402	54.8	1,464,942	53.4	338,085	62.4	96,375	52.8
Foreign or mixed parentage	1,030,783	29.7	844,910	30.8	138,150	25.5	47,723	26.2
Mexican parentage	917,614	26.5	750,909	27.4	126,120	23.3	40,585	22.2
Other and not reported	113,169	3.2	94,001	3.4	12,030	2.2	7,138	4.0
Foreign-born	534,814	15.4	431,098	15.7	65,424	12.1	38.292	21.0
Born in Mexico	468,684	13.5	373,918	13.6	59,946	11.1	34,820	19.1
Other and not reported	66,130	1.9	57,180	2.1	5,478	1.0	3,472	1.9

Source: *Persons of Spanish Surname*, U.S. Census of Population: 1960, Final Report PC(2)-1B.

employed as craftsmen, operatives (semiskilled), private household workers, service workers, farm laborers and foremen, and "other laborers" in 1960, while only 49 per cent of Anglos held such jobs. Mexican-Americans were located in large numbers in the semiskilled category: about 23 per cent of the men and 25 per cent of the women were operatives. About 16 per cent of the males were farm laborers, approximately the same as the percentage for craftsmen and for "other laborers" (see Table 3).

The Mexican-American, typically, is better off than the Negro and worse off than the Anglo in terms of income and rate of unemployment. The intermediate position of the Mexican-American may be attributable, at least in part, to the relatively greater penetration of men into the craftsman (skilled) category and of women into the clerical. The rigid discriminatory barriers which have prevented entry of Negroes into these jobs do not seem to apply in the same degree to Mexican-Americans. On the other hand, Mexican-Americans do no better than Negroes in the high-income professional categories. Only 4.5 per cent of employed Spanish surname males, identical with the percentage for employed Negro males, were defined as professional, technical, and kindred workers.

It is impossible to determine, with any precision or confidence, the extent to which the occupational distribution of Mexican-Americans

TABLE 3

Distribution by Sex and Occupation, Spanish Surname and "Anglo" Populations, Five Southwestern States, 1960

Occupation	Spanish surname				"Anglo"*			
	Male	Per cent	Female	Per cent	Male	Per cent	Female	Per cent
Professional, technical and kindred	28,955	3.9	14,683	5.5	805,595	13.6	433,769	15.4
Farmers and farm managers	16,442	2.2	482	0.2	253,603	4.0	12,759	0.4
Managers, officials, and proprietors, exc. farm	32,010	4.3	6,744	2.5	806,000	13.6	153,416	5.4
Clerical and kindred	33,866	4.6	54,362	20.4	411,234	6.9	1,031,662	36.6
Sales	24,933	3.4	20,183	7.6	481,467	8.1	252,075	8.9
Craftsmen, foremen, and kindred	116,578	15.8	3,273	1.2	1,221,760	20.7	32,740	1.1
Operatives and kindred	68,497	22.9	66,212	24.8	933,176	15.8	251,215	8.9
Private household	878	0.1	28,514	10.7	5,925	0.1	125,197	4.4
Service, exc. private household	52,749	7.2	41,189	15.4	305,734	5.2	347,942	12.3
Farm laborers and foremen	117,688	16.0	10,319	3.9	131,818	2.2	17,792	0.6
Laborers, exc. farm and mine	106,409	14.4	3,006	1.1	281,317	4.8	8,864	0.3
Occupation not reported	37,763	5.1	17,688	6.6	266,519	4.5	149,499	5.3
Totals	736,768		266,655		5,904,148		2,816,930	

Sources: *Persons of Spanish Surname*, U.S. Census of Population: 1960, Final Report PC(2)-1B; *General Social and Economic Characteristics: Arizona, California, Colorado, New Mexico, and Texas*, U.S. Census of Population: 1960, PC(1) Series.

*"Anglo" represents the total employed in each category *minus* the Spanish surname and Negro totals.

has been influenced by the direct or indirect discrimination which has undeniably occurred. One fact is clear: many American employers, particularly those in agriculture, have long regarded the Mexican population (domestic and foreign) as a source of cheap and "dependable" labor. The flow of Mexican nationals into and out of this country has been regulated (or unregulated. as in the case of the "wetbacks") in accordance with the needs of domestic employers. The inflow has increased enormously in wartime and during other periods of labor shortage and, in turn, many Mexicans were returned to Mexico by force during the Great Depression. In 1954-1955, prior to inauguration of the bracero program, public pressure forced the return of thousands of illegal entrants to Mexico. At this writing, the bracero program appears doomed to well-earned extinction at the end of its current term; however, the complex and specialized problems of agricultural labor are beyond the scope of this article.

A particularly disturbing trend in urban areas is the increasingly widespread employment of Mexican-Americans, often women, in low-paying service or semiskilled jobs. Small firms, such as laundries and garment manufacturers, in highly competitive industries employ Mexican-Americans in large numbers. Union officials charge that many employers take advantage of language barriers, low levels of education, and unfamiliarity with legal rights to exploit these workers. Some garment trades unions in Texas have been decimated by such tactics. The Amalgamated Clothing Workers, among others, has launched a campaign to organize these employees in the Los Angeles area. The difficulties are great and it is still too early to judge how successful the program will be.

Overt discrimination against the Mexican-American (or Latin-American) is more common in Texas than in California, although California is not blameless. Fair Employment Practices laws have provided a degree of protection to the Mexican-American in California which does not exist in Texas, a state characterized by antiunion laws and an absence of civil rights measures. Testifying before a subcommittee of the U.S. Senate Committee on Labor and Public Welfare in late 1963, Congressman Henry B. Gonzalez of San Antonio declared that Mexican-Americans in that state suffer discrimination both in employment and in education. He pointed out that Mexican-Americans are often concentrated in types of industry, such as agriculture and small firms, which are not covered by minimum wage and other protective laws and are usually nonunion: "It is not uncommon to find Latins in Texas who earn less than fifty cents an hour, or even less. Laundry workers, for example, often make less than fifteen dollars for a forty-four to forty-eight hour week." Noting the absence of an FEPC law in Texas, Congressman Gonzalez cited specific examples of discriminatory job specifications, taken from employment ads in San Antonio newspapers. Among the examples cited are these: "Maintenance: 30-45 Anglo, local, married, $250 . . . "; "Neat, dependable Anglo short order cook . . . "; "Waitresses, Colored or Latin . . . "; "Latin tire changer . . . "; "Counter Attendants, under 35 . . . Anglo . . . ."

The testimony of Congressman Gonzalez contains further examples of discriminatory treatment in pay scales, housing, and education. He cited the case of a young Mexican-American woman who held a clerical position at a local library, was highly skilled and educated, and spoke only English. Yet she was paid $25 per month less than her coworkers doing the same job. Her employer explained that "the other girls would quit if I paid her as much as they make."

Congressman Gonzalez and many others emphasize the critical role of poor education in blocking the economic progress of the Mexican-American. Two problems confront most Mexican-Americans in Texas: (1) school districts with high Mexican-American concentrations tend to be poor and thus offer inferior and oftentimes segregated facilities, and (2) cultural factors and unenforced school attendance laws make it especially difficult for Mexican-American youngsters to benefit from a school program directed to the English-speaking. The result is that the illiteracy rate among the Texas Latins is extremely high.

The Mexican-American would be at a disadvantage in the labor market because of the inadequacy of his education and training, even were there no discrimination. Mexican-American youngsters drop out of high school at an alarming rate, and their lack of a diploma disqualifies them from apprenticeships and other training programs. A high, though indeterminate, proportion of the dropouts actually are pupils who have been categorized as ill-behaved or unmotivated and have been invited to leave. In addition, Mexican-American schools experience relatively high transiency rates, which impair the quality of instruction received by the youngsters.

Unfortunately, in all too many cases the pupil receives little encouragement to stay in school. Parents and peers alike pressure him to drop out (sometimes for economic reasons), and the school itself may consider him "burdensome" for one reason or another. He does not fit easily into the mold created for the Anglo student, nor does the typical school program offer special help to youngsters having difficulty because of language problems or cultural differences. Employers and school officials have remarked to the author, on several occasions, that the problems of the Mexicans would vanish if only they became "Americanized," i.e., exactly like the Anglos. The author, of course, does not share this naive view.

Programs of vocational education and training have had little impact thus far on Mexican-Americans. Most unemployed Mexican-Americans fall into those age and education brackets which are proportionately under-represented in the training programs inaugurated under the

Manpower Development and Training Act. Existing classes do not enroll many young people who have dropped out of high school, have little or no employment experience, and do poorly on standard examinations. When language problems are added, it becomes clear that the Mexican-American is not yet in a position to benefit significantly from such programs.

Nor is there consensus either among experts or among Mexican-American families as to the value to Mexican-Americans of vocational programs in the public schools. A few parents undoubtedly resist the assignment of their children to vocational courses because academic or college-oriented programs have greater prestige. It is a commonly held belief within both the Mexican-American and Negro communities that minority youngsters, including many with college potential, are unfairly categorized as vocational pupils. Others feel that the school system does not offer enough vocational training. Whatever the merits of these respective claims, most specialists agree that vocational counseling and the teaching of vocational subjects in nearly all schools are seriously deficient, largely because there is inadequate liaison between industry and the schools and pitifully little awareness by counselors of job requirements and trends in the labor market.

Mexican-American spokesmen, employers, and educators generally agree that education is the key to a solution of the Mexican-American's employment problems. However, there is little agreement on how responsibility for such improved education should be divided or on the proper function of the educational process in serving the particular needs of a bilingual youngster. The schools tend to blame Mexican-American parents for allegedly failing to motivate the children to take advantage of educational opportunities, while Mexican-American spokesmen charge the schools with failure to meet the needs of students other than the favored Anglos.

The predominant view among employers, as expressed to the author, has been suggested previously: that the Mexican-American must be persuaded to drop his attachment to the Spanish language and Mexican culture. It is undeniable that the Mexican-American who speaks English fluently and exclusively and adopts "American" (Anglo) customs has a considerable employment advantage over his less Americanized compadres, especially if he is also light-skinned. But two important questions arise here: is this single-focus approach realistic for the vast majority of disadvantaged Mexican-Americans, and quite aside from realism, is it genuinely desirable to subvert a cultural heritage simply because its values may sometimes conflict with those of an Anglo majority?

So far, the most concrete programs for improvement of Mexican-American employment opportunities have been aimed at young people. Probably the largest and most noteworthy single project yet undertaken is the "youth employability" program financed initially by a half-million dollar grant from the Office of Manpower, Automation, and Training of the U.S. Department of Labor and administered by the Youth Opportunities Board of Greater Los Angeles in the overwhelmingly Mexican-American East Los Angeles area. The purpose of the project is to provide training, counseling, and guidance for youngsters, particularly high school dropouts, who otherwise might join the ranks of the hard-core unemployed.

Even at an early stage, project officials have had some success in persuading dropouts to return to school and in placing some of the unemployed, but the critical tests are yet to come. Based on interjurisdictional cooperation among the California State Employment Service, the city and county schools, the city and county governments of Los Angeles, and various community agencies, the program seeks to: identify youngsters in the 16-21 age bracket who are unemployed or underemployed and who meet certain other criteria; provide counseling by experienced staff of thy State Employment Service and the schools; locate jobs which offer "reasonable expectation of employment;" and gear training and placement programs to such jobs.

Certain of the school districts are now initiating long-overdue programs to improve counseling and teaching of Mexican-American pupils, combat excessive dropout rates, develop and introduce books or materials directed to the non-Anglo students as well as to the Anglo, and build closer ties with the Mexican-American community. The Los Angeles Board of Education has recently established an Office of Urban Affairs, empowered to undertake programs of this nature, and has adopted policy statements favoring increased instruction in Mexican history and culture, remedial English classes, and similar offers. Much remains to be done, however. Counseling is a major problem area, and the standard methods of communicating with parents continue to yield meager results in a community, like the Mexican-American, which has little background of participation in school affairs. The problem is further complicated by a severe shortage of bilingual teachers, counselors, and administrators at all levels of the school system.

A significant aspect of the current push for more and better jobs for Mexican-Americans is that it coincides with, and probably has been stimulated by, the movement in the Negro community toward the same goals. This timing, in the context of an economy which has high levels of persistent unemployment, creates obvious problems. Some Mexican-American spokesmen seem uncertain whether the Negro push for equality of opportunity is a boon or a hindrance to the corresponding efforts of their community. Neither the Negroes nor the Mexican-Americans have yet resolved the question of how much they can or should work jointly in programs to break down employment barriers. Some Mexican-Americans strongly oppose any consolidation of efforts, while others urge further cooperation. The anomalous position of the Mexican-American, who is neither fully accepted nor fully rejected by the dominant Anglo community, makes this decision harder. There are some, fortunately a minority, within the Mexican-American group who deny the existence of serious problems and condemn all those who are organizing for action.

The degree of cooperation between the minority communities appears to differ from one state to another. In Texas, Negroes and Mexican-Americans have long tended to work together, politically and otherwise, for common goals. In California, by and large, the two groups have acted separately. Tentative gestures to increase collaboration have been made on both sides, but political clashes have recently engendered antagonism and an occasionally expressed fear that Negroes may be getting jobs at the expense of Mexican-Americans. The evidence for this is tenuous and elusive at best. But despite signs of tension, no basic cleavage seems imminent at this writing.

The critical need for public programs which would increase the general level of employment is certainly clear in this context. The economic difficulties confronted by Mexican-Americans and by Negroes stem from the general unemployment situation as well as from specific problems of discrimination, cultural differences, and lack of training. It would appear that the two communities have a strong common interest in generating support for measures to restore full employment.

One major difficulty has been that the Mexican-Americans, unlike most other minorities, have not supported permanent, adequately financed organizations concerned with community problems. There is no Mexican-American equivalent of the Urban League, and no single organization which can legitimately claim to speak for a large segment of the community. Fragmentation and internecine warfare have rendered many Mexican-American groups impotent. Furthermore, those identified as "leaders" are often detached from those most in need of assistance and either cannot or will not back strong demands for action.

Basically the Mexican-American community faces the same problems as does the Negro, except in a more subtle form. Direct discrimination does not hit the Mexican-American as severely, but he has arrived at the same dead end by a different route. Like the Negro, the Mexican-American is found mainly in blue-collar jobs, the category most vulnerable to automation. Like the Negro, the Mexican-American lacks the education and training to give him sufficient adaptability in a dynamic labor market. Like the Negro, the Mexican-American suffers an excessive rate and duration of unemployment. And, even worse than the Negro, the Mexican-American is placed at a disadvantage by the absence of community organizations powerful and united enough to secure a redress of grievances. There is evidence, however, that the old order is changing and that the Mexican-American will no longer be a "forgotten man."

DISCRIMINATION AGAINST MEXICAN AMERICANS IN PRIVATE EMPLOYMENT*

ALBERT ARMENDARIZ

Discrimination directed against the Mexican American in private industry is an every-day fact of life in these United States. It rears its ugly head in every facet of private employment, from the smallest menial task to the highest paid executive position, so long as it involves competition with an Anglo-American for such a position.

Undoubtedly, if the choice of a subject for this paper had been mine, I would not have used the word "discrimination" in it. This is because we need the cooperation of our Anglo counterparts in our society to alleviate the situation and they do not admit that there is any discrimination. I would have labelled my contribution, "The Problem of Preferential Treatment of the Anglo Worker over the Mexican American in Private Industry in the United States." When you charge discrimination, the defense begins and the cooperation ends. My first recommendation, therefore, is that the word, "discrimination" not be employed in any phase of this work; it will only bring on excuses as are illustrated by the following examples — no results:

The representative of a large Corporation in Corpus Christi, who insisted that the reason that only eight out of a total of 883 employees in his Company are Mexican Americans is not discrimination, but the fact that he has experienced difficulty in obtaining qualified applicants.

The School Administrator who answers the charge of illegally segregated Mexican American Schools is not due to discrimination, but due to the conglomeration of Mexican Americans in certain districts, when he knows that a mere change in the direction of district boundaries would completely alleviate the situation.

*The Mexican American: A New Focus on Opportunity, Inter-Agency Committee on Mexican American Affairs, U.S. Govt. Printing Office, Washington, D.C., 1967, pages 239-244.

The Newspaper Editor who cites editorially the advance of what is but a minute percentage of Mexican Americans in the professions, business and politics as proof of the non-existence of discrimination in his area, failing to state in such editorial that a large percentage of the poverty stricken in the same area today is found in the Mexican American population.

Another School Administrator who answers the charge of segregation of Mexican Americans in his system with the assertion that his district obeys all of the mandates of the Courts, while its Board spends Public School Funds in the litigation and appeal of all orders requiring integration. (This District receives approximately $8,000,000.00 in Federal Funds, not counting OEO Funds on Special Projects in Head-Start and Remedial.)

The Union Official who testifies that his Trades Council does not discriminate in refusing to accept applications for training under OEO programs from applicants of Mexican American extraction, but states that his Union requires a High-School education and a special test as qualifications for house painters.

The large Corporation Personnel Executive who insists that Mexican Americans are not promoted because they are not qualified when his roster has Anglo-Americans in the desired positions with less education and fewer qualifications.

Yes, they deny that they practice discrimination, but statistics tell the story. These figures, unfortunately, are typical wherever there is a large concentration of Mexican Americans:

In the City of Los Angeles, where we find the largest concentration of Mexican Americans in the world, the top fifteen Industries hired only 9.7% Mexican Americans. Of these, only 4% have been hired in white-collar jobs; 68.3% of these were in the lower wage scales and clerical jobs.

In the great State of Texas, where 16% of the total population according to the 1960 census is Mexican American, only 4.7% are white-collar workers; 80% of these are in the lower wage scales and clerical jobs.

The Texas Advisory Committee to the Civil Rights Commission reports that in three of the largest Corporations around a certain city with heavy concentration of Mexican American population and a large number of Government Contracts, out of a total of 1350 persons employed, only nine are Mexican American.

Large percentages of Mexican American families live in poverty and have an income under $3,000.00. The numbers range from 86% in some Counties of Texas, to 24% in some Counties in California.

The effect of the above conditions reflects itself in our people. Large segments of children drop out of school. Those who continue are materially behind in their age-grade cycles, products of indifferent school systems (so far as the Mexican American is concerned). In many instances, High School graduates are from three to six years behind the Anglo Graduate in educational attainment, and certainly no match for the Anglo in this competitive world. This is a sad commentary on our times and as one Educator put it: "In the process of serving up the Latin the nearest thing to no education at all . . . the Anglos are serving their own children a third grade education on a silver platter of racial glory."

Our Anglo counterpart in this society is generally a fair-minded, God-fearing individual. He is, we must admit, THE BOSS. He is the one who must open the doors to our group to reach equality of opportunity in industry. Because we are not a militant group, because we are too proud, too shy or too scared to join many marches, because we know that our advances in our society must be achieved in a dignified manner, we should recognize that a major portion of our job is to find effective ways to appeal to the Anglo's sense of justice and fair play with renewed vigor and persistence from every angle. When this has been given a test of short duration, we must demand that the governmental agencies involved refuse government funds to those who remain unconvinced.

I find that twenty years of living with our problems does not necessarily ease the difficulty of proposing solutions. There is no easy answer. Decades of toil have created the problems. The mortar that cements the roots of the evil lays fast, dry and hard. Our fathers before us have faced these same problems, for more than a century, and the mortar remains unyielding as we place our shoulders to the task of its destruction. For destroy it we must.

There are those in our group that feel that all of our problems would disappear with the simple expediency of changing all of our names to Jones. Indeed, many of our group have done exactly that. We know that this is not likely to occur to any great extent, but the theory behind this movement remains sound. In order to achieve equality of opportunity based on qualifications alone and without regard to race, color or creed, the Negro has demanded the removal of racial designation from all applications for employment and from all employment records. In his behalf, American Industry has granted this concession to a very large extent. This has resulted in the placement of many Negro Americans in jobs which were previously denied to them on the same excuses used against our ethnic group. It is practiced in the majority of Federal Job Placement services with the same result. Our surnames are what give us away, for which prospective employer does not know that Juan Pistolas, job applicant (original or promotional), is a Mexican American?

Solution.—Require that all applications for employment, original or promotional, together with all applications for training, enrollment in training schools, applications for Employment in OEO projects, enrollees for training, or enrollment in schools established for the purpose of training or rehabilitation be strictly based on number systems such as those used in College entrance examinations. Also remove the requirement that a picture be necessary.

Rationale.—This simple, inexpensive change in procedures removes the suspicion that determination and placement is based on any other factor than that of qualifications and experience. The argument that it is not practical to hire a person that is not seen is, at best, suspicious, and is not sufficiently strong to overcome the great harm done to equality of opportunity under the present system.

While discrimination in public employment is the subject of another presentation at this conference, comparative statistics reveal that the evil of preferential treatment exists in public employment at all levels, federal, state and city, including administrative bodes such as school administration and police departments. This presentation would not be complete if I did not mention the effect of this preferential treatment on the private employer.

Solution.—All the majesty of the Federal Government should be brought to bear on all public agencies, the majority of them heavily financed by Federal funds, to immediately terminate preferential treatment of the Anglo worker.

Rationale.—Example is the best teacher. More important, how can we expect private industry to respect governmental policy and orders requiring equal opportunity when equal opportunity is not available in public employment?

Responsible Mexican American leaders agree that the problem of the education of our children, if solved, offers the greatest avenue for the solution of our overall problems. Make of this youngster a qualified, trained person, and we are on our way. These same leaders are almost unanimous in their belief that the educational system that is provided to accomplish this task has completely failed. This is not an unfair nor unfounded appraisement of the educational problems that face us when we consider the huge number of Mexican American applicants who have attended these educational institutions, and have been denied opportunity and training because they do not academically qualify. This statement is not limited to school dropouts alone, but includes many holding high school diplomas whose academic attainments are as much as four years behind their Anglo co-student. We shall examine a few of its faults and present a few possible solutions:

School boards and school administrators in the present school systems are members of the ruling power structure that has paid little heed to the educational necessities of this large minority group. It has established its bus lifts to assure that integration does not occur and has laid out school boundaries to assure that the Mexican American pupil attends classes in his school. Their standard excuse for the poor quality of their product is that the Mexican American is different, and that he has a language problem that prevents his complete development as a pupil to his propensities to learning. We must convince these school officials, one by one, in groups or in unison, that the concern and the demands of this ethnic group are serious. That we no longer can, nor will we tolerate a second class education for our children. We must make it known to them that the Federal government agrees with us. The following are a few suggestions that might accomplish this serious but necessary task:

a. Invoke the authority of the Federal Government in any form. Include in this the H.E.W. Department in an all out effort to convince local school boards that de-facto segregation of our children must end. To those that will not listen to reason, direct the attention of the Attorney General to file suits to quickly achieve total integration of the Mexican American child in all school systems.

Rationale.—The segregated school or classroom presents no challenge to the Spanish speaking child. When confronted by an integrated group, he is required to learn English if he is to get along. Necessity, it is said, is the mother of invention — it also teaches little Spanish speaking children the English language. Once he learns English, his ability to grasp the subject matter of classroom work is materially enhanced.

b. Through these same contacts, make a new effort to convince more school systems to adopt the bi-lingual system of study for these pupils being careful that it is not installed as a shield to the classroom segregation of our children.

Rationale.—The effectiveness of this educational concept has been studied and reported by many leading educators. It is the subject of funding in at least one Congressional bill of recent vintage. The concept is based on the reasonable principle that education in subjects such as arithmetic can proceed to be taught in English to these pupils so that they may be prevented from getting behind on their school work while they are learning the English language.

c. Through these same contacts, attempt to convince the school systems to re-install the use of the kindergarten or pre-school year. This would be an excellent place to use the funds now going to the little school of the 400 or the Head Start programs. I can speak from personal experience here, for my own education began at a time when I did not speak a single word of English. Yet, fortunately for me, it began in the kindergarten grade of a public school which itself was integrated. By the time I left kindergarten to advance to the first grade, I knew enough English (the majority of it, I must admit, learned from my Anglo schoolmates) to be able to compete on an equal or nearly-equal basis.

Rationale.—There is no valid reason for having the Head Start programs as separate and distinct "extras" available to only a few children who start their school careers as something distinct and apart. A mandatory pre-school year, at least in districts with large Mexican American population, will remove the stigma of specialized attention and can be, according to studies, incorporated into the regular curriculum of schools. This can be done at a cost far less than is being spent on the Head Start program. In addition, it will notably prepare the child for the first grade if experienced and capable teachers (their experience and capabilities will expertize them in a few semesters) are used. It will reach *all* children in such districts, not only those who are recruited.

d. Through these same contacts, and suits, if necessary, convince the school systems to fully utilize trained personnel of Mexican American extraction in their systems, especially in areas where this problem is evident. Guaranteeing to this element, there should also be opportunities for advancement within the system, including the position of school principal and other top administrative and policy-making positions.

Rationale.—If the problem involves the Mexican American, it is logical that Mexican American educators are more aware of the problem and its possible solution. With a guarantee of promotional equality, more and more of these trained Mexican Americans will join our school systems as teachers, assuring a constant flow of talent to carry out these programs.

e. Up to now, emphasis of all educational programs has been upon the "academic" aspect of education, or, stated another way, preparing the high school graduate for college. This is in spite of the fact that up until recent years, the Latin American comprised less than 1% of the total college population. Very little emphasis is given to technical or vocational teaching. This is the slot which the Federal programs can best serve the present deficient, uneducated, and thus disqualified Mexican American: by using Federal funds to help private schools in technical and vocational training; by using more funds, with supervision to guarantee no discrimination against the Mexican American in unions or on the union programs of remedial and technical training.

Rationale.—The Mexican American has a traditional adeptness in the use of his hands. This natural skill could be channeled into a great service to the industrial effort of this country if properly trained and prepared. The absence of academic proficiency can be minimized to the technical data involved in the specific field. This technical data can be taught either in Spanish or in English or both. It is the quickest answer to the personnel executive quoted above that the Mexican American is not qualified to take the jobs that he offers.

It should be noted here that what I am referring to in this part of the presentation is the enigma that the Mexican American faces in this modern industrial world. He depends on the Anglo to teach and prepare him to be qualified so that the Anglo Industrialist will be able to utilize him in his business. He depends upon the Anglo establishment to teach and train him in a mandatory school system, when such a system is not geared to the needs of the said industrialist.

f. Federal remedial funds should be channeled to private or government agencies engaged in the solution of the problem of remedying this training and education gap.

Rationale.—It defeats the very purpose of the remedial funds spent when they are given to the same agency that created the deficiency which is sought to be corrected.

Employment

Our group is very thankful that a Mexican American was appointed to the Commission on Equal Employment Opportunity. We are also deeply troubled by the ineffectiveness of that Commission in finding a remedy to the situation. It is also true that the biggest disappointment that we have suffered is in its apparent failure to stop the preferential treatment of private employers, especially those that enjoy large government contracts. Let us examine a few of the possible solutions to this problem.

a. The problem of proof is of paramount importance here. If the Mexican American must carry the burden of proof in his allegations of unfair and unequal treatment in employment and employment opportunities, he is lost. We do not have the funds, the machinery, the organization, or perhaps not even the personnel to do this. We must depend on the Commission, which does have all of these elements that we lack, to pursue the matter fearlessly against the offending employer. This initiative on your part includes the bringing of charges.

Rationale.—It requires the use of the prerogative given by the law to initiate investigations without complaint. If this is not done, the office of Equal Employment Opportunity will remain ineffective to our needs. For example, one report shows that in a series of complaints against a telephone company, 2,500 were filed by Negroes, while only 25 were made by Mexican Americans. Efforts in having printed instructions in Spanish on how to file a complaint were noble, but of little use.

b. We admit, of course, that the most effective way to combat the problem lies in the bringing of prompt complaints from those personally affected. We must find new ways to make them come forth. When they do, we must find ways to protect them from any repercussions thereof.

Rationale.—It is difficult enough to make them come forth, and when they do, as in the case of a public utility facing such complaints, the workers were promised that their names would not be revealed to their employers. Their employers found out and as a result, their lives are now miserable. Their families will not have a working breadwinner very much longer after the investigation is over with. The investigators have gone back where they came from, and the worker is left "holding the bag." It is not reasonable to expect complaints under these conditions.

c. Adequate publicity must be given to the fact that a certain company is receiving government contracts and requires workers in certain categories and that it is bound to the principles of Equal Employment Opportunity.

Rationale.—If these facts are publicly known, more people will apply for these job availabilities, and there is less likelihood that the usual absence of applicants will occur. This is one of the standard excuses for the disparity in numbers between the workers in the two groups.

We are equally disappointed in the failure of the Office of Economic Opportunities to reach the needs of the Mexican American community. We were keenly aware that the benefits from the many programs that the O.E.O. offers had not reached us because they had been placed in the hands of the very power structure which we have discussed hereinabove. In fact, one of the outstanding facts was that in the book-form report printed by the O.E.O. and covering each of its related agencies, we were able to find only *one* Mexican American surname as the director of an O.E.O.-sponsored project.

My final contribution is a recommendation that programs such as SER be established and maintained in all areas of OEO and EEOC sphere of influence. Operation SER was conceived and programmed by the G.I. Forum and the League of United Latin American Citizens. I am quite aware of the trials and tribulations experienced in putting the program into operation and obtaining its approval and financing. This program was created by those that were working on the problem long before there was any hope of receiving any pay. It is dedicated to the service, employment, and redevelopment of this ethnic group. It has received approximately $500,000. This is the only OEO money directly handled by the two largest organizations which have been chipping at the tough mortar with very poor, blunt instruments. We need more. As Dr. Julian Samora, Head of the Department of Sociology, University of Notre Dame, said:

> For many years many of us have been working on less than a shoestring trying to do something about the variety of problems which confront the Spanish-speaking people and over the years we have been unable to attract funds from agencies or foundations to help in this most important work. Most other minority groups, either through the government or foundations, have received encouragement and assistance in the resolution of their problems and ironically enough the Spanish-speaking who have been in the Southwest longer than any group, and who constitute the largest Ethnic group in the Southwest if not the United States, have been totally neglected.

CIVIL SERVICE AND THE MEXICAN AMERICAN*

JUDGE ALFRED J. HERNANDEZ

The Civil Service Commission, in the preface of the 1966 study of minority group employment in the Federal Government, stated that the purpose in collecting and publishing this report was to provide a means of assessing progress and identifying areas where greater efforts must be made to assure equality of opportunity. It is somewhat ironic to note that 150 pages of this report were dedicated to publishing employment statistics in the Federal Government as concerning the Negro, while only 14 pages were dedicated toward presenting the plight of the Mexican American in government today. However, I do not feel that we should really complain, but rather we should consider ourselves fortunate as the entire picture of the American Indian, the original American, was reported in 12 pages. If we are to use this report, either as a means of recording the progress or identifying the areas where positive affirmative action must be taken to assure equality of opportunity in employment with the Federal Government, it is necessary that we begin our study with the agency that compiled this report — the Civil Service Commission.

In the Civil Service Commission there are three commissioners none of whom are, or have ever been, of Mexican American descent. At the regional levels there are, to my knowledge, no regional directors of Mexican American descent and only a very small number of Mexican American investigators, among whose duties are included those of investigating alleged complaints of discrimination in government agencies and military installations.

The great need for bilingual and bicultural investigators in the Civil Service Commission can best be illustrated by the situation which occurred in the immediate vicinity of El Paso at White Sands Missile Range. At this installation complaint after complaint had been

*The Mexican American: A New Focus on Opportunity, Inter-Agency Committee on Mexican American Affairs, U.S. Govt. Printing Office, Washington, D.C., 1967, pages 227-232.

presented to the Spanish-speaking community surrounding White Sands Missile Range as well as to the Department of the Army and the Civil Service Commission. Early this year the Civil Service Commission sent a team of investigators from its regional office in Denver, Colorado to investigate these alleged acts of discrimination. The team arrived at White Sands Missile Range and spent between six to eight weeks interviewing employees of the Range who wished to present grievances to the Commission. At the end of their investigation they compiled a voluminous report and presented a copy of it to the Civilian Personnel Officer of the installation. The report served only to confuse the Civilian Personnel Officer in regard to what the actual grievances were and what actions should be taken to correct them. None of the investigators were of Mexican American descent. Shortly thereafter the Department of the Army requested that Department of Defense Contracts Compliance Office lend them the services of Mexican American community relations specialists. A team of Mexican American employees of the Department of Defense Contracts Compliance Office arrived at White Sands Missile Range, met with the Commanding General and the Civilian Personnel Officer, ·met with supervisory employees at the Range, and met with Mexican American organizations and community leaders in the cities of El Paso, Texas and Las Cruces and Alamogordo, New Mexico. Both of the investigators were bilingual and bicultural and were able to communicate with Mexican American employees as well as with Mexican American community leaders and determine the problems that existed at this facility. It must be mentioned that this facility had undertaken a program of affirmative action designed to assure equality of opportunity for all employees, and that the Commanding General of this facility was personally committed to the principles of equal employment opportunity. However, this program had not been fully communicated to Mexican Americans in the community or to their employees. At the end of one week the community relations specialists met again with the Commanding General of the installation and presented to him their specific recommendations toward correcting the problems that existed. Approximately one month later a conference on equal employment opportunity was sponsored by the Commanding General, and approximately one hundred Mexican American leaders of the surrounding community were invited. At this conference the installation's program, dedicated toward insuring equality of opportunity for all employees, was presented. As a result of the work of the community relations specialists and the conference held by the Commanding General, lines of communication have been established between the facility and the Mexican American community.

A similar incident occurred at Sandia Base located in Albuquerque, New Mexico, where the Civil Service Commission again undertook to conduct investigations of alleged acts of discrimination against Mexican American employees. Shortly Sandia Base employed a Mexican American as the Deputy Equal Employment Opportunity Officer as the first step in the solution of the problems.

Problems have arisen and still exist at many military installations which are located throughout the five Southwestern states, with the most glaring and still unsolved problems existing at Kelly Air Force Base in San Antonio, Texas. All efforts which have been made by Mexican American organizations in an effort to correct these problems have met with complete failure. Problems exist there in regard to the Mexican Americans who, although employed in large numbers at this facility, hold jobs in the lower grades and are constantly denied promotions with the reason being given that they are not qualified. It is ironic that this facility located in San Antonio where approximately fifty per cent of the population of the city is Mexican American and where the Mexican American is, by far, the largest minority group employed, only recently announced the appointment of a person to the position of Deputy Equal Employment Officer and charged him with the responsibility of meeting with and understanding the problems of minority group employees, and, yet, passed over the applications of all Mexican American applicants as not qualified. It is evident, therefore, that there exists a glaring need for Mexican Americans to be employed by the Civil Service Commission at all job levels, including those in policy-making positions, if this Commission is, in fact, going to discharge its obligations of assuring equality of opportunity.

The Department of Health, Education and Welfare, according to the 1966 study of minority group employment in the Federal Government, has a total employment of 90,695 of which 954 or 1.3% are Mexican American, and in grades GS 9-18 has a total of 23,107 of which 191 or .8% are Mexican American. This Department recently created a Civil Rights Division which embarked upon a survey to determine the number of students in colleges and universities and primary and secondary school districts by race. It prepared a report system which was forwarded to colleges and universities as well as to the secondary districts. This reporting form prepared by the Civil Rights Division of the Department of Health, Education and Welfare instructed the universities and school districts to classify Mexican American students under the category listed as "others" with the explanation that Mexican Americans are not members of the Caucasian or white race. The League of United Latin American Citizens (LULAC) vigorously objected to this reporting form and called this matter to the attention of the Civil Rights Division of Health, Education and Welfare. The form for universities and colleges was rescinded and a new one prepared which lists Mexican American students under the category of "white" with an explanation that they are students of Spanish surname. The form sent to the school districts, however, has not been rescinded and the explanation given our organization was that two months of work had already been expended into the preparation of this form and the compilation of data. It is evident, however, that two months of work, at taxpayers' expense, have been wasted on a form that seeks completely incorrect information and data. Had there been a Mexican American employee in the Civil Rights Division of Health, Education and Welfare at the time that this form was prepared, this would never have happened. It is gratifying to note, however, that since this blunder on the part of HEW, a Mexican American has been employed in the Civil Rights Division as a Special Assistant.

The Department of Housing and Urban Development, an agency that is headed by a member of a minority group and an agency that was created to help minority groups and which, therefore, should be cognizant and sensitive to the needs of all minority groups in this country, has a total employment of 14,057 of which 117 or 0.8% are Spanish American.

The Department of Labor has a total employment of 9,626 of which 85 or 0.9% are Spanish surnamed Americans. In grades GS-9 through 18, the grades which are normally those that include supervisory positions as well as positions at policy-making levels, Department of Labor has a total of 4,786 employees of whom 47 or 1% are Spanish surnamed Americans. Is it any wonder, then, that the programs established by the Department of Labor, including the Manpower Development Training Act and On-the-Job Training programs, have miserably failed to reach the Americans of Spanish surname? It is true that the Department of Labor has in existence many programs that could greatly benefit this minority group; however, until this Department sees fit to establish a special program, the primary responsibility of which is to communicate the existing programs to Americans of Spanish surname throughout the country, as well as determine the need for new programs that can benefit this minority group and establish a line of communication between this mintority group and the Department of Labor, Spanish surnamed Americans will continue to receive training under Labor Department programs for service station attendants, short order cooks, and television repairmen.

The Department of Agriculture, in 1966, had a total employment of 102,184 of which 1,448 or 1.6% were Americans of Spanish surname. In grades GS-9 through 18, it employed a total of 32,979 of whom 140 or .4% were Americans of Spanish surname. It is indeed welcome news that in the last two months this Department has embarked upon a bold and aggressive program of affirmative action designed to rectify this appalling situation and during this period has succeeded in employing 326 Americans of Spanish surname. It is evident, therefore, that whenver a Department determines that it is going to seek out qualified minority group applicants it can find them as evidenced by the above facts. It must be made clear to all government agencies that the worn out statements and tired phrase, "We do not have more employees of Spanish surname because there just aren't any qualified," is no longer acceptable to our group.

The Office of Economic Opportunity, which was created to help eliminate poverty in the United States had a total employment in 1966 of 2,637 of which 50 or 1.9% were Americans of Spanish surname. In the five Southwestern states, employment in this agency reflected a much better profile, for out of 315 employees, 33 or 10.5% were Americans of Spanish surname. In grades GS-12-18, out of a total of 79 employees, 12 or 15.2% were Spanish surnamed Americans. It was distressing to note, however, that when a vacancy occurred in the regional office in Austin, Texas for the position of regional director, Mexican American organizations submitted names of qualified Mexican Americans to fill this position. The Mexican American organizations felt that it was necessary that the person who headed this office, whose territóry included Texas and New Mexico where the Mexican American is the largest minority group, should be a person who was bilingual and bicultural — a person who could study the problems of the Mexican American and direct his actions and his agency's actions toward solving these problems. Needless to say, a Mexican American was not selected for the position, and to this date there are no Americans of Spanish surname in any of the top level positions in the entire structure of the Office of Economic Opportunity.

The Equal Employment Opportunity Commission was created by the Civil Rights Act of 1964 and charged with the enforcement of Title VII of this Act, which Title prohibits discrimination in private employment because of race, creed, color, sex, or national origin. Even though the second largest minority group in the country is the American of Spanish surname, this Commission, immediately upon its creation and during its first two years of operation, consistently ignored our problems. In 1965 in Albuquerque, New Mexico, a group of Mexican Americans, including myself, walked out of a meeting sponsored by the Equal Employment Opportunity Commission after informing the Commission of our grievances. This year the President of the United States appointed the Honorable Vicente Ximenes to serve as a member of the Commission, and it is gratifying to note that there has been a steady increase in the number of Americans of Spanish surnames that have been employed by the Commission. It is also gratifying to see a well qualified administrator such as Mr. Tom Robles occupying the position of Regional Director of this Agency in the city of Albuquerque. There is, however, room for improvement, and I believe that it is incumbent upon this Commission to establish special programs which will be dedicated toward communicating to the Spanish surnamed Americans of this country all information relevant not only to the existence of this Commission, but to the rights that these citizens have under the Civil Rights Act.

The Department of Justice includes the Immigration and Naturalization Service and the Border Patrol that come in contact with thousands of Americans of Spanish surname on a daily basis. This agency has a total employment of 32,960 of which 501 or 1.6% are Americans of Spanish surname. In grades GS-9 through 18 it has a total employment of 11,695 and only 62 or 0.5% are Americans of Spanish surname. Yet, the Immigration and Naturalization Service and the Border Patrol require their officers to be bilingual and are content to spend thousands upon thousands of taxpayers' dollars teaching non-Spanish-speaking employees how to speak Spanish at their academy in Port Isabel, Texas. Right here in El Paso, a female of Spanish surname is employed as a GS-4. She performs the work of a GS 7-9 as an interpreter. She is held responsible for this most delicate and vital work, yet she is not considered to be qualified for a promotion to a GS-5.

The Department of Defense is the biggest employer in the entire United States, employing a nationwide total of 1,024,048 with 36,257 or 3.8% being Americans of Spanish surname. In the five Southwestern states, however, it employs a total of 260,611 of whom 32,205 or 13.4% are Americans of Spanish surname. In the GS-9 through 11 grades, it has a total employment of 27,429 of which 1,433 or 5.2% are Americans of Spanish surname; in the GS-12 through 18 grades it has a total employment of 14,845 of which only 257 or 1.7% are Spanish surnamed Americans. The statistics would show good employment insofar as overall numbers are concerned, but, by the same token, they are on a comparable level to all other Government agencies, in that they show a very small number of Spanish surnamed Americans who are employed or even promoted in the higher grade levels. The Contracts Compliance Office of the Department of Defense has only two Spanish surnamed Americans on its staff. Eleven regional offices have been established; however, there are no regional directors who are Americans of Spanish surname. In all fairness, it must be pointed out that the Department of Defense is the only agency that has a special program for Spanish-surnamed Americans. This special program has been solely responsible for communicating the Government's program on Equal Employment Opportunity to Spanish surnamed Americans of this country, and, in addition, it has been solely responsible for the bringing together of the League of United Latin American Citizens and the American G.I. Forum in the establishment of the first government-funded program dedicated toward the elimination of poverty in the Southwest through job training, job development, job guidance and counseling and job placement. This Department also established the first job placement centers dedicated to the placement of Americans of Spanish surname in jobs with Government contractors. These centers have been directly responsible for the placement of thousands of Americans of Spanish surname in nontraditional, nonmenial jobs. While the Department of Defense should be complimented for having this program, it should be encouraged not only to continue this program but to enlarge it, and thus insure that equality of opportunity for Americans of Spanish surname is, in fact, a reality among private employers who have contracts with the Federal Government. In addition, it should, and with an enlarged staff, continue to lend the services of members of the special programs to military installations that are encountering problems with Americans of Spanish surname in an effort to help these installations resolve the problems in a fair and equitable manner.

I could present statistics on many other departments of the Federal Government, such as the Department of Commerce where only 0.9% of its employees are American of Spanish surname; the Department of Interior which, out of a total of 69,000 employees, has 1.7% employees who are Americans of Spanish surname; Small Business Administration which employs 0.7% Spanish surnamed Americans; the Selective Service which does not have a single employee of Spanish surname above the grade of GS-8; the Treasury Department where 1.1% of its employees are Americans of Spanish surname; and the list would actually be endless in repeating the same facts and statistics, which would only repeat the tragic story that has already been presented. For each problem that exists, there has to be and is a practical solution, and I would offer the following recommendations to help alleviate this deplorable situation:

(1) It is incumbent upon the Civil Service Commission to establish a special department to deal with the problems of the Spanish surnamed American. This department must be created at a level high enough to where it can establish policy, not only for itself but for the Civil Service Commission as well. This department must be able to function as recruiters for the Civil Service Commission in an effort to find qualified applicants of Spanish surname to fill positions in all job levels of the Civil Service Commission. If the Civil Service Commission is to continue to be charged with the responsibility of enforcing the provisions of nondiscrimination in employment, promotions, transfers, and terminations in all Government agencies, it must set the example and enforce these provisions within its own system.

(2) The Civil Service Commission should take a long, hard look at the testing procedures that are currently being utilized by Government agencies as well as the merit promotion system, as both of these systems are ineffectual and outmoded. Tests should be re-evaluated to assure that administering of them is necessary for the positions which they are given. The merit promotion system, as it now stands, permits flagrant violations in promotions, in that it allows supervisory personnel to make preselections for promotions; therefore, this system is discriminatory against employees of minority groups.

(3) Each agency within our Government that is in charge of programs which will affect or benefit the American of Spanish surname

should create a special department whose primary responsibility will be to assure that these programs are, in fact, reaching the American of Spanish surname, and whose secondary purpose would be that of securing qualified applicants of Spanish surname for positions at all job levels within the agency.

(4) Every agency that is charged with enforcing the provisions of Executive Order 11246 which prohibits discrimination in employment among Government contractors because of race, creed, color, or national origin should follow the example of the Department of Defense Contracts Compliance Office and establish a special programs department staffed with bilingual and bicultural employees whose primary duty will be that of insuring that the provisions of the Executive Order, which they are charged to enforce, are applied so as to insure equality of opportunity to Americans of Spanish surname among Government contractors, and, in addition, to aid the agency itself in the recruitment of bilingual and bicultural investigators.

In conclusion, the problems which I have discussed can and must be solved. If each governmental agency and department will take it upon itself to establish a bold and aggressive program of affirmative action, dedicated to insuring that their programs are, in fact, reaching the American of Spanish surname and to insuring that Americans of Spanish surname are employed at all levels of their agency, then, and only then, will equal employment opportunity for the American of Spanish surname within the Civil Service become a reality.

EMPLOYMENT PROBLEMS OF
MEXICAN AMERICAN YOUTH*

SALVADOR RAMIREZ

Who are the Mexican American youth? What is their heritage and what is their future? What problems do they face in their daily existence which are related to the area of employment and which contribute to the development of potential delinquent characteristics and to actual delinquent behavior? What steps, i.e., creation of meaningful work programs, must be taken to solve the problems of the unemployed minority?

The following presentation represents an attempt to answer most of the above questions. Information herein presented is based on, or directly relates to the findings of the El Paso Juvenile Delinquency Study Project. This Project was designed to demonstrate methods for assisting Mexican American youth and adults in the barrio of South El Paso, Texas. This assistance has been aimed at increasing the ability of the target population to realize, cope with and find solutions to the problems caused by living under conditions of poverty, isolation, powerlessness and deprivation. The project was constructed as a "Comprehensive Endeavor," dealing with major influential factors which were thought to motivate a Mexican American youngster towards deviant behavior. Thus, component composition of the project is related to the areas of: health, education, legal service, social service, employment, adult neighborhood work and youth work.

During the first week of operation for the El Paso Juvenile Delinquency Study Project, almost one hundred South El Paso youth were received at the central office. The word had spread throughout South El Paso that the Project staff would include an Employment Counselor, and the majority of these youngsters had come to the office to receive

*The Mexican American: A New Focus on Opportunity, Inter-Agency Committee on Mexican American Affairs, U.S. Govt. Printing Office, Washington, D.C., 1967, pages 75-89.

assistance in obtaining employment. As this flow of unemployed youngsters continued and increased, it became apparent that, in fact, there was a substantial number of low-class Mexican American youth who possessed a need and/or a desire for employment; the strength of which provided sufficient motivation to *initiate* contact.

In order to secure employment, however, the youth must not only want or need a job, but must also possess the necessary job qualifications. A large percentage (approximately 65%) of Mexican American youth who seek employment are, in fact, not prepared to enter the world of work. They suffer from a multiplicity of problems or handicaps: lack of adequate job skill preparation; inadequate educational background; negative familial and environmental atmosphere; inadequate socialization to the value system of the large society: the world of work. For many, the combined effects of social, economic and cultural deprivation are manifested not only in the inability to secure employment, but also in the inability to retain a secured position.

After the initial week of Project operation, during which time it appeared that the entire gamut of problems related to employment had been revealed; the duties and functions of the Employment Counselor were expanded to fit the existing situation. There is a real and urgent need for the initiation of a comprehensive work-program not only in El Paso, but throughout the Southwest. It is not sufficient to merely coordinate or amalgamate existing "stop-gap" programs which are related to the area of employment. If these existing programs are not organically interrelated, they will remain entities with separate, disparate focii and methodology, which are connected only by a formal bureaucratic structure. In the course of this paper, therefore, we will attempt to present possible avenues of pursuit for the development of realistic comprehensive youth-work programs for Mexican American youth in the Southwest.

One of the principle characteristics of the Mexican American population of the U.S. is revealed in its age distribution. The median age is close to 20, as compared with about 30 years for the total U.S. population. According to the 1960 U.S. Census, the total Mexican American population of the Southwest constitutes approximately five million persons. Between 1950 and 1960 the Mexican American population in the Southwest evidenced an increase of 51% as compared with a 39% increase in the total population of the five southwestern states. At present, the Mexican American ethnic group represents the second largest minority in the United States.

A review of the U.S. Census data shows that the Mexican American, has become increasingly urban in residence (1960 — about 80% of population found in urban areas). However, if we examine the occupational distribution of employed urban Mexican American males it becomes apparent that the increase in urbanization has in no way been accompanied by a comparable increase in general occupational skill level. In fact, of the total number of Mexican American males employed in urban areas in the southwestern states, only five percent are represented in professional occupations. A little over three-fourths (76%) of Mexican Americans are categorized as manual workers. Because of the concentration in unskilled occupations, the Mexican American exhibits a median annual income far below most other groups in the United States.

The educational attainment of the Mexican Americans as a group corresponds to their occupational and income position. In 1960 the median number of school years completed was 8.1 for Mexican American males as compared with 10.3 for the total U.S. male population, fourteen years old and over. It should be noted that of the Mexican Americans in the five southwestern states, those in Texas rank lowest not only in the area of education, but also in areas of occupation and income.

The situation of the Mexican American youth in the Southwest today is directly related to the preceding discussion of the general socio-economic and demographic characteristics of the total Mexican American population. As has been previously mentioned, a significant characteristic of this population is its large percentage of youth. About 21% of the Mexican American population is represented by the teenage group. If the term, "Youth," is used to refer to that segment of the population, ages 15 to 19, we find that Mexican American youth constitute approximately 300,000 persons (over 153,000 are males). According to the U.S. Census definition of "labor force" (persons 14 years of age or older who are employed or employable), Mexican American youth represent three hundred thousand potential additions to the total labor force. It should be noted, however, that although the true picture of the employment situation for this segment *is* definitely related to the rate of unemployment, a more significant and perhaps more revealing area of examination can be found in the percentage distribution of occupation. For example, it was previously noted that of the total numbers of Mexican American males employed in southwestern urban areas, only five percent were engaged in some type of "professional" occupation, and that the majority were engaged in some form of manual labor. In general, the degree of employment opportunity possessed by the Mexican American youth today, reveals little hope for improvement in the imbalance of occupational distribution.

The tendency of the Mexican American to be employed as a "hewer of wood and a drawer of water" is complex in explanation. In general, we can cite four related areas of causation: (1) elements of overt and covert discrimination, (2) differences in educational and training opportunities, (3) a vicious poverty cycle, (4) language and cultural barriers. In addition, the plight of the Mexican American youth is intensified by general trends in the U.S. labor market which are presently affecting the total youth population of the United States nationwide, the steady growth in the number of youth seeking employment far surpasses the relatively static number of job openings which are available to persons of this age bracket. An obvious result has been a marked rise in unemployment among the nation's youth. At present, the unemployment rate of "teenagers" is more than twice the rate of unemployment for the total labor force.

Because of the generally low job skill level which characterizes the youth segment, and because of the steady decrease in the demand for unskilled labor, many youth either find that, in reality, they possess no marketable skills, or that they are unable to compete with older, more experienced workers for unskilled positions. Another contributing factor is the general increase in educational requirements, even for unskilled positions. A high school diploma has become the minimal requirement for most "entry" (unskilled) jobs, particularly those holding any promise of promotion. Limited education presents a severe handicap not only to Mexican American youth, but also to the entire ethnic group.

The situation of the lower class Mexican American youth presents an even more negative picture. Not only is this group the victim of limited education, but more often than not it is characterized by inferior educational preparation. Lack of education of the adult population has a real effect on the educational aspirations and on the educational achievement of the youth. Parents, therefore, seldom represent positive role models with regard to the requirements, restrictions, etc., of the greater society. Youth are not socialized to meet the demands of, or to function with any degree of effectiveness in the middle class, industrialized, urban environment. The socialization process places considerable emphasis on the internalization of the major attitudes and values of the Mexican American sub-culture. Many of these values are diametrically opposed to the value orientation of the middle class world of work. For example, in the Mexican American sub-culture emphasis is placed on the primary responsibility to family and on maintenance of family ties, on concentrating on the immediate present and consequently leaving events of the future in the hands of God. In the greater society, however, emphasis is placed on the individual and on minimal family ties so as to facilitate both physical (geographic) and social mobility; on achievement of material wealth and related status and prestige, and on future orientation, or deferred gratification.

HOW MUCH LONGER . . .
THE LONG ROAD?*

ARMANDO RENDON

Flat, dustgrey fields, burdened with fruits and vegetables, span to the right and left of Highway 99 in California; fields just like them, but broken more often by trees, spread out along U.S. 83 in south Texas; farmlands swell out over the subtly rounded earth beside Highway 49 in southwestern New Jersey; 99, 83, and 49 are major arteries of America's agricultural industry. To people who follow the crops, they signify miles of cramped, sweat-sticky travel by car or bus, dry swallows of roadside meals, the down in the gut fear of being too late or too early for a job.

How much longer this long road for the migrant farm worker? How many more the years of kneeling and picking down the rows of tomatoes or strawberries, of bending to the short-handle hoe, of being cheated out of a fair day's wage for a fair day's work, of camping on a river bank or renting a broken down shack, of pulling your children out of school before they get a chance to really learn or even make a friend?

Daily, the migrant seasonal farm worker suffers the want of physical or material goods and the denial of civil and human rights. Whatever his racial or ethnic origin, the oppressive conditions of farm labor debase him to the level of a stepchild of poverty and discrimination.

The rootlessness of his life and his dependency on external measures of supply and demand which he can neither alter nor understand have made of the migrant field worker a man on the fringe of society. His dominant fear is that he will lose his job, however lowly or poorly paid. Yet, his innermost desire is to settle down, in or out of agricultural labor, for his own and his children's sake. That he cannot really influence the course of his life may constitute the most critical injustice exacted of the farm worker.

How this situation has come about and what the current conditions of farm labor are in American have been well documented. The

*Civil Rights Digest, Summer 1968, pages 34-44.

character of farm labor has altered radically since World War II. Certain problems in the present makeup of the farm workforce owe their existence to the shortage of domestic hands during the war years and the subsequent importation of foreign workers. A more crucial issue — the farm worker's unequal standing in the organized labor movement — dates back to 1935 when, in the enactment of the Wagner Act (precursor to the Taft-Hartley Act) by the 73rd Congress, agricultural workers were explicitly excluded from the definition of "employee." Since then they have been barred from basic Federal labor law.

The introduction of modern, specialized machines into the fields coupled with the development of new and more efficient farming techniques has created new forces to displace or further undermine the wage earning potential of the human harvester. Efforts of Federal, State, and local governments — even private church, union, and civic groups — have resulted in some progress over the years in certain areas such as health, housing, education, but too often for varying periods of time and degrees of effectiveness. The inclusion in 1966 of farm laborers under the Fair Labor Standards Act might be of more lasting significance. However, even this legislation affects only 380,000 or one-fourth of the farm workforce, restricts farm workers to a top minimum wage projected for 1969 of $1.30 an hour, and excludes them all from overtime provisions afforded other workers covered by the Act.

The farm worker's situation is complex but generally it can be understood as consisting of three major trends, two within the migrant stream, one in the external development of equitable rights and treatment under law. As to the stream, some individuals are striving to drop out, to learn new job skills, to upgrade their education, to establish a permanent homebase; others will continue or join the stream for seasonal work, preferring the work they know best and rural living to the city, but desiring a better life where they are. Outside the stream but closely related to it, is the provision through legislation of rules and regulations governing work and wage conditions and other essential services or programs which afford the farm worker, whether he is getting out or remaining in the stream, the same extensions of the law as are due other workers. Given this complex situation, it is apparent that simply raising wages to an arbitrary level which is inherently discriminatory cannot begin to affect realistically and broadly enough the fundamental farm labor issues.

To arrive at any clear conclusions or recommendations for action about so complex an issue is difficult. Where do you start? What are the facts? What insights can be provided the concerned person? The very routes farm workers travel to harvest the Nation's food and fiber provide at least an itinerary for gathering information and placing the issues in perspective.

California's Central Valley is one of America's richest agricultural areas. The State boasts some of the largest farm corporations in the country; its economy is one-third dependent on farming for jobs; its income at farm level annually amounts to more than $4 billion. In such an economic setting the California farm worker would be expected to do relatively better than his counterparts in other States. *Relatively,* this is true: in 1967, hourly farm wage rates were highest in California and Connecticut at $1.62. The average wage rate nationwide for farm workers, however, was $1.33 an hour last year, 40 cents lower than the average for laundry workers, traditionally a low wage group. (Four southeastern States paid fieldworkers an average wage below the $1.00 minimum of 1967.) Work patterns, too, are somewhat more stable since there are many of the seasonal farm workers who move generally within the State or have developed a year-round farm work pattern. Also the opportunities for non-farm or even farm-related jobs are greater in the Golden State. Nevertheless, the California fieldhand is still at the bottom of the social pyramid, short on job skills, basic education, decent housing, and income.

Why is this so in such a valley of plenty? In Delano, a farm town between Bakersfield and Fresno, a farm workers' union and grape growers have been engaged in a crucial economic encounter since September 1965. The United Farm Workers Organizing Committee (UFWOC) has been on strike against major producers of wine grapes during the first two years and most recently against fresh table grape growers. The union is headed by Cesar Chavez, a Mexican American farm worker. During the nearly three years of strikes, there have been several incidents of friction and physical clashes between growers and union members or supporters, unrelenting opposition to the union from many sides, and legal encounters as well. Contracts have been won from nine growers, often at great hardship.

The 1968 Report (No. 1274) of the House Committee on Education and Labor dealing with Coverage of Agricultural Employees under the National Labor Relations Act (NLRA), noted, that "the strike for recognition, with all its disastrous consequences, has largely become a thing of the past — in manufacturing, in transportation, entertainment, publishing, food processing, broadcasting, retailing — in all industries but agriculture. There, the law of the jungle which generally prevailed 33 years ago still exists." The Committee report recalls a strike by 5,000 cottonpickers in Corcoran, California, near Delano, which in 1933 resulted in mass evictions, mass picketing, mass arrests, and the death of two workers when a union meeting was forcibly broken up. "Labor unrest on the farm to varying degrees, continues to this date — in California, in Texas, in Florida, in Michigan, in Ohio, in Wisconsin, and elsewhere . . . And the testimony before this committee indicates that in the absence of law, it takes ugly forms which can harm the employers, the employees, and the community."

The "law of the jungle" described by the committee is due in large measure to the fact, then, that farmers and farm workers are outside the jurisdiction of basic labor law and therefore subject neither to the benefits nor the prohibitions of Taft-Hartley.

It was the first day following an agreement by the Immigration and Naturalization Service of the Department of Justice with the United Farm Workers to enforce a regulation of the Department of Labor prohibiting immigrant Mexican citizens in the United States with Alien Registration Cards (greencard workers) from being brought into the country as strikebreakers when the Secretary of Labor has certified a bonafide labor dispute.

On that Friday, April 26, *la migra,* as the Border Patrol is known throughout the Southwest, performed its usual function of scouting by air for suspected aliens, relaying information to a ground team, then chasing suspects down in the fields by jeep or on foot. Early that morning at a farm road intersection outside Delano, two border patrol officers engaged in a brief and heated exchange with Chavez and Roberto Bustos, a union captain. One officer questioned the two union men, asking for their papers, their names, what their purpose was. Chavez refused to give any information and charged the officers with neglecting their duty in the fields. In an apparent effort to intimidate the two men, the officer asked, "Do you want to get arrested?" Shrugging the ploy aside, Chavez replied, "No, but if you want to arrest me, go ahead." The two officers returned to their car and as they drove off, Chavez called out: "What's your name so I can report you to your boss?" The officer behind the wheel retorted, "I'm not telling you my name if you don't tell me yours."

Later that afternoon, *racimos,* or small groups of union members were assigned to strategic exits of one of the fields owned by Giumarra Vineyard Corporation, largest of the 24 table grape producers being struck in the Delano area. The racimos were to pursue strikebreakers seen leaving the fields for their homes. The "scabs" would later be shamed out of the fields by the union through various means: leaflets, word-of-mouth, and door-to-door marches in towns such as Earlimart, Richgrove, McFarland, all near Delano. The United Farm Workers has also been conducting a nationwide boycott of all California grapes in an effort to force its primary target, Giumarra, to the bargaining table. There have been mass arrests, beatings, and economic intimidation by the growers, the farm workers have alleged and charged in various court suits.

Perhaps the open hostility toward the strikers and the counter reaction of unionization tactic such as the "scab" hunt would persist, but the damaging effects to both sides from the recognition strike and the secondary boycott as well as the physical clashes would be mitigated or entirely obviated by amendment of the NLRA. Efforts in Congress to do this, in House Bill 16014 and Senate Bill 8, however, so far have been stymied, one in the House Rules Committee, the other in the Senate Labor and Public Welfare Committee. If farm workers are included in the basic legislation, coercion by either side would be a prohibited unfair labor practice and when voluntary recognition does not occur, 30 percent of the workforce can demand an officially supervised election to decide whether the union will be the sole bargaining agent for the employees.

Chavez asserts that through the union, the farm worker can achieve economic, health, housing, and education standards equivalent to those of workers in other industries. "It is an error to think of programs; this is not what we're after because taking handouts merely destroys the individual. Programs don't mean anything, education doesn't mean anything, unless you have bread on the table. Migrant workers must be given a chance to form a union. The Government can provide the rules; let the workers do the rest."

Other union members echoed Chavez's thoughts. Waiting under the harsh sun, an old traveler of the migrant road crinkled his eyes as he peered along the glaring roadway. "The union is the only way," he said. "My wife and I have four children and a home in Delano. I am getting too old to travel. The oldest girl is in high school and we hope she will graduate. One of my boys is not doing too well but may make it. But I don't want them to follow me."

The woman resting against a vinebush was telling about the years she had spent among the grapevines. Her fingers were distorted and calloused from the work, her skin dust brown from the sun. Her joy was a son who, she said, was especially bright and looking forward to college and an engineering career. "It's hard our being on strike because we want to help our son get through college. He's a very smart boy. He's never had to work out here and I hope he never will. There's a chance of him getting a scholarship that will help."

A grizzled, work-creased man, the father of eight children, recalled the eight years he had spent in San Antonio, Texas, in various city-type jobs, some of them good-paying, but that he had returned to farm work and rural life where he felt more at ease. "I had enough of that city life. It's too fast and mean. I like working out in the field. I'm strong and I can do the work. But I think we can have it a little better here in Delano. I liked Chavez and the union from the beginning. I've been in the union since before we started the strike — I walked from here all the way to Sacramento where we had the march two years ago. I think we're doing the right thing to get our rights."

A crucial factor that must be considered in amending the NLRA, of course, is the extent of coverage of farmers under the new legislation. A key criticism and stumbling block to the inclusion of farm workers in NLRA has been the contention that small, family farms might be affected adversely by such a change. In fact, House report No. 1274 anticipates that coverage under the wording of House Bill 16014 would extend only to about 30,000 American farms, "roughly nine-tenths of 1 percent of the 3.2 million farms in America," — only those farms which employed at least 12 employees at a time and paid a wage total of at least $10,000 in the past year according to the proposed amendment.

Given these conditions, the House report added, only 44,000 farms were found to fall within the minimum annual expenditure figure of $10,000 according to the Bureau of the Census, Agriculture Division. This number (1.4 percent of all American farms) in the peak final week of May 1966, employed 622,000 farm workers — 60 percent of the 1,083,000 who worked on farms that week.

Under the limitation of 12 or more employees, the total number of farms that might expect to be affected by new legislation, the report stated, falls to 30,000 since "most livestock, dairy, and poultry farms" having an annual wage cost of $10,000 or more probably do not hire a dozen or more hands. The 30,000 farms which would be affected by Taft-Hartley, then, would be the fruit and nut, vegetable and cotton growers, who, in turn, hire the most peak harvest workers and, therefore, expend larger amounts in wages.

It is a fact that the UFWOC has been striking, not the small farmer, but the biggest grape growers in the country. These same producers of the grape, it is significant to note, who can best afford the move, are turning in the direction of eliminating, completely if possible, the hand picker, the hoer, and the gleaner from the fields.

Mechanization, a mounting threat to the agricultural laborer in many areas or crops, is less of a specter to Chavez, however, than the strikebreaker, of whatever variety — domestic, greencard, or illegal alien. "The growers are trying to kill the union by scaring us with talk of mechanization," he stated. He said of a grape harvester being developed at the University of California at Davis that even if the machine is perfected, it will pick only one of 22 kinds of wine grape.

Basically, it could be sensed from Chavez' words and the comments of farm worker after farm worker, that to the man who picks the crops, the union or community organization in general is the only way that their lives will be improved, that they will be able to exercise their rights fully. As one of the union captains put it, a key objective of the workers is to make the union a major issue on which everyone will have to take sides, on which no one can be neutral. Literally, to them, the union is a life or death issue.

Along the Rio Grande, U.S. 83 runs the gamut of poverty. Appalling conditions of hovel housing, hunger, economic dependence, lack of opportunity, unemployment, injustice are in permanent residence here. Highway 83 is a main artery of the migrant stream flowing from south Texas through New Mexico into Arizona and California or up through the Texas Panhandle into the Rocky Mountain States. Main portions of the migrant population move upward to the Great Lakes Region, the North Central States, and some to Florida.

In the Rio Grande Valley, a community movement is groping its way into becoming an independent, self-help organization under the name,

Colonias del Valle. Its headquarters in San Juan, a small one-street town east of McAllen, operates as the Valley Service Center.

Colonias in this part of the country are small housing developments, subdivisions sold lot by lot to local migrant people who build their own houses or contract with the developer. Many are small, tidy homes but with few if any of the modern conveniences. Most are unfit for the people who live in them because they are usually vermin or rodent infested, offer little protection against weather, and are too small for the number of people they shelter. In colonias such as El Gato and El Rincon, the thatch-roofed *jacal* is common, shacks pieced together with strips of tin, wire, sticks, odds and ends of boards. There are no paved streets here, no street lights, running water, or indoor plumbing. Water must be hauled into the colonia in many cases, because wells pump up a bitter, salty brew. Yet in certain areas, too much water, in a flash flood of the Rio Grande, can severely damage crops and communities.

In September 1967, Hurricane Beulah roared into south Texas, killing and maiming people on both sides of the border. The hurricane also devastated fields, churning them into sloughs, wiping out, too, many of the already scarce jobs available to the valley residents. The wage-depressing influx of greencarders into this valley has forced families to seek work as far away as Washington and New York — Beulah turned the economic clamp about the farm worker several more notches. From January 1967 levels, farm jobs fell by about two-thirds in 1968 in Hidalgo County alone.

The fear that dominates the migrant is that of losing a job, of not finding the job available that he had last year because of mechanization, demise of a farm, or arriving too late for the first good pickings. Here, in south Texas, the fear begins — fear for the few days of hoeing or running a tractor, for the prospect of out-of-state jobs, how soon to leave, where to go, getting a loan in time.

Amador is the father of four children; his wife is pregnant. The cooling system in his pickup truck had needed repairs lately and then for two days the vehicle had been missing, stolen. When it was found, the engine was burned out. The cost to repair the engine, he had learned, was more than he could earn in a month on the road. How could he move out now without transportation? For three years he had been among the more than 86,000 people who had engaged in interstate travel out of Texas, and among 39,000 who had ventured out of only four Rio Grande Valley counties: Hidalgo, Starr, Cameron, and

Willacy. (Other figures compiled by the Texas Employment Commission and the Texas Bureau of Labor Statistics indicate that in 1966, more than 100,000 families or groups left the State while 129,000 sought farm work within the State.)

The story of Amador can be multiplied with minor alterations thousands of times over. The oldest of six children he began field work at the age of nine. He dropped out of school in the 10th grade. At present, only the youngest child, a girl, has a chance to finish high school, the first and only person in the family to do so. For a time he enrolled in an adult education program in Starr County where he could earn some money while learning, but he had to leave to join the harvest.

Now Amador's chances are dwindling. Perhaps he'll fix his pickup or find another job, or he may have to leave his family, join a single men's group to hunt work in the Great Lakes area or even in Chicago where he lost a finger last year in a potato packing plant. He was an early member of the *huelga,* the strike in Starr County which pitted the No. 2 local of the UFWOC against the large farm employers along the Rio Grande. If he happens to get a job in south Texas now, Amador believes, he would be out of a job as soon as the employer learned about his union activities. But he asserts that it had been a lack of education that made his parents think that earning $13 a day or less in the fields was enough. "We think differently now," he says. "We have to work together and defend ourselves to better ourselves."

The persistent pressure exerted by the need for work had enveloped Amador. It appeared, too, in the dry, matter-of-fact words of an old man wielding a hoe in a jalapeno field for $1 an hour: "If we leave now, the children won't learn anything, and they'll end up here." The time was toward the end of May, school was almost over, and many families were already gone, or waiting till the last school bell rang. Their homes would be left, boarded up, at the mercy of weather or anyone who might break in, take what little might be there. Forces pulled at them, pressing them into the stream. Yet, a chunky farm worker could still look ahead as he slapped on a thin coat of white paint to protect the clapboard sides of his home. The next night, as soon as he could sign up with the Farm Labor Service in McAllen, he would be on his way.

Beyond the vagaries of weather and timing, the south Texas Mexican American, who makes up a good part of the 103,000 persons of Spanish-surname who migrate for work, must contend with the presence of the greencarder, not by the tens, or hundreds, but by the thousands.

The border crossing at McAllen-Reynosa, one of the major crossings in the area, teems with people from Mexico, dressed for field work, of all ages and sizes, male and female. The people come to work in the U.S. because wages are higher than in Mexico and since the American dollar is worth more in pesos, it is extremely beneficial for a Mexican to obtain a greencard and work on this side during the day, returning to his home in Mexico at night.

Yet, annual income per capita in Starr County, for example, is about $1,500, and according to the report, Hunger, U.S.A., by the Citizens Board of Inquiry into Hunger and Malnutrition in the U.S., Starr County's percentage of poor families was 71.4 and its newborn death rate was at 9.7 per 1,000 in comparison to the national rate of 5.9 per 1,000. There is also evidence of greater numbers of illegal entrants into the U.S. Notably since the termination of Public Law 78 (the "bracero" program), the number of Mexicans deported for illegal entry increased to 14,248 in 1965, nearly half again the number that had been deported just the year before, and was up to 24,385 in 1966. The actual number of illegal workers is difficult to gauge but it is possible to surmise a total twice the 1966 figure of those who are not caught.

Of major importance in evaluating the impact of the greencarder is that apart from the loss of jobs to resident workers and the suppression of wages, the situation forces upwards of 75 percent of the Mexican American population out of the area to find work. The migrant is thus deprived of opportunities in education, job training, housing, and the exercise of certain civil rights. As long as he must leave home for three to six months of the year, he cannot build a sound and solid base of political and social involvement in his home community. The Colonias del Valle, however, point toward a method by which the migrant can maintain an organization from which will flow the kinds of activities and services other regions take for granted. Ed Krueger, a United Church of Christ minister doing non-denominational work in the valley since 1966, has been like the rock fallen into the stream which little by little catches branches floating down willy-nilly until an island, even a dam is formed. Twenty colonias have formed self-help committees since October 1967. In turn, the colonias have set up a joint council to work on common problems. It is still too early to become too enthusiastic about the colonias' organizing efforts, Krueger said, and summer will be the first major test of the new movement.

There are signs in Starr County that things are changing for the better, he added. For example, a coalition of the poor people, the United Farm Workers local in Rio Grande City, led by Gil Padilla, national vice president of the union, and some teachers and business-men concerned with the conduct of government, ousted several county officials and elected two people to the school board in the May primary elections.

A coalition like this had never succeeded before in south Texas; the current efforts may fail, or be long in making changes but a new start has been made in which the farm worker himself is crucially involved. A colonia leader, who had a large family and who could ill afford to migrate, said: "We are fighting for the children. We must keep faith in one another — that is what counts. We face indifference everyday here but even though we've never united before, we know that this is the only way to change our children's future."

The highways of the migrant stream inevitably lead back to the legislative and administrative problems which slow progress or block change for the itinerant farm worker. A detailed and comprehensive program which would affect most phases of the farm worker's life is set forth in the February 1968 Report (No. 1006) of the Senate Subcommittee on Migratory Labor of the Committee on Labor and Public Welfare. Suggestions for revisions or provisions in the law dealing with collective bargaining rights, foreign workers, voluntary farm employment service, unemployment insurance, workmen's com-pensation, old age, survivors, and disability insurance, residence requirements for public assistance and for voting eligibility, and for a National Advisory Council on Migratory Labor — all of these basic factors — are covered by the Senate Report.

From the evidence in Delano and south Texas, perhaps in the future for the Garden State, the migrant farm worker may yet obtain the essence of the American dream: self-determination through personal participation in the forces which shape our lives. He will have to do this in spite of the indifference and resistance of certain sections of society, but he is becoming more aware that he can achieve a measure of dignity through his own efforts. The migrants, one realizes, are among the most oppressed and disadvantaged people in America. On the other hand, their economic deprivation could be the easiest problem to resolve. How a man can be brought back to self-respect, self-confidence, is another thing. Perhaps, it is only through unionization and community organization that this is possible. As long as inequities of law and practice persist, farm workers will continue to be denied rights and opportunities even while other groups are achieving them. They simply will not have the choice to stay on or to abandon those highways of misery.

"LA MULA NO NACIÓ ARISCA"* . . .

ERNESTO GALARZA

When I am asked to take part in conferences or meetings in which the topic is the Mexican-American in California, I ask myself: "Why the Mexican-Americans?"

It may be that our liberal conscience demands that we talk publicly about this sick spot in our society. Nevertheless, we should not think that the presumed Mexican-American problem can be reduced, by public discussion, to the dimensions of one state, abstracting it from those of the nation and of the world. Nor should we think that it can be understood by using an intellectual tool that is comfortable and disarming but untenable: the concept of the subculture.

My working definition of culture runs like this: A culture is characterized by: a) the uses it makes of its material environment; b) the accepted or tolerated relations between the individuals that compose it; c) the symbols, conventional signs, and utilities of every-day behavior; and d) the values by which the society measures its moral performance.

By this rule-of-thumb I see only one culture in the United States: it is the culture of the American people — all of them.

Thus, I do not think we can legitimately presume that there is a sub-culture of Mexican-Americans which explains their depressed conditions of life, or that there is a sub-culture of Negroes which explains their economic deprivation these past three hundred years.

What the concept of sub-culture implies, but does not say in so many words, is that alien cultures of a lower grade somehow intruded themselves into the American super-culture. If the Negro family today, for instance, is too often damaged by the absentee father, the working mother, and the delinquent youth, it is said to be a characteristic of their sub-culture. The concept shines most brightly when we talk about the discomforts of American society — dilapidated housing, crime, and unemployment. It is upon minorities that these discomforts fall most heavily. It is they, to be sure, who populate the ghettos, but it is our entire society, the American society, that spawns slums and breeds poverty.

*Center Diary, September-October 1966, pages 26-32.

I am not attempting to lay blame. I am trying to discover connections and relationships. What I see is that, among Negro and Mexican-American minorities, what shows up vividly as local color and dramatic contrast are, in truth, cracks and tears in the seamless fabric of American society.

It is not the sub-cultures that are in trouble. It is the American culture itself.

And what have been some of the major strikes against Mexican-Americans and Negroes?

One is the pattern of land ownership, control, and use that has developed in America during the past half century. Out of this pattern came the tractoring-out of the southern sharecropper, the withering of the family farm, and the massive importation of foreign agricultural laborers.

The resulting flight from the soil took millions to the cities, which were already suffering from urban cramps. We have begun to call these cities "ports of entry." The term has happy connotations: it suggests the migrant minority is on its way to better things — that is has *made* connections, not *broken* them.

But, in fact, the minority man finds the port congested with people like himself. They, like him, are becoming obsolete as a result of mechanization, automation, and cybernation — American cultural products that are radically altering job requirements, opportunities, and tenure. He finds that those sections of the big city where he has found transient refuge are also becoming obsolete. Here, another American culture concept, acted out with bulldozers, awaits him — urban redevelopment. As soon as a section shows speculative promise, it attracts speculative capital and entire neighborhoods go under. The Mexican-American poor move with their anxieties to another place.

These and other massive social decisions are not for the Mexican-American poor to make, or even take part in. These choices, and the complicated devices by which they are applied, are not even understood by the poor. To understand them, they would need an educational system that would deal factually and critically with them. But the Mexican-American, on the average, barely gets through eight or nine years of school, so that even if the high schools and colleges were undertaking the task, which by and large they are not, they would not be reaching the minority man.

Mexican-Americans in California *have* made progress since the Forties. They are subject to less ethnic discrimination. They have also begun to climb the lower rungs of the economic ladder. Ninety per cent of the people I knew as a boy were farm workers; now, far more than 10 per cent of us work as professors, journalists, bureaucrats, and so on. This change is only recent, but the process is increasing in scope and pace. With new jobs has come an ability to articulate. Today perhaps we even have too many spokesmen. In any event, the time is past when the Mexican-American was not heard from. Now he says what he wants.

So far, we have been testing the mechanics of American democracy. Those of us who have climbed two or three rungs up the ladder have had opportunities to learn how Anglo-Americans do things — how they run political parties; how they caucus; how they lobby; how they manipulate all of those niceties of political contrivance, some clean and some unclean; how they use them, sometimes for personal benefit and sometimes for the good of the commonwealth. And two general kinds of Mexican-American leaders have emerged: those who conclude that the American political system doesn't have to be tested with values — it works for 195,000,000 people and what more could anyone ask; and those of us who are trying to see whether it really works in terms of human values.

At the same time, the Mexican-American community has lost ground — important ground. Our leadership has been dispersed. Political appointments have sent men of distinction to Sacramento, Washington, and abroad. Distance does something to these men: their values and ideas change; politically and ideologically, not just residentially, they are separated from the community. Individuals are entitled to personal satisfaction in life, but, for the community, political dispersal has meant and means political decapitation.

Strains have also occurred within the community. Mechanization and automation, in industry, agriculture, and trade services, have thrown many thousands of Mexican-Americans out of work. In farming, machines now pick tomatoes, grapes, oranges, and so on. Where the packing houses and canneries used to employ 85,000 people at the peak of production, they now employ around 45,000. Large groups of Mexican-American families have had a steady income cut away, and have been forced to disperse and be mobile. These nuclei of community have broken down as a result.

Marginal workers have not been helped by the trade union movement. Indeed, the trade union leadership helped destroy the farm labor union we organized in the Forties. We had posed the twin issues of power and exploitation in agriculture, but the union leaders shrank from their responsibility to help farm workers, leaving thousands to a cruel fate. However, they taught the Mexican-American community a lesson: the trade unions cannot be a taproot of our salvation. They are interested only in workers who are continuously employed, even though vast numbers of people are now unemployed and probably always will be. Lose your job, or stop paying union dues, and you are no longer "sir" or "brother."

The disintegration of the Mexican-American community is apparent in the numerous "shoestring" and "doughnut" communities in which thousands of Mexican-Americans live. The "shoestrings" grow along the banks of irrigation ditches, where water is available and land is cheap; here, displaced migrants have pitched their trailers and shacks, and the profile of their settlements is a shoestring; the classical example is South Dos Palos. The "doughnut" type is found in the city, in places like *La Rana* (The Frog) in Torrance. There, as in many other places, Mexican-American families settled as farm workers, but now they are surrounded by progress, and they can only wait to be pushed out by urban redevelopment. This community, one might say, is a hole where poor people live surrounded by people with dough.

Among Mexican-Americans, the proportion of wasted, discarded, obsolete, or unneeded workers is growing higher. Personal and family anchorage to work they can do and to people they know is becoming more precarious. For these men and women the closest thing to an economic taproot is seasonal hiring in the fields and cyclical employment in the cities. The prevailing mood in the poverty pockets is thus one of puzzlement, insecurity, and resentment. And as insecurity deepens, puzzlement is giving way to the conviction that there is no way out, and resentment is heightening to the point where life is fulfilled not by making progress toward a goal but by shooting at a target.

The welfare services designed for the Mexican-Americans and other minorities, diverse and ingenious as they are, are no answer or substitute, for around them no sense of community can arise, no organization of interests can emerge, and from them no effective action can result. Each social service, gigantic like everything else in American, is institutionalized; and each institution asserts its jurisdiction over a slice of the individual or the family. In the battle of jurisdictions, the human meaning of integration, of integrity, is lost.

Vertical integration no longer means a man standing securely upon and belonging to the earth — free of mind and responsible of spirit. It has come to mean the putting together of economic components into smooth-running financial and technical mechanisms.

The demands of the economy and the palliatives of social welfare are manifestations of the American culture as a whole, not of any supposed sub-culture within it. They originate in the centers of real power and of effective decision. No program for action with regard to the Mexican-American minority, or any other minority, therefore, can be more than a provisional tactic to gain time (if there is much left).

What is this provisional tactic? It is the grouping of the poor through organization, around the resources provided by the federal government in various Acts, notably the Economic Opportunity Act of 1964.

As a result of this Act, the Mexican-American minority, to take it as an illustration, has the legal opportunity to participate in the initiation, planning, and administration of social services that have heretofore been of the hand-me-down type. Local residents are now able to create a cluster of activities around which democratic organization can take form, and within which they will be able to maintain responsible relationships. The politics of power, inescapable in any event, can be reduced to more manageable proportions.

But if the federal resources are to be subordinated to local community action, local residents must be provided with organizers responsible to them. I am not talking of organizers who are deft with the gimmickry of community organization, but of those who are skilled in recognizing what the vital interests of poor people really are. These interests will in many respects coincide with the services that the federal government stands ready to finance. When they do, the objective of the local community becomes the preparation of action programs and the organization of the neighborhood around them. Into these programs the Mexican-Americans themselves must move. Their training must begin from the moment they take on a role, however modest, in a program.

What is the ultimate goal of such action programs? It is simply the re-creation of a human web of relations that will serve to produce a genuine community. Community is all that man has been able to invent to give him at least an approximation to security in his transit through life. I say re-creation deliberately, for there have been times and places in the American past when such relations did exist and did function. But the web of community, these last fifty years, has been strained and rent. If it is to be patched now and perhaps rewoven later, men must do it by their own efforts. I realize that it is only a patching that I am suggesting. It is only the choice of a road, not the end of a journey. But it may be the only road not beset by anger, despair, and violence.

The war on poverty is, at this stage, a mere skirmish. It cannot become a war until Congress appropriates the money to mount. a massive attack on unemployment. The problem is not simply to create jobs but to influence the basic decisions, like the allocation of resources, that society makes. Decisions about where the money is to be invested, for instance, are what creates jobs. And to these decisions the poor are not a party.

Discrimination must be ended, in employment and in every other phase of social relations.

We must also battle for "anthropomorphic education." This is a terrible phrase, but what I mean is that schools have to teach children, not systems. Experiments in Los Angeles have proven that one teacher with fifteen pupils and one expert assistant can do a much better job than one teacher with forty pupils and no assistant. Remarkable discovery! We have to press to make that teacher-student ratio universal because it will mean that the status and authority of the upper strata of administrators will be downgraded and the greatest prestige and largest salaries will go to kindergarten teachers. We cannot give an inch in this battle.

Private wealth can provide a cutting edge in the reconstruction of communities. It could start projects at those points where the government says "no" — and the government can do this without ever really saying "no." There are a lot of experiments the Congress is not going to finance, and there áre areas in which federal funds and services either are a handicap or are useless, anyway. Some indispensable things will never happen if we wait for federal funds.

Does the Mexican-American community merely want to catch up with the Anglo-American culture? The question is important, and we had better be careful before we say "Yes." My experience — in farm labor, in academic work, in politics — has taught me a lot of things about the Anglo-American culture that I do not like. Its economic system, for instance, produces certain values and behavior that I don't want to catch up with! Mexican-Americans have an opportunity to discriminate between the different values, behavior, and institutions in the pervading culture, and we had better choose wisely.

All my life I have heard that the trouble with the Mexican-American is that he is too apathetic. As a boy, in Mexico, I lived among people who, viewed from the outside, were extremely apathetic. Nobody was interested in knowing who was going to be the next president of Mexico, or who the military commander of our zone was. Nobody cared about the location of the nearest college or high school. They were interested in tomorrow's ration of corn.

When we came to California, Anglo-Americans preached to us about our apathy and scolded us. And I thought: Are we really so? Of course we are not. What is mistaken for apathy is simply a system of self-defense inherited by people with a long history of being kicked around. And if they don't inherit it, they learn quickly. They learn that they are surrounded by hostile men and forces that will do them in at every turn. They naturally become indifferent and unresponsive. But it is not apathy: it is self-protection. "La mula no nació arisca" — the mule isn't born stubborn, he's made stubborn.

In the village where I was born, men carried a money belt tied around their waists, and in it they kept all the money they possessed. They worked with the belt on, and they slept with it; they trusted nobody. As they progressed a little farther, they put their money in a sock, which was purchased specially for the purpose; since nobody wore socks. Their circle of confidence had increased, but still they hid the sock under the corn crib in their cottage and left their women to protect it. Still a little farther along came the piggy bank, which they usually placed on a shelf. Their circle of confidence had expanded further: all the family was trusted, friends too, even strangers who would drop by. Finally there came the sign of maturity: the bank account. Now, not only men were trusted but also a system, run by men who were not seen or even known.

These four stages of social evolution illustrate the so-called apathy of Mexican-Americans. How can anybody accuse that villager who kept his money in a belt tied around his body of being apathetic? Considering the circumstances, he was a pretty smart Mexican.

It is often assumed that Mexican-Americans need to be "emancipated"; after all, a lot of us used to live in a different culture in Mexico, and survived a feudal economy and society. The mayor of San Francisco remarked once that his city was going to build such a wonderful cultural center that it would make Los Angeles look "like a little Mexican village." Well, what's so wrong with that village? I have some good memories of Janco, my birthplace. There were no electric lights there, but in the evening, as the sun went down, people would sit in front of their cottages and talk by the twilight. And when it was dark the kids were sent to bed, and later the young men and women. Then the men would talk, not about small things but important ones. Some nights we heard a rumble of voices, lasting far into the morning. When I would awaken I would go to the yard and count the number of slits made by machetes in the hard-baked earth, and I would know how many men had gathered. It was these men who sparked the revolution in my village. And it was villages like these that started one of the most portentous events in the history of the Americas: the Mexican Revolution. In my yard.

I have not really been talking of fundamentals here. Not until the economy provides all men with sufficient incomes; not until mothers can stay home and take care of their children; not until massive investments of money are made in places like Watts; not until urban development becomes a weapon for something other than ·transferring doughnut communities from one part of the landscape to another, will the job of reconstructing communities have begun.

Are Mexican-Americans ready? That I don't know, but some of us intend to find out.

FAMILY AND RELIGION

FAMILY AND RELIGION

Institutions are the organized, formal normative, accepted means by which man meets his major needs. No two are more important in understanding a society, community, culture or subculture than the family and religion. In a book such as this, these two institutions must be singled out, for in addition to their importance they are the institutions where the Mexican American subculture shows some variance from the norms of the majority culture.

The norm of the Anglo culture is the conjugal family, parents and children; the norm of the Mexican culture is the consanguine family, the extended kinship group; the norm of the Mexican American subculture lies between those of its parent cultures. As was pointed out in the selection comparing the Mexican American subculture to the subculture of poverty, the Mexican American family differs to some degree from the Anglo norm in the parental roles, attitude toward children, sexual permissiveness, family stability, and extended family interaction.

In his book *Across the Tracks,* Arthur E. Rubel, an anthropologist, describes life among Mexican Americans in a town in Texas a few miles north of the Mexican border. The description is excellent but is typical only of border areas where the influence of Mexican culture remains strong. It is not intended to apply to the life of urban Chicanos in San Antonio, Denver, Kansas City, New York, Omaha, or Los Angeles. The selection included here is a shortened version of his chapter on the Mexican American family in this town which he calls "Mexiquito." In this chapter the different roles assigned to men, women, and children in the family are shown, and the reader who understands Anglo culture may make a comparison. He also analyzes courtship and marriage, which contain some elements which are unique when compared to Anglo culture, at least in degree. However, the relation of the family to neighbors is radically different from that in Anglo towns of comparable size, and the institution of *compadrazgo* is virtually unknown to Protestant Anglos.

Intermarriage is one of the most interesting aspects of intergroup relations. Such marriages between groups are defined as exogamous, while marriages within the group are called endogamous. An excellent indication of assimilation of a minority group is the rate with which it intermarries with the majority group, and one of the better indices of the social acceptance of a minority group is the rate at which majority group persons intermarry with them. In the study "Ethnic Endogamy— the Case of Mexican Americans" Frank G. Mittelbach and Joan W. Moore, both professional sociologists, present a three-generational analysis of marriages involving Mexican Americans in Los Angeles County. Their study shows relatively high rates of exogamy; rates are higher for women than for men; and rates increase with removal from immigrant status. A definite pattern of generational endogamy was found and also a strong suggestion that social distance between generations may be as important as social distance between the ethnic group and the dominant society. Exogamy is more prevalent among higher status individuals. With some exceptions, occupation appears to be a better predictor of exogamy than generation. Generally, the older the groom, the more "Mexican" the spouse, though the pattern is not the same for brides. These findings have important implications for assimilation of the Mexican Americans and for understanding processes of assimilation.

In Mexico, a sizeable number of persons are functionally "unchurched," a few belong to Protestant denominations, and the large majority are nominally Catholic. Those who profess Catholicism range in religious interest and participation from very devout men and women who rigorously practice the Church's rites to those whose physical contact with a church is confined to baptism, marriage, and burial. All of these types have emigrated to the United States. As a generalization, part of the present culture change shows a weakening of the hold of the Catholic church, especially upon those whose relationship was never more than nominal. There has not been and there are no indications that in the forseeable future there will be a great exodus of Mexican Americans away from Catholicism. On the other hand, the gains being made are by various Protestant groups. Because of this, and because Mexican American Catholics do not seem to differ greatly from most other immigrant Catholics, the selection which follows deals with the area of change; i.e., the rise of the Protestant church among Mexican Americans. The author, Dr. Margaret L. Sumner, is an anthropologist.

THE FAMILY*

ARTHUR J. RUBEL

The contemporary society of Mexiquito is comprised of a number of bilaterally-oriented small families, to which individuals acknowledge their only binding allegiance. The strength with which a person is bound to his family so overshadows all other bonds in importance that it contributes to the atomistic nature of the neighborhood. Socially, if not spatially, each household stands alone, separated from others.

The nuclear family stands out in sharp relief from the rest of kin, and it is characterized by denotative kinship terminology, which contrasts with the generally classificatory usage of the system. An individual's essential social unit is comprised of his parents and his parents' brothers and sisters. Particularly important to an individual are his mother's sisters. In the second ascending generation — that of an individual's grandparents — both sets of grandparents are revered, but not the siblings of the grandparents. In the individual's generation his own siblings (*hermano, hermana*) are conceptually separated from others, as are also his first cousins (*primos, hermanos*), who are separated from other, farther removed cousins (*primos*). In all contexts a reference to a first cousin on either side pointedly distinguishes that class from other classes of relatives. *Primos hermanos* are said to be somewhat like one's sisters and brothers.

In Mexiquito a domestic group comprised of a nuclear family is not only the unit most commonly found but, also, serves as an ideal.

A couple never gets along with the husband's mother, so you are better off living far away from her. That's because when the wife and her mother-in-law are angry with one another, the poor man is caught in-between. If he sides with his wife, his mother will slap him, and if sides with his mother, the girl will leave him.

A young college student volunteered the information that:

> If I had to choose, I'd live near-by my wife's folks. The trouble with the Latins is that the mother favors the son; she knows what his likes and dislikes are.

*Rubel, Arthur J., *Across the Tracks,* Austin, University of Texas Press, 1966, Chapter 3.

If you live near your mother, then its hard on the wife. She would always be interfering. I know my mother! It's easier on the girl to live near her mother. If you live near her mother, then she'll see that the girl works hard for you. But the best thing of all, if you had the chance, would be to live away from both parents.

The trouble with the Latins is that they stay around the family too much. That's why you see those people who go to California but don't stay there. They always come back here at the end of six months. They pay taxes out there and they pay them here, but still they come back because their family is here. That's why so few kids go out of the Valley to college.

The respect for one's elders is a major organizing principle of the Mexican-American family. When coupled with the principle of male dominance, the pattern of ideal relations within the family is produced. "In *la raza*, the older order the younger, and the men the women. It is difficult to establish with certitude the extent to which the respect of younger for older was practiced in years gone by, but certainly such behavior is presently extolled, while, at the same time, it is almost universally agreed to be a thing of the past. The expected attitude of humility is no longer present, although vestiges of that attitude remain among some "old-fashioned" families.

Men of the Family

A household is the residence and center of activity of a nuclear family, over which a husband and father is expected to dominate. With very few exceptions those who pay social calls to a household are persons whose range of conduct is quite circumscribed. They are either close kin — parents or siblings of the residents — or else are related by virtue of ritual kinship. Whosoever is permitted to visit in a household is expected to behave in decorous and deferential manner toward the residents. A man's home is his castle; the home is a sanctified locality, within which one's womenfolk are safe. At the head of the household is the father or, in the event of his death or absence, the oldest son. "In my home," says a sixty-year-old, "I am judge, jury, and policeman."

The husband and father of a family is expected to be firm but just he is the *jefe de la casa* (boss of the house). Abel remembers that one winter, when he was a youngster of ten, he and his brother were taken by their father to the river. Bade by the stern parent to undress and enter the chilling waters they swam about until almost numbed by the cold. This was to make men of them, they were advised. When commanded to emerge from their swim they could hardly stand on the river bank, and wished only to approach the fire their father had been careful to prepare. However, before he would permit them to dress, the old man insisted on rubbing down each of his sons "so that we might not catch cold." Whether this story is apocryphal is of little importance. It sketches the *jefe de la casa* as gruff and firm, yet neither capricious nor tyrannous. That portrait is painted by other informants.

The father tells the child only once what to do, and so it is to be. He manages all the social affairs engaged in by members of the family, as well as all financial matters. One father always told his daughters, "We are your best friends," meaning the family. At this point a daughter-in-law interjected: "You know, some of that old stuff still goes on here in New Lots among the more ignorant people." Indeed, one young key informant continues to distinguish one of his older brothers by the affectionate term *el oso* (the bear) precisely "*because* he played with us even though we were younger"; he displayed the affectionate side of his nature to his younger siblings as well as acting in the sterner role of an older brother.

In those days there was no one else but the father who gave the word on the family actions. He would say what had to be said just once; there was never any second time! His word was an order. But now things have changed. It is still true that the man's word is carried out, but it is not so strict as it once was. My father was a very proper [recto] man! Nowadays a man and his wife may talk things out; they might try to put the things of the two minds together to solve something which bothers them. In those days there was only one word.

A father, as *jefe de la casa* or *jefe de la familia* represents his household to the world outside; it is he who mediates between domestic group and outside agencies. Correspondingly, the conduct of each of the members of his family reflects on the *jefe de la familia*.

Although it was suggested that the father represents a gruff and correct (*muy recto*) figure to the others of the household, his actions appear to be motivated neither by caprice nor arbitrariness. Nevertheless, young people speak of their fathers *as if* they acted in a capricious and arbitrary fashion.

The chicanos, especially the young men, carry an image of their fathers as stern, gruff, and domineering personages. When young men speak of their fathers, their attitude tends to have a resentful note, albeit respectful. Without exception, direct observations note the warmth and affection exhibited by fathers with their young sons and daughters, children under ten years of age. In several instances the field notes comment that the father was, in fact, far more gentle with his children than was their mother. On other occasions it was noted that fathers were observed feeding children from bottles while holding them in their arms.

In the case of a household in which the father is deceased or absent, the oldest son becomes his surrogate. Ideal behavior between an older and younger brother is in many ways similar to that which is expected between fathers and sons. Brothers don't play together. We just never did . . . [But] just wait until a brother gets hurt by someone or gets into a fight, that's when he knows that he has a brother! When you're in trouble and need someone, then your brother lets you know that he's there! In the less serious day-to-day activities brothers participate together in minimal degree. Playful interaction is never conducive to respect of one another. One of the means elected to avoid the ever-present threat of insult, intentional or otherwise, is to avoid those situations in which one encounters brothers to whom decorous behavior is prescribed. The best and easiest manner in which to prevent abrasive relationships is for fathers and sons, and older and younger brothers, to go their separate ways.

Women of the Family

In contrast with the husband-father of a household group, or his surrogate, the oldest brother, a wife and mother is, ideally, submissive, unworldly, and chaste. She is interested primarily in the welfare of her husband and children, and secondarily in her own requirements. Both the mother and father of a household are accorded extraordinary respect by their children, but the restraint shown in relation to each is derived from different sources. The father must be respected because of his authoritative position at the head of the household, whereas the mother is respected because she minimizes her own necessities in order to better provide for those of her family. She devotes herself to her family. The relationship between a daughter and her mother is of great importance to women of all ages, and it perdures throughout a woman's married life. Couples who had moved returned as often as possible. When asked the purpose of the visit, they usually phrased their response to indicate a desire to be with the mother or the sisters of the wife. The strength of the bond between sisters is such that sisters' husbands are separated from all other relatives-in-law of the same generation. They are considered as being in a special kind of bond and are spoken of as concuños. Sisters of whatever age and marital status are closely knit in their affections.

Courtship and Marriage

Informants in Mexiquito took pains to emphasize the extent to which a girl is confined to the home of her parents until she is married, and then is restricted to the household of her husband. Oftentimes a married woman advises that until she married her husband she had not looked him in the eyes, much less gone out with another man. Such statements present a highly idealized version of real behavior; they are the moral norms of conduct, which are more or less adhered to by women of Mexiquito.

Social norms prescribe the circumscription of courtship by highly ritualized behavior. Ideally, the young man is expected to communicate with the parents of the girl when he wishes to announce his intentions of matrimony, for example, and a kiss or other bodily contact is forbidden between the courting couple. The girl is expected to become acquainted with her suitor by means of a protracted exchange of correspondence, either in the form of letters or by utilization of carefully chosen intermediaries. Persons highly respected in Mexiquito's social system are much in demand as intermediaries in marriage arrangements, for the more exalted the status of the intermediary (*portador*), the more weighty his brief for the suitor. Therefore the more revered the position of the *portador*, the more difficult it is for the girl's parents to refuse his petition pointblank. The *portador* thus invests something of his own personal prestige in winning a spouse for a client. (Schoolteachers occupy positions at the apex of the occupational system. They share that status with the physician and the priest, the latter being most exalted of all as *portador*).

It used to be that when a boy's father went to the home of the girl to ask her father for his daughter's hand that the girl's father would say:

"Well, I don't know. I'll tell you what. Send your boy over to my house for two months and we'll see how he works. We'll see what we can expect from that young man!" Then the father of the boy would agree to do this. But he would tell the father of the girl that he, also, wished to see how the girl behaved and what kind of worker she was. He suggested that the girl come to his house for two months. That way there was an exchange (*intercambio*).

The girl would get up at three in the morning and see what kind of condition the *nixtamal* (*tortilla* dough) was in, and she would set the fire, bake the *tortillas*, and tidy up the place. At her family's home the boy would be working himself to death; he would be walking in from the fields with a load of sweet cane over one shoulder, and a load of corn on the other shoulder. People knew how to work and keep house then! After two months, when the parents had seen how well the children were able to work, they would give them permission to wed.

When a proposal was accepted the boy was not expected to serve a test period in the home of his fiancée's parents. In lieu of that service the youth was expected to send food or money to her parents — a custom called the *diario*. In order to demonstrate his ability to care for the girl, the boy sent food and clothing or money for a period of eight months between the acceptance of the proposal and the actual marriage. Then after the marriage the young couple lived with the parents of the girl. If the two couples proved compatible, the younger pair would build or rent a home next door to the home of the wife's parents.

An enterprising Catholic priest remarked that a high incidence of elopements (*robamientos*) existed in Mexiquito. He blamed the high rate on two causes, the first the excessive cost of the wedding celebrations demanded by local customs. The priest pointed out that such celebrations were prescribed by what he called "local folklore"; they were by no means required by canon law. The second practice contributing to elopement was frequent disapproval of the match by the parents of the girl. The priest claimed that he had established channels of communication through which he was informed when a couple planned to elope. He then contacted one of the pair and usually suggested that they elope directly to his church. After he married them, he accepted as *his* responsibility notification of the irate parents. By such means he made certain that the young couple had been married in church.

The importance of the system by which one uses a *portador* to represent his virtues to the parents of the girl is now in sharp decline. Nevertheless it continues to serve as a normative guide for courtship in Mexiquito. At first glance it seems odd that the very moment for which a girl has been prepared throughout her life — marriage and motherhood — should be fraught with hard feelings and conflict. Why should a middle-aged woman recall that when *she* wished to marry, she had expected *the trouble* with her parents? What does the marriage of a daughter imply to her parents?

The girl has been brought up in such a manner that she represents herself as a paragon of virtue, a woman fit to mother the children of a respectable male of *la raza*. Early in her life she was made aware that she represented her household group fully as much as she represented herself, an individual. In all instances her claims to enjoyment were made secondary to the claim of propriety. In other words, hers was a road carefully planned from girlhood to womanhood within the tight restraint of family discipline. Her comportment reflected the abilities of the parents as taskmasters of the children.

When properly undertaken, courtship and marriage are triumphant phases in the life of the domestic group. The passage of the girl from the home of her parents to that of her husband is accompanied by rites and fanfare, which make public the announcement that the girl *and* her parents have adequately met their obligations. The approaching wedding of a daughter is publicly announced at a dance sponsored by *her* parents, and there at the dance the parents of the girl are introduced to the gathering by the master of ceremonies. Their obligations toward her met, *they* are honored as well as she. The financial outlay for such an announcement is considerable, but after all, it is a life's work to prepare a daughter to become a worthy wife and mother.

The place of a woman is within the confines of the home. Her friends and confidants are restricted to her mother, her sisters, and her close female relatives; initiation of acquaintanceship beyond that very narrow group of kinswomen is deterred. The striking dependence of a Mexican American woman on a minimal unit of femal relatives is intensified by the enjoined aloofness between the woman and her close male relatives. Consequently the emotional needs of a woman in this society are funneled to a microcosmic group of other women. Given the little world of familiars upon whom an adult woman is forced to depend, each of the others in that group is of critical importance to her. Therefore, the marriage of a daughter threatens to fracture a group already overstrained by interdependency.

Courtship and marriage are by no means blissful for the households concerned. Each family has too much at stake. Courtship itself is enveloped in a ritualistic behavior, whose delicate procedures are often carried on by emissaries in order to avoid direct confrontation of the parties. The contemporary custom of the *diario* and the past customs of bride and groom service in the homes of the prospective in-laws are mechanisms best described as attempts by the two families to accommodate themselves to impending change. The relatively elaborate, ritualized behavior and language in which courtship is enmeshed is best understood as a means of cushioning the loss of a son or a daughter. But those cultural mechanisms are inadequate for the task. Courtship and the early years of marriage are periods of stress to those persons immediately involved.

The Mexican-Americans have been quite aware that their patterns of courtship and married life differ from those of the Anglos. It has been especially difficult for young chicanos to understand patterns of dating whereby a girl will go out with a boy on one night, another on the following night, and still another on the third night.

The young women on the other hand find "serial dating" attractive. Moreover, chicano youths of both sexes find the close chaperoning of the girl irksome; Anglos of the same age move about quite freely, and the young chicanos are beginning to emulate them.

Another quality of Anglos courtship and marriage which young Mexican-Americans find attractive is the autonomy allowed a romancing youngster in electing his or her own spouse. This conflicts with the older pattern by which chicano parents arranged strategic marriages for their children. Each of the newly introduced alternative techniques of courtship and marriage which are products of processes of acculturation and urbanization, conflict sharply with more traditional customs. Moreover, adoption of new courting techniques by some members of the society, but not others, has led to conflict between expectations and values of one generation with another, as well as between those held by young men and young women.

However, neither process of change — neither acculturation nor urbanization — helps to explain "the trouble" which is associated with the periods of courtship and early marriage of the chicanos of Mexiquito. To consider *that* particular stress a product of some sociocultural change phenomenon proves fruitless. On the contrary, the more rigidly conservative the adherence of a parental couple to the normative values of the culture, the more stress is found associated with the marriage of their daughter. And, it seems likely that the smaller the number of females in a household the more disturbing to the household group the marriage of a daughter will be. Rather than a consequence of change, "the trouble" is a consequence of conflicts built into the indigenous social system.

Ritual Kinship

Although Mexiquito's social system contains built-in conflict, it also provides institutionalized means to contain it. One institution which chicanos utilize to confine conflict is ritual kinship (*compadrazgo*).

Older couples will soon be requesting assistance from their married children, an expectation known as *el deber de los hijos*. Yet, when the young married couple gives assistance to one set of parents, the others think themselves deprived. On the other hand, the two older couples will also share equally in rights to their grandchildren. The ambivalence of their feelings toward one another — antagonism on the one hand, shared interest on the other — is resolved by the inauguration of ritual kinship, which permits the two couples to interact, albeit in a manner remarkable for its constraint.

Another example of the way in which chicanos utilize ritual kinship as a means to restrain conflict occurs in the following: "Sometimes when someone is afraid that you are going to sleep with his wife, he'll make you his compadre. That way you can't do it."

Compadrazgo lends itself so well to the containment of conflict because chicanos expect that those so related will treat one another with respect and deference. Whether the expected punctilio of respect and deference is emphasized by the two parties depends to a great extent on the motivations which led them to contract their relationship. For by no means all such ritual bonds are contracted in order to constrain potential conflict and ambivalence. In many instances individuals seek to make a friendship more firm and lasting by contracting fictive kinship ties. However, so salient are the qualities of decorum which obtain in this relationship that whether one intended to increase or to diminish the ranges of his interaction with the other by means of a *compadre* bond, those who enter into such an alliance must maintain their distance. Of all the kinds of *compadre* relationships into which chicanos may enter, the one in which qualities of respect and deference are most demanding is initiated at the time a child is baptized. The sponsors and the biological parents become *compadres* (coparents).

Although an infant is linked to his baptismal sponsors (*ahijadopadrinos*) and they inaugurate a fictive kin relationship with the child's biological parents (compadres-compadres), their relationship does not under any condition extend to the infant's siblings.

It is possible, however, for an individual to sponsor more than one child from a single family. This multiple relationship is described as making the sign of the cross (*haciendo la cruz*) because those families which countenance multiple sponsorship insist that it be limited to three children.

In any case, the importance which chicanos attribute to the baptismal triad — *padrino-adhijado-compadre* — cannot be overemphasized.

When you choose a compadre, you have to call him *Sir* in a way. You say *Usted*. Ritual kinsmen are also expected to assist each other in a more material fashion. An infant's baptismal *padrinos*, for example, are obliged to furnish their godchild's ceremonial clothing, to defray the costs of the rite, and to commission a portrait of the child by a local photographer. In the case of a wedding, those who act as sponsors assist with the costs of the bridal outfit, and meet the cleric's fee. Whatever are the original reasons for initiating such a relationship, those who are ritually allied to an individual, together with his nuclear family, constitute his security system.

Neighbors

The Mexican-Americans conceive of their households as places of security, from which the residents look out on a hostile world. Good fortune is attained in spite of the malice and invidious sanctions which are directed by neighbors against one's family. One of the most important aspects of the ethos of Mexiquito is a gnawing fear of these invidious sanctions. The householders are convinced that a successful year in the fields, a season without sickness, a journey free from occurrence of serious accidents, all provoke the invidiousness of other Mexican-Americans. Whenever the serenity of the family is disrupted by unseasonable weather which interferes with the wage earner's gainful employment, or a family member is afflicted by illness, or someone is incapacitated by a serious accident, such disturbances may be assumed to be the projection of willful malice by neighbors. In this society it is human, not suprahuman, forces with which the householders must contend.

Visiting between households in the neighborhood is discouraged. If a male not included in a category of relationship in which respectful behavior is prescribed pays a visit to a home, he is presumed to have sexual designs on the women of that household.

Many times the observer hears women express this value-laden sentiment, "I don't like to visit with my neighbors; if we have something to discuss, it is better done in the yard." In fact, during the two years, only two cases were discovered in which a woman regularly visited the home of another to whom she was not related. In both instances the visiting pattern was asymmetric, that is, only one of the pair was the visitor, the other was always the visited. Neither of the visiting women had kin in town except those related through their husbands; one of the visitors had long since been deserted by her husband. Each of the visitors conceived of herself as a social isolate, for whom life was meaningless, hopeless, and without order. In fact, one of the women was contemplating suicide at the time of our acquaintance. In each of these two instances of irregular visiting, the husband of the visited woman peremptorily forbade his wife to admit the visitor any more. His action was a direct consequence of the gossip which arose from the unusual pattern.

Of the people of Mexiquito it may be said that apprehension and anxiety increase as the distance between neighbors decreases. The closer the sites of two homes the less the degree of esteem between the residents. Relationships between immediate neighbors in Mexiquito tend to be unusually unpleasant.

People don't want anyone to improve themselves. The trouble with the Mexican people is that they cut each other's throats.

Mingo, a young man of Mexiquito, remarked that he had been sent through elementary and high school with the assistance offered by an Anglo family and that he had attended college with the assistance of another Anglo. When he had won his college degree he sought employment and was recommended for a well-paying job by still another Anglo. But the personnel manager of the firm to which he was recommended was a chicano, like himself, and Mingo was turned down for the position. "That's the way Mexicans are."

Stories of witchcraft (*mal puesto*) are not uncommon as examples of invidiousness among neighbors.

Raúl, a young man of Mexiquito, reports that he was once requested by a woman to take her to a curer because she was having trouble with a neighbor. The neighbor was a bad sort, the woman told Raúl, and was "doing something to her." The *curandero* she consulted advised her to go out of her house at midnight, when she was to stand between the two houses and recite a number of prayers, including several "Our Fathers." Then she was advised to take two seeds given her by the curer and to place one of them at each corner of her home on the side which fronted on the house of the suspected neighbor. According to Raúl, the woman did this and now she is no longer troubled by her neighbor.

Another story which describes the view that residents of Mexiquito tend to hold of their neighbors is recounted by Orlando:

> Some years ago my brother eloped with a seventeen-year-old girl, a very beautiful young woman. The girl's aunt did not like my brother because she wanted her niece to marry another.
>
> Almost as soon as the couple were married, they began to get very sick. For a very long time they had an unhappy marriage. One of them was always sick and they didn't have any children, even though both of them wanted children. In those first years they couldn't get along with one another at all, and they kept arguing and fighting all of the time. They were married in 1933 and didn't have their first child until 1936.
>
> Finally, they went to visit a curer for some advice and she told them that somebody had it in for them and they would have to try very hard to get along to overcome the malice that the other person had in his heart for their marriage.
>
> They tried harder to get along and the marriage was more successful. Then, one afternoon, when my brother's wife was cleaning up the yard she spied an old doll, and discovered that it was full of needles. She put the doll on the fire and destroyed it, and they were able to have children and they got along better together. That doll was put under the house either by the girl's aunt or else by her former boy-friend.

There are also means other than witchcraft by which individuals are thought to be projecting their malice against neighbors in Mexiquito. During a ten-day period in 1958 a number of households received telephone calls of a calumnious nature from anonymous persons. The language of the callers was so vile and the insinuations so dastardly that those who answered the telephone were left shaken and ill. After receiving such calls several families petitioned a change of telephone numbers from the company. After inquiries revealed the reasons for the petitions, the company notified the police. Because none of the families would sign a formal complaint the police could not inaugurate an investigation. Although the persons called, quite reasonably, were reluctant to divulge that they were the targets of such vilification, some of the circumstances associated with the calls were put together as described below. The nature of the matter indicates something of the quality of interpersonal relations in Mexiquito.

Those members of the maligned families with whom I talked attribute the telephone calls to invidious motivations of a family whose social mobility has not kept pace with that of those whom they telephoned.

But insulting telephone calls and witchcraft do not exhaust the techniques which Mexiquito residents assume are used by their acquaintances to project hostilities. It is a common belief in the neighborhood that arresting officers of the United States Border Patrol often act with such prescience about the illegal presence of one's friends and relatives that the agents must have been tipped off by neighbors.

The people of Mexiquito peer out from the security of their homes at a society which they view with distrust, suspicion, and apprehension. The fears of invidious sanction, witchcraft, tips to the Border Patrol, and calumnious telephone conversations all attest to the anxiety and apprehensiveness with which social relations in Mexiquito are viewed. In actual fact there are bases in reality for such anxieties and apprehensions. Only within his or her own home is the Mexican-American in an environment in which he or she trustingly participates with others.

Summary

In Mexiquito the most important social units are the nuclear families, which consist of parents and their children. Ideally, each nuclear family resides in a separate household, although sometimes a widowed parent of one of the spouses lives with them. Visiting between households is discouraged, except by members of the close family or ritual kinsmen.

Within the household, interaction between family members is guided by well-marked channels of respect and deference. Status and role behavior are clearly marked for each member of the nuclear family, and the individuals interact with assurance, if not with ease. The older order the younger, and the men the women. Those values which order the conduct of the residents enjoin exhibition of levity or frivolity. The home is a place for serious demeanor, it provides an appropriate environment for one's wife and daughters.

The confinement of females within the home gives rise to a closely knit group of a mother and her daughters, a relationship which endures throughout the lifetime of the individuals. The imminence of a daughter's marriage appears to provoke stressful consequences in the life of the domestic group. It is hypothesized that a daughter's impending marriage is stressful because it threatens to rupture the microcosmic group of interdependent women who reside together.

The individual households stand isolated from each other, socially if not spatially. Families perceive members of Mexiquito society other than close relatives as dangerous and antagonistic. Improvement in the well-being of an individual or his family is accomplished in the face of opposition from others of the society. The themes of invidious sanction and malevolent intent are incessant in Mexiquito, and the means by which such hostile intentions are believed to be projected are manifold.

MEXICAN-AMERICAN MINORITY CHURCHES, U.S.A.*

MARGARET L. SUMNER

Can or should a church be 'indigenous' in terms of the local ethnic group when that group constitutes a minority and is looked upon — even by its members — as occupying an inferior position with respect to the dominant society? is the query posed by Dow Robinson. Ralph Winter raises the question: Is not this sort of context as subject to ethnographic analysis as any other? And may it not be as helpful to understand the ecclesiastical dynamics of a situation as the other cultural factors?

Ecclesiastical dynamics and the total social situation of a local congregation are indeed subject to ethnographic analysis, and that without such analysis the social and psychological consequences of becoming a Protestant in a Catholic community cannot be properly understood. Material will be presented below on three of these "indigenous" (Spanish language) Protestant congregations, with two objectives in view.

It is suggested that attention to secular processes and problems in the field will enable directors of missionary programs to take account of and compensate for the social isolation of Protestants in a pagan or Catholic society. It appears that the fewer the coreligionists in an area, the more disruptive are the consequences of withdrawal from the religious community of the majority. For example, in a psychiatric study of a disturbed Mexican-American, the author observes: "A Mexican . . . who has embraced a Protestant faith, as in the case to be presented, has done almost as much as one can do to isolate himself from the main body of his people. This is a rather strong statement about an extreme case, but it draws attention to the problem of religious isolation and its social and psychological consequences in a plural society.

Although the ministers of the three congregations studied have been more concerned with the "Christianization" than the "Americaniza-

*Reprinted from *Practical Anthropology*, Volume 10, Number 3, May-June 1963.

tion" of their Mexican-American members, the two processes can scarcely be separated. All members of the churches are residents, and most of them are citizens, of the United States. Accepting a form of Protestantism reflects a tentative identification with American predominantly Protestant culture; the repudiation of Catholicism involves at least a partial rejection of a Mexican past.

The basic Protestant reliance upon individual experience and conscience has been acted upon in the embracing of the new faith. Church membership provides the basis for new responsibilities for self-government, and a more equalitarian relation to authority and to society. Moreover, contact with "American" Protestants has been established. Thus experience in a Protestant church might be expected to lead gradually to a complete acceptance of what might be called the "American" world view with its emphasis upon activity in this world, control over the self and nature, a hopeful view of the future, and stress on individual responsibility. These orientations are not the exclusive property of any particular religion, but they have been historically associated with Protestantism, in the United States and Elsewhere.

New Social Networks

This paper will not deal with the overall problem of the type and extent of culture change induced in these three congregations; it will focus on the social bonds which are severed, and those which are newly established, in a social network involving: (a) Protestant subgroups of the Mexican-American society, (b) the predominantly Catholic Mexican-American community as a whole, and (c) the dominant "American" society, particularly that large sector of it which shares a common religious orientation with the Protestant-Mexican minority. Since transmission of ideas and standards of behavior occurs along the lines of such a network, it is important to know who is in contact with whom. It was predicted that Mexican-American Protestants would have reduced contacts with the Catholic section of the *Colonia,* (what the Spanish-speaking community calls itself), and increased ties of intimacy with "Anglos" of the same denomination or church, a situation favorable to acculturation. Is this actually the case?

The city in which the study was made is in Northern California, with about one-tenth of the population of Mexican origin or descent.

The presence of a fluctuating and uncounted number of illegal immigrants makes difficult the estimation of the proportion of foreign born; it is probably about twenty per cent. In general, elderly people speak only Spanish, or speak it far more easily than English. Most persons in their thirties and forties are bilingual, though Spanish is generally preferred for situations of friendship and intimacy. Some parents make a point of speaking English at home so their children will not suffer the language handicaps they themselves suffered; others insist on the use of Spanish at home, to preserve the cultural heritage. Children of school age speak so little Spanish, and are so unaccustomed to reading it, that Sunday school instruction for the very young is usually given in English "so that they can understand," even in the churches which prefer instruction in Spanish. A surprising number of teen-agers, however, perhaps half, chatter together in an Americanized Spanish argot.

In comparison with the greater number of persons of Italian birth and descent in the city, the "Mexicans" present marked linguistic and cultural conservatism. In addition, they are farther than the Italians from "prestige" appearance, since many of them have a dark skin or other indicator of Indian ancestry. Although manifestations of anti-Mexican prejudice are not as servere here as in the Southwest in general, "Mexicans" rank low in the social scale, and they know it; only Negroes are below them. The social and economic fences around the Anglo society, and the cultural conservatism of the "Mexicans," which is partly a consequence of those barriers, combine to produce considerable separation of the two cultures and societies. Friendships, courtships, and marriages are usually within rather than across the ethnic lines. At school and on the job, there are plentiful contacts with "Americans" of all sorts, but most relationships across the ethnic lines are of the impersonal type, with the Mexican-American in the subordinate status: employee-employer, patient-doctor, client-welfare agent, suspect-policeman, and so on.

Protestants and the "Colonia"

The "social tone" of the *colonia* is that of a Roman Catholic society. The best known and most admired men of the *colonia* are almost all Catholics. Families and business associates are linked by ties of *compadrazgo* 'coparenthood.' Public exercises are opened by a priest, almost never by a Protestant minister. Menus for social or civic dinners provide for fast days. The serving of alcoholic drinks, particularly beer, marks almost any gathering that can be considered a fiesta. Fund-raising dinners and dances depend heavily upon the sale of liquor for their profits. Since the Protestant churches of the *colonia* emphasize "temperance," this difference in consumption patterns tends to set Protestants apart from the social and civic life of the *colonia*.

Although some Catholics say they admire the Protestants because they are "more dedicated," most of them are vague about the beliefs and activities of the Protestant churches. Some of the unacculturated believe that Protestant rites include deliberate desecration of representations of the Virgin. Others refer to all non-Catholics as "Aleluyas," since their only acquaintance is with the services of the emotional sects. One civic leader is known to be a Methodist and a 33rd Degree Mason. His achievement in Masonry is generally admired; his Methodism is ignored. Thus while Protestants are not exactly a "despised minority within a minority," they are at a social disadvantage with respect to all Anglos, and "Mexican" Catholics.

Differing standards of food and drink consumption restrict social intercourse between the varieties of Christians in the *colonia*. Protestant use of time is different, too. The more frequent the services, prayer meetings, classes, and suppers connected with the church, the less the time and energy available for friendships or social and civic activities outside the local congregation. Needless to say, converts are sometimes quite estranged from their Catholic kinsmen, and spend more time with their new "brothers." Finally, teen-agers are in a particularly isolated position if they are of a puritanical sect in which dancing, cards, movies, and similar entertainments are forbidden. This is especially true for girls, of whom good behavior is more seriously demanded. The "new" puritan demands, if grafted onto conservative Mexican ideas concerning the sequestration or chaperoning of daughters, leave many Mexican-American girls almost completely out of the social life of the public school. For example, they are unable even to attend picnics and other *fetes* considered acceptable by the majority of both societies. If there is a large and active group of teen-agers at the church, their social needs may be provided for here, but this is not always the case. Moreover, a marriage with a "Christian" partner may not be possible, since the number available is so limited.

Thus the degree of isolation of the Protestant minority from the Catholic *colonia* is largely a function of sectarian exclusiveness.

Differing standards of behavior as well as belief set these persons apart as a Christian "elite." On the other hand, the degree of integration with Anglo Protestants of the same denomination is largely a function of ecclesiastical polity, as will be indicated below. There are also an undetermined but relatively small number of persons of Mexican descent who have joined English-speaking congregations. This solution is not open to all; those who have joined dominantly Anglo churches are usually highly acculturated and socially aggressive. "Shyness" is characteristic of "Mexicans," and, in fact, the welcome they are so mistrustful of finding is very often withheld.

The majority of Mexican-American converts to Protestantism have been members of Spanish language churches, which have offered one kind of solution to the linguistic and social difficulties involved. Does this solution meet the needs of the acculturating members? Are they compensated for their sacrifice of shared values and mutual esteem within the Catholic community by being assisted to become Americans with self-respect, and Protestants with satisfactions and responsibilities beyond the boundaries of the ethnic group?

Three Protestant Congregations

The denominations studied will be called A,B, and C. These congregations all have English language counterparts in the same city. Two of the ministers were born in Mexico, one in Colorado of Spanish ancestry. They were all raised as Catholics, and were converted at approximately the age of twenty.

The A church is characterized by the greatest degree of sectarian exclusiveness, the most rigorous self-discipline of members, and the closest communication with Anglo members of the same denomination. This group is by doctrine and puritan discipline most remote from the Catholic community, and is indeed most anti-Catholic. Its members are isolated from the *colonia* by a variety of restrictions on behavior and dress, including observance of the Sabbath on Sunday. It also offers the greatest number of opportunities for friendly contact and cooperative endeavor with members of the denomination from other communities and ethnic groups. The treasurer and an elder of this church are bilingual Anglos, as is the director of youth activities. Non-Mexican visitors were noted at every service attended by this observer; many of them addressed the congregation in Spanish. (The emphasis on linguistic training for missionary work provides a large number of "American" A's who speak good Spanish.)

Some children from the Spanish-language church attend the A school and seminary nearby, occasionally on scholarships contributed by the English-language congregation. The women's welfare society, youth camps, Bible teacher training courses, and other units in a network of closely integrated "societies" offer opportunity for participation in local English-language activities of the church.

The A church appears to be most successful at integration because it is most closely organized and disciplined. It is important that they should be so, since A's are set apart by belief and custom, not only from the rest of the *colonia,* but from American society as a whole.

The B faith is characteristically American; there are thousands of churches and millions of members throughout the land. There are in this city about a dozen of these congregations, including another Spanish-language church, which was not studied. While they may be linked by belonging to associations or conventions, they are basically autonomous, and the management of any one congregation is beyond the formal control of any superior body. They "hire" and "fire" their own minister. This Spanish-language church is affiliated with other Spanish-language churches in the state, but it does not fit into a hierarchy which also includes English-language churches. Thus these members have the greatest opportunity to take responsibility for their own affairs, and have been markedly successful in doing so, even operating without any minister for the better part of a year following the death of the pastor.

The price they pay for this autonomy is lack of any systematic cooperation with English-speaking B's. There is a loose association of "sponsorship" with one "English" church, but it does not appear to have been of great effect. One member reported: "We asked them for Sunday school teachers and they sent us some old magazines." Never did this observer happen to see any other Anglos at the services. When the minister died, hundreds of mourners from all over the state came to his funeral, but they were almost entirely of Mexican background, including several non-Protestants. Two English-speaking B pastors from the town attended, and one made a brief graveside address. The tone suggested this was an official act rather than one of personal friendship.

The C church is the smallest, partly because it is the most recently established. It began as a mission of a large, hierarchically organized church which is firmly, though not exclusively, associated with the American middle class. The congregation manages its local affairs, subject to the control of entirely "American" ecclesiastical and administrative superiors. It does not select its own minister. This church contains the fewest recent converts from Catholicism, and the highest proportion of high school and college graduates. Like the others, it also includes elderly persons who are purely Spanish-speaking, some of whom are illiterate or semi-literate. Most of the latter show the opposition to a "worldly" morality, and to Catholicism, which characterizes many American Protestant sects. The minister himself and the younger members are oriented to a "socially creative" rather than a "self-restrictive" discipline. Although raised in Mexico and least American in speech and manner, this pastor has had the broadest education, since he attended a California college. He presents a harmonious blending of Latin humanistic and American middle-class intellectual values.

Membership in this church is potentially the least isolating from the *colonia* and least conflicting with the dominant variety of American middle-class culture, yet the social separation is marked. There are two highly acculturated members who act as liaison with an English C church. The minister has engaged an Anglo choir director, and insisted his Sunday school teachers take training in classes given by the local Council of Churches. He is eager for more formal and informal contacts with the American C's. He has expressed a wish that some-where, somehow, he could find some "American" couples who would be willing to participate in the affairs of this church. The church stands open to the C's of this city, yet they do not know of its existence. Although only a few miles away from them, it is practically in "another world."

Need for a "Sponsor"

When he first came, the minister stated, It is my business to make Christians of them, not Americans." Now he has come to realize that the "indigenous" church can no longer meet the needs of an increasingly acculturated Mexican-American community. (The C church is, in theory, "integrated," but in fact the segregation remains.) He suggests that some more intimate and systematic cooperation between C's of the two traditions is important for his congregation.

The successor to the first pastor of the B church, American born and oriented, holds the same view. He would like to see a voluntary sponsorship between an "English" and a "Spanish" church, of a type he experienced in a Kansas town. In that case, church buildings and teaching facilities were shared. Services were given in both languages, seriatim. There were separate Sunday school classes in Spanish for those who needed them, while English-speaking classes were attended by some of the Mexican-Americans. An arrangement of this sort, he believes, is the best solution to the problem of "indigenous" churches. It utilizes buildings and personnel most efficiently, it leads to greater integration, and provides for the ultimate dissolution of the Spanish-language congregation.

The answer to the question, "Do Mexican Protestants withdraw from the life of the *colonia*?" is "On the whole, yes." These three congregations show varying degrees of isolation from Catholic society. All are somewhat set apart by their frequency of interaction within the congregation, and have different values, especially those concerning leisure time and entertainment.

The question "Are they increasingly integrated into groups of Anglo Protestants?" must be answered, "As church members, very little." The class stratification of Protestant congregations in the United States is mirrored and intensified in the separation of "Mexican" from "American" congregations of the same church. Initially, this separation was justified by the language difference. As acculturation proceeds, the separation is less and less necessary and merely enforces an increasingly artificial separation between Protestants of different ethnic backgrounds.

Christians presumably have a creative function in a society, but in order to function in any society it is necessary truly to belong to it. Christians value "fellowship" because they are aware that the sharing of beliefs and ideals is made meaningful — and sustaining to the individual — only through genuine companionship. Traditionally, immigrant groups have been welcomed to the American melting pot by being allowed to battle their way in. It appears that the Protestant churches of this country could devise more effective ways of actively inviting them in.

It has been suggested that in a sponsor-oriented society like that of Mexican Indians, a church-sponsor relationship with a larger body is a genuine need. American society has not traditionally been sponsor-oriented, stressing instead a responsible individualism for persons and for groups. The study of the "indigenous" churches of this California city suggests that some sort of vigorous and responsible sponsorship relation between "Spanish" and "English" churches should be directed toward more complete cooperation and assimilation at this time.

ETHNIC ENDOGAMY—THE CASE OF MEXICAN AMERICANS*

FRANK G. MITTELBACH AND JOAN W. MOORE

Theorists concerned with problems of social differentiation have generally taken the endogamy rate of a subpopulation as an indicator of the rigidity of boundaries around it. (Boundaries are, of course, due both to prejudice against the group and to the group's internal cohesiveness.) As Merton argues, this is justified theoretically because exogamous marriages disrupt the network of primary-group relationships that underlie the cohesiveness of any population. In some respects, this is a functional as well as a motivational explanation in that the threat of disrupting primary-group relationships acts as a deterrent to exogamous marriages.

Empirical studies of intermarriage between subpopulations in this country have in some cases emphasized the significance of external boundaries imposed by prejudice, as, for example, in the analysis of Negro exogamy. In other research, as in the analysis of upper-class endogamy and endogamy of European ethnic populations, much literature assumes the boundaries internally maintained by in-group solidarity to be the important factor.

This paper examines the Mexican Americans, the nation's second largest disadvantaged minority and a group which has often been portrayed as distinctively unassimilated and unacculturated — that is, one which has unusually strong boundaries around it. Though these boundaries are most frequently attributed to in-group cohesiveness, Mexican Americans have also experienced considerable prejudice and discrimination. In short, analysis of patterns of intermarriage among this group, which shares minority status with Negroes and shares ethnic distinctiveness with other foreign immigrant groups, offers some promise of fruitful insight into the processes of boundary maintenance and dissolution.

The paper has two purposes. The first is to increase understanding of the current status and future prospects for assimilation of this population, and the second is to amplify general propositions about condi-

*American Journal of Sociology, Vol. 74, July 1968, pages 50-62.

tions under which exogamy occurs. The two purposes reinforce each other: Mexican American patterns of endogamy are best understood in a general context, and the analysis of this unusual case may help extend the theoretical frontiers slightly.

Previous studies of Mexican American endogamy are comparatively rare, but all show extremely low rates of exogamy, supporting the notion of the group as distinctively unassimilated. Panunzio's study of individuals born in Mexico and marrying in Los Angeles between 1924 and 1933 showed that only 9 per cent of the individuals (and 17 per cent of the marriages) were exogamous. An analysis of Spanish-surname persons in Albuquerque from 1924 to 1940 indicated that only 8 per cent of the individuals (and 15 per cent of the marriages) were exogamous. Finally, a more recent study of Spanish-surname persons in San Antonio marrying between 1940 and 1955 showed exogamy rates of no more than 10 per cent for persons (and 17 per cent for marriages) in any of the years sampled. Considering that many of these persons in Albuquerque and probably in San Antonio are native born of native parents, the image of this minority as distinctively unassimilated gains much support from these studies. And considering that these studies were prepared in different places and times, the notion that the low rate of assimilation is due to unusual strength of in-group bonds also gains much support.

Both social scientists and journalists have tended to emphasize the special strength of Mexican American ascriptive bonds — especially to kin and "la raza" (diffusely, the ethnic group) — in interpreting the slow rate of acculturation and assimilation in the population. However, this kind of interpretation does not help much in our analysis of intermarriage in contemporary Los Angeles. The Los Angeles patterns are understandable only in the light of general propositions about the process of assimilation. The data, for example, illustrate the effects of the considerable and growing internal differentiation within the population. They suggest that this differentiation has differentially weakened the holding power of the ascriptive bonds of "la raza."

In addition to pointing to the effects of this growing differentiation within the Mexican American population, the study — whose findings depart so notably from the three cited above — strongly indicates the importance of the environing social system. The contemporary Los Angeles milieu is far less hostile to Mexican Americans and offers far more economic opportunity than any of the other milieus studied.

These data thus compel the analyst to give consideration to external-system as well as internal-system effects on boundary maintenance of this group.

Data and Milieu

The data which form the basis for our analysis consists of 7,492 marriage licenses issued in Los Angeles County during 1963 from a total of over 47,000 licenses. These 7,492 licenses include all marriages in which one or both spouses carry a Spanish surname. By the definition adopted, a total of 9,368 Mexican American individuals were identified. Of these 2,246 (or 24.0 per cent) were first generation or born in Mexico; 3,537 (or 38.2 per cent) were second generation, with one or both parents born in Mexico, and 3,585 (or 38.2 percent) were third generation, defined as Spanish-surname individuals whose parents were born in one of the five Southwestern states where Mexican Americans are concentrated.

The Mexican Americans hold a very special position in southern California, both as the major local minority and as compared with Mexican Americans. elsewhere. In many respects they appear to be a "typical minority." Mexican Americans constituted slightly less than 10 per cent of the total Los Angeles County population in 1960, but more than 80 per cent were born in the United States. Though it is thus no longer an immigrant population, it is one which has been locally defined as a problem for more than two generations. Memories of the zoot-suit riots of the 1940's are still alive, and segregation from both Anglo whites and Negroes is sharp, great enough so that three Los Angeles area high schools are predominantly Mexican American — a factor certainly important in the availability of marriage partners. However, prejudice against the population in Los Angeles is comparatively low and opportunities for status advancement quite high in comparison with other parts of the American Southwest. From the point of view of the environing social system, then, Los Angeles is an environment which facilitates interaction with the larger system.

Findings

A. *Sex and generational differences.*—The over-all rate of exogamy in these data was much higher than anticipated. Forty per cent of the marriages involving Mexican Americans were exogamous, and 25 per cent of the Mexican American individuals married outside their ethnic group. Although statistics in the field are notably difficult to find, it is clear that exogamy in Los Angeles today is much higher for Mexican Americans than in the past or in other urban areas. Interestingly, the Mexican American exogamy rate is roughly that of the Italian and Polish ethnic populations in Buffalo, New York, a generation ago. Both of these populations are now assimilating rather rapidly.

The results for men and women by generation are presented in Table 1. They show the sex gradient to be as expected for a subpopulation occupying a low status. Women are more exogamous than men, with the respective over-all rates for individuals of 27 and 24 per cent.

TABLE 1

Percentage of In- and Out-Group Marriages of
Mexican Americans, Los Angeles County, 1963

SPOUSE	Mexican-American Grooms			Mexican-American Brides		
	Foreign Born, Mexico (1)	Foreign or Mixed Parentage, Mexico (2)	Natives of Native Parentage (3)	Foreign Born, Mexico (4)	Foreign or Mixed Parentage, Mexico (5)	Natives of Native Parentage (6)
Foreign born, Mexico						
Foreign born, Mexico	*51.9*	13.8	*48.5*	14.5	14.5	6.9
Foreign or mixed parentage, Mexico	22.8	*34.5*	23.8	21.8	*36.7*	27.0
Natives of native parentage	12.2	28.4	*38.9*	9.7	23.2	*33.8*
Subtotal, Mexican American	86.9	76.7	69.5	80.0	74.4	67.7
Hispanic,[1] foreign or mixed parentage	2.9	1.5	0.8	4.0	1.6	1.3
Other [2]	10.2	21.9	29.8	15.9	24.0	31.1
Total	100.0	100.0	100.0	100.0	100.0	100.0
(*N*)	(1,086)	(1,826)	(1,667)	(1,160)	(1,711)	(1,918)

Note.—Generationally endogamous cells are italicized.

[1] Excludes foreign stock from Mexico; includes foreign stock from Central and South America, the Philippines, and Spain.

[2] Includes natives of native parentage with Spanish surname with parents born outside the five southwestern states, natives of native parentage without Spanish surnames throughout the United States, and foreign stock outside of Mexico and other Hispanic countries.

The generational gradient suggests that exogamy will probably increase in the future as relatively more Mexican Americans move out of immigrant status. The most exogamous are third-generation women (32 per cent), and the least exogamous are first-generation men (13 per cent). The generational gradient is steady (Table 1, "Subtotal" row). Sex differences are maintained within each generation, with women more exogamous than men. Similar findings were discovered in a recent two-generational analysis of Puerto Rican exogamy, and their interpretation there, as here, was made within a social-class context.

Most significantly, there is a pattern of endogamy within each generation as well as within the ethnic group. It is apparent that individuals of every generational status tend to marry those with the same generational background.

More important, the data indicate that marriage of second- and third-generation Mexican Americans are assimilationist. Both men and women are more likely to marry "Anglos" than to marry immigrants from Mexico. Among third-generation persons, the chances are actually higher that he or she will marry an Anglo than either a first- *or a* second-generation Mexican. Further evidence can be found related to this generalization. In Table 2, persons with foreign or mixed parentage have been sorted out into those with both parents and those with only one parent born in Mexico. Clearly, Mexican American men and women with both parents born in Mexico are more likely than those with mixed parentage to marry first- and second-generation spouses and less likely to marry third-generation spouses. By this indicator, the social distance between generations of Mexicans is greater than the social distance between some categories of Mexicans and Anglos. This apparently low degree of solidarity inside the ethnic group is not only contrary to much popular opinion but also to general sociological expectation about this group.

This three-generational gradient and the intra-Mexican variations may well exist in other ethnic groups, but to our knowledge it has not been previously demonstrated. It gives a hint to the processes that take place as assimilation of a subordinate population progresses. The data suggest, for example, that members of an ethnic group become less "attractive" to the native born as they appear to be more "ethnic." Conversely, they may become more "attractive" as they become more similar to members of the host society. As differentiations between them and members of the host society become fewer, exogamy may be facilitated.

TABLE 2

Percentage of In- and Out-Group Marriages of Second-Generation Mexican Americans by Nativity, Los Angeles County, 1963

SPOUSE	Second-Generation Mexican-American Grooms			Second-Generation Mexican-American Brides		
	Both Parents Born Mexico	Father Only Born Mexico	Mother Only Born Mexico	Both Parents Born Mexico	Father Only Born Mexico	Mother Only Born Mexico
Foreign born, Mexico	17.9	10.7	9.1	18.1	11.9	9.8
Foreign or mixed parentage, Mexico	36.5	31.5	34.0	38.6	34.2	36.6
Natives of native parentage	24.1	33.8	30.0	17.8	28.8	26.8
Subtotal, Mexican American	78.5	76.0	73.2	74.5	74.9	72.2
Hispanic foreign or mixed parentage	1.2	1.2	2.5	2.1	1.5	0.7
Other	20.3	22.8	24.4	23.4	23.6	26.1
Total	100.0	100.0	100.0	100.0	100.0	100.0
(N)	(885)	(588)	(353)	(811)	(605)	(295)

Note: For both categories (brides and grooms), X^2 significant past .001.

B. *The influence of occupational status.*—Some of the sources of this tendency toward assimilation are suggested by the occupational gradient in Mexican American marriages. The only indicator of general social-class standing available on Los Angeles marriage licenses is the occupation of the bride and the occupation of the groom (parents' occupations are not reported). Because women's occupations are notoriously poor indicators of their social-class standing, we will here only examine the groom's occupation; that is, both brides and grooms are grouped according to occupational status of the groom. Thus, the kinds of generalizations we can draw from the two sets of data are more limited in the case of women than of men. In both instances, however, they are consistent with findings from earlier studies and, most saliently for our analysis, are also comparable with Fitzpatrick's data for Puerto Ricans.

Within these limitations, the analysis in general reaffirms the social-class context of exogamy (Table 3). Generally, the higher the socioeco-

TABLE 3

*In-Group Marriages Among Mexican Americans
by Occupational Status of Groom*

OCCUPATION GROUP OF GROOM AND GENERATION	Grooms		Brides	
	Percent In-Group	N	Percent In-Group	N
High[1]				
Mexican born	66.2	74	57.6	99
Mexican parents	63.1	187	49.3	207
Native of native parents	51.4	138	44.6	177
Total	59.6	399	49.3	483
Middle[2]				
Mexican born	87.5	353	75.3	413
Mexican parents	76.0	766	74.1	703
Native of native parents	75.6	870	69.0	1,039
Total	77.9	1,989	71.9	2,155
Low[3]				
Mexican born	88.7	626	87.3	612
Mexican parents	80.4	810	82.1	750
Native of native parents	65.6	593	71.3	624
Total	78.6	2,029	80.3	1,986
All[4]				
Mexican born	86.9	1,086	80.0	1,160
Mexican parents	76.7	1,826	74.4	1,711
Native of native parents	69.5	1,667	67.7	1,918
Total	76.4	4,579	73.1	4,789

[1] Includes professional, technical and kindred workers, managers, officials, and proprietors (except farm).

[2] Includes clerical, sales and kindred workers, craftsmen, foremen and kindred workers, and farm owners and managers.

[3] Includes operatives and kindred workers, non-household service workers, private household workers, laborers, and farm workers.

[4] All marriages include also those where occupation not reported, unemployed persons, students, and others with no occupation.

nomic status of the groom (or the new family of procreation) the greater the rate of exogamy. For Mexican American women, slightly more than half of those marrying high-status grooms married exogamously, with only 49 per cent marrying Mexican American men. Once again, as with generation, the gradient is remarkably steady. The most exogamous are women marrying high-status men, agreeing with Fitzpatrick's findings and probably his interpretation that "it is likely that . . . women are marrying up as they marry out." The least exogamous are the women marrying low-status men.

Within each occupational group, exogamy increases as the person is further removed from immigrant status. This is true for both brides and grooms. Within each generational group, exogamy increases steadily with the socioeconomic status of the groom. This is true for each generation. Although the lowest rate of in-group marriage for men appears among the high-status third generation, the percentage of endogamy in the middle-status group far exceeds the endogamy of the lower-status group.

In most cases, Mexican American women show a higher rate of outmarriage than do men. Generally, women of lower status levels have more restricted opportunities for forming social relationships outside the narrow limits of kinship and long-standing friendships.

The results tabulated in Table 3 show generally that both generation and occupation are relevant in Mexican American exogamy. To gain some insight into whether occupation or generation is more important in influencing endogamy, we begin by ranking the percentages in Table 3 in a new tabulation by generation and by occupation (Table 4). Then, if occupation is more important than generation in exogamy, the rank order will emphasize occupation (with the generation ordered within each occupation, as in col. 3). If generation is more relevant, it will emphasize generation (with the occupation ordered within each generation, as in col. 4). The results show that actual rankings conform much more closely to the hypothetical rank order emphasizing occupation (Table 4, cols. 1 and 2).

We note two departures from the hypothetical ranking among the men and one among the women. Interestingly, both Mexican American men and women in the low-status, third-generation group marry out more than would be hypothesized from the influence of social class (or occupational status alone). Possibly this group is more acculturated and comfortable with Anglos than occupation alone might suggest. Perhaps

TABLE 4

Rank Order of Out-Group Marriage Rates by Sex, Occupation, and Generation

RANK, FROM MOST TO LEAST OUTMARRYING	Actual				Hypothetical			
	Rank, Males (1)		Rank, Females (2)		Rank of Occupation More Important than Generation (3)		Rank if Generation More Important than Occupation (4)	
	Occupation	Gen.	Occupation	Gen.	Occupation	Gen.	Occupation	Gen.
1	High	3	High	3	High	3	High	3
2	High	2	Middle	2	High	2	High	3
3	Low	3	High	1	High	1	Low	3
4	High	1	Middle	3	Middle	3	High	2
5	Middle	3	Low	3	Middle	2	Middle	2
6	Middle	2	Middle	2	Middle	1	Low	2
7	Low	2	Middle	1	Low	3	High	1
8	Middle	1	Low	2	Low	2	Middle	1
9	Low	1	Low	1	Low	1	Low	1

the effect of being native born of native-born parents counteracts the cultural isolation of a low-status blue-collar job. It might also be an age-associated pattern. Possibly, low-status third-generation persons marry earlier than middle- and higher-status persons in the same generation.

We do not feel these exceptions disturb the general conclusion that occupation is more significant than generation in explaining outmarriage for both Mexican American men and women. Since only the occupation of the groom is reported, it further supports the suggestion that women's exogamy is probably associated with their upward mobility. One complicating factor does exist. The conclusions previously reached are on the basis of three generations. The full impact of the third generation may not yet have appeared, and it is possible that when it does its thrust will be somewhat different than is presently shown. When we drop out the third generation completely and compare only two generations, we find that generational primacy does, in fact, assume considerable importance.

It is plain that within an ethnic population consisting largely of immigrants and their children, the ethnic culture and the kinship relations of the family are closely interwoven. This seems true whether one considers two generations or three, except that with the addition of a third generation, other kinds of social relationships and distinctions undoubtedly become more important. In the relatively open social system of Los Angeles, it is not surprising that occupational status is so significant.

C. *Age at marriage.*—Earlier research has shown that age of a man or woman at marriage is definitely patterned by ethnic and social-class subcultures. It is reasonable to expect that Mexican Americans in Los Angeles also show such patterns. The aggregate data, including all cases where neither party had been previously married, indicating that the median age is 22.0 for Mexican American grooms and 20.3 for brides (Table 5). This is slightly below comparable figures for the

TABLE 5

Median Ages of Grooms and Brides by Ethnicity
(Neither Party Previously Married)

GENERATION OF BRIDE OR GROOM	Born Mexico	Parents Born in Mexico	Third or More Generation	Not Mexican American
		Groom's Median Age		
Bride:				
First generation	25.9	26.1	22.0	23.3
Second generation	24.0	23.2	21.3	23.1
Third or more generation	21.8	21.2	20.8	21.8
Subtotal, Mexican American	24.9	22.3	21.1	N.A.
Subtotal, not Mexican American	22.4	22.0	21.0	N.A.
Over-all	24.7	22.2	21.1	N.A.
		Bride's Median Age		
Groom:				
First generation	23.7	22.1	19.4	19.8
Second generation	22.6	21.0	19.3	19.5
Third or more generation	20.7	19.8	19.1	19.0
Subtotal, Mexican American	22.4	20.6	19.2	N.A.
Subtotal, not Mexican American	21.7	21.5	19.9	N.A.
Over-all	22.3	20.8	19.4	N.A.

Note: Generationally endogamous cells are italicized.

nation, although they have not been completely standardized. Nationally, median age of bride at first marriage in 1963 was 20.4 for women and 22.8 for men. But the aggregate results conceal important generational differences.

First- and second-generation Mexican Americans tend to be notably older and third-generation spouses notably younger than the average American at time of marriage. This gradient is not entirely unexpected in light of the variations in age composition of the first, second, and third generations. For example, in the Los Angeles SMSA, in 1960, only 13 per cent of the Spanish-surname population born in Mexico and over fifteen years of age was in the marriageable ages from fifteen to twenty-four. By comparison, individuals with native- or Mexican-born parents, respectively, accounted for 36 and 26 per cent of this marriageable age group.

Given the differences in age composition, we find that among persons of every generation, the more "Mexican" the spouse, the older the bride or groom. Without more study one might accept the notion that persons who marry spouses close to immigrant status are marrying into an older population and are themselves likely to be older than those who marry native-born Mexican Americans. Further examination of the grooms suggests that this is not entirely sufficient as an explanation.

Table 6 holds both age and generation constant for Mexican American grooms and examines the distribution of marriages by ethnicity and generation of brides. The data strongly suggest that in any particular generation of grooms, age has a stronger influence on mate selection by Mexican American men within the ethnic community than on the endogamy rate proper. In every one of the three generations, older Mexican American men tend to marry women close to immigrant status.

The Mexican American men who married Anglo women tended to be somewhat younger than the men who married first- and second-generation brides and older than those who took third-generation brides, although differences are minor. Among the brides who married Anglo men, the pattern is more mixed, although for neither brides nor grooms are there strong reasons to believe that the exogamous spouses are necessarily older (Table 5). (The explanation for these patterns might be cultural or demographic. Present data on this issue are not available.)

TABLE 6

Percentage of In- and Out-Group Marriages of Mexican Americans by Age of Grooms, Los Angeles County, 1963

BRIDES	Grooms, Foreign Born, Mexico			Grooms, Mexican Parentage			Grooms, Natives of Native Parentage		
	Less Than 25	25-34	Over 34	Less Than 25	25-34	Over 34	Less Than 25	25-34	Over 34
Foreign born, Mexico	42.1	56.4	61.6	8.0	18.1	24.8	5.8	8.9	14.1
	(49.7)	(63.1)	(71.0)	(10.3)	(24.3)	(32.4)	(8.2)	(12.9)	(26.7)
Foreign or mixed parentage, Mexico	23.0	24.8	19.8	30.5	37.7	40.7	23.6	25.8	20.0
	(27.2)	(27.7)	(22.8)	(39.2)	(50.6)	(53.1)	(33.4)	(37.4)	(37.8)
Natives of native parentage	19.6	8.2	5.3	39.3	18.7	11.1	41.2	34.2	18.8
	(23.0)	(9.2)	(6.1)	(50.5)	(25.1)	(14.5)	(58.4)	(49.6)	(35.5)
Subtotal, Inmarriage	84.7	89.4	86.7	77.8	74.5	76.6	70.6	68.9	52.9
	(100.0)	(100.0)	(100.0)	(100.0)	(100.0)	(100.0)	(100.0)	(100.0)	(100.0)
Foreign or mixed stock:									
Hispanic	2.0	3.7	3.4	0.5	2.6	2.6	0.8	0.7	1.2
Other, Outmarriage	13.3	6.9	9.9	21.7	22.9	20.8	28.6	30.4	45.9
Total	100.0	100.0	100.0	100.0	100.0	100.0	100.0	100.0	100.0
(N)	(444)	(379)	(263)	(973)	(546)	(307)	(1,280)	(302)	(85)

Note: Percentages in parentheses are based on endogamous marriages only.

How can we explain why younger Mexican Americans are as likely to marry exogamously as are older persons? It is possible that the younger people are more antitraditionalist in their orientation than the older persons. One piece of data supports this contention. Preliminary results from field surveys show the prescriptive age of marriage for men to be rather high in this population. This would argue that the young are departing from the norms of the community. It is possible also that other studies which found the rate of exogamy to rise with age dealt with groups where the prescriptive age for marriage is low, where those who defer marriage until economically and socially established are antitraditionalist in their lives. One might also suggest that the opportunities for wide contacts and social mobility are much greater among the young. Our cross-sectional study captures persons in different age brackets. Thus, the twenty-one-year-old Mexican American marrying an Anglo in 1963 may have had quite different experiences from the thirty-one-year-old person marrying a Mexican-born bride in the same year. Relationships with the larger Anglo society have changed considerably in the past decade.

Implications

At the outset, we stated that our paper had two purposes. The first was addressed to the probable future of a particular population — the Mexican Americans. We feel that our findings strongly suggest the assimilative potential of the population when external barriers are comparatively low, though this potential has been generally depreciated. We must not, of course, make the mistake of confusing a cross-sectional three-generational study with a longitudinal study; the internal differences in endogamy rates imply that the assimilative potential is related to nativity and rate of advancement in the group, and both of these may shift.

We also feel that this anlaysis strongly supports the responsiveness of Mexican Americans, along with other ethnic groups, to milieu — that is, to variations in both prejudice and opportunities, which themselves are associated.

More generally, these data can be interpreted as indicating underlying processes which occur in the breakdown of mechanical solidarity in an increasingly open system. Mexican Americans have been unusual in maintaining strong ethnic boundaries, in part because of many isolating mechanisms associated with their initial contact with Anglo populations. These mechanisms include the structural and emotional effects of two wars fought with neighboring Mexico within a hundred years, both of which impinged particularly heavily upon Texas, an area that still contains a large proportion of the nation's Mexican Americans. General "race" prejudice and severe educational and work segregation have been still other factors. The population is also quite segregated by religion. That is, Catholicism is the prevailing faith in a predominantly Protestant region. However, Catholic *practice* is far less equivocal in the Los Angeles area. Less than half of the marriages considered here, for example, were validated by Catholic ceremony. There is evidence that in other regards as well the religious practice of this population in the country falls far short of the Catholic norms. The population is also segregated by residence, both in rural and urban areas. In New Mexico, even more stringent historical and political circumstances have insured little contact with the surrounding Anglo population; the high endogamy found in Albuquerque is not surprising, despite the fact that the "Spanish" population is actually older than the relatively "new" white settlers from the East and North.

These kinds of isolating experiences were historically accompanied by considerable — almost exclusive — reliance on kin as principal sources of emotional and other support and also by considerable similarity in outlook and style of life. However, the extent of this isolation is generally declining — though only slightly in some parts of the Southwest, more substantially in others, like Los Angeles.

As isolation declines and as both upward and horizontal mobility become more common, there come to be many more varieties in style of life. Most important, primary-group relations decline in functional importance and they even cease to be maintained mechanically, that is, by style of life. Thus, the socializing and identity-maintaining structures of the ethnic group — and particularly the family — are structurally weakened. Intrafamily dissimilarity increases.

This kind of interpretation seems applicable in our case especially to the third-generation families living in the relatively open opportunity structure of the type found in Los Angeles, and helps explain their notable propensity toward assimilative marriage (whereas if ethnic loyalty were maintained, the generation of partner would have little relevance). Increased experience in the larger system — especially rewarding experience — decreases the saliency of the ethnic group as the prime source of identity, in turn weakening the control of the primary group over the social relations of its members. Ascriptive identity decreases in salience.

The particular history of this population warrants further exploration on this and other topics; the peculiar blend of minority and ethnic statuses provides an especially fertile ground for the development of hypotheses concerning the combined effects of a variety of social differences. This study, based on the severely limited data available in marriage licenses, appears to call for increased attention to the group not only as a social problem but as a sociological problem of interest.

SOCIAL AND POLITICAL BEHAVIOR

SOCIAL AND POLITICAL BEHAVIOR

The social interaction occurring within any group is a significant factor in its total ethos and may have much to do with the "tone" of a subculture, as seen by both insiders and outsiders. Part of the stereotypes held by one group about another — or by members of the group about themselves — are predicated upon observations of social interaction. For example, the Zuni are characterized by most people who have studied them as non-violent, purposefully cooperative, and opposed to conflict. New England Yankees speak of themselves, and are spoken of by others, as being highly independent in thought and action. Mormons generally are considered by their neighbors as hard-working, religious, and cooperative with each other to the point of clannishness. Such generalizations, derived from within and without the group in question, invariably have exceptions. If they are proper generalizations, however, they will be more often correct than incorrect.

Those from within and without the Mexican American group who attempt to characterize their social and political behavior into generalizations do not always agree, but usually the differences in description relate to degree rather than to kind and are the type that represent continuous rather than discrete variation. Many specialists agree that Chicanos tend to be more personal in their social relations than Anglos; that they tend to become more emotionally and partisanly involved in issues or differences of opinion; that often they take a narrower "I and mine" outlook as compared to a broader "we—group" outlook. They tend, comparatively, to be disputacious and argumentative, and as a result their friendship patterns are likely to be comparatively deep and narrow and especially important with the family. They have comparative difficulty in setting up viable organizations that are both strong and enduring. They are politically fragmented and, despite frequent and eloquent talk of devotion to *la raza* rarely are able to unite in large numbers behind a leader, a political candidate, or an organization. A verifiable political consequence is the extreme scarcity of Mexican American elected officials, even in areas where the Mexican American population is large or a majority. A successful but cynical Anglo politician, who lived in a county whose population was over half Spanish-speaking, told the author, "As long as they don't outnumber us more than two to one, we'll usually win."

251

Studying the current scene, one is tempted to say that what Chicanos lack in organization they make up for in enthusíasm. This may be true in the case of social organizations whose major purpose is achieving satisfying interpersonal relations or helping support one's ego. Yet even in this context one can observe real political campaigns for the officerships of Spanish-speaking "knife and fork" clubs, whereas in most Anglo clubs such elections are a matter either of "passing around" the offices or of finding people who are both capable and willing to accept the positions, which persons, after a nominating committee's report, commonly are elected unanimously and immediately.

The most prominent Mexican American organizations include the old and powerful League of United Latin American Citizens (LULAC), the G.I. Forum, the Political Association of Spanish-Speaking Organizations (PASO or PASSO), the Mexican American Political Association (MAPA), the Community Service Organization (CSO), and student organizations such as the Mexican American Student Association (MASA), the Mexican American Youth Organization (MAYO), and the United Mexican American Students (UMAS).

One fact is very clear. The "new Chicano," often but not necessarily youthful, is convinced of the need for political participation; he is an activist; he sees organizations as essential to achieving his own goals and those he has for *la raza.* He dislikes to admit it, but he has learned a great deal from Black militants, many of whose tactics he has copied with both greater and lesser success. To use a proverb, the older Mexican Americans disliked being aggressive, being a "squeaky wheel." The "new Chicano" is aggressive and believes that only by being a "squeaky wheel" will he get any "grease." The selections which follow point out clearly both the older, folk pattern, and the newer, urban pattern, the latter undoubtedly demonstrating the trend of the future political and social activity of Mexican Americans.

"Perceptions of Social Relations" is an edited chapter from the book *Across the Tracks* by anthropologist Arthur E. Rubel. In this chapter Dr. Rubel describes social relations among Chicanos in a South Texas border city. The folk Mexican culture is still strong, and the people are not yet assimilated into urban or Anglo culture. He finds anxiety and disaffection common. The nuclear household is seen as a refuge from the threatening larger society and the chief unit through which to pursue social and economic ends. The *palomilla* is a network of dyadic relationships serving emotional and psychic ends. The high degree of personalism in the Chicano social system is the major difference between it and the Anglo social system, as well as the chief source of the anxiety and disaffection found in Chicano social interaction.

Paul Sheldon, a prominent sociologist, in "Mexican American Formal Organizations," speaks generally of Chicano organizations and describes several specific groups, mostly in California. He reports on the ephemeral nature of many smaller organizations, the personalization of organizations as a weakness, and the problems caused by lack of funds, diffuseness and variation in activities and goals, and fragmentation.

Because Mexican Americans are becoming "news," and because the Anglo majority often is not up-to-date on the conditions of that group, *The Atlantic Monthly* commissioned Helen Rowan to summarize recent Chicano history and conditions, and to shed some light on their recent militancy. This, Miss Rowan does in the selection "A Minority Nobody Knows." She reports that Mexican Americans are increasingly an urban people, despite the focus on Cesar Chavez and the farm-labor strike and grape boycott. They are politically disorganized, partly because the nebulous quality of discrimination permits some Mexican Americans to move into the Anglo middle class. Considering their size and concentration, they have very little elected representation, and do not demonstrate the likelihood of any immediate change. For the future, one of the worst influences is the uniformly poor education and counseling which Mexican American children receive.

Some insight into the political situation in the Mexican American community can be gained from the findings of the selection by George Rivera, Jr., "Recognition of Local-Cosmopolitan Influentials in an Urban Mexican American Barrio." He reports that with one exception no cosmopolitan influential and only three local influentials were even recognized by over 50% of a representative sample from a Houston barrio. Real influence, of course, is far less than mere recognition. There is leadership in the Mexican American community but it tends to be local.

Not always have Mexican Americans shunned demonstrations and violence, and a small but increasing minority of young Chicanos are self-consciously militant. One of the largest "incidents" occurred in 1968 in East Los Angeles, involving high school and college students and drop-outs. Two selections describe this phenomenon, Dial Torgerson's " 'Brown Power' Unity Seen Behind School Disorders," and "Uprising in the Barrios" by Charles A. Ericksen. Both articles describe the new militancy in general, and analyze specifically the high school walkouts, and the extreme militancy of the Brown Berets. The focus of this particular militancy is education, where the situation of Mexican American students is demonstrably bad. The great majority of the militants are young, and "have-nots," which in no way differentiates them from other minority militants. Like other young militants they are more sophisticated in "revolution" than their predecessors of ten or twenty years ago.

For several years some of the Mexican American top leadership have sought a White House Conference on Mexican Americans. In this they have not yet been successful, but in 1967, in El Paso, a large, federally sponsored Conference took place. It was addressed by dozens of Mexican Americans, each with a special point-of-view or topic. An equal number of Mexican Americans opposed the Conference vocally or in print. In the lengthy article "La Raza—Today not Manana," Armando Rendon, associate editor of the *Civil Rights Digest* presents the background of this Conference, and the opposition to it. He reports on the La Raza Unida Conference held independently but at the same time and city. He describes various Mexican American organizations and their recent roles. Finally, he presents in summary the gist of most of the hearing statements, a summary available in this form in no source other than the selection which follows.

PERCEPTIONS OF SOCIAL RELATIONS:
A COMPARATIVE ANALYSIS*

ARTHUR J. RUBEL

Numerous observers report that Mexican Americans attach qualities of anxiety and disaffection to their perceptions of social relations, and Mexican Americans themselves state — and deplore — this as a common characteristic, something so frequent it almost seems inherent. An excellent illustration is the folk tale about the Mexican shepherd who astutely discovers the principle of the steam engine only to meet death at the hands of his envious neighbors. One finds the constantly recurring theme that Chicanos cannot get along with one another, that neighbors are against one. This theme is expressed in a number of diverse ways ranging from accusations that Chicanos do not want others to succeed in school or business to a fear of neighbors and strangers as agents of such dangerous illnesses as *mal de ojo* and *mal puesto.*

No attempt is made here to evaluate the truth of the deposition by Chicanos to the effect that they are more disputatious than other people, or that a Chicano cannot in fact maintain a viable partnership or work crew with one or more other Chicanos, or that any success on the part of an individual incurs negative sanctions from his friends and neighbors. (For the record, I found these Chicanos a thoroughly likeable, friendly group of individuals.) Those are problems which lend themselves to the experimental techniques of the social psychologist, not to the methodology which was employed in this study. My effort here is to provide an anthropological explanation of why these Chicanos perceive social relations in a framework where anxiety and disaffection are prominent features. Finally, no claim is advanced that the following interpretation is definitive. The ethnographic data remain ready at hand for colleagues who find another explanation more cogent and economical.

To begin, the distributional patterns of anxiety and disaffection have several interesting facets. In the first place, they appear in association

*Rubel, Arthur J., *Across the Tracks,* Austin, University of Texas Press, 1966, Chapter 8.

with relationships between an individual and persons who are not members of his nuclear family, but not between family members. Two illustrations of this skewed distribution adequately demonstrate this fact. In the preceding chapter it was determined that although anyone, inclusive of members of the same household, is believed capable of inflicting *mal de ojo* on another, there appears not a single instance in which victim and agent are members of the same household. The same can be said of the data on *mal puesto*, from which it is learned that whereas the relevant belief system assumes that every Chicano individual is considered capable of deliberately causing harm to another by means of witchcraft, in actual fact none of the case histories include an accusation by one member of a nuclear family against another. Anxieties associated with conceptions of these two folk illnesses seem clearly to demarcate the nuclear family as an individual's basic security unit, from which he peers out at an unpredictable world.

Secondly, individualistic anxiety and disaffection are never attached to Chicano-Anglo relationships. A Chicano never presumes an Anglo to have inflicted *mal de ojo* or *mal puesto* on himself, or a member of his household. Nor does a Chicano aver that in the very nature of things a Chicano cannot maintain a viable working relationship with an Anglo or that "Anglos are against *one*." When discord arises between an Anglo and a Chicano the latter attributes it to the nature of intergroup relations which obtain in this region. For example, a Chicano employee fired from his job by a Chicano supervisor perceives the action as simply one more example of the inability of Chicanos to work together, one additional bit of evidence that in the very nature of things Chicanos are pitted against one another. If the very same man were to be discharged by an Anglo supervisor, he would interpret it as proof of the thesis that the Anglo group has its foot "on our necks," in other words the Anglos as a group are perceived as intent on maintaining the Chicano group in a subordinate' role.

In either instance, the end result is that a Chicano's perception of his nuclear family household as a place of security is strengthened and, to the same degree, his understanding of the larger society as threatening receives support. The depiction by Chicanos of the nuclear family household as a place of security and, contrarywise, an observed prominence of anxiety and disaffection which attaches to extrafamilial relationships suggests the utility of assuming an association between the type of social system which orders behavior in Mexiquito and the prominence of the emotional qualities now being discussed. Accordingly, a brief summary of the important organizing features of this social system follows.

Briefly, the social system may be described in terms of three major organizing features. First, a Chicano thinks of his nuclear family as the only formally organized unit in terms of which he should pursue economic and social ends. Outside the family the male Chicano has his palomilla, but this aggregation serves emotional rather than instrumental ends. The activities in which a palomilla engages and the information communicated between participants are not such that assist an individual in earning a living, acquiring a wife, or caring for his family.

A palomilla is best conceptualized as a network of informal dyadic relationships, some of which may be formalized by initiation of ritual kinship (*compadrazgo*) bonds. Thus, the second major organizing principle of this social system is that relationships beyond the range of the family are between one individual and another, rather than between an individual and a *group* of others.

Third, relationships between a Chicano and others are characterized by a high degree of personalism. Probably, if one were to seek one single principle by which to contrast most markedly the Chicano social system and its Anglo counterpart it would be the extent to which the former seeks to invest his social activities with personal characteristics and the opposite tendency by those who live South of the tracks.

The above sketch of Mexiquito's social system, suggests that it evolved over a period of time to function most efficiently under circumstances in which members of the society knew personally most of those with whom they came into contact, and nuclear families were self-sufficing and independent — economically, socially, and spatially. Needless to add, the densely populated neighborhood of Mexiquito and the fact that every Chicano inhabitant is required to work for or with others in pursuit of a livelihood makes this kind of system maladaptive and dysfunctional.

Moreover, the presence of a very considerable populace of Anglo-Americans, who control economic, political, and social resources for which Chicanos strive, and whose own social system contrasts sharply with the one described above, exacerbates the difficulty encountered by Chicanos as they attempt to secure valued goals by means of social techniques which are maladaptive.

Because most Anglo-Americans in the city and the lower Rio Grande Valley are members of Protestant Churches, they are not amenable to the establishment of formal godparental relationships, an instrumental technique so important a part of the Chicano's society. And, the ability of Chicanos to control their social environment in strategic ways is even further diminished by the almost total prohibition by the dominant Anglos of intergroup marriages.

Finally, there is the question of whether Chicanos may join Anglo social groups and thereby manipulate the behavior of them to their own satisfaction. In fact, many religious, secular, and fraternal groups in New Lots' Anglo society remain closed to Chicanos. In a total of more than fifty secular groups, five have small proportions of Chicano members, none of whom hold leadership positions.

The tendency of Anglos to form organized groups in order to carry out tasks for common needs, their essentially impersonal approach to social relations, and their unresponsiveness to the social techniques which derive from kinship and personal relationships of the Chicanos make extremely difficult any effort of the latter to gain from the former the social and economic goals to which they strive.

It is now hypothesized that the anxious and disaffective qualities which are so apparent in Mexiquito may be understood as a function of the incongruity which obtains between the atomistic social system for which the Chicanos are socialized and the wider and far more complex society with which they must *really* contend. That is, during the course of growing up a Chicano is taught to act as if there were no solidary ties required between his family unit and the remainder of the society. It is as if one were trained to interact only with close relatives and yet, realistically, social circumstances require individuals and their families to adapt their needs to those of other individuals and groups not members of their own family unit. The hypothesis argues that the incongruity between their expectations and the reality with which they must cope gives rise to anxiety and disaffection. Moreover, as the materials which follow indicate, the hypothesized relationship between an atomistic social system and a prominence of anxiety and disaffection may be extended to other Mexican-American societies in the lower Rio Grande Valley, as well as to some societies which are historically unrelated to Mexiquito.

Because social systems remarkably like Mexiquito's exist in societies otherwise unrelated to this neighborhood, and inasmuch as they recur in association with a prominence of anxiety and disaffection, I am prompted to write of a type of society which is atomistic. An atomistic-type society is here defined as one in which the social system is characterized by an absence of cooperation between nuclear families; in which qualities of contention, invidiousness, and wariness are paramount in the perceptions which nuclear families hold of one another.

In construction of such a cross-cultural type of society, reference is made to three criteria:

1.   A cross-cultural type is characterized by selected features rather than by its total element content.

2.   The selection of diagnostic features must be determined by the problem and the frame of reference.

3.   The selected features are presumed to have the same functional interrelationships with one another in each case.

Unlike Steward, however, I do not conceive of these interrelationships as of a cause-and-effect nature, but, rather, as correlates of one another, or "adhesions" as E.B. Tylor phrased it. Neither need one follow Steward in stressing economic factors as necessarily possessing the status of independent variables in such correlations.

In order to avoid a major pitfall of comparative research, I selected several societies which share with Mexiquito a prominence of anxiety and disaffection, but which do not share history, economic base, or acculturation pressures with this south Texas neighborhood.

However, rather than attempt to compare a single settlement of Mexican-Americans with such broad spectrums as, for example, Italian and Algonkian ways of life, it will be shown that the fundamental features of social life in Mexiquito recur in other Mexican-American settlements. Furthermore, studies of several towns in widely separated areas of Latin America show that the covariance of the type of social system characteristic of Mexiquito and a prominence of anxiety and disaffection is not restricted to the United States-Mexico border regions; quite the contrary.

Other Mexican-American Settlements
Frontera

While I was doing field work in New Lots, another anthropologist, Dr. Octavio Romano, was studying the people of Frontera, Texas. This village is located approximately twenty-five miles west of New Lots, and the two settlements have a great deal in common.

Frontera was founded early in this century by refugees from the unsettled, revolution-torn states of Nuevo León and Tamaulipas in northeastern Mexico. A few were native-born citizens of the United States. The refugees were attracted to Frontera by employment opportunities for unskilled workers in construction and land-clearing operations. Those who settled Frontera were Spanish-speaking and Roman Catholic. Thus, the historical and cultural roots of Frontera and Mexiquito are similar.

In some other aspects, though, Frontera is unlike Mexiquito. In the former live several hundred Mexican-Americans. Immediately adjacent to the unincorporated village is the home of an Anglo family. By contrast, Mexiquito's population comprises more than nine thousand Chicanos who live in an incorporated municipality, which is also home for six thousand Anglos. Despite the demographic dissimilarities, the relations of each Chicano populace to Anglos is similar. In Frontera the Anglo family owns and manages the principal source of Chicano employment, and in Mexiquito all major sources of employment are controlled by Anglos. In each settlement Chicano society is therefore dominated by its Anglo counterpart.

Romano's description of social behavior in Frontera is in substantial accord with my findings in Mexiquito. There, also, a Chicano finds security only within his immediate family; he withdraws from interaction with others. Romano finds recurrent the isolation of individuals from nonkindred and, with a single exception, the absence of groups larger than the isolated nuclear family. A mutual benefit society includes a number of adult males, but its meetings and procedures are consistently rent by dispute and disaffection. The life history of an average Chicano of Frontera shows an employment record notable for its inconstancy. According to Romano, its unusually high labor turnover is caused by distrust of the employer and a fear that the latter is taking advantage of his employee.

The social system of Frontera includes only one intense, consensual bond, that of the *amigo de confianza,* but even then, it is said: "Your friend today may be your enemy tomorrow."

A great amount of verbal communication is devoted to duelling, and the most innocent conversation in Frontera is feared; it may contain innuendos designed to cast doubt on the virility or social competencies of the other.

The quality of social relations, aside from those binding close kin, is characterized by features of threat and anxiety. Outside the kindred " . . . the most basic premise which governs behavior holds that the world is fickle and undependable." Human relations are acted out in an ambient of generalized distrust and defensiveness. For example, in a rare moment of cooperation, funds were collected among residents for construction of a Frontera church. To guard against pilferage and misappropriation, three treasurers were appointed. So regnant was mistrust of others, that the designation of three guardians was not enough to prevent quick dissolution of the movement.

The socioculturally mobile in Frontera are beset by a concern for the opinion of others; a fear of invidious sanction pervades the atmosphere. More severe invidiousness is presumed to be transformed into witchcraft, which is considered to be an instrumentality of the envious. Similar attitudes are recorded in Mexiquito.

Border City

Ozzie Simmons describes social life in another Chicano society of Hidalgo County, focusing his attention on the relationship between a dominant Anglo group and subordinate Chicanos. Simmons' material includes valuable observations of the social system and ethos of Chicanos in Border City. The Chicanos he describes from the majority of the population of a city of approximately twenty thousand people, Chicanos and Anglos.

The history of Border City is very much like that of New Lots; each was founded on a site hacked out of a thornbrush forest. The cities were constructed to service irrigated Anglo farms which were developed at the turn of the century. Each locality was settled by Mexican-Americans and by Anglo-Americans. The former were attracted to the new cities by opportunities of employment as unskilled laborers. Most were emigrants from the northern Mexican states of Tamaulipas and Nuevo León seeking refuge from the insecurities of a region beset by furies of revolution and drought. The Anglo population was composed mostly of Americans and Candians induced by salesmen to purchase lands in the newly developed tracts. With very few exceptions, the Anglos did not speak Spanish, nor were the laborers competent in English. The former were members of Protestant churches, the latter Roman Catholics.

Today the situation in Border City remains basically the same, although a large proportion of the Mexican-American population is bilingual, and many of the Chicanos are engaged as professionals in medicine, the ministry, and education. Another sector of the contemporary Chicano population is successful in commerce. Despite the fact that Border City's occupational status hierarchy is relatively open, and many Chicanos are socially mobile, personal interaction between members of the two ethnic groups is limited. For example, intergroup courtship or marriage is rare, and they are discouraged.

Simmons describes the Chicano society as home-centered. The father-husband dominates the household, presenting a rigid, gruff, and authoritative figure to the others. The mother is idealized as a nurturant and self-effacing person. The world of the Border City Chicanos is described as extremely personal, where egos are easily hurt by the slightest criticism, and insults are remembered forever. Simmons also writes that extrakin relations are brittle and easily broken.

Demographic features in Frontera on the one hand, Mexiquito and Border City on the other, are dissimilar. Moreover, the inaccessibility of powerful Anglos in the larger towns contrasts with the situation in Frontera. Nevertheless, social life in the societies seems quite uniform. The recurrence of behavior patterns and themes permits one to make some general statements about social life of Chicanos in the lower Rio Grande Valley.

In Chicano society individuals are ranked, some higher than others. No matter how highly ranked a Chicano, he is subordinate to Anglos. In Mexiquito, members of the formerly prestigious, landed families are referred to sardonically as *los tuvos* — those who once had. Elsewhere, as well, the ranking system of the Mexican-Americans is overshadowed by the dominance of the Anglo-Americans.

Until 1940 the great majority of Mexican-Americans were occupied as unskilled and semiskilled workers. They worked in fields of produce or citrus, in canning and processing plants, and in heavy construction. Occupation is today emerging as an important criterion which ranks intragroup and intergroup status. An increasing number of younger Chicanos in Mexiquito and Border City are employed in professional and white-collar tasks. The pattern is emergent in Frontera to a lesser extent.

In the two larger settlements achieved occupational status with its requisite antecedents — formal educatioon and English-language skills — emerges as an ascendant criterion in the social-status system. In Frontera, ascribed status based on sex, age, and the power to dispense favors, remains unquestionably paramount.

In spite of the apparently immutable restrictions on intergroup marriage, and the barring of Chicanos from membership in a number of fraternal and religious organizations, the social system of the region, or any one of its component towns, remains relatively open. The next few years will determine whether, in fact, equivalence of income, occupation, and English-language competencies generate a true open-class system, or whether ascribed ethnic characteristics will remain ascendant criteria of social rank. If the latter condition prevails, one foresees a nativistic response by upwardly mobile Chicanos. If the former condition emerges as the dominant criterion, Chicano energies will be devoted to attainment of superior status in the system of social stratification.

No settlement in the Valley exists as a unit isolated from the total society. Residents are attached to others outside of the settlements, together with all other Chicanos they comprise the *chicanazgo*. The *chicanazgo* perceives itself a solidary unit vis-à-vis Anglos. But, the Chicano residents of any specified settlement such as Mexiquito, for example, do *not* perceive themselves as an unique unit vis-à-vis Chicanos of other towns, Border City, for example. Absent is any indication that Chicanos of Border City, Mexiquito, or Frontera feel allegiance or loyalty to the town in which they reside. In each town the presence of a superordinate Anglo society creates a sense of solidarity among the Mexican-American residents, where none would have existed otherwise. Anglo-Chicano conflict erects boundary-maintenance devices around the Chicano villages and quarters. Remove the Anglos from the region and the Chicanos' sense of in-gruop solidarity would disappear. The perception of a community as deserving of allegiance or loyalty is alien to the Mexican-Americans. The Chicano confines his loyalties to his narrow and shallow kin group.

In Chicano society the nuclear family stands forth clearly and distinctly. The loyalties of the Chicanos are home-centered. Ties which bind him to his nuclear family also bind him to its locality. All decisions are subject to the approval of the male head of the household. Among Chicanos, "The older order the younger and the men the women."

In a household in which a father-husband is absent, the oldest son substitutes. Early in life the children commence to learn their sex-typed roles.

In both Mexiquito and Frontera the palomilla engages much of the time of a virile member of society, but none of his loyalties. Palomillas are a logical product of complementary congeries of values, which provide behavioral expectations for young men. Values which govern behavior in the home proscribe frivolous activities such as dancing, smoking, drinking, and levity. Verbal expression of those behaviors are frowned on. Yet other values direct a youth to validate his manhood at every opportunity; virility and its proper expression are extolled. The participation in palomillas of youthful males enables such validation while preserving the sanctity of the home. No matter what the extent of his interaction with a palomilla, a young husband retains and exercises effective control of family affairs. At approximately forty years of age, a Chicano diminishes the frequency of his interaction with a palomilla, and engages more actively in the management of household affairs.

In Romano's description of Frontera, social life is depicted as remarkably similar to that of Mexiquito. Likewise, Simmons' observations of Chicano life in Border City contribute to a generalization: Social behavior of Mexican-Americans in the lower Rio Grande Valley is organized in small units, of which the nuclear family is of overwhelming importance, and relationships outside the family are arranged by means of dyadic relations based on personal esteem of the parties involved. Interaction between adults is characterized by a high evaluation of the autonomy of the individual, a factor associated with the reported brittleness of nonfamilial social relations. Each case reports anxious feelings attached to relations between Chicanos not members of the same household; in Frontera and Mexiquito there is reported to be an important quality of disaffection. From Border City, Simmons reports a tendency to withdraw from interpersonal relations and to seek safety in the haven of the home, but one does not receive an impression of the degree of threat and danger impinging the Chicanos of Border City as is reported from Frontera and Mexiquito.

It has been suggested that in a society whose members strive to achieve valued goals by means of incongruous instrumental behavior, qualities of disaffection and anxiety will be prominent. More specifically it was suggested that such qualities appear in association with participation by individuals who have been socialized in an atomistic social system but who are seeking to achieve highly evaluated goals, which are controlled by individuals not members of the nuclear family.

Simmons proposes an alternative explanation, offering distrust generated in a fragile ego as an antecedent variable. He hypothesizes that in Border City the ease and regularity with which social relations are fractured depends on the sensitivity of the adult ego. In Border City, writes Simmons, adult egos are hurt quickly by the slightest criticism, and insults are remembered forever. He postulates that brittleness of relationships is a consequence of fragile egos which, in turn, are caused by discontinuity during socialization. In infancy and early childhood a youngster is the center of attention in a Chicano home in Border City, and Simmons describes those places as infant-centered. After the first years of childhood a father's relations with his child changes from warm affection to brusqueness and coolness. A similar developmental sequence is noted in Mexiquito. If Simmons' explanation of the connection between the ethos and the social system characteristic of Border City is acceptable, then it also serves to explain the connection between the two in Mexiquito.

First, Simmons' post-factum explanation is reasonable and credible, although it contains several difficulties. One of these lies in his contention of a discontinuity in the relationship between a father and his children in Border City; I have noted the same phenomenon in Mexiquito, but there discontinuity is confined to the bond between the father and his child, and does not seem to extend to others of the family. Furthermore, quite unlike her brother, a girl is not thrust into a presumably hostile world outside the home where she would be expected to fend for herself; just the reverse. In each of the respective populations, relations between a child and its mother, or its female siblings, is *not* characterized by discontinuity. Indeed Simmons describes Chicano children in Border City as carried everywhere by their mother or older sisters. The warmth of the relationship between a mother and her children is readily observed and endures over many years. Although there is no quarrel with Simmons' observations of the relationship obtaining between a father and his child, the observed *continuity* in the socialization of a child by its mother and sisters makes difficult a conclusion that discontinuity in socialization gives rise to generalized disaffection and a sense of unpredictability in social life.

It is discovered that although anxiety and disaffection are prominent features of perceptions of social relations, they are confined to relations between an individual and persons not members of his nuclear family. Consequently, a thesis is advanced that the anxiety and disaffection which recur with such frequency when Chicanos discuss their relationships with nonfamily are a function of the incongruity which exists between the family-oriented system for which Chicanos are socialized and the larger and far more complex society with which they must contend. It is argued that the prominence of anxiety and disaffection is functionally interrelated with what is denoted as an atomistic social system, both together forming a configuration described as an atomistic-type society.

An atomistic-type society is one in which the social system is characterized by an absence of cooperation between nuclear families; in which qualities of contention, invidiousness, and wariness are paramount in the perceptions which nuclear families hold of one another; and in which such behavior and emotional qualities are consonant with normative expectations.

Mexiquito is shown to be similar to the two other Mexican-American neighborhoods in the lower Rio Grande Valley. Nevertheless, despite the suggestiveness of the above relationships, the formulation proves not to be universally applicable. In another society — among the Parisian bourgeoisie — a prominence of anxiety and disaffection are not in evidence despite the presence of an atomistic social system, indicative of the presence of intervening variables which are still unknown. Continued research on this problem will enable researchers to factor out the particular intervening variables which modify the expectation that, in general, an incongruity between socialization toward one kind of society and the necessity to cope with very different circumstances, will be associated with a prominence of anxiety and disaffection.

MEXICAN AMERICAN FORMAL ORGANIZATIONS*

PAUL SHELDON

This paper represents part of a study carried out by the Laboratory in Urban Culture of Occidental College from 1961 to 1963 in the Los Angeles area. The main part of the study comprised approximately 300 interviews in depth.

There are scores of organizations whose membership and purposes are concerned with Mexican Americans. In 1961 the local Spanish language newspaper recorded 85, the published directory of the Health and Welfare Planning Council listed 47. The Council of Mexican American Affairs claimed 44 member organizations.

These include casual social organizations which give a dance or two a year, perhaps for the benefit of an orphanage in Mexico, and sickness and burial societies which may collect dues as the need arises, for example fifty cents from each member when a death occurs. There is a Mexican American Chamber of Commerce with a monthly publication. Several luncheon civic clubs meet in the areas of heavy Mexican American concentration, although the membership is mixed, frequently less than half Mexican American. One group meets weekly in a downtown hotel, alternating its name from the Table of Friendship to the Latin American Club depending on the week.

There are ephemeral clubs which organize, elect officers, plan a program and fund raising campaign, perhaps for scholarships, and somehow fail to survive the first year. In the field of fund raising there is at East Los Angeles College one of the oldest organizations, the Armando Castro Scholarship Fund, with some faculty leadership. Armando Castro was a student who was killed trying to stop a street fight between two local gangs.

At the present writing only two organizations have an office and a telephone. No Mexican American organization has a full time staff member promoting the welfare of this ethnic group. Leaders and club members express deep concern that there exist no effective organizations comparable to those financed and staffed by other ethnic groups

*Mimeographed article, April, 1964.

such as Jews, Japanese, and Negroes. There is no one organization which can speak authoritatively for the whole Mexican community. This became apparent in 1963 when the issue of cooperating with Oriental and Negro groups caused a public split among Mexican American leaders.

The larger and more stable organizations tend to be those formed since World War II, involving a high proportion of veterans and their wives. It is difficult to select representative groups, but the following accounts may give a picture of the nature of some of the current organizations. Because of the shifting and evanescent nature of the memberships, we are not concerned with the history and origins of each, but with its influence and activity at the time of the study.

The Council of Mexican American Affairs

The Council of Mexican American Affairs was founded in 1953 to represent a cross section of the Mexican American community. Its governing board consists of thirteen members at large and twelve representatives of the House of Delegates, which listed 44 member organizations. Some of these organizations are social, some are for veterans, some have community service programs. All have predominantly Spanish surname membership or orientation. It defines itself as a "non-partisan, non-sectarian and a non-profit citizens organizations dedicated to the development of leadership among Americans of Mexican descent and to the promotion of coordination of effort among all the various organizations and groups concerned with the betterment of the Mexican American in the Los Angeles region." The members are described as "interested individuals who are desirous of improving the social, economic, educational and cultural status of all persons of Mexican descent . . . and who want to contribute towards this goal their time, efforts and resources." They have included business, professional and labor leaders. In meetings and public pronouncements there has been constant emphasis on needs for cooperation, unity, and a better way of life. It was planned that the organization would be in a position to offer information and counseling services to the East Side community. Conferences were held on youth problems in relation to delinquency, narcotics, education, and jobs.

During the period of this study the organization maintained an office, a full time executive director, and a secretary. A fund raising campaign with a goal of $50,000 ($20,000 for educational scholarships) was under way. The campaign fell short of its quota, and the Council went heavily into debt. There was considerable discouragement and bitterness at this time. One officer stated that "too many Mexican American organizations are dedicated to the destruction of each other." During the period of discouragement, there was a high turnover of board members and officers. Disagreements about the plan of organization, lack of funds, and personal problems resulted subsequently in the closing of the office and the dismissal of the staff.

In 1963 there was a rebirth of interest and strength chiefly under the leadership of new board members and officers. Committees on scholarships, job opportunities and housing have been formed, but as of this writing the Council does not claim a mass base. Several of the former leaders in the Council of Mexican Affairs became prominent in other organizations such as the newly organized (1962) Educational Opportunities Foundation, whose interests include scholarships and fighting job discrimination.

Community Service Organization

The Community Service Organization, since 1947, has carried on an active campaign chiefly for and among Mexican Americans in the Southwest. Its national and local headquarters are housed in the same building in East Los Angeles. Technically non-political and non-partisan in terms of candidates, it has promoted registration of thousands of citizens of Mexican background, with a goal of 416,000 registrants of Spanish surname. The local office claims a membership of 2,000. Close ties are maintained with labor organizations. The intent is to unite the "sleeping giant" of California politics with other groups concerned to promote social action programs, including a minimum wage and medical service for migrant workers, investigation of incidents of police brutality, and unionization of migrant workers. The "C.S.O.," as it is known, considers the passage of the law making non-citizens eligible for Old Age Assistance one of its most significant triumphs. They have received assistance from labor organizations, churches, and several foundations, including the Industrial Areas Foundation, and have been able to keep a team of dedicated workers (Fred Ross, Cesare Chavez, Antonio Rios, Herman Gallegos) in the field on full or part time bases since the founding of the organization.

Their stated philosophy is to get all Americans of Mexican background to register, then to use this potential voting power to secure the passage of specific measures which will benefit all minority groups.

The American G.I. Forum

The American G.I. Forum is a national service organization of Mexican American veterans of World War II and of the Korean Conflict. It held its first California State Convention in Los Angeles in 1958. Active chapters are maintained in most of the local Mexican American communities in and around the Los Angeles area. It is a veteran's family organization with stated purposes that include "gaining first class citizenship through education" and the elimination of discrimination in all fields. Raising money for scholarships and working for fair employment practices have been major objectives. Activities have sometimes been diffuse under the motto "Education is our Freedom and Freedom should be Everybody's Business." The membership includes some of the men and women who are most active in all the Mexican American ethnic organizations in and near East Los Angeles.

Mexican American Political Association

The Mexican American Political Association was organized on a statewide basis in April, 1960 when 150 volunteer delegates gathered at Fresno, California. It was felt that a new organization and a new method were necessary to work for mutual betterment: "a non-partisan, statewide association that would be frankly political, and frankly Mexican-American." Using the slogan, "Opportunity for All Through M.A.P.A.," the following objectives were presented:

To seek the social, economic, cultural and civic betterment of Mexican-Americans and other persons sympathetic to our aims,

To take stands on political issues and present and endorse candidates for public office,

To launch voter registration drives throughout California,

To encourage increased activity within the political parties.

In practice the activities were chiefly the support of the election and appointment of Mexican Americans to public office.

The forming of a national group known as "PASSO" (Political Association of Spanish Speaking Organizations) caused considerable controversy and confusion, since the latter included Puerto-Ricans, Cubans, and people of South American background. Officially, the 1961 MAPA state convention went on record as viewing with favor the affiliation with the national group.

It is difficult to assess the effectiveness of this association, MAPA, but it was active in the campaigns which were conducted on an ethnic basis. The success of a Mexican American slate in taking over the government of Crystal City, Texas, was considered as an encouraging omen for the MAPA type of program.

The total picture presented by Mexican American organizations in the Los Angeles area suggests that the number of active ethnic leaders is small compared to that among other ethnic groups. In our interview sample of men considered active in the community, 89 per cent were members of at least three organizations. The significance of multiple memberships and activities remains to be analyzed for our larger samples.

In the reporting of meetings in the local press, the same names seem to appear regardless of the title of the organization. At a leadership conference held under the auspices of the County Commission on Human Relations in the fall of 1963, it was the consensus that "We are not yet ready for an over-all coordinating council." This situation presents a confusing image to the larger community. People of good will on the Los Angeles School Board, for example, feel frustrated in their attempts to understand and to plan programs for the Mexican American districts. When an *ad hoc* committee was appointed to advise the Board, it was immediately attacked by *The Eagles,* a publication of one of the leaders of the Equal Opportunities Foundation, as unrepresentative and weak. When representatives of the National Urban League wanted to discuss cooperation in programs with their opposite numbers, it was not possible to hold a public meeting with Mexican American leaders.

In November 1963, when a conference with then vice president Johnson and Secretary of Health, Education, and Welfare Calabrezzi was held in Los Angeles, a larger segment of the Mexican American leadership boycotted the meetings and made plans for a separate meeting in 1964, partly because they felt that too much attention was being paid to other minority groups.

The same aggregate of fifty to one hundred names appear at the memorial dinners, the meetings of boards, the political promotion dinners. There are certain people who refuse to work or be on the same committees with certain others. There are many successful Mexican Americans who do not choose to be identified with any ethnic organization. Some of these are considering forming new, more conservative groups to improve their status.

These organizations are somewhat lacking in mobility but the mere fact of the existence of Anglo-type Mexican American young persons with dedicated leadership is in itself a phenomenon of recent years. It represents a breaking away from the traditional working class pattern of limited and only informal relationships outside of the extended family. Perhaps a phenomenon of the emerging middle class may also be related to acculturation, of growing awareness of methods needed to be effective in Urban Anglo society.

RECOGNITION OF LOCAL-COSMOPOLITAN INFLUENTIALS IN AN URBAN MEXICAN AMERICAN BARRIO*

GEORGE RIVERA, JR.

Since Robert K. Merton conducted his classic study of local-cosmopolitan patterns of influence, there has been much attention given to this area of analysis. Alvin W. Gouldner has utilized Merton's typology to study the orientations of college professors, and Joyce Ladner has focused her attention on the orientations of Black Americans toward Black leaders. However, Merton's typology has not been applied to Mexican Americans. Thus, this study will focus on the recognition of Mexican American local and cosmopolitan influentials in an urban barrio.

If at every stage of a social movement, the given social movement is dependent upon leaders, then a study of leadership patterns of influence might serve as one indicant of a movement's status. In retrospect, one can analyze the Black Movement in America as one which gained impetus only after cosmopolitan influentials appeared to lead the masses; thus, local influentials must be able either to break their ties of local orientation or to give way to changing leadership if their movement is to survive. It is from such a perspective that the Mexican American Movement should also be studied.

The neighborhood where this research project was conducted is known as Magnolia; it has a tradition of being the oldest ethnic enclave in Houston, Texas.

Magnolia was selected as a research site for the following reasons: (1) the area is a community which is exclusively Mexican American; (2) the area has well defined boundaries; (3) several generations of Mexican Americans live there; (4) the area is highly residential and noncommercial; (5) the majority of residents work in or near the community; (6) the community has great internal cohesion. In all respects, Magnolia is typical of urban Mexican American barrio life.

*This is an unpublished paper prepared for this publication in 1969. A simplified version of this paper was published in the Chicano Press Association newspaper, *Compass*, Volume III, Number 5, May, 1969.

Over two thousand Mexican American families live in the area. A twenty per cent regular interval sample was selected for study in the summer of 1967. Thus a sample of 415 heads of households were finally interviewed.

The Mexican American population of Magnolia had, in 1959, less education as well as less income than the total Houston population. Although there have been relative increases in income and education for Mexican Americans, the gap between the Mexican American and the Anglo remains the same; the forgotten people are still forgotten.

The respondents were given a list of Mexican American influentials and were asked whether or not they recognized the names. A brief description of each listed influential follows:

(1) Henry B. Gonzalez: A Mexican American Representative to the U.S. House of Representatives who is from San Antonio.

(2) Reyes Lopez Tijerina: A militant Mexican American from New Mexico who is attempting to recover land grants to Hispano citizens as specified in the Treaty of ·Guadalupe Hidalgo.

(3) Lauro Cruz: Area Representative to the State House who campaigned and established his headquarters in Magnolia.

(4) Roy Elizondo: A local Houstonian who is the state chairman of the Political Association of Spanish-Speaking Organizations (P.A.S.O.).

(5) Al Hernandez: A Mexican American Poverty Program official whose job includes serving local Mexican American poverty areas including Magnolia.

(6) Rev. Antonio Gonzalez: A local priest whose church was located in central Magnolia and who also was very active in the state's Valley March on Austin by South Texas farmworkers.

(7) Rev. James LaVois Novarro: A Local Baptist minister who monitors a Mexican American Baptist hour and who also was active in the state's Valley March on Austin.

(8) Frank Partida: A local resident who is a board member of a local Poverty Program and who also is the president of the

United Organizations Information Center (U.O.I.C.) created to represent city Mexican Americans.

(9) Ernest Nieto: A Mexican American Poverty Program official whose efforts have focused on the social problems of Magnolia.

(10) Ben Canales: A local Mexican American who is employed by the Legal Aid Agency to work with local Mexican Americans.

Recognition of influentials can be studied on a local-cosmopolitan classification (See Table 1).

Seven of the influentials were classified as "locals" because local Mexican American leadership, although sometimes obscured by temporary state involvement, was their prime role requirement and commitment. The remaining three influentials were classified as "cosmopolitans" because their major loyalty was not to the Mexican Americans of Magnolia, but rather to a multiplicity of communities beyond the barrio.

TABLE 1

Mexican American Influentials Classified
by Pattern Type of Orientation

Influential	Classification*
Henry B. Gonzalez	(C)
Reyes Lopez Tijerina	(C)
Lauro Cruz	(L)
Roy Elizondo	(C)
Al Hernandez	(L)
Rev. Antonio Gonzalez	(L)
Rev. James LaVois Novarro	(L)
Frank Partida	(L)
Ernest Nieto	(L)
Ben Canales	(L)

* Robert K. Merton's classification of "local" (L) and "cosmopolitan" (C) is used; the chief criterion for distinguishing the two is found in their orientation toward the local community or the greater society outside of the community.

TABLE 2

Influentials by Percentage Recognition

Influential	% Recognition
Lauro Cruz	66.1%
Rev. Antonio Gonzalez	64.9%
Henry B. Gonzalez	54.1%
Frank Partida	50.5%
Rev. James La Vois Novarro	44.0%
Al Hernandez	37.2%
Ernest Nieto	29.8%
Reyes Lopez Tijerina	27.6%
Ben Canales	21.1%
Roy Elizondo	20.0%

The percentage recognition in rank order is presented in Table 2.

Lauro Cruz, a local influential, received the highest percentage recognition (66.1%) and Roy Elizondo, a cosmopolitan influential, received the lowest percentage recognition (20.2%). With the exception of Henry B. Gonzales, those influentials with more than fifty per cent recognition were all locals in orientation. Reyes Lopez Tijerina and Roy Elizondo, both cosmopolitan in orientation, ranked very low in recognition by Magnolia residents.

In addition, the clergy which has, in the past, been the traditional leadership, ranked high in recognition (64.9% and 44.0%). Rev. Novarro's high rank might be indicative of Protestant trends in the Mexican American community. However, as is shown in Rev. Gonzalez' rank, Catholicism still has its hold on the barrio. It should also be noted that Federal Government employees tended to be ranked low in recognition which suggests that the local Poverty Program is not communicating with the barrio poor. Furthermore, the state chairman of the Political Association of Spanish-Speaking Organizations, Roy Elizondo, ranked very low in recognition. This might suggest that P.A.S.O.'S long mentioned middle class focus bypasses the needs of the barrio. Thus, the barrio lower class does not recognize its representative because he, as well as the organization, does not step into the barrio community where the masses are.

Although the findings of this study are only one index of the status of the Mexican American Movement, they are indicative of the continuing Chicano crisis. Though many writers seem to try to convince the public otherwise, these findings suggest, contrary to the literature on Mexican American leadership, that there *is* leadership in the Mexican American community. Leadership does exist even though it might be of local rather than cosmopolitan orientation.

The Mexican American Movement is strongly becoming *the* most crucial social movement; social change within the barrio is occurring rapidly as the movement gains momentum. Although the leadership trends suggest a high recognition of Mexican American local influentials, even this is constantly changing. With the advent of the Chicano Press Association, newspapers across the Southwest are exposing Mexican Americans to competent cosmopolitan leaders. With the growth of concerned, responsible leadership in the Mexican American barrio, the *patron* and the *jefe politico* may no longer have the power of exploitation; the "sleeping giant" is awakening.

"BROWN POWER" UNITY SEEN
BEHIND SCHOOL DISORDERS*

DIAL TORGERSON

"We want to walk out," a group of students at Lincoln High School told teacher Sal Castro last September. "Help us."

The students, like Castro, were Mexican-Americans — at a mostly Mexican-American school deep in the belt of east-of-downtown districts which together comprise the United States' most populous Mexican-American community.

"Don't walk out," Castro told them. "Organize."

And — as has now been seen — they did.

What resulted was a week-and-a-half of walkouts, speeches, sporadic lawbreaking, arrests, demands, picketing, sympathy demonstrations, sit-ins, police tactical alerts and emergency sessions of the school board.

It was, some say, the beginning of a revolution — the Mexican-American revolution of 1968.

In the midst of massive walkouts and police alerts, Dr. Julian Nava, only Mexican-American on the Los Angeles Board of Education, turned to Supt. of Schools Jack Crowther.

"Jack," said Nava, "This is BC and AD. The schools will not be the same hereafter."

"Yes," said Crowther, "I know."

First Mass Militancy

And, in the vast Mexican-American districts of the city and county of Los Angeles — the "barrios" (neighborhoods) where 800,000 people with Spanish names make their homes — leaders of a movement to unite what they call "La Raza" swear the barrios will never be the same, either.

Since World War II the Mexican-American community has had leaders calling for unity, change, better education, civil rights, eco-

Los Angeles Times, March 17, 1968, page 1, Section C.

279

nomic opportunity and an end to what they called second-class citizenship.

But the community never backed them up. Except for a few instances of picketing, nothing happened.

Then came the school walkouts, the first act of mass militancy by Mexican-Americans in Southern California. "Viva la Revolucion," the youngsters' signs read. "Viva la Raza." (Raza translates "race" but is used in a sense of "our people.")

And, surprisingly to some, stunningly to others, the community backed them up.

The men and women of the once-conservative older generation jammed school board and civic meetings, shouting their approval of what their children had done. Parents of students arrested during demonstrations even staged a sit-in in the Hall of Justice.

"The people are with us, now," one young leader says.

Observers within the community say it heralds the entry of a powerful new force on the American scene: a newly united Mexican-American movement drawing a nationalistic, brown-power fervor from 4.5 million people in five Southwestern states.

With underground newspapers, cooperation with Negro groups, plans for political action and economic boycotts, leaders say they will show the country a new type of Mexican-American: one proud of his language, his culture, his raza, ready to take his share of U.S. prosperity.

Some experts, less swept along in the spirit of the movement, say they'll wait a while before they'll believe a few thousand school children can lead the typically divided, splintered Mexican-American millions into becoming a unified power.

But there's no doubt at the grassroots levels, where earlier pleas for unity never reached before — in the minds of the younger men and women on the streets of the barrios, from East Los Angeles to Pico Rivera, from the fringes of Watts north deep into the San Gabriel Valley.

Listen to the voices there of La Raza — and the message observers say these voices bring to the Anglo world:

. . . the scene is a rainy sidewalk outside East Los Angeles Junior College. A white panel truck halts and four young men in brown berets and mixed, cast-off Army fatigues and boots jump out, craning their heads left and right to see if they are pursued, and then file into the campus for a meeting.

They are members of the Brown Berets, the most militant of East Los Angeles Mexican-American groups. They have been accused of inciting high school students to riots, using narcotics, being Communists. There are several hundred of them here and in the Fresno area, their leaders say.

Frankly Admiring Students

"The deputies and the cops have really been harassing us," said David Sanchez, a college student who dropped out to be chairman of the Berets. "Sixty-five Brown Berets have been arrested in the past month. There are warrants out now for five of us because of the school walkouts."

The four sit on a concrete bench and speak in quiet voices to a newsman, glancing at times down the wet, windswept walkway toward the street, nodding in reply to greetings from frankly admiring students with the slightly superior air of young men slightly past 20, slightly revolutionary, and slightly wanted.

"Communism? That's a white thing." said Carlos Montes, mustachioed minister of public relations for the Berets. "It's their trip, not ours," said husky Ralph Ramirez, minister of discipline. Added Montes:

"It's pretty hard to mix Communists and Mexican-Americans. Che (Che Guevara, the late Cuban revolutionary some Berets seem to seek to resemble) doesn't mean a thing to the guy in the street. He's got his own problems."

Despite their vaguely ominous look, the Berets claim wide community support. "A lot of mothers' clubs help us with contributions," said Sanchez. "Men's clubs, too. They're happy to see there is finally a militant effort in the community. And they like what we're doing with the gangs."

In each barrio there are kids' gangs (The Avenues, the Clovers, the White Fench, Dog Town, Happy Valley) which have long shot up each other, and whole neighborhoods, and senseless warfare.

"Gang fights are going out," said Montes. "We're getting kids from all the different gangs into the Brown Berets. It's going to be one big barrio, one big gang. We try to teach our people not to fight with each other, and not to fight with our blood brothers to the south."

Police say the Berets were among the "outside agitators" who helped cause the student disturbances. "The Chicano students were the main action group," said Sanchez. (Chicano is a term for Mexican-Americans which members of the community use in describing themselves.)

"We were at the walkouts to protect our younger people. When they (law officers) started hitting with sticks, we went in, did our business, and got out." What's "our business?" "We put ourselves between the police and the kids, and took the beating," Sanchez said.

Significance Explored

What significance lies behind the militant movement?

"They've given these people a real revolutionary experience," said Dr. Ralph Guzman, a professor of political science at Cal State Los Angeles. "No Marxist could do better. They're making rebels. When they see police clubbing them, it's the final evidence that society is against them — that existing within the system won't work."

"I don't know what's going to happen. I'm worried. I think there will be violence. I'm not predicting it. But from what I've seen — I saw riots in South America and India when I was with the Peace Corps — I think we all have a potential for violence."

. . . The scene is Cleland House, a community meeting hall in East Los Angeles. Two hundred people, most of them adults, jam the hall, facing representatives of police and the sheriff's and district attorney's office invited there by a civic group.

Student Gives Version

"We were at the alley, just breaking out, when the cops charged at us," said Robert Sanchez, 17, a student at Roosevelt High. "If I could be allowed to express myself with dignity, I'd do so. But if they're grabbing me, or hitting me, and there's a rock or a brick there, I'd throw it."

"The only reported injury," said Police Inspector Jack Collins, head of the patrol division, calmly, "was a police officer hit in the eye with a bottle . . . "

"Parents got beat up, too!" yelled a man's voice.

"Now try to get out of that one!" shouted Sanchez.

In an office, later, Lincoln High teacher Castro explained the walkouts:

Teacher Tells His Story

"It started with the kids from Lincoln," said Castro, 34 a social studies and government teacher who himself grew up in the East Los Angeles barrios. "They wanted things changed at the school. They wanted to hold what they call a 'blowout' — a walkout.

"I stopped them. I said, 'Blow out now and everyone will think it's because you want short skirts and long hair. Organize. What do you need?'

"They said they needed some help in making signs, printing up demands, things like that. We got them help from college kids — mostly from the United Mexican-American Students at the different colleges. A blowout committee was established at each of the four East L.A. schools. And there was one committee with kids from each school.

Original Plan

"The original plan was to go before the Board of Education and propose a set of changes, without walking out — to hold that back to get what they wanted. Then, at Wilson High Friday (March 1), the principal canceled a play they were going to do ("Barefoot in the Park") as unfit, and the Wilson kids blew out. It was spontaneous.

"Then Roosevelt and Lincoln wanted to blow, too. Garfield, too. Later on (March 8) Belmont, which was never in on the original plan, came in, too.

"These blowouts in the other schools, like Venice and Jefferson, weren't connected with the Chicano blowouts, but they may have been in sympathy. Some of the kids from schools uptown asked us to send representatives to tell them how to organize.

"What do you think of that! The Anglo schools asking the Chicano kids to help them organize. They should've told them 'Ask your dads how they organized to oppress us all these years.' "

Significance Weighed

And what significance lies behind the sudden surge of student activism?

"These things weren't thought up by the kids," said Philip Montez, western program director for the U.S. Commission on Civil Rights.

"Eight years ago the Council on Mexican-American Affairs was asking for bi-cultural education, one of the things the youngsters want now.

"But all attempts to move the community were abortive. Movements would start and peter out. We could never get a commitment. We were dealing with older people, conservative, with livings to make, kids to raise.

Up 'til now the Mexican-American community hasn't had the sophistication for organization or movement. But things are different now.

"The kids are close to being anglicized and middle class — which is apparently what it takes to bring them closer to being able to work a system. That's why they're the leaders.

Identity-Seeking

"Tied in with it is an identity-seeking process. These kids say proudly: 'I'm a Mexican, and I want to learn about my culture.' It used to be, when I was a kid, we'd play it pretty cool about that Mexican thing. Someone would say, 'Are you a Mexican?' and you'd say, 'Well, y'know . . . ' and change the subject, or make a joke.

"But the society has changed, too. Always before in the Mexican-American community there was a faith and belief in the Democratic society, that through good graces you'd achieve success. Be conservative. Family-oriented. Know God is on our side.

"But they don't believe it any longer. There's a higher level of sophistication. They don't want to sit around and wait. They see they've got to make it work. That you've got to grease the wheels of democracy.

"That's what the kids were doing when they walked out — and it caught the imagination of the adults. Now, for the first time, the community is behind them. And the adults are asking: 'Why did the kids have to show us why we make mistakes?' "

. . . The scene is Belmont High School, on the other side of the Civic Center from the East Los Angeles barrios. Only one-third of the students there have Spanish names, as compared with 90% of some Eastside schools. Yet Belmont, too, joined the demonstrations.

"I was arrested," said Frances Spector, 16, an A12 at Belmont who was charged with disturbing the peace. She has light brown hair and blue eyes, but feels strongly about the demonstrations — and what happened to her. "I was told to go home by a school official, and police stopped me on the street and put me in the police car. They said they were taking me home. But we went to the police station."

(Ten of the 15 persons arrested during the demonstrations were picked up during the Belmont walkout, in which police say outsiders played a large role: of the 10 arrested, 9 were nonstudents.)

View on Demands

How does she feel about the student demands?

"At Belmont," said Frances, "you look at the industrial arts classes, and it's all Chicano and black. You look at the college preparatory classes, and it's all Anglos and Asians.

"That can't be the way they really fit! They can't be getting the right counseling. They're just putting people where they think they belong because of what color they are."

Is there any significance to students' complaints that Mexican-Americans are being pushed into shop courses, and discouraged from taking academic courses?

"I was graduated from Roosevelt High in 1945," said Dr. Nava, now 40, who got his Ph.D. from Harvard in history. "I was told to take auto shop. And I did. I did as I was told. Then I went into the Navy — and I wasn't a Mexican anymore, I was just Julian. It opened my eyes.

Served in Navy

"But, then, in the Navy I was an auto mechanic — so I can't say that the advice was all bad. A lot of those decisions were based on what the high school counselors considered 'a realistic assessment of the chances of success.' They realized the chances, then, of a Mexican-American getting through college.

"I'm just worried for fear they're still making those 'realistic assessments.' I just wonder how many other Julians have ended up in an auto shop, somewhere. And stayed there.

"They had me believing my oldest kid, Hector, wasn't too bright," said Charles Ericksen, whose wife came from Mexico and whose children went to East Los Angeles schools before he became a public relations man in Sacramento. "All he could get were Cs."

"The counselor told me Cs were fine, all we could expect. They said he had no leadership potential. He never had any homework. Then we moved to Sacramento, and he went into a school where he's the only Mexican-American. They call him 'Taco.' And he gets all As and Bs and is president of his class."

"It's wrong when people say, 'We have a terrible school system,' " said Dr. Guzman. "All in all, it has an excellent reputation in our country. But it may not be effective in certain corners of society. The policy is established downtown for all the areas and all the schools.

"But, in some areas, such as the Mexican-American areas, they find that somehow these rules don't apply. Their tests don't work. And they wonder why. You know why? They don't understand our people. They're not trying to."

Scene at UCLA

. . . the scene is UCLA, where, late last month, hundreds of delegates from 25 different Mexican-American groups gathered at a symposium sponsored by the Associated Students of UCLA and the United Mexican American students.

"Integration is an empty bag," said Rudolfo (Corky) Gonzales, of Denver, head of the Crusade for Justice, a Colorado civil rights group he says numbers 1,800. "It's like getting up out of the small end of the funnel. One may make it, but the rest of the people stay at the bottom.

"Our young people reject politics. All the new leaders we developed a year ago are now working for the poverty program. They were bought out. They are not provoking a revolution. They're putting water on fire. Young leaders! Don't spend your time trying to educate a racist majority. Teach your own people. Tell them to be proud of their names, their values and their culture.

Willing to Die?

"Ask them if they're willing to fight for their rights and dignity. And ask them: are they willing to die for it?"

"The violence in New Mexico was the moment of awakening for La Raza," said another speaker, Reies Tijerina — "El Tigre," the Tiger, leader of the militant Alianza (Alliance) of Indio-Spanish peoples of northern New Mexico. (Because their ancestors date to Spanish conquistador days, before there was a Mexico, Tijerina's followers prefer Indio-Spanish to Mexican-American. Often, in Colorado, New Mexico and Texas the term "Spanish-American" is used.)

Tijerina came to the symposium while free on appeal bond for his conviction on charges of aiding and abetting an assault on two federal officers — forest rangers held by Alianza members when they invaded a national forest in October, 1966. Last June raiders shot up the courthouse at Tierra Amarilla, N.M. and Tijerina is charged with numerous counts on which trial is still pending.

"Since Tierra Amarilla," said Tijerina in Los Angeles "there has been a closer association. People realize the need for closer cooperation in different parts of the Southwest. As we get closer to danger, the brotherhood tightens in closer.

"I myself am not a violent man. I don't believe in outright violence. But in dealing with our government, we find it urgent and natural to make our demands in a different way from 30 to 40 years ago."

Bert Corona, head of the Mexican-American Political Association, urged the Mexican-American community to fight for power politically — but the militancy of the meeting, which primed much of the young Chicano leadership for the demonstrations of March was best illustrated by Luis Valdez:

"We're in the belly of the shark," said young Valdez. "In occupied California."

He worked for a time helping efforts of Cesar Chavez, leader of the United Farm Workers Organizing Committee, in Delano. Chavez achieved notable success in unionizing Mexican-American farm workers in the San Joaquin Valley — and then, disturbed by threats of violence by some Mexican-Americans he said were "seeking a short-cut to victory," went on a highly publicized 25-day fast to dramatize his nonviolent approach.

He had been scheduled to speak at the UCLA symposium, but couldn't because of his fast. That same week Tijerina was making numerous appearances in the Los Angeles area, flanked by Brown Beret bodyguards, embracing and praising Black Nationalist leaders, and stirring young militants with hints at violence and calls for valor and a willingness to die, if need be, for La Causa — the cause.

Valdez, wearing a Che Guevara type costume, attacked the "bagachos" — a Mexican-American term for Anglos — and showed a militancy more characteristic of Tijerina than Chavez:

"It's time for a new Mexican revolution," he said. "And which Chicanos are going to lead the next revolution? The ones in the belly of the shark! Nosotros! We're going to lead that revolution!

Denounces 'Lousy' System

"We've got to stand up and talk straight to the gabachos — say, hell, no, I won't go, to their whole lousy system. I won't go to your suburban barrio. I won't talk your language. I won't eat your foot!"

Amid cheers, he added: "Support Tijerina! And Viva la Raza!"

Has this revolution, as some say, already started? Were the New Mexico raids and the San Joaquin Valley strikes a prelude to the beginning of a real grass-roots movement in Los Angeles?

"These things sometimes appear in a flash," said Dr. Leo Grebler, an economist who is chairman of the committee for the Mexican-American Study now underway at UCLA. "And, then, they disappear in a flash.

'Hard to Tell'

"Since it is so new, it's hard to tell. I don't know of any criteria to predict if it will be a permanent force. In the past, attempts to unite, to draw in other Spanish-speaking people, have been flashes. I maintain an attitude of skepticism. I have to think in my terms, and my terms are skeptical, based on past performances.

"But, then, the Mexican-American population is younger than the rest of us (50% of the community is under 20), and youth feels the social issues more severely than the older leaders.

"Numerically, the importance of the young will stay with us for at least this generation. The young are here, and they'll stay with us. What they'll do with their power we'll have to wait and see. I'd like to take a look, say about 1970 or 71, and see what changes occurred.

"But we can't predict it. All we can do is wait, and see, and then record it."

At the end of the week the Brown Power movement had achieved one objective — the school board had agreed to meet in East Los Angeles. Will it all end there? In the barrios they say no. Next, they predict, will come economic boycotts, political drives, perhaps more demonstrations.

The history Dr. Grebler plans to write is already under way, they say. Because history, say Southern California's young Chicanos, is something which is happening now.

UPRISING IN THE BARRIOS*

CHARLES A. ERICKSEN

In California's cities the natives are restless. The ethnic kin to the Cabrillos and Serras, to Joaquín Murrieta and Jose de la Guerra are confronting the power structure with demands for educational change. They want it now. They tell you that they don't intend to be stalled or sidetracked or bought off with a job or a raise, a new title or a fingerful of *atole*.

They are activist Mexican-Americans. Their awareness of what the American educational system has done to the bilingual, bicultural Mexican-American is acute. They know that in California he lags nearly four years behind the Anglo, two behind the Negro, in scholastic achievement. They know that the worst schools in cities like Los Angeles — measured by dropout statistics — are the de facto segregated Mexican-American schools.

The day when a lazy "educator" with a glib tongue dazzles them with doubletalk about "language problems" and "responsibilities of parents" is past. They know better. They've done their homework. And while they don't claim to have all the answers, they do know that solutions don't lie with the status quo.

Instant change is the only hope, or many thousands more brown children of the United States will be destroyed by the system, California's activist Mexican-Americans tell you.

Who are these activists?

They are Sal Castro, schoolteacher; Miguel Montes, dentist; Manuel Guerra, college professor; Esther Hernandez, housewife; Moctezuma Esparza, student. The list in Los Angeles alone could fill a book and encompass every trade and profession from newspaper boy to electrical engineer.

The commitment of each varies, of course. In part it is proportionate to the time each has left over from his obligation to job and family, or in the case of some who exploited or downgraded their own race, *raza,* to "make it," proportionate to their personal guilt. Or maybe it is in direct ratio to how much they have been Americanized and made aware of their individual rights.

*American Education, November 1968.

Some send in a dollar. Some work at it 24 hours a day and go to jail for *la causa*.

The growth of Mexican-American militancy in California has been rapid. Its focus is education. Dominated by youth, it moves in spurts.

Last March several hundred Mexican-American students participated in a series of peaceful but widely publicized walkouts from their high schools in East Los Angeles. Their orderly protests brought praise from some members of the Los Angeles board of education and called the community's attention to urgently needed educational programs after adult discussion had failed to do so.

Underground newspapers, with Mexican-American reporters in their teens and twenties, are sprouting in cities up and down the length of California. They take on the police, the alleged *Tio Tomases* of their communities, the growers, the selective service system. But the main meat they feed on is the educational system. In East Los Angeles there are two such newspapers: *La Raza* and *Inside Eastside*. They have been instrumental in exciting youth's passion for change.

In the past regular community newspapers circulating in the Eastside and other Mexican-American *barrios* throughout the Greater Los Angeles area studiously avoided social controversy. Today they have changed. They report controversial matters, column upon column, because the community demands it. It wants to know what's going on.

In Los Angeles a few years ago the first significant organization of Mexican-American teachers was founded: the statewide Association of Mexican-American Educators. It flourishes today, and its leaders speak out frequently and boldly. Most of its teacher members are in their twenties and thirties.

Soon after the teachers organized, the students did, too. Today the college and high school students from Los Angeles' Mexican-American community have several organizations to choose from. Most prominent among them: the United Mexican-American Students, the Mexican-American Student Association, and the Brown Berets.

When the Los Angeles district attorney's office charged 13 Mexican-American activists with conspiring to cause the East Los Angeles high school walkouts (to walk out is a misdemeanor; to conspire to walk out is a felony), United Mexican-American Students and Brown Beret members were among those arrested, as was a member of the Association of Mexican-American Educators.

The action brought an immediate response from the Mexican-American community and its leadership. Miguel Montes, a member of the California State Board of Education, termed the arrests "an imprudent attempt to keep students and teachers in line . . . unjust and highly partial application of the law."

Francisco Bravo, prominent medical doctor and president of the Pan-American bank, reacted to the arrests with an open letter to the district attorney: "I wish to take hard issue with you in this matter . . . ," he began. Referring to "the continuing mental maiming of our children which has been in existence these many decades in our local educational system," Bravo explained, "While we wish to be responsible citizens, yet we must also ask . . . that our government be responsible and responsive to the needs and to the problems of our people . . . .'

On the issue of education, California's Mexican-Americans speak with an unfaltering, united voice. Yet five years ago only a few dared to speak out, and they, with rare exception, were quickly discredited.

Why the sudden shift to militancy?

The success of the Negro civil rights movement in American unquestionably had a lot to do with it.

Today's activist in the Mexican-American community is the one who is most Anglo in his attitudes. He's more aware than his neighbors of his rights as an American and more sophisticated in his knowledge of the machinery of our democracy. In other words, he knows what happens to the squeaky wheel."

Sillas and other committee members spent two days in the heart of the East Los Angeles *barrio* last year, listening to the testimony of intense young Mexican-Americans about civil rights problems in their community. Typical was the commentary by Rosalinda Mendez, a graduate of an East Los Angeles high school:

"From the time we first begin attending school, we hear about how great and wonderful our United States is, about our democratic American heritage, but little about our splendid and magnificent Mexican heritage and culture. What little we do learn about Mexicans is how they mercilessly slaughtered the brave Texans at the Alamo, but we never hear about the child heroes of Mexico who courageously threw themselves from the heights of Chapultepec rather than allow themselves and their flag to be captured by the attacking Americans.

"We look for others like ourselves in these history books, for something to be proud of for being a Mexican, and all we see in books, magazines, films, and TV shows are stereotypes of a dark, dirty, smelly man with a tequila bottle in one hand, a dripping taco in the other, a serape wrapped around him, and a big sombrero.

"But we are not the dirty, stinking winos that the Anglo world would like to point out as Mexican. We begin to think that maybe the Anglo teacher is right, that maybe we are inferior, that we do not belong in this world, that — as some teachers actually tell students to their faces — we should go back to Mexico and quit causing problems for America."

"What is an activist anyway?" "Our 'conventional' activists are the ones who become involved in the PTA, who get wrapped up in community projects or walk the precincts for one political party or another. Maybe they'll form a housewives' picket line around City Hall to get a street light on a dark block, or maybe they'll bake cakes to raise money for a new church building.

"Whoever they are, whatever they do, they're working to bring about change. They possess special knowledge and have a special point of view. They introduce an idea to the community, and they campaign for it. This is a basic process of democracy.

"Mexican-American activists are no different than any other American activists. The issue of education is one that affects them most intimately.

Rodriguez contends that these people are vital — just as a PTA is vital — if Mexican-Americans are to get their full share of the American educational system.

"Remember," he says, "the Mexican-American is not talking about destroying the system. He wants to improve it."

"If Mexican-American children have a higher dropout rate than any other comparable group in the Nation — and they do — the schools cannot explain away their failure by belaboring the 'Mexican-American problem.' The problem, simply, is that the schools have failed with these children."

Howe pointed out that Federal funds flow through title I of the Elementary and Secondary Education Act into many school districts in which Mexican-American children go to school. "You and your fellow citizens with a particular concern for Mexican-American children should bring every possible pressure to bear to ensure that title I funds provide education which allows Mexican-American children to have pride in their heritage while learning the way to take part in the opportunities this country has to offer. Title I funds are not appropriated by the Congress to promote 'business as usual' in the schools.

They are appropriated, instead, to help the educationally deprived get a fair chance.

"The funds enabled us, for the first time, to focus on the needs of the disadvantaged Mexican-American child — to zero in on some of his problems," says Wilson Riles, California's State director of compensatory education. "Students in our title I programs have averaged about a year's gain for each year of instruction. Before title I, they averaged about seven-tenths of a year's progress in a year."

The problem, Riles states, is in having insufficient funds to reach all of the eligible children with a saturated program. "We require districts to concentrate their programs. We try to reach the most severely deprived areas. Spread the money too thin, and you see no results."

Federal monies for migrant education projects also flow through Riles' office. Ramiro Reyes, who coordinates California's plan for the education of migrant children, says, "We're helping 50,000 children, and 85 percent of them are Mexican-American."

Through special migrant education projects some school districts are discovering that they can structure a regular summer school program capable of attracting significant numbers of migrant children. Reyes cited the community of Mendota, in fertile Fresno County, as an example of this:

"They had never had summer schools there before. They started when our program came in, and the youngsters turned out in droves. Many children of migrants from Texas were able to be absorbed into the program."

Another federally funded title I program of importance to California's two million Mexican-Americans is English as a Second Language '(ESL). Manuel Ceja, consultant in program development in the State's office of compensatory education, sees ESL as the first step which districts take in recognizing that there is a problem and that other subjects should be taught bilingually too.

"Many of today's ESL programs are steppingstones to true bilingual programs," he says.

In September, Santa Monica started using some title I funds for a 10th-grade bilingual class in reading, math, and English for recent immigrants as well as native-born Mexican-Americans.

Rodriguez points out that the Federal Government has made a national legal and moral commitment to bilingual education.

"The commitment must be taken up by the States and implemented, regardless of how many dollars will be forthcoming through the new bilingual legislation, or when they will become available," he says. "There are sufficient monies available now through a variety of other Federal programs. It's up to local school districts to re-examine their priorities as to which are the most effective programs and to initiate bilingual teaching."

California's Miguel Montes of the California school board agrees that true bilingual programs must be given top priority. He sees them as intertwined with priorities for expanded preschool programs and projects to prepare teachers for the cultural differences of the Mexican-American child:

"The entire history of discrimination is based on the prejudice that because someone else is different, he is somehow worse," says Commissioner Howe. "If we could teach all of our children — black, white, brown, yellow, and all the American shades in between — that diversity is not be feared or suspected, but enjoyed and valued, we would be well on our way toward achieving the equality we have always proclaimed as a national characteristic."

Armando Rodriguez sees this as the challenge. "The more completely we develop this bicultural resource — the Mexican-American — the better he will serve our Nation. That's the goal: to educate the total Mexican-American, not just parts of him."

When this happens California's Mexican-American activist will stay home and bake a cake.

A MINORITY NOBODY KNOWS

HELEN ROWAN

There are some five million Americans of Mexican descent or birth. About four a half million live in five Southwestern states: Arizona, California, Colorado, New Mexico, and Texas. Between them, California and Texas account for 82 percent of the Southwest's total, with California holding the edge.

Census statistics and the other studies show the Mexican-Americans in the Southwest to be worse off in every respect than the nonwhites (Negroes, Indians, and Orientals), not to mention the dominant Anglos (everybody else). They are poorer, their housing is more crowded and more dilapidated, their unemployment rate is higher, their average educational level is lower (two years below nonwhite, four below Anglo).

What is extraordinary about the situation is not so much that it exists as that it is so little known. In California, Mexican-Americans outnumber Negroes by almost two to one, but probably not one Californian in ten thousand knows that simple fact. It is an easy one to overlook if you measure a minority's importance by the obvious signs: poverty programs, education, and job-training activities geared to its situation, the elected and appointed officials it can number, the attention directed to it by the press, politicians, and even textbooks, and the help given it by do-good organizations. By all these measures, the Mexican-Americans have been slighted.

The Johnson Administration is beginning to pay them some attention, though in a fitful and nervous manner. Mexican-Americans have been demanding such baubles as jobs, federal appointments, and Great Society programs tailored to their needs. Since they justifiably consider themselves to be the nation's best-kept secret, they would like some national visibility, preferably through the lens of a White House Conference focused on their many problems. This the Administration has been loath to give them, though it has tried to appease them for a couple of years by holding out the possibility of such a meeting. Still, there are signs that the *federales* are thinking of some programs specifically designed for Mexican-Americans. While their first needs

are the same as those of a lot of other people — money and jobs —
there are certain issues which clearly affect them in a special way.

The Mexican-American birthrate is 50 percent higher than that of
the general population; the community's average age is already ten
years younger than that of the total population. The school dropout
rate is higher than that of any other group, and very few of those who
do graduate from high school move on to college. Even in California,
with its vaunted and supposedly inclusive system of higher education,
only about 2 percent of the four-year college enrollment is Mexican-
American, while Mexican-Americans constitute about 10 percent of the
total population and a much higher percentage of the school-age
population. Delinquency and drug addiction rates are high. Residential
segregation is increasing. As far as jobs go, the old devil, overt
discrimination, has been largely replaced by the new devil, automation,
and by more subtle "cultural discrimination" in the form of tests
which penalize the Mexican-American first as a student and then as a
prospective employee. Finally, there are signs of increasing family
change. In the Spanish-speaking ghetto of east Los Angeles, for
instance, 26 percent of all children under eighteen are not living with
both parents (the figure is only 13 percent for Los Angeles as a whole).
This is a particularly serious development for the Mexican-American
community, which springs from a culture in which the family is the
strongest of all institutions.

If they think of them at all, Easterners are likely to think of
Mexican-Americans in terms of wetbacks who cross the border to
fester in farm shacks for the miserly wages paid to migratory workers.
In fact, Mexican-Americans are heavily urbanized. Almost 80 percent
in the Southwest live in cities and towns, a proportion fully as high as
the Anglo concentration and considerably higher than the nonwhite.
For every Mexican-American picking fruit in California's Central
Valley there are scores working as hod carriers and busboys in Los
Angeles. For every stereotypical migrant who follows the crops, there
are dozens crowded into the *colonias* and *barrios* that cling to the
fringes of innumerable Southwest towns. The recent urbanization of
such a group, given its low educational level and other characteristics,
must represent social, economic, educational — and potentially political
— significance of a high order.

But the Mexican-Americans' few successes in bringing themselves to
national attention have had to do with the farm-labor issue, which is

appropriate yet somewhat ironic. The farm workers, with an average annual income of about $1500 and generally unspeakable living and working conditions, are worse off than anybody else. In the past two years, Cesar Chavez managed to organize and sustain a successful strike of grape pickers. The strike was dramatic, colorful, and immensely appealing, and it drew the support of activist Anglos from all over. Pilgrimages to the Central Valley were undertaken by Bobby Kennedy and youngsters from SNCC, by correspondents of the New York *Times* and television crews from national networks. Bay area liberals who had never set foot in San Francisco's Mission District or in east San Jose made the 550-mile round trip to Delano, the strike headquarters, carrying money, food, and clothing. And many middle-of-the-road Californians did not eat so much as one grape for months, so as not to risk patronizing a struck vineyard.

The condition of the farm workers is obvious and desperate. But Chavez himself is said to have urged urban leaders not to allow the farm-labor issue to deflect their attention from the more complex problems of the *barrios*, which are bound to grow worse as the ghettos continue to receive steady influxes of Mexican immigrants (almost a thousand a week) and displaced domestic farm workers.

East Los Angeles is one of those areas that Eastern eyes would never recognize as being poor. The low dwellings (though there may be as many as three on a tiny lot) have yards around them, and flowers, and on smogless days the nearby mountains stand out beautifully. There is a color that is heightened by the leftover symbols of other peoples for whom the area earlier served as a port of entry: Orientals, Italians, and then Russian Jews, Mexicatessens offer kosher *burritos* and Okie *frijoles* and Winchell's Do-Nut House features a Taco Fiesta. Youngsters cruise around in beat-up cars for which they buy gas by the quarter's worth. An "Operator Wanted" sign in a curtained storefront window signifies that yet another small sweatshop has opened where the illiterate (and perhaps illegal) immigrant or school dropout may find a few days' work sewing blouses or shirts.

Following the riots in nearby Watts, a special census was made of that area and east L.A. What attention the survey got was mainly directed to the part on Watts, but those who read the rest of the report could find that in east L.A., too between 1960 and 1965 real income slipped by 8 to 10 percent, housing deteriorated, home ownership declined.

Of the two courses that Mexican-Americans might follow to bring themselves helpful attention, one they have been unable to take and the other they have been unwilling to take. They have not been able to organize into an effective political bloc, and they have not been willing to riot and burn. One federal official describes them as "the most disorganized ethnic group in the country." The federal establishment, according to some officials, is so desperate to find a real leader to treat with that it would even welcome the emergence of a Mexican-American Stokely Carmichael.

There are good reasons for the Mexican-Americans' lack of political clout, but they escape anyone who tries to understand the Mexican-American experience in terms of other ethnic groups. Ernesto Galarza, a distinguished scholar and writer, points out that historically Mexican-Americans have not been seen as a great constitutional and moral issue, as were the Negroes, nor as an ordinary immigrant group to be acculturated or assimilated. They have been looked on simply as an ever replenishing supply of cheap and docile labor.

For Mexican-Americans do have in common with the Negroes a long history of discrimination, but they were never enslaved and no war was ever fought over them, though one was fought over their land. Harsh as the discrimination was, including lynchings and segregation in schools and other public facilities, it was spotty (you could get into a swimming pool if you weren't too swarthy) and varied from place to place and from time to time.

The somewhat nebulous quality of the discrimination — and the concomitant fact that a lucky Mexican-American could "make it" into the middle class — helps explain why the Mexican-Americans have not yet produced the spontaneous leadership or found the unifying force of the civil rights movement. And the very institutions which might have been expected to recognize the condition and champion the cause of the Mexican-Americans — the Roman Catholic Church, labor, the Democratic Party, liberal groups, educational institutions, and the Eastern philanthropic and press establishment—have been by and large deaf, dumb, and blind on the subject. "For the Mexican-American," says a college professor, "there are no liberals."

This is not literally true, of course. Some individuals such as Carey McWilliams have for years written and spoken vigorously on the problem, and twenty years ago Fred Ross, supported by Saul Alinsky's Industrial Areas Foundation, began community organization efforts in Mexican-American sections of California. Other individuals and groups have done effective work on a small scale, and a few priests (though often at the cost of being silenced or sent away by their superiors) have been fairly militant spokesmen for the Mexican-Americans.

But there has been no wide-scale involvement. The white liberals who at one time helped to lead and to bankroll the Negro movement had few Anglo counterparts working with and speaking out on behalf of the Mexican-Americans. Many Southwestern Anglos supported the Negro movement, however, and even some Mexican-American college students confessed to me that they became active in the Negro cause before they caught on that there was work to be done closer to home.

The lack of outside interest and help (spelled m-o-n-e-y), combined with the fact that until recently the group was overwhelmingly rural and had very few educated members, has given the Mexican-Americans of today very little political leverage. Social, fraternal, and thinly disguised political organizations appear and disappear with startling rapidity, but there has never been a Mexican-American equivalent of the NAACP or Urban League, let alone SNCC or CORE. Even the sturdiest and longest-lived of the organizations have very little in the way of paid staffs. If you want to see the head of some group, you phone his place of business or his house, because it is quite likely that there isn't any headquarters. There is no effective clearinghouse or information center, and communications within the community are weak — among the leaders, and also between them and the poverty-stricken of town and country.

Chavez is the most authentic leader in the traditional sense: a charismatic man sprung from a rural proletariat whose understanding and loyalty he commands. What is questionable is whether the basis of his appeal — a combination of religious pageantry, evocation of the heroes of the Mexican Revolution, and nonviolent civil rights techniques — could successfully be transferred from the fields to the city streets.

"There are dozens of Chavezes hidden in the *barrios*," a city spokesman said sadly, but presumably these buried Chavezes will have to find new ways to rally the new urban proletariat. For whatever the culture of the *barrios* may be, it is certainly a hybrid one, neither classical Mexican nor traditional Anglo urban.

"It's always my parents telling me to be proud I'm Mexican and the school telling me to be American," a junior high school student cried out. For the city youngsters (50 percent of the Mexican-American population is under twenty), the goodies offered by the industrialized society are all too visible and unavailable. "The thing to do is learn how the *gringos* keep you down," they say. And the residents of the *barrios* are sophisticated enough to recognize that it is the future they have to fear more than the present.

"They are teaching my boy nothing in that school, *nothing*," a mother said to me with a despair that is impossible to convey in writing. "What will happen to him. What will he do."

Considering their numbers in California (now estimated at nearly two million), the Mexican-Americans have a singular dearth of elected representation. There is one congressman of Mexican descent, Edward R. Roybal, a Democrat from Los Angeles. No Mexican-American sits in either house of the California legislature, or on the city council, or elected board of education in L.A. Roybal became the first of his community since 1881 to serve on the city council when he was elected in 1949, but when he left for Congress in 1962 his seat was contested: by four Mexican-Americans and one Negro, with the result one might expect.

What the Mexican-Americans have lacked in elective political muscle they have tried to make up for by extracting promises and appointments from Anglo politicians. Here again they are handicapped: the Democrats have taken them for granted (traditionally, about 90 percent of the relatively small registration votes Democratic), and the Republicans haven't bothered much until recently. Most Mexican-Americans agree that Democratic Governor Pat Brown did more for the group than any previous governor. Still, it wasn't enough.

During the last campaign the Reagan forces made some successful overtures to the community, and the Republicans made some electoral inroads, notably around Los Angeles, but the Democrats believe that overall they managed to hold on to about 75 percent of the Mexican-American vote. The defections in California and the rest of the Southwest, however, apparently worried the Democrats (they hastily appointed a Mexican-American to the National Committee), and they should be worried; while they may have no place else to go now, the Mexican-Americans are looking around. A mutually satisfactory political marriage will not easily be achieved. The one thing that Anglos and Mexican-Americans do most certainly for each other is to provide inexhaustible sources of frustration. The Anglo litany of complaints about Mexican-American political behavior, to abbreviate it drastically, runs like this:

They can't get organized, they can't agree among themselves, there aren't any real leaders, and the so-called leaders can't deliver. ("They'd come to us with talk about 400,000 votes," one of Governor Brown's campaign managers said aggrievedly, "but some of those guys couldn't deliver their own families.") The community is uninvolved, and it is difficult to find out what it wants. An assistant to a southern California congressman says that when he sends out invitations to a meeting with the congressman — say 250 to the Negro community and 250 to the Mexican-American — about 150 Negroes usually turn up, and about 30 Mexican-Americans. "And the first question, sometimes the only question, they ask is: 'How many Mexican-Americans on your staff?' If it was 100 percent it still wouldn't be enough," he adds glumly.

This leads to another Anglo complaint: that many Mexican-Americans view the American political process with an eye to appointments and that politics for them becomes a superficial numbers game, with little attention paid either to the potential importance of the jobs or the ability and effectiveness of the appointees.

Finally, Anglos complain that many Mexican-American spokesmen prefer to compete among themselves for elective or appointive jobs instead of working out ways and means for achieving at least a show of unity, a drive for a cause. All too often four or five Mexican-Americans insist on running for an office, thus dividing the vote.

Beyond the Anglo politicos, who have special and self-centered interests in view, others who are highly sympathetic and have no political axes to grind are appalled by the amount and ferocity of infighting that goes on and the fact that it is so often caused not by ideological but by purely personal differences. So strong is the role of *personalismo* in Mexican-American politics that, as one sympathetic observer commented: "They wouldn't even vote to establish a postal system unless they knew who would be the mailman on the block."

Although there is much evidence to support these complaints, they do not take into account a number of relevant factors, including the Anglo role in perpetuating disunity and ineffectiveness within the group, whether intentionally or heedlessly. The Anglo politicians who criticize the lack of Mexican-American political organization make the very decisions that render such organization nearly impossible. In California, the Democrats, apparently thinking they knew a safe thing when they saw it, gerrymanded the Spanish surname sections of Los Angeles and San Francisco so as to make Spanish-speaking voters the pivotal but never the controlling factors in their various districts. This makes it difficult for Mexican-Americans to vote as a bloc and cuts of incipient leadership.

While the Democrats complain that they have to deal with leaders who have no followers, they have not financed the kind of block-to-block canvassing and voter registration that would produce organized constituencies. In search of votes, they woo the heads of the Mexican-American organizations and other community leaders in the hope that the leaders can exert personal influence over the community; it has to be personal, since the organizations themselves lack the money or manpower to organize real constituencies.

In making appointments, too, Anglos seem to set up situations which inevitably cause trouble in and for the Mexican-American community. Because they want to get the maximum political mileage from the few appointments they are willing to make, Anglo officials undertake elaborate though clandestine efforts to procure the perfect all-purpose Mexican-American, then assert that no man can be found to meet the wildly unrealistic qualifications established for the job.

Anglo officials make incessant demands for unity among Mexican-Americans, the implication being that the Anglos are unable to do anything until they can discern an unmistakably clear picture of exactly what the community wants. While there are real frustrations involved in dealing with a group as fragmented as the Mexican-Americans, there is also real cynicism involved in the way so many Anglo officials in positions of power, at all levels seize on the condition as an excuse to do nothing. It should not be necessary to identify genuine leaders or take a poll of the grass roots to guess, for instance, that no group "wants" to have urban renewal accomplished at the price of its own removal (in at least one border town the Mexican-Americans were renewed right over into Mexico); that no community "wants" to be slashed into chunks of hideous freeways (as has happened in east Los Angeles); that few people "want" their children to attend a school run by someone who could remark, as the former principal of an east Los Angeles high school did in the presence of an Anglo friend of mine, "We couldn't run this school without the dropout rate. They don't belong here anyway — they belong in the fields."

The truth is that the endless jockeying, delaying, rumormongering, and playing of the cat-and-mouse game simply elicit and intensify the very kind of behavior the Anglos deplore: dissension and a flying off in all directions. The entire protracted handling of the on-again, off-again

White House Conference is a perfect case in point.

In the fall of 1965, some Mexican-Americans, having heard of plans for a major civil rights conference in Washington, asked to be included. They were given to understand, in writing, that a separate conference would be held for Mexican-Americans or possibly all Spanish-speaking Americans. From then on there were unanswered telegrams from this group, unanswered letters from that one, understandings and misunderstandings, and joint attempts by the leaders of Mexican-American groups to apply pressure. A year ago the President had a few spokesmen to dinner and left them with the impression that there would be a conference. Others of a group that considered itself the prime negotiating committee were not invited. Their exclusion, of course, strained relations among the Mexican-Americans as well as between them and the *federales*.

No more was heard of the much-wanted conference until late October of 1966, when high officials of the Administration found time, despite, or because of, the imminence of the elections, to meet with about sixty Mexican-American spokesmen in "preplanning" discussions of the real conference. Since then official silence has been accompanied by comic-opera goings-on. A small group with Labor Department leadership and the use of White House stationery — but with offices in neither place — is known to be "doing something" about Mexican-Americans and other Spanish-speaking Americans. A receptionist answers its phone "National Conference" but is unable to say on what, or where, or when, or for whom any conferring is being or is going to be done. So rumors fly, consternation and frustration increase among the Mexican-Americans, and much of their attention, time, and energy, and that of a number of federal officials, is diverted from the real problems, which continue to grow more malignant.

The school systems of the Southwest have totally failed the Mexican-American community," says Dr. Miguel Montes of California's state board of education. The cold statistics alone make his case.

What is striking is that so little has been done or said until recently, despite the fact that a few educators such as Dr. George Sanchez of the University of Texas have for years been urging bilingual instruction, a revision of the curriculum and textbooks to appeal to the interests and to strengthen the sense of cultural identity of Mexican-American students, decent counseling and guidance, and teacher training that might produce instructors capable of reaching and educating Mexican-American children.

In most of the states, among them California, it is against the law to use any language but English as the medium of instruction, though the law is openly flouted by the few teachers who can speak Spanish. The psychological and educational implications of such a policy is clear. By denying the child the right to speak his own language (in some places children are still punished for speaking Spanish even on the playground), the system is telling him, in effect, that his language, his culture, and by extension he himself, are inferior. And he rapidly becomes truly inferior in achievement, since the teachers must perforce water down the subject matter, such as arithmetic or social studies, for use as a vehicle for teaching English rather than the subject itself.

Counseling in the schools is notoriously bad, and constitutes a special source of bitterness for the Mexican-Americans who have survived it — that is, defied it. "Realistic" counselors say, in effect: college costs too much; besides, you couldn't make it anyway; besides, you couldn't get a good job when you finished. Congressman Roybal was advised to become an electrician on the strength of an A in his ninth-grade algebra class (he was lucky to get into algebra; "general math" is usually considered sufficient). Julian Nava, a young professor at San Fernando Valley State College with a Ph.D. in history from Harvard, was advised to take, and did take, body and fender courses in high school in east Los Angeles. There are plenty of current stories of this sort.

The inadequacy of ability tests when applied to many groups is also notorious; the question is how, when the fact is so well known, school officials can summon the arrogance to brand young children as mentally deficient when it is the tests and the schools that are deficient. In California, Negro and Mexican-American children are overwhelmingly overrepresented proportionally in classes for the "mentally retarded." A former education official (an angry Anglo) told me of visiting a school in the San Joaquin Valley where he saw records listing one child as having an I.Q. of 46. Wanting to learn more about how such a mental basket case could function at all, he inquired around and found that the child, a boy of eleven, has a paper route, takes care of his four younger brothers and sisters after school, and prepares the evening meal for the family. He also speaks no English.

Many Anglo educators claim that they cannot make headway against the problems of language, culture, and parents. The stereotype has it that Mexican-Americans are not interested in having their children get an education, though every bit of evidence I found suggested just the reverse. In fact, many Mexican-American adults have an entirely unwarranted respect for the wisdom of teachers and principals, which is one reason why they have allowed their children to be pushed around for so long. There are problems, but they are by no means insurmountable. Actually, they have been used as a mask, and not a very effective one at that, for the real attitudes of the Anglo community at large.

"The schools are the places where Anglos and Mexican-Americans come to learn and act out the roles they will later play," says Theodore W. Parsons, an anthropologist at the University of California. He recently spent months studying the schools in a California town where the population is about 57 percent Mexican-American; practices similar to the ones he observed there are followed in many schools all over the feudal Southwest. The children — Anglos are called "Americans" and Mexican-Americans are called "Mexicans" — are conditioned for their respective roles in the adult world from their first day in school to their final one, when at graduation the Mexicans march in last and sit at the back of the platform. "This makes for a better-looking stage," a teacher explained to Parsons, adding that it allows the Americans, who have all the parts in the program, to get to the front more easily.

"Once we did let a Mexican girl give a little talk of some kind," Parsons was told, "and all she did was mumble around. She had quite an accent, too. Afterwards we had several complaints from other parents, so we haven't done anything like that since. That was about twelve years ago."

The Negro revolution has stimulated, but by its great drama has also obscured, already existing ferment within the Mexican-American community. Spokesmen have had increasingly stormy sessions (and nonsessions — the walkout is becoming something of a fad) with federal, state, and local officials.

Many Anglos seem to dismiss the volubly expressed anger of Mexican-American leaders as not being "representative" of the feelings of the masses, but it is foolish to do so. No Mexican-American I know of has even threatened that blood will run in the streets if conditions continue to grow worse, but thoughtful spokesmen acknowledge that no one can predict what outlet the growing hostility will find, a hostility that may be the more malignant because it has been so long suppressed.

"Man, if east L.A. ever blows, it will *really* blow," one said, and Herman Gallegos of San Francisco, a highly responsible leader, reports that some Mexican-Americans decline to join picket lines or other peaceful demonstrations because they fear they could not remain nonviolent. There is undeniable resentment of not only Anglos but Negroes: "If they don't move over, they're going to find footprints on their backs," one temperate Mexican-American said. He and other sophisticated Mexican-Americans realize that it is not the Negroes' "fault" that they are getting a little bit more of not enough, but there is the dangerous tension that always exists when poor people are set to scrambling for the few crumbs tossed out by the affluent society.

The fuel that could set off a Watts-type explosion is present in ample supply. Perhaps one day it will be ignited by some incident. Or perhaps the youthful population will simply retreat into increasing withdrawal, alienation, and addiction.

There is also, of course, a third possibility: that Anglos will give up their cynical game of divide and rule, listen to the growing number of articulate Mexican-American spokesmen as they define the community's problems, and allow Mexican-Americans the tools they can use to carry themselves into the mainstream of American life.

LA RAZA – TODAY NOT MAÑANA*

ARMANDO RENDON

History has been made by Mexican Americans this past year by events which serve as guideposts to understanding the mounting drive for unity among these people who cherish the value of a heritage grounded in the history of two motherlands, both born in revolution, and of the birthrights of language and culture which have proven at one time a barrier and at another a safeguard in coping with the demands of a different and often conflicting American way of life.

Two major events which took place on the last weekend of October 1967, in El Paso, Texas, represent not only the culmination of recent efforts by Mexican American leaders but also a new starting point of opportunities in every field for La Raza.

One dominant theme — the concept of La Raza as a people striving for its rightful place as a contributing partner in American society - linked the two apparently diverse events which occurred that weekend: the Cabinet Committee Hearings on Mexican American Affairs convened in El Paso's most sumptuous settings and La Raza Unida Conference of grassroots organizations called together in the border town's worst slum barrio.

Four Cabinet members and directors of several Federal agencies "came to listen" in unprecedented simultaneous hearings which covered major problem areas for the Mexican American: agriculture; labor; health, education, and welfare; housing and urban development; antipoverty; and economic and social development.

Coordinating the three-day event was the Interagency Committee on Mexican American affairs, a Washington-based agency established only five months prior to the hearings. Texas-born Vicente T. Ximenes, a past national president of the American G.I. Forum, had been sworn in as a member of the Equal Employment Opportunity Commission and as director of the Interagency Committee on June 9, four months before the El Paso hearings.

Any thoughts that Ximenes and his staff may have had of easing into their new roles were completely forgotten in the flurry of activity

*Civil Rights Digest, Spring 1968, pages 7-17.

which followed the President's announcement setting a deadline only eight weeks away.

Among Mexican American groups, the proposed hearings precipitated immediate reactions. Various preliminary conferences were held all over the Southwest. Discussions and debates probably affected a more widespread portion of the Mexican American community than any previous issue. To understand this reaction clearly as well as to assess more concretely the value of the hearings and conference for the Mexican American, the context of prior events in which the President's request was made must be recalled.

For all of its special importance as an event without precedent, the El Paso convocation of Cabinet members and the several hundred Mexican Americans invited to attend must be viewed in the wider perspective of the Mexican American, the "chicano," as he calls himself, enduring the evolutionary process of group identification through recognition and acceptance of a common heritage, of common goals, even if not of methods by which to achieve them. This process, truly a "movement" in its own right, is capturing daily the imagination of more chicanos as it awakens in them an awareness of the need for personal involvement and commitment to this "cause."

The Mexican American, no less than the advocate of Black Power here in America or the fighter for independence in the emerging nations of the world, is caught up in a revolution that is sweeping the world through which people are striving to become a cohesive and self-assertive force so as to participate and help shape the processes and trends of local, national, and international policy and opinion.

Mexican Americans are moving from a position in which they were considered by the dominant culture as a predictable, subservient social mass, the harmless and pliable descendants of a conquered people, into a demanding, implacable force, valuing their cultural and historical heritage and their language as priceless birthrights from which spring their present energy and drive toward a better life and a full sharing in the American dream of equality for all men.

This quest for equality was mirrored at El Paso in the fact that two events, reflecting the major aspects of the "movement," were taking place at the same time, and in many instances involved the same people, and yet, despite any apparent conflict, established the same goals. If the hearings were, as one Interagency staff member put it, "an opportunity from which the best and the worst can be expected," they were also the catalyst for what may be the most important outcome of those three days when La Raza met in El Paso.

To Mexican Americans familiar with the verbal turmoil of the past two years, the phrase "White House Conference" quickly incites heated debate. Chicano groups through their leadership reacted vigorously when in the fall of 1965, preplanning sessions for the White House Conference "To Fulfill These Rights" were convened but excluded consideration of the problems of the Mexican American as well as chicano participation. A Washington, D.C., group, the National Organization for Mexican American Services, among others, wrote the President at that time, criticizing the proposed conference. In his reply, the President suggested that he would call a similar conference dealing with the problems of the Mexican Americans in the not too distant future.

In March 1966, 50 Mexican Americans walked out of an Equal Employment Opportunity Commission (EEOC) conference in Albuquerque, N.M., charging that the session was "rigged" with too tightly structured speeches and how-to meetings, leaving little time for discussing concrete employment needs and solutions. The group also charged the EEOC with discrimination because no Mexican American was a member of the Commission. An ad hoc committee, composed of some of the 50 who walked out in Albuquerque, coalesced to press for a growing list of demands including a White House Conference on the Mexican American, the appointment of a Mexican American to the EEOC, increased employment of Mexican Americans by Federal agencies, inclusion in the June 1966 White House Conference "To Fulfill These Rights," and a meeting of Mexican American leaders with the President.

The chicano coalition threatened to picket the June 1966 White House Conference, but in May the President eased the tension when he met privately with five prominent Mexican American leaders of large and well-organized groups. The five were Bert Corona of Oakland, California, president of the Mexican American Political Association (MAPA); Roy Elizondo of Houston, president of the Political Association of Spanish-Speaking Organizations (PASO); Augustin Flores of Riverside, California, past president of the American G.I. Forum; Dr. Hector Garcia of Corpus Christi, Texas, founder of the G.I. Forum, and Judge Alfredo Hernandez of Houston, past president of the League of United Latin American Citizens (LULAC).

A sub-task force was set up shortly after this meeting involving representatives of various agencies to lay groundwork for a conference. In September 1966, David North, formerly with the Department of Labor, was detailed to direct the work of a small staff of the Committee on the White House Conference on Mexican American Affairs. In September 1967, he was officially transferred from the Department of Labor to the Interagency directorship.

Given an official address and office space and with staff borrowed from other agencies, the committee achieved Cabinet-level status on June 9 and changed its name as well. The secretaries of Agriculture, of Labor, of Health, Education, and Welfare, and of Housing and Urban Development, the Director of the Office of Economic Opportunity, and Ximenes were named by the President to comprise the Cabinet Committee on Mexican American Affairs.

The advent of the El Paso hearings apparently did not smooth nor allay the objections of many chicano individuals or groups. A Los Angeles newsletter, Carta Editorial, put the question bluntly: "Is this the White Conference? Or is this meeting being held in lieu of such a Conference?" La Raza, an East Los Angeles barrio newspaper, displayed bitter sarcasm when it devoted the front page of its prehearings edition to describing "the newest game: El Paso . . . different from any other game in that it has no rules."

Young chicano militants, meeting in Albuquerque the weekend before the hearings, formed a national organization, established an information center in Los Angeles, and planned as their first major action the picketing of the hearings. In early October, more than 200 Mexican Americans convened at Camp Hess Kramer near Los Angeles to draw up a list of grievances and proposed solutions to present at the hearings. The MAPA board of directors, however, voted 58 to 5 to boycott the hearings, Al Pena, a city commissioner in San Antonio, Texas, had publicly criticized the hearings and threatened to boycott the proceedings but relented to head a delegation to El Paso. The tension and bitterness which had begun to crystallize into formal action in the fall of 1965 was reaching a peak by the time the hearings were called to order on Friday morning, October 27.

Ximenes, evaluating the hearings shortly after they had been concluded, stressed their nature as a series of hearings and not as a conference. He pointed out that much conflict arose because of confusion on this point. "There was no need for resolutions since the

Cabinet head was sitting in front of you with no bureaucrats in between," he said. "It was our main objective that for the first time we would get Cabinet-level directors, including the Civil Service Chairman, to come together to hear the Mexican American. These people usually come to talk, not to listen," he noted.

"Now we should be able to tell anybody what can be accomplished immediately or on a long term basis," he said, "No one had given the Mexican American credit for any intelligence," the EEOC Commissioner remarked, but it has now been proven, he added, that the Mexican American "can conduct Cabinet-level hearings and present good information."

Realizing that when the President called the El Paso hearings "we were not going to have a White House Conference" of the kind held in June 1966, Ximenes relates that he attended several conventions of major Mexican American organizations to explain the nature of the hearings. He recalls that at the last such meeting he attended, before the MAPA State membership in Riverside, "I put the question before them: do you want such a hearing? — and I got a good reaction."

As for the possiblity of the much sought after White House Conference, Ximenes declined to speculate but added: "When the agency was created, the President said that the Cabinet members and I would hear the problems and seek solutions concerning the Mexican American. As chairman of the Interagency I had particular interest because the job given us by the President was very specific." In line with the President's mandate, he said, "Hearings are ten times better than any conference especially if we can get the Cabinet people to attend. There is ten times more promise in these hearings than in a conference."

Echoing the concern of most Mexican Americans, whether they were critical of the hearings or not, Ximenes suggested that within the next few months, the real impact of the hearings would become apparent. Effects of the hearings on department policies, both in hiring practices and in providing programs and services to the Mexican American, should develop to an appreciable extent in six months at least, he said.

The Interagency itself, meanwhile, was to develop a list or scorecard based on specific recommendations made during the hearings and on commitments made by government officials. "The things asked of the department people are not unreasonable," Ximenes said. "Many require merely rules and regulations." By late January, a memorandum had been submitted to the President summarizing the El Paso hearings and restating in general terms the suggested solutions provided by the hearing participants.

An early return on one Cabinet hearing at which John Macy, Chairman of the U.S. Civil Service Commission, presided, was the appointment of Richard L. Romero of Denver, Colorado, as director of the U.S. Civil Service Commission's Equal Employment Opportunity Project. Ximenes attributed the appointment to remarks made by Judge Hernandez and Armando Quintanilla of San Antonio, Texas, drawing attention to specific problems in the employment of Mexican Americans within the Civil Service agency itself. The Department of Housing and Urban Development also recently set up a task force to step up hiring of Mexican Americans.

In the final moments of the 90th Congress, a Bilingual Education Act was passed as Title VII of the Elementary and Secondary Education Amendments of 1967. Results from this new legislation are still many years away from fruition but its passage represents the first recognition by Congress of the basic need for bilingual instruction in many of the Nation's schools.

Besides this major undertaking of followthrough on the hearings, the Interagency will continue to implement its three basic functions which Ximenes says are: to redirect old programs, to create new programs, and "to hear the mexicano." Most attention is being focused on the first and third areas, Ximenes admits, where there is "a lot of redirecting to do" of many agency programs whose personnel are not aware of the "unique" needs of Mexican Americans. He believes that the Interagency serves as "a sympathetic ear" for the mexicano to which he can voice a complaint, seek direction on how he can gain redress, apply for jobs or be referred for job openings, and even get assistance in obtaining funds for specific projects.

Commenting on a major problem area brought up frequently during the hearings, Ximenes suggested that the Interagency should not be the only source for Mexican Americans to air their grievances or to seek assistance. "Mexican Americans are needed in all agencies," he said. "Services and personnel should be incorporated into each department" to fulfill the Federal agency's responsibility in understanding and meeting chicano needs and problems, he explained.

Ideally, that would take care of the Mexican American's problems: Increase job opportunities and job training programs, open up labor union apprenticeship programs, promote bilingual and bicultural instruction in schools heavily attended by Spanish-speaking children and change attitudes in both the public and private sectors toward the Mexican American.

But, the chicano, as events in El Paso bear out, is a realist.

While witness after witness presented his case and was duly recorded, a radical turn was being taken in the Mexican American movement. A conference, La Raza Unida, functioning much like a political rally, with oratory, slogans, cheering, and even a march through downtown El Paso, covered the same issues and problems that were being discussed in the hearings but without the sophisticated programing. Nevertheless, La Raza Unida Conference centered on what may be the most important issue for the Mexican American to resolve — and which only he can resolve — the quest for unity.

On the surface, it would seem that the two events were in conflict, but in reality they complemented each other. Commissioner Ximenes, informed by the conference planners of their intent to conduct a separate conference noted that "the group didn't hurt us, it didn't want to and stated so . . . . We had a series of hearings; the other group attempted to have a conference whereby an organization could be established, that's fine. There were other meetings as well, of legislators and educators, which didn't detract from the hearings."

A deep significance can be read in Ximenes' words since frequently militant factions of a minority group might be expected to resort to physical means to disrupt such proceedings. On the contrary, some of the major protagonists of La Raza Unida Conference, which barrio people called "la verdadera conferencia," read their own incisive papers before Federal officials then boycotted the rest of the sessions.

Among chicanos who rejected invitations from the Interagency Committee but came to El Paso to exert strong roles in the conference were Corona, MAPA president, and Rodolfo "Corky" Gonzales, head of the Denver-based Crusade for Justice. Of those invited who did not come to El Paso at all, the one whose absence was most significant was Cesar Chavez, director of the United Farm Workers Organizing Committee in Delano, California, considered by many chicanos as the leading figure in the rise of Mexican American aspirations. Making up the majority of La Raza Unida participants were people of the barrio.

Presiding at La Raza Unida Conference was Dr. Ernesto Galarza, of San Jose, California, economist, author, and farm labor organizer whose efforts date back to the mid-1940's. A Mexican American, whose face and hands bore the marks of long hard hours and years in the fields described Dr. Galarza as "el apostol de los campesinos," the apostle of the fieldworkers.

Only last April, Dr. Galarza had asserted at a conference on legislation before more than 500 Mexican Americans in Sacramento, California, that the mexicano must "imitate and beat the Anglo politician at his own game." His comments on the El Paso hearings echo this political orientation, for he noted that the hearings had "gotten together a lot of people who wanted the opportunity of exchanging ideas and enabled some of us to report on what was happening within the Mexican American community in general." La Raza Unida Conference provided "a stimulus for many people and insights into how the national Administration operates, something they wouldn't have gotten if the hearings hadn't been held," he said. Galarza, as others at the conference, attacked the "Administration's point of view and technique" in setting up the hearings. Chicano criticism, he said, centered on three main contentions: that the presence of two Presidents in El Paso for the signing of the Chamizal Treaty drew national attention away from the hearings; that the hearings themselves permitted only a minimum of audience participation; and that invitations had excluded the poor and youth to the degree that these groups were forced to resort to demonstrations before being allowed to participate. On the first point, the fact was cited that Saturday morning hearings were abruptly cancelled so that participants could be bused to the International Airport where President Johnson and President Gustavo Diaz Ordaz of Mexico addressed them.

Characterizing the hearings as a political manuever, Galarza said: "At issue is whether the Interagency Committee is merely a label and Ximenes a front for Johnson or whether we can count on them — right now my feelings are entirely negative."

With a new agency to develop, Ximenes had been "entitled to a fair chance," Galarza said, adding; "I was opposed to a boycott of the hearings and I think the papers presented were excellent and made an impressive indictment of the injustice existing in the areas covered." The conference, picketing, and demonstrations that did occur, he pointed out, "show how much tension exists among Mexican Americans."

"The White House Conference is not a dead issue," Galarza believes, "but I have no idea what the White House intends to do.

Fundamentally, when we get through all the gestures and all the loud noises, we're saying 'close the doors to the ghettos.' If the young people are cut off and not listened to, and if the administration keeps trying to suppress the poor, I can predict how they will react. If the Administration had the brass to try the kind of moves they pulled on people like myself and representatives of 50 other organizations, I hate to think of what they will try on people in the ghetto."

A direct result of La Raza Unida Conference, Galarza reported, was the formation of the Southwest Council for Mexican Americans which is seeking funds to provide what he believes the conference participants were in most urgent need of: "machinery to unify and to communicate."

What the Cabinet hearings lacked in color and drama, La Raza Unida Conference made up for and surpassed. Two general sessions were held on Friday and Saturday in the parish gym of Sacred Heart Catholic Church, located in "El Segundo," the south El Paso barrio where adobe shack and brick tenement conditions rival the worst urban slums in the Nation. In vigorous, resounding speeches, orators expressed frustrations, anger, and bitterness, but all of the speakers called for unity. Each gave the same basic message, of the urgent need to unit and to demand the rights due the Mexican American and solutions to his problems on the chicano's terms.

As never before, the voices of young people were raised, insisting on their rights and for increased opportunities particularly in education and employment. They showed little patience with the efforts of the veteran chicano leaders. One youth, Jose Angel Gutierrez of San Antonio, president of the Mexican American Youth Organization (MAYO) which manned picket lines from the start of the hearings along with about five other youth organizations, challenged the crowds in the barrio gym: "We are going to march and you can join us. But if you don't, you will be left behind." Another, Phil Castruita of the United Mexican American Students at California State College, remarked matter of factly: "The young chicanos see this conference (the hearings and La Raza Unida) as the last chance you older chicanos have to come through. If nothing happens from this you'll have to step aside or we'll walk over you."

Still another student, John Garcia of San Jose State College, who represented the Mexican American Student Association (MASA), spoke passionately of his sense of identity with the Mexican American culture, indicating that it had only recently begun to inspire his loyalty and commitment to the cause of La Raza. Speaking in Spanish, he declared: "We want our rights, not as gifts from the whites but as citizens. We have to stand up against injustices and demand they be stopped. You must let youth speak because the problems of the mexicano are not just the problems of the old people." He concluded that a new realization and acceptance of themselves as Mexican Americans were being generated in youth chicanos like "a fire . . . a fire that will not go out."

UMAS, MASA, and another activist group, the Brown Berets, can be credited with inspiring student walkouts on March 5 at five dominantly Mexican American high schools in East Los Angeles. The three groups had issued a 15-point set of grievances in February demanding removal of fences around Garfield High, inclusion of Mexican American history and culture in textbooks, easing of crowded conditions, and new schools. Planned for but spontaneously set off at Garfield when students rebelled at the cafeteria's lunch menu, the walkouts triggered student-police clashes, arrests, picketing, sit-ins by parents, and emergency school board sessions.

It is apparent in retrospect that the El Paso hearings brought into sharp focus the external problems facing the Mexican American and disposed high government officials to help alleviate them by, at the very least, "rules and regulations." But even more, it now appears that the hearings served as a catalyst to crystallize for the mexicano the pattern of internal difficulties underlying the more obvious issues: Lack of communication, lack of group awareness, lack of political "clout," lack of clear definitions of purpose and methods of operation, along with the need for coalitions with other minority groups for common objectives.

In a preamble to La Raza Unida Conference, the proclamation is made that "the time of subjugation, exploitation and abuse of human rights of La Raza in the United States is hereby ended forever . . . ." The conference "affirms the magnificence of La Raza, the greatness of our heritage, our history, our language, our traditions, our contributions to humanity and our culture . . . pledges to join with all our courageous people organizing in the fields and in the barrios. We commit ourselves to La Raza, at whatever cost."

These same aspirations were evident in and out of hearing rooms in conversations which pondered La Raza, in terms of "brown power" and "chicano power." There were buttons in evidence, too, with the most popular ones, an orange button showing a Mexican sombrero and crossed bandoleras (cartridge belts) reminiscent of the 1910 revolutionists in Mexico, another with the words, "Adequate programs and funds for Our People First then Viva Johnson," and the red button bearing the black eagle of "La Huelga," the farm labor organizing movement.

The hearings themselves provide a detailed rendering of the countless difficulties obstructing Mexican American aspirations throughout the Southwest and, perhaps of great surprise to move people, in good-sized chicano communities wherever Mexican Americans have settled, usually dropping out of the migrant stream, in places such as Chicago, Illinois; East Chicago, Indiana; East St. Louis, Illinois; where large "pueblos" exist; and in smaller communities in Wisconsin, Kansas, Indiana, Nebraska, Iowa, Michigan.

Maclovio Barraza of Tucson, Arizona, executive board member of the Mining, Mill & Smelter Workers Union spoke first before Undersecretary of Labor James Reynolds and Assistant Secretary Stanley Ruttenberg, substituting for Secretary of Labor W. Willard Wirtz who had to remain in Washington on personal business. (Barraza dropped out of the rest of the sessions, devoting his time to the La Raza Unida Conference. On Saturday he was chosen to act as temporary chairman of the Southwest Council.)

"Whatever other reasons many may have for distrusting the intentions of this conference," he told the Labor officials, "perhaps the most central is that we Mexican Americans are very disappointed with the performance of all levels of government. In spite of the many studies and voluminous reports, the many conferences and the big promises, we have yet to see any significant evidence of the kind of action needed at all levels of government to correct the legitimate grievances of our people." Citing recent civil rights measures, the antipovery and medicare programs and a mine safety bill as promising avenues for the Mexican American, he added:

"But what the Mexican American is saying is: It's not enough and it barely touches the many problems that beg attention. Our people are saying that before we shout Viva Johnson, there better be a Viva la gente mexicana program. There must be a bridge built immediately between the well-intentioned promises and some real positive action." Perhaps no other speaker spoke as strongly on the nature of the hearings nor pinpointed more forcefully key employment problems. Barraza called for inclusion of farmworkers under the National Labor

Relations Act and under the Fair Labor Standards Act, abolition of section 14b of the NLRA (the "right to work" provision), recruitment of Mexican Americans for Federal jobs, stronger enforcement of equal employment statutes by the EEOC, and evaluation of apprenticeship and training programs by the Department of Labor's Bureau of Apprenticeship Standards.

Barraza declared: "Along with the other disadvantaged people, the Mexican American is growing more and more restless. He's patient but it's running out. He may soon be forced to seek dramatic alternatives to his patience—alternatives that seem to bring more generous responses from government than obedient restraint in face of adversity and injustice." El Paso, itself, he said, has been described as a "powder keg . . . which could explode into violent riots far more intense than those of Watts, Detroit, or other cities."

Data presented by Hector B. Abeytia, of Fresno, Calif., then State director of the OEO-funded Manpower Opportunities Project in California, showed that according to 1960 census figures, Mexican Americans represent the largest minority group in the State, 9.1 percent of the population. Yet Mexican Americans completed fewer years in school than the next largest minority group, held fewer Federal jobs, generally set unemployment rates two percentage points greater than Anglos, enrolled less than half the numbers of Anglos or Negroes in Manpower Development Training programs, and were hired by federally financed contractors at a rate far below their proportion in the State.

Abeytia cited three "realities" under which MDT programs must be formulated: (1) Mexican Americans are at the bottom rung, (2) the bottom rung is continually being replenished by new poor from Mexico, (3) two permanent cultures—Mexican and Anglo—coexist in the Southwest. Strongest criticism of the commuter or green card worker situation along the United States-Mexico border came from Henry Muñoz, Jr., director of Equal Opportunity, Texas AFL-CIO, and Robert Sanchez, a McAllen, Tex., attorney. Muñoz called it "a national scandal that U.S. citizens who work for as little as 25 cents along the Texas-Mexican border have to compete with 90,000 Mexican-Alien green card commuters in all job classifications—this is the primary cause of unemployment and underemployment." In support of their charges, Judge Philip M. Newman of the Los Angeles Municipal Court stated that the Immigration and Naturalization Service "has established the fiction of the commuter without any statutory authority. . . . Their rationale has been 'to equate employment with domicile.'" Enforcement of the Alien Registration Receipt card (form I–151) by insisting on actual residence in the United States or terminating a holder's card after allowing a reasonable period for establishing residence, was viewed by the speakers as a "humane solution" to the problem.

A detailed analysis of the problems of chicano youth was presented by Sal Ramirez, director of the South El Paso Boys Club Juvenile Delinquency Project. Median age of the Mexican American population is 20 years, he said, and because 80 percent of all Mexican Americans live in cities, young Mexican Americans are consequently city dwellers, too, he indicated. "Inadequate educational preparation, low socio-economic status, limited monetary resources, cultural conflict, language barrier, prejudice, and discrimination," he stated, are obstacles which abort their chance for gainful employment, and "its subsequent benefits for social mobility, advancement, achievement, and recognition."

He suggested that work programs pertaining "more directly to the post-placement performance of the individual" and "geared" to the existing labor market," would be of greater aid than "a proliferation of 'stopgap' employment programs." He concluded that "it is the responsibility of the Mexican American and the Anglo American population segments to find solutions to community problems. . . . The opening of new horizons, new opportunities, cannot wait for another generation of Mexican American youth to join and increase the ranks of the disadvantaged."

One of the most controversial issues of the day, the land grant conflict in northern New Mexico, drew the attention of four main speakers in the hearings on agriculture presided over by Secretary of Agriculture Orville L. Freeman.

The most controversial figure in a highly publicized case, Reies Lopez Tijerina, was absent from this hearing. The leader of the Federal Alliance of Land Grants, as his northern New Mexico organization was originally called, had not been invited to participate in the hearings but he came to El Paso anyway. At the time of the hearings, the 41-year-old Tijerina was facing trial in Las Cruces on five charges related to a takeover of the Echo Amphitheater campgrounds in Rio Arriba County, N.M., in October 1966, by a band of Spanish Americans. On November 11, 1967, Tijerina and four members of the Alliance, recently renamed the Federation of Free City-States, were convicted on at least one count each. On December 15, the Alliance leader, convicted of assaulting two Forest Service officers, was sentenced to two years in prison. The decision is on appeal.

Tijerina, a Texan by birth, still faces another trial on charges filed following a raid of the Tierra Amarilla Courthouse on June 5. All the facts have still to be sifted out but basically Tijerina and 18 of his followers were charged with armed assault on a jail after occupying the courthouse, wounding or beating three officers, and taking two persons as hostages. At a preliminary hearing on January 29 in Santa Fe County District Court, kidnapping charges were reduced to false imprisonment, all charges dropped against 10 Alianzistas while the rest, including Tijerina, were bound over for trial but released on bail.

To La Raza Unida audience which included one man who wildly strummed a guitar as he approached the microphone, Tijerina said: "Reform of the land started on June 5 in Tierra Amarilla. Fear is gone in New Mexico as of June 5. We have learned from those militants [black power militants] that the government respects nothing more than power. We need a spark to fire our movement—that spark is not communism but justice," he declaimed. "Without union, we will continue to keep getting the powdered milk of services. We must unite and fight for justice, not justice in books, but justice in our culture, our language, and in the land. We have discovered the valor that is in the land and in justice," he concluded.

During the hearing on economic and social development conducted by John Macy and attended by Ximenes and William L. Taylor, Staff Director of the U.S. Commission on Civil Rights, Dr. Clark Knowlton, chairman of the department of sociology at the University of Texas at El Paso, stated:

"Until [Spanish Americans] as a people, experience the physical return of all or a good part of the land taken from them or receive what they define as an adequate compensation, the deeply rooted burning emotions of resentment and of having suffered historical injustice will continue to exist. The poisonous abscesses of alienation, rejection of Anglo American society, and poverty . . . should be lanced. If they are not, the accelerating slide of the Spanish Americans toward rural violence cannot be halted," he said.

A laissez faire policy, he stated, would perpetuate the serious conditions of poverty in northern New Mexico and southern Colorado. "Outmigration will continue to send out of the region hundreds of poorly educated, unskilled, semi-acculturated workers to add to the social problems of our larger cities. It is far easier to struggle with the problems of rural New Mexico and southern Colorado than it is with the problems of the large slums and ghettos. Time is running out. The land issue has reached a crisis point. If it is not resolved soon, Spanish American desperation will increasingly find an outlet in violence."

Conflicting viewpoints underlie the New Mexico land issue, stated Tomas C. Atencio, associate director of the Colorado State Migrant Council in Boulder, Colorado. "Land tenure and land use are perhaps the most prominent areas in which conflict between the government bureaus and the native population of northern New Mexico exist. The traditional subsistence stock farmer continues to perceive that the land surrounding his community that was there for his ancestors, is there for him to enjoy. Forest Service officials have informed him to the contrary and have imposed procedures consistent with their own priorities," he said.

Fiscal obligations for 1968 in Colorado provide $242,868 for range and revegetation but more than $2.4 million for recreation facilities, and in New Mexico $240,753 for range and revegetation but $1.2 million for recreation, with similar differences to be found in California, Arizona, and Texas, he reported. Atencio suggested a thorough reexamination of Forest Service programs and services with the purpose of evaluating them according to the culture and values of the Spanish surname American.

In the same Cabinet hearing, Dr. Sabine Ulibarri of the University of New Mexico, insisted that the Spanish cultural heritage of the Southwest should be preserved and nurtured through the use of the Spanish language in the schools as well as instruction in the culture, the history, and social contributions of Spanish-speaking people to America.

The Federal Government "has a responsibility to support daring, imaginative, and possibly ridiculous research" to find solutions to the social problems of the Southwest, said Ralph Guzman, a member of the faculty of California State College at Los Angeles and formerly assistant director of the Mexican American Study Project sponsored by the University of California at Los Angeles. He added that government must "dare to trust the poor to direct their own lives, dare to trust them to administer programs, to establish direction, and to make decisions."

Bilingual education for the Mexican American child was the major focus in the Health, Education, and Welfare hearing held by John W. Gardner, at that time Secretary of Health, Education, and Welfare.

Funds must be earmarked for specific programs dealing with the Spanish-speaking child from preschool years through college, a number of speakers asserted. For example, Dr. Julian Nava, member of the Los Angeles Board of Education, suggested that curricula should be revised "to give proper attention to Hispano-Mexican contributions to Western civilization and America." He suggested that precollege aid be given Mexican American students and that admission policies be modified to admit youths who may not meet formal academic standards but show potential and motivation to complete college studies.

"A militancy for higher education" was advocated by Priscilla S. Mares of Denver, Colorado, executive director of the Latin American Educational Foundation, to promote the desire and the ability of Mexican Americans to attend college. She cited Weld County, Colorado, as having not only one of the lowest income levels of Spanish surname families in the State but also the lowest median school year level of 15 counties with large Spanish surname populations — six years. From 50 to as high as 80 percent of Spanish surname adults in most counties of the State had not advanced beyond the eighth grade, she added.

Augustin Flores of Riverside, California, past president of the American G.I. Forum, delivered a paper before the Housing and Urban Development hearing headed by Secretary Robert C. Weaver which covered four major areas of concern to Mexican Americans. On financing, Flores suggested the lowering of loan requirements to more realistic levels, adjustment of financing requirements to cost-of-living demands of the target area, and the lowering of interest rates and extension of loan periods. On personnel, he cited the need for bilingual Mexican American staff. On policy, he urged participation of people in target urban renewal areas to determine their wishes. On research, he suggested formation of a national advisory committee on housing needs of Mexican Americans and provision of adequate research grants to document these needs.

The relationship of education and employment needs to substandard housing conditions was shown by Lorenzo A. Chavez, an attorney of Albuquerque, New Mexico. Citing statistics from a study of Bernalillo County, New Mexico, in 1966, by Philip Reno, he pointed out that of 10 census tracts surveyed having large Spanish surname representation, families with less than $3,000 annual income ranged from 20-46 percent, adults with less than 8 years schooling from 23-60 percent, and percentage of substandard housing from 15-69 percent. Unemployment ranged from 4.7 percent to 14.5 percent.

Jose Morales, Jr., of New York, Puerto Rican Community Development Project executive director, reported on the mounting problems in housing faced by the more than 600,000 Puerto Ricans in New York City alone where the number of low-rent apartment units has been steadily decreasing.

Carlos Truan of Corpus Christi, an attorney, added: "Programs should be geared to helping not only the children, but the parents as well. Head Start is good, but the adult poor wants dignity and worth today, not 20 years from now!" Involvement of the poor in decision making processes of Community Action Programs was an essential ingredient of the antipoverty campaign and must be preserved, Truan said.

Daniel R. Lopez, East Los Angeles Service Center director, recommended the multiservice center format as a proven means of providing coordinated agency services to the poor. He called for full appropriation of requested funds for the war on poverty, continued centralization of OEO programs under the Office of Economic Opportunity, more flexibility for local poverty agencies in the use of funds, and legislation to permit component agencies of service centers to share costs of intake operations on a prorated basis.

Census surveys for 1960 and 1965 in the East Los Angeles area showed an increase of from 66.1 percent to approximately 76 percent in the Spanish surname population out of a total of 228,000, Lopez noted. The influx, attributed by Lopez largely to former farmworkers, "further aggravated . . . the dangerously overcrowded conditions of already poor housing" conditions that "defy the imagination."

Poverty conditions in an area such as East Los Angeles, Lopez said, are illustrated by health district figures: TB case rate, 31.6 percent as compared to 20.6 percent in Los Angeles County; TB death rate, 6.2 percent to 2.8 percent for the county; syphilis case rate, 122.7 percent above 1958 figures to 88.7 percent for the county.

The direction and speed of the Mexican American movement is still difficult to gauge at this moment. Indications since the Cabinet hearings and La Raza Unida Conference give the generation picture of a people re-evaluating and regrouping. But no one is taking the challenge offered by the El Paso event lightly.

Efforts of the Interagency Committee and of proponents of La Raza Unida so far indicate that yet another period of debate and of action is in the offing. Both elements should serve as a yardstick and a spur to each other. The Interagency has its program of watchdogging agencies and advising government departments on the Mexican American.

Keeping La Raza Unida on the move, the Southwest Council met in Tucson in mid-December on the same weekend that various chicano youth groups were conferring in El Paso. A meeting stressing legislative and political involvement was held in January in San Antonio, Texas, two others in March in Laredo, Texas, and Sacramento, California, and will be followed by other meetings soon in other Southwest States.

It was Corky Gonzales of Denver, Colorado, before a La Raza Unida session, who called for a declaration of independence for the Mexican American. "We have to start judging our lives with new values," he said. "The Anglos consider us conquered citizens, but we are not second class citizens. We must declare that our rights under the Treaty of Guadalupe-Hidalgo be recognized, that the educational system be changed and include bilingual teaching and the history of the Mexican American. Que viva la raza y la revolucion!"

Gonzales refers in his statement to the Treaty of Guadalupe-Hidalgo which was formulated in 1848 to conclude the war between the United States and Mexico. Provisions in the document, especially Articles 8, 9, and 10, treat of the political or civil and land rights of the Mexican people who remained to become American citizens within the new boundaries established by the treaty. Many Mexican American leaders have publicly called for the Federal Government to live up to those provisions and trace many of the troubles confronting Mexican Americans today to violations of that treaty.

The conclusion of Maclovio Barraza in his speech before the Cabinet hearing on labor is perhaps the best summation of the challenge which the chicano — and the Nation — faces: "Our government and our institutions are confronted with a challenge to meet the crisis in our own country. The Mexican American is eager to make this Nation faithful to its democratic tenets.

"If we accept this challenge as an opportunity to perfect our way of life, we will succeed in making this Nation and the world a better place for all people. If we continue to be blinded by prejudice and selfishness of a few, do we deserve the place of world leadership that destiny has thrust upon us? We must start now towards our avowed national goals. Mañana is too late."

HEALTH

HEALTH

Health can be studied from a socio-cultural point of view in terms of epidemiology, of attitudes, values and practices, or of statistical measures, and this can be done for both physical and mental health. One can count and report illnesses and causes of death for a group; beyond this, what is most important is that group's characteristic attitudes and behaviors toward health matters.

Statistically, Mexican Americans show higher than average rates of tuberculosis, infant mortality, chronic disease, and illnesses associated with poverty and lack of adequate medical care. Studies of specific Mexican American communities show that over half the pre-school children did not receive immunization, that half of the families had no family doctor, and about 85% did not own health insurance. Many Mexican Americans are geographically mobile, which hampers health care for any group.

Among Mexican Americans more than among Anglos, the family itself tries to treat illnesses. This conforms to Mexican culture norms, to the norms of the subculture of poverty, and to social expectation and definition of the situation in extended family cultures. Other than this, the major difference in middle class Anglo culture and the Mexican American subculture is the prevalence of the belief that some types of illness are of supernatural origin. It is not that all Mexican Americans do not recognize the germ theory of disease and the desirability of pills and injections, but rather that some Mexican Americans and Spanish Americans still recognize an additional source or factor in illness. Mental illness in particular and "unexplained" illnesses in general are more likely to be treated as having supernatural causes.

The major interest of Dr. William Madsen, an anthropologist, when he made a study of a county on the Texas-Mexican border, was in the relationship between society, culture, and health. The selection reproduced here is his chapter on "Health and Illness" from *Society and Health in the Lower Rio Grande Valley*.

In recent years the relationship of mental health to culture has come under close scrutiny, and in general the findings show a close and significant relationship. Studies by anthropologists and sociologists on

327

"Mental Illness Among the . . . " are increasingly common, and uniformly fruitful. The selection "Perception of Mental Illness in a Mexican-American Community" is authored in part by Dr. Marvin Karno, a research psychiatrist who is probably the outstanding authority on mental illness among Mexican Americans. His co-author, Dr. Robert B. Edgerton is on the research staff of the UCLA School of Medicine.

SOCIETY AND HEALTH
IN THE LOWER RIO GRANDE VALLEY*

WILLIAM MADSEN

Health and Illness

The illness of an individual is always a matter of concern for the extended family. No member of a Mexican-American family is regarded as ill unless the head of the family agrees that he is. No major treatment is ever accepted for a sick person unless the head of the family has approved of it. The health worker is not dealing with a single individual but with an extended family which often includes distant relatives and compadres.

A. Concept of Illness

The family usually is reluctant to relinquish its responsibility for sick members and frequently resists hospitalization. The impersonal environment of a hospital or mental institution seems cold and unpleasant to the Mexican-American who values the affective interpersonal relations of his family environment. Hospital schedules and unfamiliar food are distasteful to the Mexican-American patient. Finally, the hospital is feared as "a place where people go to die."

Mexican-American folk medicine diagnoses illness on the basis of its natural or supernatural causation. Most mental illness is believed to be of supernatural origin. Diseases of supernatural origin fall into three main categories: 1) those sent by God or a saint as punishment for misdeeds; 2) those caused by witchcraft or the evil eye; and 3) fright sickness caused by seeing ghosts. These theories of disease are most prevalent among the lower classes but also permeate the entire class system. Middle or upper class families and anglicized individuals often deride supernatural concepts of illness, but it is common practice for such avowed skeptics to cite cases of witchcraft which they have witnessed.

All local variations of Mexican-American disease theory and treatment in South Texas cannot be described here, but the general pattern

*Published by the Hogg Foundation for Mental Health, The University of Texas, Austin, 1961.

will be presented. A variety of illnesses is believed to be the result of witchcraft. An individual who wants to harm his enemy may hire a witch who specializes in the magical causation of "daños" (harms). A leading motive for bewitchment is "envidia" or envy of the prosperous individual who indulges in conspicuous consumption, to the discomfort of his less fortunate neighbors. Other motives are sexual jealousy and the desire to avenge an insult.

Witch-sent illnesses are called "enfermedades mal puestas." The magical techniques for causing illnesses are supposed to be professional secrets known only to witches. Some herb stores sell books on black magic and the necessary paraphernalia to laymen, but the amateur is never sure that his magic will work, whereas most witches guarantee their results. Whether the magic is amateur or professional, there is always a method of notifying the victim that he has been hexed, causing him to suffer from shock.

Mental illness is the most common form of disease inflicted through witchcraft. There is a strong belief that certain individuals are more susceptible than others to mental illness, bewitchment, and venereal disease. The mental illness called "demencia" (insanity) is said to come from an "aire" — an evil element put into the air by a witch — directed at the victim. Symptoms of demencia include amnesia, hallucinations, and guilt or persecution complexes. A victim of the most extreme form is called "loco de remate" and is believed to be incurably insane. He is committed to a mental institution only if he becomes violent.

A milder mental disturbance caused by bewitchment is called "miedo" (fear). The victim is so frightened that he imagines seeing frightful things that do not exist and cannot be observed by normal people. The ailment known as "visiones" causes the victim to see visions of the menacing witch and his client who are sometimes reported to leave their teeth marks or scratches on the patient's body. The Mexican-American distinction between these two witch-sent illnesses is that the victim of "miedo" just imagines seeing things while the victim of "visiones" sees real visions of those who are harming him.

Evil-eye sickness ("mal de ojo") is caused unintentionally by certain individuals who are born with a powerful magic force in their eyes. When such an individual looks with admiration or desire at someone, his look releases an evil force which enters the person's body and causes illness. If the individual with the evil eye admires an object such as a vase, it may crack. Today, it is said in the Valley that people with the evil eye have much "electricity" in them. The victims of evil-eye sickness are usually children. Young animals are also susceptible to this disease.

Fright from seeing ghosts is called "espanto" and the victim is described as "espantado." Symptoms of this illness are restlessness, sadness, nervous tension, dizziness, and weakness. The patient's mind and vision may both be clouded.

Natural illnesses are caused by improper diet, emotional upsets, night air, drafts, fatigue, and injuries. Any ailment which seems minor at the outset is presumed to be natural illness amenable to treatment with home remedies. But there is always the possibility that a seemingly natural illness or injury, such as a broken arm, may have been caused by God as a punishment for immoral behavior. The illness or injury may also be inflicted on the sinner's child to make his parents realize that their wrongdoings harm others.

Common emotional illnesses of natural origin are "susto" and "bilis." Susto is an illness caused by any natural fright such as seeing a poisonous snake or witnessing a murder. The symptoms are similar to those of "espanto" but much less serious and easier to cure. The adult afflicted with "susto" suffers a general malaise and frequently has horrible dreams about the fright that made him ill. Symptoms of the disease manifested by children are crying, whining, sadness, insomnia, and nightmares. Tuberculosis is believed to be a complication of advanced susto ("susto pasado") that has not been treated. If the susto is cured, the tuberculosis will respond to simple home treatment according to Mexican-American disease theory which does not classify tuberculosis as a communicable disease. Most Mexican-Americans do not understand the medical insistence on isolating cases of tuberculosis. This disease is called "tis" by the Spanish-speaking population.

Strong anger ("coraje") causes the illness known as "bilis" which produces an overflowing of yellow stomach bile that results in diarrhea, vomiting, and sometimes a yellowish complexion. This concept is a survival of the Hippocratic theory that sickness results from an imbalance of the four bodily humors: blood, phlegm, choler (the yellow bile that causes anger), and melancholia (the black bile that produces gloominess). An imbalance of the humors is characterized by an overheated or underheated body which must be restored to its normal temperature by proper diet. A sick person whose body is too "hot" must consume foods and herb medicines classified as "cold," while a cold body needs "hot" foods and medicines. The categories of "hot" and "cold" have no references to the actual temperature of the foods but refer to the supposed effects of the foods on the human body. Hippocratic medicine was introduced into Mexico by the Spaniards in the 16th century and is still a basic part of Mexican folk medicine but is of little significance in Mexican-American folk medicine of South Texas. Minor stomach upsets are believed to be caused by eating too many hot or cold foods in most communities, but the hot-cold complex is completely lacking in some localities.

A draft called "un aire" or "un golpe de aire" can cause a common cold or the flu which are both regarded as natural diseases. Night air ("sereno") is dangerous to anybody although it is especially dangerous to children. Particular care is taken to see that no windows are open in the room where a baby sleeps. A child's head must be covered if he is taken out at night.

Children are subject to a number of other ailments. Even in his mother's womb, the unborn child must be protected from dangers unknown to Anglos. An expectant mother fears that the full moon may injure her fetus causing it to be born with a harelip or some other defect. To protect her child, she may wear a string around her waist holding a piece of metal over her abdomen. A nursing mother who again becomes pregnant gives contaminated milk which causes the child to have digestive disturbance and anger. The mother is then called "chipilesa" and the child "chipil." Any emotional extreme experienced by a child may endanger his health. Heart disease is believed to be possibly a complication of anger or fright.

Any fall or bump suffered by an infant can cause the illness known as "caida de la mollera" which occurs when the fontanelle "collapses" inward toward the brain. The fontanelle is regarded as a loose and movable thing because one can feel it throb. A baby's head is always carefully cushioned and protected to prevent fallen fontanelle. This condition produces sadness and lack of appetite.

When a child becomes extremely thin and has a protruding belly, he is called a "panzon." The actual cause of this condition is usually intestinal parasites, but Mexican-Americans believe it comes from overeating.

B. The Medical Referral System

When a minor illness presumed to be of natural origin does not respond to home treatment with herb remedies, patent medicines, and prayers, outside help is sought. Lower or middle class families may solicit the aid of a neighbor or compadre who has had some experience with curing if the patient does not seem too sick.

In the event that the patient still fails to improve, his family may consult a diviner ("adivino") to determine the nature and cause of the disease. Diviners also sell their services to help locate lost objects or foretell the future. After diagnosing the case, the diviner often recommends a specific "curandero" (folk curer) or undertakes treatment himself if he happens to be a curer as well as a diviner. Upper class anglicized Mexican-Americans consult physicians, naturopaths, or chiropractors instead of diviners or curanderos.

Professional physicians are viewed with suspicion and hostility by conservative members of the lower class who generally regard the germ theory of disease as a fraudulent scheme to help Anglo doctors and nurses extract exorbitant fees from the gullible. The Mexican-American skeptic in this case reasons that germs which cannot be seen cannot exist. He often refers to germs as "animalitos" (little animals). Furthermore, he knows that physicians lack the knowledge needed. to treat illnesses of supernatural origin. He may even doubt the physician's knowledge of natural diseases. He points out that a curandero "knows" how to treat a patient, but a physician has to consult books, colleagues, or rely on x-rays to discover the cause of an ailment. A curandero petitions God and the saints for aid in the cure but a physician generally ignores the possibility of divine help. As one Mexican-American put it: "Doctors act as though they know more than God who created them."

The typical physician and nurse fail to achieve the close affective relationship with Mexican-American patients which is so characteristic of curandero-client relations. The most obvious reason for this failure is the language barrier between the Anglo physician or nurse and the Mexican-American patient who speaks little English. A second reason is the authoritarian relationship which the physician and nurse assume with the Mexican-American patients. The patient feels that the doctor and nurse are unconcerned with his welfare, his feelings, and the obligation of his family. As a final insult, the physician may ridicule the patient's self-diagnosis made in terms of folk disease theory.

The curandero maintains close relations with both the client and his family. He patiently explains the cause and nature of the affliction and the reasons behind each step of the treatment. These explanations are meaningful in the context of the Mexican-American world view and great interest is taken in them. The curandero often uses great skill in manipulating interpersonal relations within the family so as to relieve pressures that produce stress and anxiety in the patient. In several documented cases, curanderos have cured mental illness after psychiatric treatment has failed.

The conservative Mexican-American consults a physician only as a last resort when all other curing techniques have failed. His attitude is comparable to that of an educated Anglo who places his life in the hands of a faith healer when his physician has told him his disease is fatal and incurable. Even as a last resort, the Mexican-American makes little or no attempt to understand the physician's diagnosis and treatment because he is used to carrying out orders without question in this type of role relationship with an Anglo.

The fact that many Mexican-American patients come under a physician's care only when the disease is far advanced lowers the chances of a successful cure. Every failure to restore the health of a Mexican-American patient is widely cited as evidence of the inefficiency of scientific medicine. While the patient is under the physician's care, his family continues to appeal for divine aid and administers folk remedies to him at home if his case does not require hospitalization. When the patient does not improve quickly, his family may transfer him to the care of another doctor or back to a curandero.

The term "curanderismo" refers to the entire system of disease theory and curing techniques associated with the curandero whose healing powers are believed to be a divine gift from God. The curandero or curandera is a highly respected individual who often receives the honorific title of "don" or "dona." Most curanderos learn some of their techniques from older folk curers.

Patients are received in the parlor of the curandero's home which is furnished with an altar containing images and pictures of Christ and the saints. All cures involve offerings of flowers and vigil lights. Similar offerings accompanied by prayers are made by the patient's family at his home altar. By the altar, there is a container of holy water, frequently prepared merely by the blessing of the curandero, who uses it in many of his treatments. While some curanderos charge a standard fee for each treatment, others make no request for payment but expect the patient to leave a monetary offering on the altar before leaving. The amount left is usually one dollar.

The general curandero handles a wide variety of cases but specializes in diseases of supernatural origin, with the exception of bewitchment illnesses which are treated only by witches, spiritists ("espiritistas"), and spiritualists ("espiritualistas"). Cases of critical illness usually are refused by the general curandero who refers them to a physician or a hospital in order to avoid the legal embarrassment of having a patient die under his care.

Some curanderos also are believed to possess powers of witchcraft or black magic which are believed to come from the Devil rather than from God. The witch-doctor is called a "brujo" or "bruja." He is said to have the power to change himself into an owl which can fly. Witches are feared and disliked to the point of being physically attacked on occasions. It is believed that a witch who bleeds profusely from a wound will lose his evil powers.

In addition to witches, there are a number of other specialists including the midwife ("partera"), the herbalist ("yerbero"), and the bone setter ("huesero"). Spiritist and spiritualist curers will treat almost any kind of illness but their services are sought mainly in cases of bewitchment. They must undergo an extensive period of training at centers in Mexico or by taking correspondence courses in order to become proficient in their curing techniques which are different from those of the general curandero. They divine and cure with the aid of spirits of the dead. Their fees are much higher than those of the general curandero.

Any curandero must demonstrate his abilities by a series of successful cures in order to enjoy a large clientele. A novice just starting in the business is suspected of being a fraud until he proves that he is not. Unless his first cases are cured, he receives no more business and may be forcibly driven from the community.

The most common techniques of curing practiced by the general curandero are: "cleaning" the patient's body with a handful of medicinal herbs and an unbroken egg to draw out the contamination which is causing the illness; administering herb teas; reciting prayers; and making offerings of flowers and candies to God or the saints. The cleansing ("limpia") ritual is used to treat espanto, susto, evil eye, and some kinds of bewitchment.

The curandero's procedure may be illustrated by a typical treatment for espanto. The patient suffering from this disease must be taken immediately to a curandero or witch doctor who is skilled in treating espanto. The diagnosis is based on the patient's pulse beat. The patient lies on a dirt floor while the curandero outlines his figure in the earth with a knife. After the sick person rises, the curandero scoops up the dirt from the marks of the outline, mixes it with water, and gives the mixture to his patient to drink. Next the patient drinks an herb tea made with a few sprigs of pennyroyal ("poleo") boiled in water. Finally, the curandero cleans his patient with a handful of herbs including pennyroyal and rosemary ("romero"). Throughout the treatment the curandero recites the Lord's prayer and chants Hail Marys. This treatment must be performed daily for nine days or repeated three times a day for three days. During this period, it is the duty of the patient's family to urge the offending ghost to return to purgatory and seek eventual rest. God is asked to reclaim the ghost from this world. Prayers are accompanied by offerings and vigil lights placed on the home altar. The family tries to obtain a photograph of the man whose ghost is causing the illness. If they succeed, the picture is sprinkled with fresh flowers dipped in holy water every day during the period of treatment. A much simpler cure for fright from natural causes involves cleaning the patient with an unbroken egg and giving him herb teas.

Recovery from any serious illness may be effected through a patient's vow to make a pilgrimage to a holy shrine in return for divine help. The most important shrine in Texas is that of Don Petro Jaramillo, in Fulfurrias. The spirit of this dead curandero is now revered as a saint by thousands of Mexican-Americans. Two popular pilgrimage centers in Mexico are the shrine of the Virgin of San Juan de los Lagos in Jalisco and the shrine of El Chorrito in Nuevo Leon. The most sacred shrine in Mexico is the Basilica of Our Lady of Guadalupe.

Recommendations

Improvement of health facilities and practices in South Texas presents the two-fold problem of gaining Mexican-American acceptance of scientific medicine without disrupting the social organization and creating unnecessary tensions.

New practices can be introduced in any society by: 1) attempting to make the new form compatible with the established value system of the receiving culture; or 2) attempting to change that value system in order to replace it in part with both the form and associated meaning of a complex concept. Trying to "sell" people on both the form and meaning of an innovation is a difficult and time-consuming process which is likely to arouse hostility. In dealing with health and welfare problems, the best approach is to begin with the first method by adapting scientific medical services to Mexican-American culture patterns. In due time, it may be possible to increase the acceptance of modern medical theory without arousing widespread antagonism between the advocates of scientific medicine and the advocates of Mexican-American folk medicine.

Specific suggestions for an integrated program of health service improvement among the Mexican-American population are presented below:

1. *Improve communication between health workers and Mexican-American patients by making a concerted effort to overcome the language barrier.*

Although the ultimate goal should be for all doctors and nurses who deal extensively with Mexican-American patients to learn Spanish, the immediate goal can be limited to: a) placing a few Spanish-speaking personnel in key positions in every clinic and hospital; b) assigning house-calls to Spanish-speaking health and welfare workers; c) hiring a health or welfare department translator who would be on call to accompany Mexican-American patients to the doctor's office; and d) improving the teaching of English in the public schools.

2. *Increase knowledge and understanding of Mexican-American folk culture among health and welfare workers.*

This immediate goal could be achieved by means of short but intense courses given periodically by an anthropologist who has worked in South Texas. The course should include the basic concepts of: culture, cultural relativity, culture conflict, culture change, and culture integration. In applying these concepts to Mexican-American culture, stress should be placed on the importance of observing the Latin rules of etiquette that govern the conduct of interpersonal relations. Health and welfare workers must know how to deal with Mexican-Americans as individuals and as members of a family group without offending them. Reference books on Mexican-American culture should be available for the professional staff.

3. *Improve the physical appearance of the clinics, making them more attractive to Mexican-Americans so that they will associate modern health services with pleasant surroundings.*

The typically drab walls of the clinics could be painted in pastel colors and decorated with simple religious symbols. Flower pots placed around the waiting rooms would appeal to the Mexican-American fondness for flowers. Where feasible, low background music featuring Mexican songs would be appreciated. A comfortable reading room with pictorial magazines and literature on health problems should be provided for patients and the relatives who accompany them to the clinic.

4.   *Treat illness in addition to the practice of preventive medicine at those clinics where it is feasible.*

The idea that one can prevent illness by certain health precautions is difficult to communicate to the many Mexican-Americans who still believe that any illness may have a direct supernatural origin. Such a fatalistic theory of disease makes no provision for preventive medicine, and indeed, may occasionally serve as a deterrent to modern public health practice since human attempts to thwart divine will are regarded as sinful. This common belief that illnesses of a supernatural origin cannot be prevented by any kind of medicine severely hampers the effectiveness of a public health clinic which is restricted to public education and preventive measures. Despite the belief in supernatural causation, once an illness is recognized it is the duty of the family to seek treatment. To the extent that modern medicine can demonstrate curative effectiveness, the Mexican-American will turn to it for help.

5.   *Show respect for Mexican-American beliefs about health instead of ridiculing them as "superstitions."*

Do not discourage or ridicule appeals for divine aid and the use of herb teas which are certainly harmless and may be beneficial. Suggest that the patient also try the physician's recommendations *in addition* to these folk remedies.

6.   *Combat the notion that clinic patients are accepting charity.*

This goal can be achieved by: a) charging a token payment (e.g., 25 cents a visit) and giving the patient a receipt to prove that he did not accept charity; or b) hang signs on the wall saying that this clinic is supported by the people through the taxes that they pay on income and luxuries. The Mexican-American value system prohibits the direct acceptance of charity. Since the clinics are commonly associated with charity cases, the Mexican-American often feels that going to a clinic might make him lose face with his neighbors.

7.   *Establish friendly doctor-patient and nurse-patient relationships in place of the authoritarian relationship that now exists between the Anglo doctor or nurse and the Mexican-American patient.*

The doctor or nurse should greet the Mexican-American patient cordially, shake hands, and chat pleasantly with him for a few minutes. The doctor should suggest treatment, not give orders.

8. *Deal with the family as well as the patient.*

Encourage expectant mothers to bring an older female relative with them to classes. Before treating illness, request consultation with the patient's parents and obtain the permission of the male head of the family to try a particular treatment.

9. *Protect the Mexican-American patient's strong sense of modesty.*

Avoid physical exposure of the female patient before a male doctor and the male patient before a female nurse whenever possible. The same principles should be followed in instruction courses utilizing illustrations.

10. *Publicize the advantages of scientific medicine.*

An occasional open house at the clinic should present talks on modern medical facilities by respected Mexican-Americans, including patients who have been cured by scientific techniques. The open house should be a festive occasion accompanied by refreshments, mariachi or band music, and movies. Conferences with priests and ministers should suggest their advocacy of modern medical facilities.

11. *Add a Mexican-American interviewer to the staff of each clinic and hospital to act as an intermediary between the doctor and the patient.*

The interviewer must be a respected local resident, preferably one who holds the honorific title of "don" or "dona." He should be the first member of the staff to receive the patient and his family in a private room. The clinic interview, conducted in Spanish, should obtain the patient's case history including his self-diagnosis, symptoms, and previous treatments for the present ailment. The interviewer then accompanies the patient to the nurse or doctor who merely greets and examines the patient. The interviewer then describes the symptoms to the doctor who in turn will explain the recommended treatment to the interviewer. He returns to the interview room with the patient, calls in the family, and explains each step of the recommended treatment in terms that are meaningful to the Mexican-American. He remains with the patient during the treatment given at the clinic. He would also accompany nurses and doctors on house-calls and make follow-up calls by himself to see that the treatment is being carried out. The hospital interviewer would receive the patient and explain hospital procedures to him on admittance. He would visit the patient daily and make reports to his family. A curandero (but not a witch doctor) would be the person most likely to have the prerequisites for this job.

12. *Clinic lectures should be given in Spanish in terms that are compatible with the concepts of Mexican-American folk medicine.*

For example, penicillin can be described as a gift from God to man enabling man to help cure himself. Lectures on germs should not be illustrated with cartoons. The existence of germs can be most convincingly proved by live demonstrations with microprojection so that the "animalitos" can actually be seen. Displays of biological specimens are also effective in illustrating talks. Lectures on nutrition should stay within the bounds of Mexican-American eating customs and avoid recommending diets that the clinic patient cannot afford or finds distasteful. Clinics should not try to teach Anglo child-training practices which are incompatible with Mexican-American culture.

13. *Make the Mexican-American patient more comfortable in a hospital.*

Allow his family to visit him for longer periods of time, if possible, and allow the mother of a hospitalized child to stay with him at night. Serve the patient Mexican-American food or allow his family to bring him food. The "tasteless" quality of Anglo cooking in most hospitals is almost nauseating to the Mexican-American. The availability of a hospital altar and holy pictures would also make him feel less apprehensive. Children appreciate any kind of entertainment, such as television cartoons, in the hospital. The adult patient who adheres to the concepts of folk medicine will have far more confidence in the successful outcome of his hospital treatment if his curandero or the Mexican-American interviewer is allowed to visit him under a program of joint treatment supervised by the physician.

14. *Improve relations between medical personnel and curanderos.*

Direct oral and legal attacks on curanderos should be avoided wherever possible. If curanderismo is driven underground it could become much more difficult to manage. One excellent way to establish a working relationship with selected curanderos would be to give them brief courses permitting them to qualify as practical nurses. They could be given impressive diplomas, allowed to wear uniforms or emblems, and given simple medicines such as aspirin for their patients. They could be taught to work with physicians and to bring their patients to clinics and hospitals. Their cooperation in this way would undoubtedly increase the number of cases referred to physicians. Cooperation between physicians and curanderos could be particularly valuable in those cases of mental illness which would respond to treatment better in a home environment than in an institution. The value conflicts often present in the Mexican-American ex-patient when he returns from the Anglo-oriented mental hospital to his home environment would be minimized by the presence of a properly trained practical nurse or social worker.

It may be impractical to apply all of these recommendations simultaneously in any one area. The most suitable suggestions can be combined in drawing up workable programs adapted to local situations. If these programs increase Mexican-American confidence in modern medical services, then Public Health workers will be in a much more favorable position to explain the scientific bases of preventive medicine, sanitation measures, and disease treatment.

In concluding, it seems appropriate to emphasize the fact that U.S. culture is the product of peoples from many lands. Our Mexican-American heritage deserves understanding and respect. In this era of high divorce rates, mental breakdowns, and suicides, we have much to learn from our Mexican-American citizens about family solidarity, child rearing, respect patterns, and religious values.

PERCEPTION OF MENTAL ILLNESS IN A MEXICAN-AMERICAN COMMUNITY*

MARVIN KARNO, M.D., and
ROBERT B. EDGERTON, Ph.D., Los Angeles

There are almost 2 million persons of Mexican birth or descent in California, about 10% of the state's population. Mexican-Americans also represent about 10% of the 7 million residents of Los Angeles County, forming a larger ethnic minority group than the Negro population in both the state and the county.

Like Negroes, Mexican-Americans have been the objects of prejudice in the United States. Tenacious stereotypes of, and discrimination against the Mexican-American have been the focus of scattered attention, but extensive documentation has not yet been provided.

Both peoples continue to be characterized by a chronically depressed socioeconomic status marked by a low educational level with a high degree of functional illiteracy, crowded and deteriorated housing, a high incidence of communicable disease, limited employment opportunities, and limited political power until the recent period of rapid growth of political strength.

Mexican-Americans, however, are a unique people in many ways. The difficulties of their situation derive, at least in part, from the limited knowledge of English possessed by a large proportion of this population; the relatively recent migration from Mexico of many; the frequent and enduring survival of rural cultural traits (readily understandable in view of the quite limited urbanization and industrialization of Mexico even at the present time); and, the continued family, community, and national ties to Mexico reinforced by heavy two-way traffic across the border.

The Epidemiological Paradox

Large scale urban psychiatric studies have repeatedly indicated that the life conditions of poverty are associated with a high incidence of mental illness, especially psychosis. There is also evidence to suggest

*Reprinted from the *Archives of General Psychiatry,* February, 1969, Volume 20. Copyright 1969, American Medical Association.

that the experiences of migration and acculturation pose special threats to mental health. Characterized as it is by life conditions of poverty, problems of acculturation, and experiences of prejudice and discrimination, the Mexican-American population must be expected to suffer a high incidence of mental illness, and in particular, major mental illness requiring hospital care.

Paradoxically, however, Mexican-Americans are strikingly underrepresented as psychiatric patients in public outpatient and inpatient facilities throughout California. For example, in fiscal year 1962-1963, Mexican-Americans accounted for 2.2% of State Hospital admissions, 3.4% of State Mental Hygiene Clinic admissions, 0.9% of Neuropsychiatric Institute (state centers for teaching and research) outpatient admissions, and 2.3% of inpatient admissions to state-local jointly supported facilities. On June 30, 1966, Mexican-Americans comprised only 3.3% of the resident population of California's state hospitals for the mentally ill. The expected figure in each of the preceding instances would be 9% to 10%. In contrast, Negroes are represented as patients in public mental health facilities in percentages proportional to their population in California.

The finding of a similar underrepresentation of Mexican-Americans among patients admitted for psychosis to hospitals in Texas, led the sociologist, E. G. Jaco, to conclude that Mexican-Americans suffer from less mental illness than Anglo-Americans. He expressed the belief that the existence of a cultural pattern of a warm, supportive, extended family with strong values of mutual acceptance, care and responsibility, tended to protect Mexican-Americans against the development of major mental illness. Jaco's provocative inference is, of course, only one possible explanation of this underrepresentation, but it serves to emphasize the epidemiological paradox posed by the Mexican-American population. It is this paradox which led to the present research undertaking.

The Research

This report is our introduction to a forthcoming series of papers that will present the findings of more than five years of collaborative work which initially involved a formal, social psychiatric research investigation concerning mental illness among Mexican-Americans in east Los Angeles. Our initial and major goal was to account for the paradoxical discrepancy between the reported low incidence and what we suspected was a much higher *true* incidence of mental illness in that population. The motivation for this research grew out of an earlier study in which we found a similar underrepresentation of Mexican-American patients in a university-based, low-cost psychiatric outpatient clinic in Los Angeles. In the particular clinic studied, it was found that the Mexican-American patient, compared with white, third generation Anglo-American patients of similar social class characteristics, selectively tended to be excluded or to exclude himself from treatment, especially intensive psychotherapy.

Research Strategy. — Before attempting to confirm or challenge the hypothesis that the low reported incidence of mental illness among Mexican-Americans reflects a low true incidence, we decided that a prior question must be asked and answered: viz, how do Anglo-Americans and Mexican-Americans of similar socioeconomic status, living in the same community at the same time, perceive, define, and respond to mental illness.

We suspected that groups of people sharing common social characteristics, but distinguished from each other by distinctive cultures, might differ in their perceptions and definitions of, and hence in their responses to, mental illness.

Prior Findings and "Explanations." — It has often been alleged that the family within the Mexican-American subculture might commonly protect mentally ill family members from exposure to alien and feared social institutions of the Anglo community, thus serving to exclude significant numbers of mentally ill persons from being defined as such in any psychiatric census. Such a social pattern has been noted or suggested in studies from Texas, New Mexico, and California, although it has never been systematically documented.

It has also often been reported that Mexican-Americans seek help from ethnic folk curers for relief of folk-defined illnesses that consist largely or wholly of psychopathologic symptomatology. This pattern could offer a source of diagnosis and treatment for significant numbers of mentally ill persons who again would be excluded from any formal mental illness statistical reporting.

Explanations of the puzzle at issue are many and diverse. The more common of these explanations, in addition to those already mentioned, are summarized in the following outline.

1. Mexican-Americans suffer as much as or more from psychiatric disorder than do Anglos, but this disorder is less visible because it is expressed in criminal behavior, narcotics addiction, or alcoholism.

2. It is expressed as psychiatric disorder per se, but is still less visible, because:

A.   Mexican-Americans perceive and define psychiatric disorder differently than do Anglos. Specifically, they are more tolerant of idiosyncratic and deviant behavior and hence are less likely to seek professional help. A common variation of this viewpoint is expressed in the belief that Mexican-Americans are simply ignorant about what more educated persons know, viz — the signs and symptoms of mental illness; they are also presumed to be ignorant about why or how to seek professional help. This is seen (by some who cite this view) as being largely a reflection of the very limited development of mental health resources and education in Mexico itself.

B.   Mexican-Americans are too proud and too sensitive to expose more personal problems to public view; they feel too much shame or stigma attached to an admission of need for professional mental health assistance. One variety of this view stresses the long prior history of humiliation experienced by Mexican-Americans in their relationships with Anglo agencies and institutions. Another stresses the conservative, rural value system of the Mexican-American.

C.   Clinics and hospitals which offer psychiatric services do not operate in ways which fit the needs of Mexican-Americans and hence are little used by them. For example, the cost is too high, the distance too far, the hours are inappropriate, and the staff do not demonstrate respect, promote self-dignity, nor evidence cultural sensitivity.

D.   In place of formal mental health services, Mexican-Americans utilize the services of priests, family physicians, and other persons for psychiatric disorders.

E.   Mexican-Americans who develop psychiatric disorder frequently return to Mexico to reestablish kinship or other emotionally supportive ties, or to seek folk or professional help in a familiar context.

F.   Mexican-Americans who are citizens of Mexico, or who are U.S. citizens but have family members in the United States (legally or illegally) who are Mexican citizens, avoid any contact with the "establishment" which may threaten the security of their (or their relatives') presence in the United States.

G.   The majority of Mexican-Americans speak only Spanish, or prefer to or can only communicate in Spanish concerning intimate or affectively charged matters; there are very few or no personnel in mental health facilities who speak Spanish.

These alleged factors were all considered in planning and carrying out of the research and all will be commented upon in future reports.

The Research Method

We developed two separate but complementary approaches to the problem. The major effort was devoted to a systematic household interview which was administered to Anglo and Mexican-American residents of two east Los Angeles communities. This survey was designed to gather quantitative data concerning perceptions of, definitions of, and responses to mental illness which could be compared across the two communities. Simultaneously, ethnographic field studies were carried out in the two communities to obtain additional qualitative information and to lend essential social and historical context to the interview responses.

The home interview survey and the ethnographic studies were both carried out in two subcommunities in the larger east Los Angeles area – Belvedere and Lincoln Heights. Belvedere, a traditional center of Mexican-American culture, has long been a major site for initial settlement by Mexican immigrants, and about 95% of its approximately 45,000 inhabitants are of Mexican birth or descent. Lincoln Heights, a more cosmopolitan community, has slightly over 30,000 residents, approximately 50% of whom are Mexican-Americans. The latter reflect a wide spectrum of acculturation. We maintained our central research office at the UCLA Neuropsychiatric Institute on the "west side" of Los Angeles, but located our field office in a long-established settlement house located in the residential heart of the east Los Angeles Community.

The Survey Interview. – The survey interview was developed and pretested over a year's time. The final version was 18 pages in length and included approximately 200 questions directed toward biographic, demographic, and attitudinal information, in addition to a variety of items dealing directly with mental illness. The core content of the interview was formed by small vignettes describing in everyday language, imaginary persons who were depicted as suffering from what psychiatrists generally consider to be psychiatric disorders. This technique was originally developed by Star at the National Opinion Research Center, and comprised the major content of an interview schedule administered to 3,500 respondents in a national survey of attitudes toward mental illness in the early 1950's.

In our pretesting we tried out a number of vignettes, our own and Star's, representing a variety of diagnostic categories. We discovered that the vignettes aroused and sustained interest in our respondents and we developed a series of largely open-ended questions, different from those used by Star, which followed each vignette and probed the respondent's perceptions and definitions of the behavior described.

Eight vignettes were included in our final interview format. Five of them, representing paranoid behavior in an adult male (Star's original), severe depression in a middle-aged woman, marital discord between a formerly happy couple, an acute schizophrenic reaction in a teen-aged girl, and aggressive, delinquent behavior in a teen-aged boy, formed the core of our interview. The latter four vignettes were our own creations. The three remaining vignettes were included to elicit preferences regarding at-home versus out-of-home treatment.

Interviews were carried out in either English or Spanish, depending upon the preference and/or capacity of the respondent. Consequently 260 of 668 interviews were carried out in Spanish.

We did not attempt to sample a representative cross-section of the entire east Los Angeles Mexican-American population. We confined our study to Belvedere and Lincoln Heights. A block sampling design within each community was employed for the random selection of households. Within households, adult members were selected as respondents by a random probability technique.

The interview was not identified to the respondent as dealing with either health or mental health. It was, rather, identified as a university-based study concerning the kinds of problems which can arise in peoples' lives. (The first question to deal with mental illness did not occur until about half way through the interview.)

Interviews lasted between one and two hours, rapport was typically good, and the refusal rate (although higher for Anglos than Mexican-Americans) was within acceptable limits. In the highly "Mexican" community of Belvedere, over 200 interviews with Mexican-Americans were completed. In Lincoln Heights, over 200 Anglos and over 200 Mexican-Americans were interviewed.

We arbitrarily decided that for the purposes of this study, "Mexican-American" respondents must have been born in Mexico; or, if American-born, be of bilateral Mexican descent. Persons of Latin American descent other than Mexican were excluded as respondents. "Anglo" respondents were restricted to white, American-born persons not of Mexican or other Latin American descent. The 12 interviewers were all fluent in English and Spanish, were mainly housewives or students, and were trained and directed under the supervision of a full-time field director.

The Ethnographic Studies. — A second feature of the investigation was the provisions for ethnographic field studies to complement the home survey interview. Data of a wide variety were collected, including: information on income, occupation, religion, education, residential mobility, crime, health and welfare; social-historical material contained in published and unpublished documents and personal histories; and autobiographical and narrative hand and tape recorded accounts from elderly residents born in east Los Angeles as well as recent immigrants concerning the routine of everyday life, at home, at work, and during leisure hours.

Results

In an introductory report of this kind, it is possible to discuss only a few of our findings, all of which are subject to elaboration and refinement.

Of the 444 Mexican-Americans interviewed, approximately one half were born in Mexico. They came from all parts of Mexico and from farming settlements, villages, towns, and metropolitan centers. The majority of the Mexican-born respondents had come to the United States as adults. The Mexican-American respondents had had much less formal education than the Anglos (about 40% of them had completed less than seven years of schooling). The comparable Anglo figure is about 10%. Education appears to be an important determinant of the nature of responses given to questions concerning mental illness. About 40% of the Mexican-Americans speak only or mainly Spanish, the rest describe themselves as bilingual. Only one Mexican-American respondent out of 444 claimed to speak only English. Answers to our many questions concerning language habits and attitudes toward language, confirm the often expressed belief that there is great pride felt in the use and knowledge of Spanish by persons of Mexican birth or descent.

Approximately 90% of the Mexican-Americans are Roman Catholic, compared to about 30% of the Anglo respondents. However, religious identification does not appear to be an important factor influencing responses concerning mental health or illness.

The first vignette in the interview is that of the depressed woman.

Mrs. Brown is nearly 50, has a nice home, and her husband has a good job. She used to be full of life; an active, busy woman with a large family. Her children are now grown and in recent months she has changed. She sits and broods for hours, blames herself for all kinds of bad things she thinks she has done, and talks about what a terrible person she is. She has lost interest in all the things she used to enjoy, cannot sleep, has no appetite, and paces up and down the house for hours.

When asked the first and very general question, "What do you think about this woman?" Mexican-Americans more than twice as often as Anglos, spontaneously replied that the woman was ill. When questioned as to what kind of illness it was, Anglos tended to call it "mental" illness, whereas Mexican-Americans called it a "nervous" or "emotional" illness. Mexican-Americans were more likely than Anglos to recommend that the woman see a physician.

Our representation of an acutely schizophrenic young woman reads as follows.

Jane Walker is 17 and in her last year of high school. She has always been a moody girl and has never gotten along well with people. A few months ago she began to cry all the time and to act very afraid of everyday things. She has stopped going to school and stays at home. She screams at her parents and a lot of the time doesn't make any sense at all. She has talked about hearing voices talking to her and thinks that she is really somebody else than herself.

A considerably higher percentage of Mexican-Americans than Anglos spontaneously (i.e., before the question of illness was raised) attributed her behavior to illness, although both groups recognized to a high degree that she had a serious problem which required professional help.

When asked, "As far as you know does a psychiatrist really help the people who go to him?" Mexican-Americans somewhat more than Anglos said yes. Mexican-American respondents were also somewhat more optimistic than Anglos about the curability of mental illness. Considerably more Mexican-Americans than Anglos believed that mental disorders begin in childhood.

Eighty percent of both Anglos and Mexican-American respondents were unable to identify, name or locate a single psychiatric clinic, yet 80% of both groups expressed the belief that a psychiatric clinic could help a person with a psychiatric disorder. In regard to current medical care, it is important to note the finding that about three out of four

Mexican-Americans have regular family physicians, as compared to two out of three Anglos.

A preliminary consideration of the complex variables affecting responses to our interviews, and analysis of the many forms of "soft" data gathered in our investigations, have led us to three tentative and general conclusions.

Conclusions

The underutilization of psychiatric facilities by Mexican-Americans (at least those who reside in east Los Angeles) is not to be accounted for by the fact that they share a cultural tradition which causes them to perceive and define mental illness in significantly different ways than do Anglos. Our initial analyses indicate that there are remarkably few statistically significant differences between the interview responses of Mexican-Americans and Anglos revolving perceptions and definitions of mental illness.

We do not believe that the underrepresentation of Mexican-Americans in psychiatric treatment facilities reflects a lesser incidence of mental illness than that found in other ethnic populations in this country. For example, our data indicate that large numbers of Mexican-Americans in east Los Angeles seek treatment for obviously psychiatric disorders from family physicians. In responses to our interviews, it might be added, Mexican-Americans in our study communities expressed the conviction that they often suffer from psychiatric disorder.

We believe that the underrepresentation of Mexican-Americans in psychiatric treatment facilities is to be accounted for by a complex of social and cultural factors. These factors have very different weightings in their relative influence. Some of the heavily weighted factors include: a formidable language barrier, the significant mental health role of the very active family physician; the self-esteem reducing nature of agency-client contacts experienced by Mexican-Americans; and the marked lack of mental health facilities in the Mexican-American community itself. Of moderate weighting are such considerations as: the open border across which return significant numbers of Mexican-Americans seeking relief of emotional stress, and the threat of "repatriation" attached to a variety of perceived-as-threatening institutions and agencies of the dominant society. Of relatively lesser weighting are such matters as folk-medicine, folk-psychotherapy, and "Mexican Culture" in general.

CLASS AND STATUS

CLASS AND STATUS

Social differentiation exists in every community and society and in every complex society there is a social stratification system and pattern. In this America is no exception, and despite an often-referred-to history of free upward mobility, actually it is a society where stratification is both common and important.

Minority groups always have two patterns of stratification. One is that of the large society, which places the modal member of the minority somewhere on a vertical stratification scale. In general, the more assimilated and upper class the minority person then the higher will be his individual position on this majority group stratification scale. Each person has a separate status in each group of which he is a part. When we speak of "social status" we are speaking of a weighted amalgam of all the group positions of a person. It is not the most accurate designation in America to speak of a person's "class," since true class is relatively weak in modern American culture. That is, class implies discrete variation, of which we have little. Rather, Americans tend to fill all positions in the spectrum of the social stratification scale, an example of continuous variation.

Thus each minority group has a modal band on an all-society stratification scale, with not all the individual members necessarily falling within that location. Considerable overlapping is the rule rather than the exception. In addition to the above scale, each minority group has its own private stratification system. The individual's position on this scale, which is also an example of continuous variation, depends on his statuses in the groups of which he is a member. In both cases the theory is the same, and broadly speaking the mechanisms are the same, but the bases on which high or low status is assigned in a minority group scale may or may not bear any relation to those which give high or low status in the majority stratification system.

All this applies specifically and observably to the Mexican American. There is enough uniformity of values that some uniformity of status may be predicted. That is, a Mexican American who is vice-president of a large bank receives a high status from this factor in both societies. The same·man however, may not participate at all in the life of the *barrio*; therefore, although the Anglos may consider him a "leader," the *Chicanos* who willingly accord him high status economically, consider him of low status as a member of *la raza* and possibly less of a leader than a semi-literate laborer who is known to have always *la raza* at heart. Confusion often occurs. The Mexican American who is socio-economically upwardly mobile wishes high status in both communities. What is helpful in one community may not be helpful in the other. With care, increasingly high status can be achieved in both communities, and some men do. Others find it easier to turn their backs on one or the other of the communities and seek status only in the other.

Dr. Celia Heller, a sociologist, in "Class as an Explanation of Ethnic Differences in Mobility Aspirations," presents a comparison of the occupational, educational, material, and other mobility aspirations of Mexican-Americans with those of the larger society. She finds the mobility aspirations of the Mexican Americans much like those of other ethnic groups, although with a possible time lag. Dr. William V. D'Antonio and Dr. Julian Samora, both sociologists, are the authors of the other selection in this section, "Occupational Stratifications in Four Southwestern Communities." This study examines the place of Spanish-name personnel in the occupational structure of ten hospitals in four southwestern communities. The authors discover that a small number of the Spanish-name population are in high status positions, a sizeable number are in medium status occupations, and the largest number in low status occupations. That at least some Spanish-name persons are in high and medium status occupations is considered evidence of progress toward assimilation.

CLASS AS AN EXPLANATION OF ETHNIC
DIFFERENCES IN MOBILITY ASPIRATIONS*

THE CASE OF MEXICAN AMERICANS

CELIA STOPNICKA HELLER

The aim of this paper is to challenge the indiscriminate use of "class" as an explanation of ethnic differences in mobility aspirations. The fact that some differences between given ethnic groups and the majority population can be *statistically* accounted for by class is often interpreted to mean that class adequately explains these differences. Our contention is that such an interpretation is both unwarranted and incorrect.

Although the usual procedure involved in the explanation we are questioning is well known, it seems appropriate, for the sake of clarity, to begin briefly by summarizing it. Its first step is to compare the occupational, educational, material or other mobility aspirations of a given ethnic group, in which the researcher is interested, with that of the majority population. When substantial differences are discovered, the factor of class is controlled. If the differences disappear when class is controlled, "class" is treated as the explanatory factor. If, on the other hand, they do not disappear but shrink, "class" is considered an important factor and the remaining differences are treated as being due to the "ethnic" factor (unique characteristics of the group studied).

We proceeded initially in the same manner in our study of aspirations and the means of mobility of Mexican American youth, to seniors in ten Los Angeles high schools. These were chosen as a representative sample of the Metropolitan area. Of the entire sample of male students 12 per cent turned out to be Mexican American.

In comparing the answers of the Mexican Americans and the white non-Mexican boys, referred to as Anglo Americans, we found substantial differences in their occupational and educational expectations, and also in their I.Q. scores. Over twice as many Anglo Americans as Mexican Americans expected to enter a *profession* (36.8 and 15.4 per cent respectively) and, conversely, the proportion of Mexican Ameri-

*The International Migration Review, Vol. Two, 4, Fall, 1967, pages 31-39.

cans who chose *skilled labor* was almost twice that of Anglo Americans (41.3 and 22.4 per cent respectively). The answers to the question concerning educational expectation corresponded to the above. More than twice as many Mexican Americans did not expect to go beyond high school. At the opposite end of the educational scale, the proportion of Mexican American who anticipated graduating from college or better was only one-third that of Anglo Americans.

As for I.Q. scores, the differences were still larger. The average score of the Mexican American male high school seniors was 90.5 as compared with 103.3 of the Anglo Americans. Almost half of the Mexican American students were below average in I.Q., in contrast to 13 per cent of the Anglo Americans. Only 6 per cent of them, but 30 per cent of the Anglo Americans fell into the "bright" and "superior" categories.

Following the commonly used procedure, which we are now questioning, we controlled the class factor and concluded that "class" largely explains the differences in occupational and educational expectation but does not explain I.Q. differences. This conclusion was based on the fact that when "class' was controlled, the differences in occupational and educational expectations were small, but the differences in I.Q. score remained large.

However, at this point, it must be admitted that our explanation was inadequate. The problem of ethnic differences in mobility is not solved by holding the class factor constant because the very class structure of the ethnic group is part of the *intrinsic* problem. In other words, *the class distribution of a given ethnic group, whether it differs from or resembles that of the majority population, must be accounted for.*

Since recent immigrants, as a whole, irrespective of country of origin, concentrate at the bottom of the socio-economic ladder, to make the leap which would enable them to approximate the class distribution of the majority population (let alone improve on it), they must at some point of their history exceed the aspirations of the majority population of the same class. If they simply advanced to the same degree as the majority people of the same class, the gap between their class distribution and that of majority population would continue. And yet we know that there is more than one ethnic group that has not only approximated the class composition of the majority population but exceeded it.

Among many ethnic groups, the process of moving toward the occupational structure of the majority population starts with the second generation, among others later, and among a few, such as Jews and Japanese, already in the first generation. Although the occupational aspirations of these last groups undoubtedly varied with class in their countries of origin, transplanted to a relatively mobile society they responded to the promises of that society irrespective of the class they occupied there or at the beginning of their stay here. There are indications that among these ethnic groups, in contrast to non-ethnic Americans, mobility aspirations do not differ significantly with class.

Similarly, class is not an adequate explanation if one proceeds to an analysis of the educational expectations of Mexican American youth. According to the "class" explanation, the lower educational expectations of Mexican Americans simply reflect their lower class background. The general proposition from which it follows is that the higher the education of the parents, the more likely they would be to instill motivation for upward movement in their children. Its specific reading is: The parents of Mexican American students being less educated than the Anglo American students are less likely to influence their children to obtain a higher education. And yet the argument is not entirely convincing. The confirmation of the proposition, it could be said, comes from the empirical studies of non-ethnic youth. *Parents' educational achievement and parents' influence on their children's educational motivation is not a necessary, although often found, equation.* The two cases in point are the American Jews and Japanese Americans.

The educational ambition and striving of the children of poor and uneducated Jewish immigrants have become proverbial and well documented. But why is this so? We know that in the traditional Jewish culture, sacred education was stressed as the channel of mobility open to all Jews: poor and rich, of educated and uneducated parents. The immigrants transferred their aspirations for their sons from religious to secular education. They influenced their children to want an education and helped them secure it.

Much less is known about the mainspring of the Japanese Americans' stress on education, although it is easily observed that in terms of educational ambition and achievement they resemble the Jews. The Japanese immigration to the United States was also largely a lower class immigration, even if in contrast to the Jewish one, it was mostly composed of peasants. These lower class immigrants put great emphasis on education and influenced their children in that direction. Thus, already in 1940, the educational level of the Nisei was 12.2 median years of school completed, as compared with 10.1 years for American-born white children in the Pacific Coast states.

In extreme contrast to the Jewish and Japanese stand the Mexican immigrants whose cultural heritage did not contain the goal of education for all irrespective of social class. But their relative failure to aspire or influence their children to aspire or achieve higher education must *not* be considered indicative of a low value placed on education, as some writers have argued in studying lower socio-economic groups of the majority population. Somehow, the Mexican Americans have long held on to their belief that formal education was useless for them and did not get them anywhere. They viewed it as leading their children not toward mobility, but toward frustration and humiliation. To help their children avoid the latter, parents pointed to those Mexican Americans who received an education and yet did not hold a job appropriate to it.

Finally, we should like to examine class as an explanation of ethnic differences in I.Q. While I.Q. may not depict the reality of differing innate human capacities, it does depict the reality of differing socially and culturally structured capacities, i.e., capacities of advancement in *our* society. The criterion employed in validating intelligence tests has nearly always been success in our social system.

Again, "class" is not an adequate explanation because, first of all, *I.Q. does not necessarily vary with class.* It is true that it varies with class in many collectivities which have been studied, but some empirical data support the above assertion that such variation is neither universal nor a necessary consequence of social stratification. An interesting study, conducted in London, showed that among the Jews there, I.Q. does not vary with class. According to this study, the average *non-Jewish I.Q.* dropped as the occupational index of parents fell, but the Jewish I.Q. remained on about the same level.

Even if empirical studies were to prove that some Jewish communities are the only ones among whom the above is true, the analysis of this deviant case holds the promise of yielding important clues to further our knowledge about social mobility. It suggests, for example, that in as far as a culture emphasizes intellectual pursuits for all classes as an end in itself, it equips the members of the lower classes with a powerful means for potential mobility. In a relatively non-mobile society such people are more likely to escape through the rigid boundaries of class. Even when bred in a closed system, they are at an advantage when they move to an open society. In contrast to them, lower class people formed in cultures where intellectual pursuits are expected of the upper class only, are not as well fit to seize the opportunities for advancement when they find themselves in a relatively open society. The Jews seem to represent an extreme case of the first and the Mexican Americans an extreme case of the latter.

In all complex societies there are certain traits that are considered appropriate for all irrespective of social position and other traits that are class bound. However, the traits that do not vary with class in one culture may be the very ones that differ with class in another. In the case of Mexicans, honor, respect, family obligation, and manliness are some of the elements that are deemed important for all. But these are not the values that are very conducive to mobility; on the contrary, they are obstacles in the initial stages of social advancement, however praiseworthy on other grounds. And, in contrast to the Jews, Mexicans consider those qualities that are especially suited to mobility—intellect and education—to be the domain of the upper classes.

But if some ethnic groups start sooner and proceed faster to catch up with the socio-economic positions of the population at large and few ever exceed it, all ethnic groups have eventually responded to the American ideology of advancement. Until now, the only exception appears to be that of the Mexican Americans. On the basis of his careful analysis of census data, Donald J. Bogue concludes that the Mexican American constitute *"the only ethnic group for which a comparison of the characteristics of the first and second generation fails to show substantial intergenerational rise in socio-economic status"* (italics supplied).

However, our data seem to suggest that the Mexican Americans are now entering, to borrow Walt W. Rostow's term, the 'take off stage' of mobility. We arrive at this new trend, not through holding "class" constant, but by comparing the sons with the fathers. It can now be said, on the basis of our findings, that there is a portion of Mexican American youth who, if they could fulfill their aspirations and expectations, would substantially exceed their parental generation in occupational, educational, and in self-employment status. Specifically, only 4 per cent of the Mexican American boys expect to be doing unskilled or semi-skilled labor while 42 per cent of them come from such backgrounds. Conversely, 35 per cent of them aspire to semi-professional or professional occupations while only 2 per cent of their fathers are in these occupations.

As for education, only 5 per cent come from homes where the

breadwinner attended college, but 44 per cent of them expect to do so. Eighty-seven per cent of their fathers had no education beyond high school, but only 31 per cent of them foresee not continuing their schooling.

Again, in the comparison of independent-employee status, 41 per cent of them think that they will have their own business or practice while only 13 per cent of them are from homes where the breadwinner works for himself or owns a business. Also distinctive is that, unlike the Anglo Americans, the proportion of Mexican Americans who expect to be employed, is smaller than the proportion of those whose fathers are employees.

If, as has been argued, the comparable distributions of the Anglo Americans indicate that the movement from an employee to independent status is not regarded by the majority youth as upward movement, then those of the Mexican American indicate a contrasting attitude. A shift from employee to independent status seems to mean to them what it has traditionally meant in America: going up in the world. In a sense, the Mexican Americans may only now be taking hold on the pattern which the majority population is already abandoning. Possibly, these third and fourth generation Americans of Mexican descent are showing the pattern that some ethnic groups, such as Jews, showed in the first generation. The mobility path of many immigrant Jews was to leave the factory and establish a small business.

In terms of independent-employee status, as well as in terms of occupation and education, we see that our sample of Mexican American boys do not expect to conform to the Mexican American pattern of no inter-generational difference in socio-economic status. As a matter of fact, if we use the above approach of "relative" mobility aspirations, the Mexican American boys seem quite mobility oriented.

In conclusion, the analysis of "relative" mobility aspirations suggests a change in the Mexican American group, which shows this group not to be the exception to the ethnic pattern in the United States, as it was considered to be until now. The process observed in all other ethnic groups is similarly reenacted here, although it took a few more generations to initiate it. This change could not have been detected through the technique – challenged in this paper – of controlling statistically the class factor.

OCCUPATIONAL STRATIFICATIONS IN FOUR SOUTHWESTERN COMMUNITIES:

*A Study of Ethnic Differential Employment in Hospitals**

WILLIAM V. D'ANTONIO and JULIAN SAMORA

Social scientists have long been interested in the problems of stratification and occupational mobility, especially as they relate to American minority groups. Warner and Srole, as the result of intensive studies, developed a conceptual scheme designed to place these minority groups within the general social hierarchy of American life. This scheme permitted them to predict "with some degree of success the probable degree of subordination each group will suffer, the strength of the subsystem likely to be developed by it, the kind of rank order it will be assigned, and the approximate period necessary for its assimilation into American life."[1]

The scheme was based on the proposition that the greater the differences between the host and the subordinate populations, culturally and racially, the greater would be the degree of subordination as well as the strength of the ethnic subsystem and the longer the period necessary for assimilation. Thus, a five point racial scale (from Caucasoid to Negroid) and a similar culture scale (English-speaking Protestants to non-English speaking non-Christians) were developed. Other scales were developed for the degree of subordination and social distance, the strength of the racial and ethnic subsystems and the timetable of assimilation.

Without repeating the Warner-Srole criteria for the scales, suffice it to say that for the Spanish-speaking (which is the major concern of this paper), Warner and Srole predicted that their assimilation into American life would be slow, that is "a very long time in the future which is not yet discernible." During this time they would suffer great subordination because of the kind of occupational restrictions which they would have to face, among other factors. This is explained by the fact that racial as well as ethnic features mark them off from the dominant American group. Thus, Warner and Srole note that "While

* *Social Forces,* Vol. 41, October, 1962, pages 18-24.

the Catholic Church is a powerful instrument for the conservation of the ethnic tradition, it is much less powerful than the forces of American organized 'prejudice' against the dark-skinned people."[2] At the same time, they recognized that the lighter skinned Spanish-speaking people, those of the clearly Causasoid type, would be able to rise in our social hierarchy as they lost their cultural identity.

The purpose of this paper is to consider the adequacy of the Warner-Srole scheme in the light of some data recently gathered in the American Southwest. The data are concerned with the proportion of Spanish-name persons who hold specific occupations in the general area of health and in the hospital occupational structure of four Southwestern communities. Spanish-name persons now constitute one of the largest ethnic groups in the United States with a seemingly low rate of assimilation. The community health system includes within its occupational structure the most prestigeful occupations to which United States citizens can aspire. More broadly stated, the occupations included in the American health system run the entire gamut from most to least prestigeful, from the most highly trained to the least skilled.

It would seem reasonable to expect that the index of the degree to which the assimilation process is at work among Spanish-named persons, as it has been with other minority groups would be apparent by the extent to which they are distributed throughout the entire range of the health occupation system. This will then make it possible for us to assess the utility of the Warner-Srole scheme.[3]

Although Spanish-name persons have been living in the Southwest since the sixteenth century, large-scale migration from Mexico to the United States did not begin until the late nineteenth century, with the building of the railroads, the expansion of mining, lumber and agriculture, and the beginnings of urbanization and industrialization in the Southwest. Immigration reached its peak in the years between 1910 and 1930; and although many thousands returned to Mexico during the depression years it is estimated that there are now about 4.5 million Spanish-name persons in the United States, with well over two-thirds of them located in the five states of Arizona, California, Colorado, New Mexico and Texas.

This large Spanish-name population (exclusive of the Puerto Ricans) can be looked upon as representing three smaller subgroupings: first, the Spanish-Americans whose ancestors colonized the Southwest and

Florida and who have lived in the United States since even before the English colonists. Before 1940 this group could have been characterized as predominantly rural, Catholic, low in educational achievement and highly resistant to acculturation. Since 1950 this group has become urban and has begun to make some achievements in the educational and occupational fields. The second subgroup can be called Mexican-American, and is composed essentially of those individuals and their descendants who migrated from Mexico to this country at the turn of the century up to the 1940's. These persons were predominantly of a rural peasant background, low in educational achievements and unskilled occupationally. The third subgroups may properly be called Mexican since they are the more recent immigrants to this country; the general background of the majority of this group has been peasant, unskilled and uneducated. Although the peak of Mexican immigration into the United States has passed, there continues to be a steady stream of over 200,000 legal entrants yearly.

Social scientists have given sporadic attention to this minority group, and their findings generally support the Warner-Srole hypothesis. The Spanish-name population have been found to suffer from segregation, lack of schooling and job discrimination in patterns similar to that of the American Negro. Thus, Marden

> Few opportunities existed for Mexicans in higher ranking occupations both because they were not equipped to fill them and because of the discrimination against their employment in occupations involving Anglo fellow workers or serving Anglo trade. 4

On the basis of all the evidence that was gathered between 1920 and 1940, Marden concluded that the normal American pattern of assimilation by the third or grandchild generation was doubtful, as color differences combined with cultural differences to retard the process,

> with no clear-cut signs that their assimilation will ever be complete . . . . The broad picture of Anglo-Mexican relations in the decade 1940-1950 was one of Mexicans accommodated to American life as a minority with no certain prospects of losing this status.[5]

Further documentation of the low status of Spanish-name persons was made by Talbert in 1955.[6] He found that of the total of Spanish-name persons employed in these four Southwestern states, only two percent were in professional occupations as compared with eight percent of the white, non-Spanish population. In all, he classified 12 percent of employed Spanish-name persons in high status occupations, as compared with 27 percent of the total population. At the other extreme Talbert found that 33 percent of Spanish-name persons as compared with only 15 percent of the total population were in low status occupations, i.e., those involving little or no skill and training, such as private household work and farm labor.

Greer's recent study of labor unions in Southern California supports these findings while indicating "some movement upward in occupational and educational level" with second and third generation status.[7] With the crest of Mexican migration to the United States now past, the Spanish-name population appear to be entering a period of critical importance in their quest for mobility and assimilation into American society. The Spanish-name enter this period at an unusual disadvantage according to Broom and Shevky: "Unlike other important American ethnic groups a middle class (of Spanish-speaking) is virtually non-existent." They found that in Los Angeles the number and diversity of professional and semi-professional services rendered by Spanish-name personnel "are even less adequate than is the case in Negro and Japanese-American neighborhoods."[8]

The cities selected for research in the Southwest do not purport to be representative or typical of southwestern patterns. Rather, they were chosen with three main variables in mind: (1) geographic location; (2) size; and (3) differential distribution of Spanish-name to the local population. A brief summary statement on each of the cities follows:

Tucson: A financial and commercial center of Arizona. Through annexation and immigration it grew from 45,000 to more than 185,000 during the 1950's. Spanish-name persons comprise about one-fourth of the population. Tucson contained six percent of the state's population in 1950. The median years of education completed for the city as a whole were 11.5; for the Spanish-name it was only 7.1.

San Diego: The largest city in the study, with more than 500,000 inhabitants in 1959, it has the smallest percentage of Spanish-name persons. The Spanish-name population rose from 15,490 in 1950 to about 25,000 in 1959, remaining at about 5 percent of the total population. The median years of school completed for the general population in 1950 were 12, while for the Spanish-name in the city it was 8.7.

Las Cruces: This town in New Mexico is the smallest city in the study, but with a population growth from 12,325 in 1950 to almost 30,000 by 1959. About half of its population is made up of Spanish-name persons. The median years of school completed were 9.1 for the general population and only 5.6 for the Spanish-name.

El Paso: This Texas city has grown rapidly, from a population of 130,000 in 1950 to 280,000 by 1959, with Spanish-name persons making up some 45 percent of the total. It is right on the border, across from the Mexican city of C. Juarez, and is a major port of entry into Mexico. The median years of school completed for the general population were 8.3, and for the Spanish-name it was 5.8 in 1950.

These cities are all located within one hundred miles of the Mexican border, they vary in size from the small town to the great metropolis, from the almost purely agricultural community to the modern industrial giant. The proportion of Spanish-name ranges from 5 percent in one city to almost 50 percent in two of them. All grew rapidly during the 1950's with three of them more than doubling in 'population size. The importance of these sites for this study is further enhanced by the fact that they contain all of the three types of Spanish-name persons mentioned above, old line Spanish-Americans, second and third generation Americans of Mexican descent and recent arrivals from Mexico. Thus, we have every reason to believe that we have a good sampling of Warner's mixed Latin American type, ranging from dark-skinned to Caucasoid and from strongly ethnic to non-ethnic in varied socioeconomic environments.

In three of the four cities, the proportion of Spanish-name persons to the total population is greater than the proportion for the state as a whole. And with the exception of Las Cruces, the median age of school years completed is greater for these cities than for their corresponding states.

A team of researchers systematically gathered data from these four research sites on community-hospital relations. The same interview schedule was used in all four sites, and coordination was achieved through a joint meeting followed by a visit to all sites by the field director.

The health occupational system in this study is limited to three main branches: (1) the top health professionals who practice in a particular area, e.g., from physician to veterinarian; (2) the members of the boards of directors of the several hospitals in the area; and (3) the hospital occupational system itself, from top administrator and staff physicians to kitchen help and maids. We will consider each branch in turn.

The results of our findings in this category show that Las Cruces was the only city which did not have a Spanish-name physician or surgeon; in fact, Las Cruces, with the highest proportion of Spanish-name persons in the 1950 census, had the lowest proportions of Spanish-name persons in the top health professional group. On the other hand, San Diego, with the lowest proportion of Spanish-name persons, came the closest to having proportional representation in the various professional categories. The low achievement in Tucson is somewhat surprising, particularly since Spanish-name persons in Tucson have achieved prestigeful occupations in business and government. El Paso, with 41 top health professionals, led the four cities in total numbers. The Spanish-name persons came close to proportional representation in El Paso only with respect to doctors of osteopathy. Not all of the professional categories were found in every city, but physicians-surgeons and dentists were the most frequently found.

The findings indicate that Spanish-name persons are not automatically excluded from the top ranks of the health profession. In his study of Spanish-name people in the Southwest and West, Talbert[9] found that Spanish-name persons comprised 2.9 percent of the employed professionals in these four states. Assuming that Spanish-name professionals were all employed at the time of the study, they comprised four percent of the employed health professionals in these four cities. In other words, Spanish-name persons were more highly represented among the employed professionals in the health system of these four cities than in the general professional categories of the four states taken as a whole. Here again, the data from El Paso showed more evidence of mobility; while Spanish-name persons represent only two percent of the total employed professional group in Texas, they comprised 12 percent of the health professionals in El Paso.

Hospital boards are generally made up of the successful men of the community. Examination of the occupations held by members of the hospital boards in these communities reveals that bankers, lawyers, industrialists, and merchants are the most frequently selected persons on such boards; on the other hand, boards of religiously oriented hospitals (Catholic or otherwise) are dominated by religious superiors. In the most recent years, even in the case of Catholic hospitals, businessmen are beginning to appear on boards in greater numbers. It was assumed that the presence of Spanish-name persons on such boards would be an indication of upward mobility and assimilation.

Of the ten southwestern hospitals in this study, only one had a Spanish-name person on its board, that being the Las Cruces Memorial General Hospital with one Spanish-name person on the five member board. If selection as a hospital board member may be assumed to be a reflection of achievement in a high status occupation, then the lack of Spanish-name persons in this category most effectively points up either their failure to achieve or lack of recognition of achievement; whether it also reflects a clear-cut case of discrimination is not so clear.[10]

In order to measure status in the hospital, an eight point scale of hospital occupations was developed as follows:

1. Administrator and staff physicians.
2. Residents, interns and courtesy staff.
3. Administrative supervisors and directors; kindred professional, e.g., pharmacists, social workers, technologists.
4. All registered nurses, including student professional nurses.
5. Supervisors, managers of kitchen, laundry, kindred; dieticians.
6. Clerks, stenographers, and kindred; aids, orderlies, L.P.N.
7. Maintenance supervisors and skilled workmen.
8, Unskilled labor, e.g., maids, porters.

The staffs of all major hospitals in the four cities were broken down into these eight categories according to the classification of Spanish-name and non-Spanish-name. In some cases data on Negroes were available so that a triple classification was possible. As might be expected, all four El Paso hospitals employed more Spanish-name persons both absolutely and proportionately than any other hospital in any of the three other cities of the Southwest. Table 1 gives the total number of Spanish-name employed in the hospitals within the four communities.

As one proceeds down the occupational ladder the proportion of Spanish-name in the particular category increases, with Spanish-name persons occupying 8 percent of the jobs at the top of the occupational structure in some communities, and as high as 89 percent of the jobs at the bottom of some of the structures. This pattern was followed more or less consistently in all 10 hospitals, but showed itself most clearly in the El Paso hospitals. In El Paso, Spanish-name persons were underrepresented in the top five categories and overrepresented in the bottom two categories. In Las Cruces overrepresentation occurred only

TABLE 1

*Number and Percentage of Spanish-name Persons in Each of the
Eight Strata of the Hospital Occupational Structures of
Four Southwestern Communities*

Stratum		Spanish-name		Total
		No.	Percent	
El Paso	1.	46	8	590[1]
	2.	47	19	251
	3.	17	21	80
	4.	174	33	526
	5.	9	31	29
	6.	322	50	647
	7.	20	63	32
	8.	255	89	286
San Diego	1.	10[2]	01	1048
	2.	0[2]	00	74
	3.	2	02	110
	4.	8	01	533
	5.	0	00	39
	6.	44	05	973
	7.	4	05	83
	8.	68	15	459
Tucson	1.	3	02	284
	2.	9	13	71
	3.	0	00	108
	4.	27	06	438
	5.	6	19	32
	6.	119	13	934
	7.	14	12	117
	8.	174	36	485
Las Cruces	1.	0	00	18
	2.	0	00	0
	3.	0	00	7
	4.	3	10	29
	5.	0	00	3
	6.	19	30	64
	7.	1	50	2
	8.	15	64	24

Note: Comparing again the Italian-name persons in New Haven with the data from the Southwest we find the following percentages for each stratum of hospital personnel: 1-17 percent; 2-18 percent; 3-23 percent; 4-15 percent; 5-8 percent; 6-19 percent; 7-28 percent; 8-11 percent.

[1] Since the physicians could be staff members of more than one hospital, the figures listed here are larger than those listed for the community in Table 1.

[2] Data for Strata one and two from San Diego are incomplete; two hospitals would not provide these particular data.

in the bottom category, a pattern which was repeated in Tucson and in San Diego. In San Diego Negroes and other nonwhites outnumber Spanish-name persons, and this was reflected in the greater proportion of the former in the hospital structure, including their representation in the higher occupational strata.

In order to get a clearer picture of the differential mobility patterns evident in these hospitals, the eight occupational categories were reclassified into three strata, labeled respectively high, medium and low status. High status occupations were those involving professional skills as well as managerial and supervisory tasks; this includes all the occupations in ranks one through four, from top administrator to professional nurses.

Medium status occupations are those of the lower white collar variety; i.e., clerks, and kindred, aids and orderlies, managers of alundry and kindred. These comprised categories five and six of the scale. In low status occupations were all those of maintenance and all of the unskilled jobs such as maid, porter and kindred, comprising categories seven and eight of the scale.

Table 2 shows the percentage of Spanish-name persons in each status category.

In all four cities Spanish-name persons are overrepresented in low status occupations, and underrepresented in high status occupations in proportion to their percentage of the total population. El Paso has the highest percentages in all three categories.

Another interesting finding suggested by the data is that there is differential employment of Spanish-name persons according to type of hospital. Catholic hospitals employ more Spanish-name persons and in higher occupational ranks than non-Catholic hospitals. Since Spanish-name persons are generally Catholic, perhaps a selective process occurs in employment procedures, making the religious factor very important and favorable to the Spanish-name. It is notable that Las Cruces is the only one of the four communities which did not have a Catholic hospital; it is also the most agricultural and stable of the four communities, and the data show that Spanish-name persons are least mobile within this hospital structure. On the other hand, of the Negroes who are employed in the hospitals for which data are available, the general and governmental hospitals appeared to favor them, albeit in the lower occupational ranks.

This finding about the employment of Spanish-name persons in Catholic versus non-Catholic hospitals in the communities studied is

TABLE 2

*Percentage of Spanish-name Persons, in High, Medium
and Low Status Hospital Occupations*

Status	El Paso	Las Cruces	Tucson	San Diego
High	19	5	4	2
Medium	49	28	13	4
Low	86	61	31	13
Expected*	45	49	25	5

* This is the percentage that could be expected in each status if Spanish-name persons were represented according to their proportion of the total population.

Note: None of the Southwestern communities comes close to approaching the rather even distribution of Italian-name persons found in New Haven, which is as follows for the three status categories: high = 17%; medium = 17%; low = 12%. One of the most interesting findings of the New Haven data is the small percentage in the low status category. This finding is explained by the fact that the Italians have been replaced at this level by the Negroes. While Spanish-name persons are moving up in the occupational categories, they are replaced not by Negroes but by the more recent arrivals from Mexico or the rural areas of the Southwest. This continuous movement of Spanish-name persons, which has not been adequately treated in the literature, tends to obscure the achievements in upward mobility that have been made by this population.

also supported by the .data gathered in New Haven. In the latter instance the Catholic hospital as compared to the non-Catholic hospital employed at least twice as many Italian-name persons in each of the three status categories.

It appears to the authors that the statements of Marden, Broom, and Shevky, Greer, Warner and Srole regarding the assimilation of Spanish-name persons are rather pessimistic and, to be sure, have been generally supported by their data. Progress toward assimilation by the population in question, as measured by their position within the health and hospital occupational structure was found to be uneven, but it was certainly not lacking. While the data seem to support the Warner-Srole prediction in general, certain factors which they did not account for have entered the picture to alter the situation:

1. Since 1940, with the coming of World War II, the Korean War, with the opportunities in defense industries, participation in the Armed Forces, and the opportunities offered by the G.I. Bill, the situation has changed drastically for at least some of this population. More and more are graduating from high school and college, entering the professions and business, and in general, the now familiar pattern of mobility seems to be occurring in the Southwest. Our data show this change in part.

2. Urbanism. Up to 1940 the Spanish-name population was predominantly rural; by 1950 it was predominantly urban. While this phenomenon does not suggest tremendous shifts in occupations, it does suggest gradual changes in the life-ways of the people, less geographical isolation, and greater contact both physically and culturally with the dominant society with the accompanying assimilative influences. El Paso has shown remarkable mobility for Spanish-name persons in recent years. San Diego has also risen to become one of the nation's great metropolises, and its Spanish-name persons are making some progress toward assimilation but not as much as has been noted in El Paso. Other factors seem to be suggested.

3. The location of the American city relative to the Mexican border, and the border interaction patterns that have developed there are important. Here again, El Paso is in a unique position. It is right on the border, and is a major port of entry into Mexico. C. Juarez, across from El Paso, has become an important Mexican city. The Anglo community in El Paso has gradually come to realize that it must learn to live with the international situation. Both business and political leaders have made efforts to get along with the citizens of C. Juarez, and to assimilate the Mexican-Americans. The El Paso school superintendent reported that some 60-70 percent of El Paso children enter school without knowing English. They have developed special programs for them within the regular school program. School integration has long been an established policy. In predominantly "Anglo" school districts Spanish is taught in the elementary grades. These programs would seem to promote mobility and assimilation for the El Pasoan of Mexican descent. The border can also act as a barrier to assimilation. Or as is the case of San Diego, the border may not be an influential factor.

4. The problem of skin color is a difficult one to assess. According to Warner and Srole the lighter Spanish-name persons would be the first to assimilate, since all they would have to do would be to drop their cultural differences. Of course, in a border city like El Paso, cultural differences are not so easily defined. Many ethnic patterns have become an accepted part of El Paso life. This is true to a lesser extent in the other cities. Some of the high status health professionals (Spanish-name) are indeed light skinned, but not all, and many of the nurses are noticeably Latino. Nevertheless, it seems certain (even without an accurate measure) that as one descends the occupational ladder, the skin color gets darker.

5. Warner and Srole perceived the Catholic Church as mainly a conservative force which tends to reinforce the ethnic subsystem, and as ineffectual against the forces of organized prejudice. Our data would suggest that the Catholic Church, with its well-organized structures (in this instance hospitals) may in certain situations be an effective mechanism for mobility and assimilation for qualified Spanish-name Catholics. We would propose further investigation to find out if Catholic hospital personnel (in particular physicians, nurses, and administrators) educated in Catholic schools and trained in Catholic hospitals, are able to move freely in Catholic and non-Catholic occupational structures.

Our interviews with personnel directors suggest that there is still strong feeling against the Spanish-name nurse.[11] It is an empirical question whether she would be able to move freely from one hospital to another. Whether her mobility is a function of race, name, religion, or technical competence is problematic. Nevertheless, insofar as the Catholic hospitals provide training that is certified and approved by national standards, they may be said to be preparing hospital personnel for mobility.

6. While the research concerning Spanish-name persons conducted during 1930-1950 revealed much the same pattern of prejudice and discrimination that has been found with respect to the Negro, recent research suggests that these two groups are not in fact perceived nor treated alike. Whereas the Negro is barred from many areas of life of the American society, the Spanish-name — Anglo relationship is not as caste-like. American society is open enough to permit acculturated individuals to enter its ranks and at the higher levels (witness the fact that Spanish-name persons belong to country clubs in more than one southwestern community under study). Thus, given the base established

since 1940, given the recent assimilative resolution of the Spanish-name, given the fact that as the Spanish-named overcome the language and educational barrier, they cease to be regarded as a racial minority group, one can hypothesize that the rate of mobility and assimilation will increase rapidly in the next generation.

FOOTNOTES

1. W. L. Warner and Leo Srole, "Differential Assimilation of American Ethnic Groups," in *American Minorities,* Milton L. Barron (ed.) (New York: A. A. Knopf, 1957), p. 436.

2. *Ibid.,* p. 444.

3. Occupational mobility is used here only as an index of assimilation, and we do not mean to imply that it is synonymous with assimilation.

4. Charles F. Marden, *Minorities in American Society* (New York: American Book Company, 1952), p. 134.

5. *Ibid.,* p. 146. The census data for 1950 reveal further aspects of this minority group status. For four southwestern states, the average of median school years completed for adults fourteen and over was 9.5 years, while for the Spanish-name persons in these four states the average was only 7.0.

6. Robert H. Talbert, *Spanish-Name People in the Southwest and West* (Fort Worth, Texas: Leo Potishman Foundation, 1955), pp. 68-75.

7. Scott Greer, *Last Man In* (Glencoe: The Free Press, 1959), p. 20.

8. L. Broom and E. Shevky, "Mexicans in the United States: A Problem in Social Differentiation," in *Sociology and Social Research* (Jan.-Feb., 1952), pp. 154 and 156.

9. Talbert, *op cit.,* pp. 68-75.

10. In Tucson, for example, one of the members of the Board of Trustees of the University of Arizona was a Spanish-name person. In El Paso several Spanish-name persons held important board memberships in public and private organizations, and several were members of the El Paso Country Club. These data suggest that there may be a hierarchy of prestige board memberships, and that the hospital board membership may be at the apex of this hierarchy.

11. We do not mean to suggest that this assimilation process will proceed without any further tension or conflict. The following quotations, taken from interviews held in these four cities during this study indicate some of the problems that will continue to impede the process. The administrator of one private hospital in the Southwest had this to say: "Yes, we have a time with them (Spanish-name persons) in the hospital. They want to get ahead but some patients won't have any nurse but an Anglo. This makes the Mexican nurses and aides mad. They are proud and envious. We can't put a Mexican and Anglo in the same room as patients; both complain."

The Director of nurses at another hospital explained something of the difficulties which Spanish-name personnel face: "The Latino RN's are very efficient but they are subject to insecurities due to the fact that the doctors do not feel that the Latino RN's understand the orders that the doctors give to them. The doctors feel that these nurses do not understand adequately because of their linguistic handicaps. The doctors do not give any Latino RN's orders over the telephone because of this limitation. They prefer to talk directly to these nurses. Because of this difficulty the Latino RN's are very insecure emotionally."

ACCULTURATION AND ASSIMILATION

ACCULTURATION AND ASSIMILATION

After a child is born into a society, that society sets in motion its mechanisms for bringing that child into contact with the culture. He is taught a language and skills and a variety of knowledges, traditions and norms are passed on to him as rapidly as he is able to absorb them. Sociologists call this process socialization. Sometimes it is necessary or desirable for a person to learn a new set of norms and behaviors, a new culture and social heritage. This is variously called resocialization, adult socialization, or acculturation and assimilation. Under whatever name, it is helpful to think of this process as a continuum. At one extreme is the person with little or no knowledge of the new culture. Gradually he learns more and more and he fits with ever greater smoothness into the new socio-cultural matrix. This process, acculturation, is a matter of degrees not of absolutes. One is fully acculturated when he functions in the new society with the same ease and depth as those born into it. At this stage, barring biological differences, he would be indistinguishable from the "natives." One significant difference would remain; his self-concept, his self-identity. For example, if our hypothetical person was an American who went to live in Germany and became fully acculturated, he would see himself as an American who was functioning smoothly in German society and culture; he would not identify himself as a German. Yet this final change in self-concept not only is possible but is relatively common. It has occurred to some first generation immigrants, to many second generation immigrants, and to most third generation immigrants.

At one time America held the "melting pot" theory of acculturation and assimilation, the belief that all cultures should and could be "mixed in the crucible of Americanization," and that the resulting mixture would be superior to any single culture. However sound this theory may or may not have been, for seventy-five years the practice most often was a one way street: the immigrant was expected to give up his culture and accept the "American" culture in toto. More recently strong emphasis is being placed on the theory of cultural pluralism, that in a large, complex society not all persons can share the same culture, nor is it best that they should. This attitude anticipates a number of subcultures, each differing in some degree from the host or parent culture, yet all together making up a cooperative whole which is richer and more useful and more satisfying and permits more individuality than is possible for any single culture.

Mexican Americans have not responded uniformly to the acculturating agents and agencies in the North American culture. Some largely rejected the new culture; some have not rejected it but only passively and accidently acquired its patterns. Still others actively sought acculturation as a rational method of adjusting to the new situation, but rejected assimilation; and others have become fully assimilated. It is probably correct to say that today the great majority of Mexican Americans seek the full measure of acculturation consistent with cultural pluralism and that in so doing not a few of them achieve assimilation either intentionally or unwittingly. The increasing intermarriage of Anglos with third or more generation Mexican Americans is one index of increasing assimilation.

In "The Mutual Images and Expectations of Anglo-Americans and Mexican-Americans," Ozzie G. Simmons, a sociologist, reports that Anglo Americans assume the Mexican Americans are their potential but not yet actual peers. They are still viewed as likely to possess to a greater degree than Anglos such characteristics as uncleanliness, drunkenness, immorality, unpredictability, and criminality. Mexican American stereotypes, on the other hand, tend to evaluate Anglos on the basis of their attitudes toward Mexicans, seeing them on the one hand as cold, exploitative and mercenary, or on the other hand as warm, just and friendly. Anthony G. Dworkin, another sociologist, in "Stereotypes and Self-Images Held by Native-Born and Foreign-Born Mexican Americans," describes a study in which he found that significantly more foreign-born hold favorable stereotypes and self-images than do native-born Mexican Americans. These differences he attributes to differences in the groups' definition of their present social situation as influenced by whether they employed their prior socio-economic situation or the socio-economic situation of the Anglo society as a standard of evaluation. In his "Epilogue" Dworkin reports on an additional, more recent study. In it he finds that differences in attitude and self concept between foreign-born Mexican Americans and native-born Mexican Americans still exist. The Native-born tended to have negative stereotypes of Anglos and positive self-images. One interesting characteristic of the sample was that only 3% of the Mexican Americans favored riots as a form of social protest compared to 37%

of Blacks. Native-born Mexican Americans were somewhat more likely to think riots were effective than was true of foreign-born. These findings are significant, for in this study age was held constant, and usually there is an age differential between foreign-born and native-born which itself tends to skew answers. Buford Farris and Richard Brymer are the authors of "Differential Socialization of Latin and Anglo-American Youth: An Exploratory Study of the Self Concept." They find differences in Mexican American and Anglo youth self concepts in the areas of academic achievement, extracurricular activities, peer group interests, opposite sex interests, age status, and adolescence. These differences are partly explained by the fact that the Mexican American high school students are in some ways a more "select" group than Anglo high school students. Leonard Broom and Eshref Shevky, both sociologists, in an older but classic study, "Mexicans in the United States: A Problem in Social Differentiation," point out differentiations based on economic function and mobility, acculturation and urbanization, status and assimilation, and modes of isolation and integration.

THE MUTUAL IMAGES AND EXPECTATIONS OF ANGLO-AMERICANS AND MEXICAN-AMERICANS*

OZZIE G. SIMMONS

A number of psychological and sociological studies have treated ethnic and racial stereotypes as they appear publicly in the mass media and also as held privately by individuals. The present paper is based on data collected for a study of a number of aspects of the relations between Anglo-Americans and Mexican-Americans in a South Texas community, and is concerned with the principal assumptions and expectations that Anglo- and Mexican-Americans hold of one another; how they see each other; the extent to which these pictures are realistic; and the implications of their intergroup relations and cultural differences for the fulfillment of their mutual expectations.

The Community

The community studied (here called "Border City") is in South Texas, about 250 miles south of San Antonio. Driving south from San Antonio, one passes over vast expanses of brushland and grazing country, then suddenly comes upon acres of citrus groves, farmlands rich with vegetables and cotton, and long rows of palm trees. This is the "Magic Valley," an oasis in the semidesert region of South Texas.

The Anglo-American immigration into the Valley was paralleled by that of the Mexicans from across the border, who were attracted by the seemingly greater opportunities for farm labor created by the introduction of irrigation and the subsequent agricultural expansion. Actually, there had been a small but steady flow of Mexican immigration into South Texas that long antedated the Anglo-American immigration. At present, Mexican-Americans probably constitute about two-fifths of the total population of the Valley.

In Border City, Mexican-Americans comprise about 56 percent of the population. The southwestern part of the city, adjoining and sometimes

*Reprinted with permission of *Daedalus,* Journal of the American Academy of Arts and Sciences, Boston, Mass., Spring 1961, "Ethnic Groups in American Life."

infiltrating the business and industrial areas, is variously referred to as "Mexiquita," "Mexican-town," and "Little Mexico" by the city's Anglo-Americans, and as the *colonia* by the Mexican-Americans, most of whom live in close proximity to one another in indifferently constructed houses on tiny lots. The north side of the city, which lies across the railroad tracks, is inhabited almost completely by Anglo-Americans. Its appearance is in sharp contrast to that of the *colonia* in that it is strictly residential and displays much better housing.

In the occupational hierarchy of Border City, the top level (the growers, packers, canners, businessmen, and professionals) is overwhelmingly Anglo-American. In the middle group (the white-collar occupations) Mexicans are prominent only where their bilingualism makes them useful, for example, as clerks and salesmen. The bottom level (farm laborers, shed and cannery workers, and domestic servants) is overwhelmingly Mexican-American.

These conditions result from a number of factors, some quite distinct from the reception accorded Mexican-Americans by Anglo-Americans. Many Mexican-Americans are still recent immigrants and are thus relatively unfamiliar with Anglo-American culture and urban living, or else persist in their tendency to live apart and maintain their own institutions whenever possible. Among their disadvantages, however, the negative attitudes and discriminatory practices of the Anglo-American group must be counted. It is only fair to say, with the late Ruth Tuck, that much of what Mexican-Americans have suffered at Anglo-American hands has not been perpetrated deliberately but through indifference, that it has been done not with the fist but with the elbow. The average social and economic status of the Mexican-American group has been improving, and many are moving upward. This is partly owing to increasing acceptance by the Anglo-American group, but chiefly to the efforts of the Mexican-Americans themselves.

Anglo-American Assumptions and Expectations

Robert Lynd writes of the dualism in the principal assumptions that guide Americans in conducting their everyday life and identifies the attempt to "live by contrasting rules of the game" as a characteristic aspect of our culture. This pattern of moral compromise, symptomatic of what is likely to be only vaguely a conscious moral conflict, is evident in Anglo-American assumptions and expectations with regard to Mexican-Americans, which appear both in the moral principles that define what intergroup relations ought to be, and in the popular notions held by Anglo-Americans as to what Mexican Americans are "really" like. In the first case there is a response to the "American creed," which embodies ideals of the essential dignity of the individual and of certain inalienable rights to freedom, justice, and equal opportunity. Accordingly, Anglo-Americans believe that Mexican-Americans must be accorded full acceptance and equal status in the larger society. When their orientation to these ideals is uppermost, Anglo-Americans believe that the assimilation of Mexican-Americans is only a matter of time, contingent solely on the full incorporation of Anglo-American values and ways of life.

These expectations regarding the assimilation of the Mexican are most clearly expressed in the notion of the "high type" of Mexican. It is based on three criteria: occupational achievement and wealth (the Anglo-American's own principal criteria of status) and command of Anglo-American ways. Mexican-Americans who can so qualify are acceptable for membership in the service clubs and a few other Anglo-American organizations and for limited social intercourse. They may even intermarry without being penalized or ostracized. Both in their achievements in business and agriculture and in wealth, they compare favorably with middle-class Anglo-Americans, and they manifest a high command of the latter's ways. This view of the "high type" of Mexican reflects the Anglo-American assumption that Mexicans are assimilable; it does not necessarily insure a full acceptance of even the "high type" of Mexican or that his acceptance will be consistent.

The assumption that Mexican-Americans will be ultimately assimilated was not uniformly shared by all the Anglo-Americans who were our informants in Border City. Regardless of whether they expressed adherence to this ideal, however, most Anglo-Americans expressed the contrasting assumption that Mexican-Americans are essentially inferior. Thus the same people may hold assumptions and expectations that are contradictory, although expressed at different times and in different situations. As in the case of their adherence to the ideal of assimilability, not all Anglo-Americans hold the same assumptions and expectations with respect to the inferiority of Mexican-Americans; and even those who agree vary in the intensity of their beliefs. Some do not believe in the Mexican's inferiority at all; some are relatively moderate or sceptical, while others express extreme views with considerable emotional intensity.

Despite this variation, the Anglo-Americans' principal assumptions and expectations emphasize the Mexicans' presumed inferiority. In its most characteristic pattern, such inferiority is held to be self-evident. As one Anglo-American woman put it, "Mexicans are inferior because they are so typically and naturally Mexican." Since they are so obviously inferior, their present subordinate status is appropriate and is really their own fault. There is a ready identification between Mexicans and menial labor, buttressed by an image of the Mexican worker as improvident, undependable, irresponsible, childlike, and indolent. If Mexicans are fit for only the humblest labor, there is nothing abnormal about the fact that most Mexican workers are at the bottom of the occupational pyramid, and the fact that most Mexicans are unskilled workers is sufficient proof that they belong in that category.

Associated with the assumption of Mexican inferiority is that of the homogeneity of this group — that is, all Mexicans are alike. Anglo-Americans may classify Mexicans as being of "high type" and "low type" and at the same time maintain that "a Mexican is a Mexican." Both notions serve a purpose, depending on the situation. The assumption that all Mexicans are alike buttresses the assumption of inferiority by making it convenient to ignore the fact of the existence of a substantial number of Mexican-Americans who represent all levels of business and professional achievement. Such people are considered exceptions to the rule.

Anglo-American Images of Mexican-Americans

To employ Gordon Allport's definition, a stereotype is an exaggerated belief associated with a category, and its function is to justify conduct in relation to that category. Some of the Anglo-American images of the Mexican have no ascertainable basis in fact, while others have at least a kernel of truth. Although some components of these images derive from behavior patterns that are characteristic of some Mexican-Americans in some situations, few if any of the popular generalizations about them are valid as stated, and none is demonstrably true of all. Some of the images of Mexican-Americans are specific to a particular area of intergroup relations, such as the image of the Mexican-American's attributes as a worker. Another is specific to politics and describes Mexicans as ready to give their votes to whoever will pay for them or provide free barbecues and beer. Let us consider a few of the stereotypical beliefs that are widely used on general principles to justify Anglo-American practices of exclusion and subordination.

One such general belief accuses Mexican-Americans of being unclean. The examples given of this supposed characteristic most frequently refer to a lack of personal cleanliness and environmental hygiene and to a high incidence of skin ailments ascribed to a lack of hygienic practices. Indeed, there are few immigrant groups, regardless of their ethnic background, to whom this defect has not been attributed by the host society, as well as others prominent in stereotypes of the Mexican. It has often been observed that for middle-class Americans cleanliness is not simply a matter of keeping clean but is also an index to the morals and virtues of the individual. It is largely true that Mexicans tend to be much more casual in hygienic practices than Anglo-Americans. Moreover, their labor in the field, the packing sheds, and the towns is rarely clean work, and it is possible that many Anglo-Americans base their conclusions on what they observe in such situations. There is no evidence of a higher incidence of skin ailments among Mexicans than among Anglo-Americans. The belief that Mexicans are unclean is useful for rationalizing the Anglo-American practice of excluding Mexicans from any situation that involves close or allegedly close contact with Anglo-Americans, as in residence, and the common use of swimming pools and other recreational facilities.

Drunkenness and criminality are a pair of traits that have appeared regularly in the stereotypes applied to immigrant groups. They have a prominent place in Anglo-American images of Mexicans. If Mexicans are inveterate drunkards and have criminal tendencies, a justification is provided for excluding them from full participation in the life of the community. It is true that drinking is a popular activity among Mexican-Americans and that total abstinence is rare, except among some Protestant Mexican-Americans. Drinking varies, however, from the occasional consumption of a bottle of beer to the heavy drinking of more potent beverages, so that the frequency of drinking and drunkenness is far from being evenly distributed among Mexican-Americans. Actually, this pattern is equally applicable to the Anglo-American group. The ample patronage of bars in the Anglo-American part of Border City, and the drinking behavior exhibited by Anglo-Americans when they cross the river to Mexico indicate that Mexicans have no monopoly on drinking or drunkenness. It is true that the number of arrests for drunkenness in Border City is greater among Mexicans, but this is probably because Mexicans are more vulnerable to arrest. The court records in Border City show little difference in the contributions made to delinquency and crime by Anglo- and Mexican-Americans.

Another cluster of images in the Anglo-American stereotype portrays Mexican-Americans as deceitful and of a "low" morality, as mysterious, unpredictable, and hostile to Anglo-Americans. It is quite possible that Mexicans resort to a number of devices in their relations with Anglo-Americans, particularly in relations with employers, to compensate for their disadvantages, which may be construed by Anglo-Americans as evidence of deceitfulness. The whole nature of the dominant-subordinate relationship does not make for frankness on the part of Mexicans or encourage them to face up directly to Anglo-Americans in most intergroup contacts. As to the charge of immorality, one need only recognize the strong sense of loyalty and obligation that Mexicans feel in their familial and interpersonal relations to know that the charge is baseless. The claim that Mexicans are mysterious and deceitful may in part reflect Anglo-American reactions to actual differences in culture and personality, but like the other beliefs considered here, is highly exaggerated. The imputation of hostility to Mexicans, which is manifested in a reluctance to enter the *colonia*, particularly at night, may have its kernel of truth, but appears to be largely a projection of the Anglo-American's own feelings.

All three of these images can serve to justify exclusion and discrimination: if Mexicans are deceitful and immoral, they do not have to be accorded equal status and justice; if they are mysterious and unpredictable, there is no point in treating them as one would a fellow Anglo-American; and if they are hostile and dangerous, it is best that they live apart in colonies of their own.

Not all Anglo-American images of the Mexican are unfavorable. Among those usually meant to be complimentary are the beliefs that all Mexicans are musical and always ready for a fiesta, that they are very "romantic" rather than "realistic" (which may have unfavorable overtones as well), and that they love flowers and can grow them under the most adverse conditions. Although each of these beliefs may have a modicum of truth, it may be noted that they tend to reinforce Anglo-American images of Mexicans as childlike and irresponsible, and thus they support the notion that Mexicans are capable only of subordinate status.

Mexican-American Assumptions, Expectations, and Images

Mexican-Americans are as likely to hold contradictory assumptions and distorted images as are Anglo-Americans. Their principal assumptions, however, must reflect those of Anglo-Americans — that is, Mexicans must take into account the Anglo-Americans' conflict as to their potential equality and present inferiority, since they are the object of such imputations. Similarly, their images of Anglo-Americans are not derived wholly independently, but to some extent must reflect their own subordinate status. Consequently, their stereotypes of Anglo-Americans are much less elaborate, in part because Mexicans feel no need of justifying the present intergroup relation, in part because the very nature of their dependent position forces them to view the relation more realistically than Anglo-Americans do. For the same reasons, they need not hold to their beliefs about Anglo-Americans with the rigidity and intensity so often characteristic of the latter.

Any discussion of these assumptions and expectations requires some mention of the class distinctions within the Mexican-American group. Its middle class, though small as compared with the lower class, is powerful within the group and performs the critical role of intermediary in negotiations with the Anglo-American group. Middle-class status is based on education and occupation, family background, readiness to serve the interests of the group, on wealth, and the degree of acculturation, or command of Anglo-American ways. Anglo-Americans recognize Mexican class distinctions (although not very accurately) in their notions of the "high type" and "low type" of Mexicans.

In general, lower-class Mexicans do not regard the disabilities of their status as being nearly as severe as do middle-class Mexican-Americans. This is primarily a reflection of the insulation between the Anglo-American world and that of the Mexican lower class. Most Mexicans, regardless of class, are keenly aware of Anglo-American attitudes and practices with regard to their group, but lower-class Mexicans do not conceive of participation in the larger society as necessary nor do they regard Anglo-American practices of exclusion as affecting them directly. Their principal reaction has been to maintain their isolation, and thus they have not been particularly concerned with improving their status by acquiring Anglo-American ways, a course more characteristic of the middle-class Mexican.

Mexican-American assumptions and expectations regarding Anglo-Americans must be qualified, then, as being more characteristic of middle than of lower-class Mexican-Americans. Mexicans, like Anglo-Americans, are subject to conflicts of their ideals, not only because of irrational thinking on their part but also because of Anglo-American inconsistencies between ideal and practice. As for ideals expressing democratic values, Mexican expectations are for obvious reasons the counterpart of the Anglo-Americans' — that Mexican-Americans should be accorded full acceptance and equal opportunity. They feel a considerable ambivalence, however, as to the Anglo-American expectation that the only way to achieve this goal is by a full incorporation of Anglo-American values and ways of life, for this implies the ultimate loss of their cultural identity as Mexicans. On the one hand, they favor the acquisition of Anglo-American culture and the eventual remaking of the Mexican in the Anglo-American image; but on the other hand, they are not so sure that Anglo-American acceptance is worth such a price. When they are concerned with this dilemma, Mexicans advocate a fusion with Anglo-American culture in which the "best" of the Mexican ways, as they view it, would be retained along with the incorporation of the "best" of the Anglo-American ways, rather than a one-sided exchange in which all that is distinctively Mexican would be lost.

A few examples will illustrate the point of view expressed in the phrase, "the best of both ways." A premium is placed on speaking good, unaccented English, but the retention of good Spanish is valued just as highly as "a mark of culture that should not be abandoned." Similarly, there is an emphasis on the incorporation of behavior patterns that are considered characteristically Anglo-American and that will promote "getting ahead," but not to the point at which the drive for power and wealth would become completely dominant, as is believed to be the case with Anglo-Americans.

Mexican ambivalence about becoming Anglo-American or achieving a fusion of the "best" of both cultures is compounded by their ambivalence about another issue, that of equality versus inferiority. That Anglo-Americans are dominant in the society and seem to monopolize its accomplishments and rewards leads Mexicans at times to draw the same conclusion that Anglo-Americans do, namely, that Mexicans are inferior. This questioning of their own sense of worth exists in all classes of the Mexican-American group, although with varying intensity, and plays a substantial part in every adjustment to intergroup relations. There is a pronounced tendency to concede the superiority of Anglo-American ways and consequently to define Mexican ways as undesirable, inferior, and disreputable. The tendency to believe in his own inferiority is counterbalanced, however, by the Mexican's fierce racial pride, which sets the tone of Mexican demands and strivings for equal status, even though these may slip into feelings of inferiority.

The images Mexicans have of Anglo-Americans may not be so elaborate or so emotionally charged as the images that Anglo-Americans have of Mexicans, but they are nevertheless stereotypes, overgeneralized, and exaggerated, although used primarily for defensive rather than justificatory purposes. Mexican images of Anglo-Americans are sometimes favorable, particularly when they identify such traits as initiative, ambition, and industriousness as being peculiarly Anglo-American. Unfavorable images are prominent, however, and, although they may be hostile, they never impute inferiority to Anglo-Americans. Most of the Mexican stereotypes evaluate Anglo-Americans on the basis of their attitudes toward Mexican-Americans. For example, one such classification provides a two-fold typology. The first type, the "majority," includes those who are cold, unkind, mercenary, and exploitative. The second type, the "minority," consists of those who are friendly, warm, just, and unprejudiced. For the most part, Mexican images of Anglo-Americans reflect the latter's patterns of exclusion and assumptions of superiority, as experienced by Mexican-Americans. Thus Anglo-Americans are pictured as stolid, phlegmatic, cold-hearted, and distant. They are also said to be braggarts, conceited, inconstant, and insincere.

Intergroup Relations, Mutual Expectations,
and Cultural Differences

A number of students of intergroup relations assert that research in this area has yet to demonstrate any relation between stereotypical beliefs and intergroup behavior; indeed, some insist that under certain conditions ethnic attitudes and discrimination can vary independently. Arnold M. Rose, for example, concludes that "from a heuristic standpoint it may be desirable to assume that patterns of intergroup relations, on the one hand, and attitudes of prejudice and stereotyping, on the other hand, are fairly unrelated phenomena although they have reciprocal influences on each other, . . . In the present study, no systematic attempt was made to investigate the relation between the stereotypical beliefs of particular individuals and their actual intergroup behavior; but the study did yield much evidence that both images which justify group separatism and separateness itself are characteristic aspects of intergroup relations in Border City. One of the principal findings is that in those situations in which contact between Anglo-Americans and Mexicans is voluntary (such as residence, education, recreation, religious worship, and social intercourse) the characteristic pattern is separateness rather than common participation. Wherever intergroup contact is necessary, as in occupational activities and the performance of commercial and professional services, it is held to the minimum sufficient to accomplish the purpose of the contact. The extent of this separateness is not constant for all members of the two groups, since it tends to be less severe between Anglo-Americans and those Mexicans they define as of a "high type." Nevertheless, the evidence reveals a high degree of compatibility, between beliefs and practices in Border City intergroup relations, although the data have nothing to offer for the identification of direct relationships.

In any case, the separateness that characterizes intergroup relations cannot be attributed solely to the exclusion practices of the Anglo-American group. Mexicans have tended to remain separate by choice as well as by necessity. Like many other ethnic groups, they have often found this the easier course, since they need not strain to learn another language or to change their ways and manners. The isolation practices of the Mexican group are as relevant to an understanding of intergroup relations as are the exclusion practices of the Anglo-Americans.

This should not, however, obscure the fact that to a wide extent the majority of Mexican-Americans share the patterns of living of Anglo-American society; many of their ways are already identical. Regardless of the degree of their insulation from the larger society, the demands of life in the United States have required basic modifications of the Mexicans' cultural tradition. In material culture, Mexicans are hardly to be distinguished from Anglo-Americans, and there have been basic changes in medical beliefs and practices and in the customs regarding godparenthood. Mexicans have acquired English in varying degrees, and their Spanish has become noticeably Anglicized. Although the original organization of the family has persisted, major changes have occurred in patterns of traditional authority, as well as in child training and courtship practices. Still, it is the exceedingly rare Mexican-American, no matter how acculturated he may be to the dominant society, who does not in some degree retain the more subtle characteristics of his Mexican heritage, particularly in his conception of time and in other fundamental value orientations, as well as in his modes of participation in interpersonal relations. Many of the most acculturated Mexican-Americans have attempted to exemplify what they regard as "the best of both ways." They have become largely Anglo-American in their way of living, but they still retain fluent Spanish and a knowledge of their traditional culture, and they maintain an identification with their own heritage while participating in Anglo-American culture. Nevertheless, this sort of achievement still seems a long way off for many Mexican-Americans who regard it as desirable.

A predominant Anglo-American expectation is that the Mexicans will be eventually assimilated into the larger society; but this is contingent upon Mexicans' becoming just like Anglo-Americans. The Mexican counterpart to this expectation is only partially complementary. Mexicans want to be full members of the larger society, but they do not want to give up their cultural heritage. There is even less complementarity of expectation with regard to the present conduct of intergroup relations. Anglo-Americans believe they are justified in withholding equal access to the rewards of full acceptance as long as Mexicans remain "different," particularly since they interpret the differences (both those which have some basis in reality and those which have none) as evidence of inferiority. Mexicans, on the other hand, while not always certain that they are not inferior, clearly want equal opportunity and full acceptance now, not in some dim future, and they do not believe that their differences (either presumed or real) from Anglo-Americans offer any justification for the denial of opportunity and acceptance. Moreover, they do not find that acculturation is rewarded in any clear and regular way by progressive acceptance.

It is probable that both Anglo-Americans and Mexicans will have to modify their beliefs and practices if they are to realize more nearly their expectations of each other. Mutual stereotyping, as well as the exclusion practices of Anglo-Americans and the isolation practices of Mexicans, maintains the separateness of the two groups, and separateness is a massive barrier to the realization of their expectations. The process of acculturation is presently going on among Mexican-Americans and will continue, regardless of whether changes in Anglo-Mexican relations occur. Unless Mexican-Americans can validate their increasing command of Anglo-American ways by a free participation in the larger society, however, such acculturation is not likely to accelerate its present leisurely pace, nor will it lead to eventual assimilation. The *colonia* is a relatively safe place in which new cultural acquisitions may be tried out, and thus it has its positive functions; but by the same token it is only in intergroup contacts with Anglo-Americans that acculturation is validated, that the Mexican's level of acculturation is tested, and that the distance he must yet travel to assimilation is measured.

Conclusions

There are major inconsistencies in the assumptions that Anglo-Americans and Mexican-Americans hold about one another. Anglo-Americans assume that Mexican-Americans are their potential, if not actual, peers, but at the same time assume they are their inferiors. The beliefs that presumably demonstrate the Mexican-Americans' inferiority tend to place them outside the accepted moral order and framework of Anglo-American society by attributing to them undesirable characteristics that make it "reasonable" to treat them differently from their fellow Anglo-Americans. Thus the negative images provide not only a rationalized definition of the intergroup relation that makes it palatable for Anglo-Americans, but also a substantial support for maintaining the relation as it is. The assumptions of Mexican-Americans about Anglo-Americans are similarly inconsistent, and their images of Anglo-Americans are predominantly negative, although these are primarily defensive rather than justificatory. The mutual expectations of the two groups contrast sharply with the ideal of a complementarity of expectations, in that Anglo-Americans expect Mexicans to become just like themselves, if they are to be accorded equal status in the larger society, whereas Mexican-Americans want full acceptance, regardless of the extent to which they give up their own ways and acquire those of the dominant group.

Anglo-Americans and Mexicans may decide to stay apart because they are different, but cultural differences provide no moral justification for one group to deny to the other equal opportunity and the rewards of the larger society. If the full acceptance of Mexicans by Anglo-Americans is contingent upon the disappearance of cultural differences, it will not be accorded in the foreseeable future. In our American society, we have often seriously underestimated the strength and tenacity of early cultural conditioning. We have expected newcomers to change their customs and values to conform to American ways as quickly as possible, without an adequate appreciation of the strains imposed by this process. An understanding of the nature of culture and of its interrelations with personality can make us more realistic about the rate at which cultural change can proceed and about the gains and costs for the individual who is subject to the experiences of acculturation. In viewing cultural differences primarily as disabilities, we neglect their positive aspects. Mexican-American culture represents the most constructive and effective means Mexican-Americans have yet been able to develop for coping with their changed natural and social environment. They will further exchange old ways for new only if these appear to be more meaningful and rewarding than the old, and then only if they are given full opportunity to acquire the new ways and to use them.

STEREOTYPES AND SELF-IMAGES HELD BY NATIVE-BORN AND FOREIGN-BORN MEXICAN AMERICANS*

ANTHONY GARY DWORKIN

Over the past two decades extensive research has been conducted in the Border and Southwestern states in an effort to obtain the stereotypes of the Mexican American held by the dominant Anglo-American population (Tuck,[1] Richards,[2] McDonagh and Richards,[3] Burma,[4] and Simmons).[5] A few investigators, including Simmons, have sampled Mexican-American opinion as well in order to discover their stereotypes of the Anglo. However, the literature appears to be devoid of studies which concentrate upon Mexican-American stereotypes of the Anglo together with Mexican-American self-images. It was, therefore, the purpose of the present research to provide a detailed list of stereotypes[6] and self-images held by this ethnic group.

Because of the heterogeneity of the Mexican-American population, it was decided that the group to be studied would consist of what Simmons referred to as the "low type," since they are of the greatest concern to the welfare and action agencies, and because the so-called "high type" have generally assimilated into the Anglo middle class population. The "low type" are generally portrayed as the high school drop-outs, the delinquent, illiterate mass of menial laborers who live in the Spanish-speaking, slum-like ghettos which are prolific in the urbanized areas of the Southwest. Such individuals do not meet the three criteria for assimilation: "occupational achievement . . . wealth . . . and command of Anglo-American ways."

Since there are at least two varieties of Mexican Americans in the Spanish-speaking ghetto (those who have lived there all of their lives and those who have recently come there from Mexico), it is perhaps fallacious to speak of the "low type" collectively. It might be expected that the two, having different available frames of reference for evaluating socioeconomic conditions, might picture their present social situation differently. The native-born Mexican American (NBMA) may compare his socioeconomic condition with that of the Anglo and note

*Reprinted from *Sociology and Social Research*, Volume 49, No. 2, January 1965.

his relative disadvantage; while the foreign-born Mexican American (FBMA) may compare his socioeconomic condition with conditions in Mexico and note his relative advantage. These perceptions may in turn affect the stereotypes and self-images each holds. It seems reasonable that the NBMA, who has lived in the same blighted area all of his life, and who has been unable to escape from the ghetto, may view his Anglo brother and himself in a manner different from that of the FMBA, who has recently left his home in Mexico to make a new life for himself in the United States.

Hypothesis

In light of the assumed differences between the NBMA and the FBMA in their available frames of reference for defining the situation, the following hypothesis was formulated: That the Mexican American born in Mexico, who has recently come to the United States, employs more positive, or favorable, stereotypes in describing the Anglo American and more favorable, or optimistic, self-images in describing himself, than does the Mexican American born in the United States, who has lived in the same blighted area all of his life.

The hypothesis is reasonable if one considers that the FBMA has successfully endeavored to leave a poorer socioeconomic condition (life in Mexico is usually worse than in the Spanish-speaking ghetto) and has voluntarily come to live in a country where the Anglo is dominant, while the NBMA has not.

Of course comparisons made between these two groups are valid only if the socioeconomic variables are controlled, and consequently, both samples needed to be drawn from the same neighborhoods. Furthermore, it must be remembered that since literature on Mexican American stereotypes and self-images is sparse, the present investigation serves more the function of an exploratory study, calling for future research, than as a crucial experiment which would solve once and for all a theoretical problem.

Subjects. The 280 subjects (*S*s) employed in the present investigation were partitioned into two groups: 50 individuals were Mexican-American college students and 230 were residents of the Mexican-American community. Both the student and the community samples were obtained from the predominantly Mexican-American sections of East Los Angeles and San Gabriel, California.[8] The students were selected on a volunteer basis, but the community sample was obtained by a more exacting method. To select the *S*s in the community sample, a table of random numbers was applied to the addresses, obtained from the city directories, which were occupied by individuals with Spanish surnames. Thus, an essentially random sample of Mexican American residents was obtained.[9]

Procedure. In order to test the experimental hypothesis it was necessary to assemble an interview schedule which would be sufficiently unstructured to permit the *S*s to discuss their attitudes openly; yet, at the same time, organized in such a fashion to obtain an accurate set of stereotypes and self-images. Because the free association method most nearly met these criteria, the stereotypes and self-images were first obtained in this manner.

The 50 Mexican American students were asked to write down upon a sheet of paper as many words as they could think of, in a period of 30 minutes, which they felt accurately described the "personality," "appearance and physical features," "mannerisms," "family and religious life," "intelligence," "educational experience," "socioeconomic status," "ambitions," and "activities" of the Anglo-American and the Mexican American populations. The students were given a working definition for the two groups they were to describe.[10]

Because students have a tendency to employ stereotyped thinking less often than the general public, and because nearly all of the students had lived in the same community all of their lives, and so, did not satisfy the requirements for testing the hypothesis, it was necessary to present the free-associated words to the residents of the Mexican American communities. The students had been quite satisfactory for the compilation of the initial stereotypes and self-images, as they were a homogeneous group (nearly all were NBMA) which would provide a consistent set of stereotypes and self-images.

From the hundreds of words obtained from the students' free associations, two lists were compiled for presentation to the community residents. The first list contained 58 words, while the second list contained 60 words. Both lists were available in Spanish if the *S* could not understand English. The words were selected either because they appeared in more than ten per cent of the students' free associations, or because the words had been found in previous studies (the latter applied only to the stereotypes of the Anglo).

Each of the residents of the communities was presented with one of the lists and asked either to agree or disagree with the students' free associations. Half of the *S*s in the sample received one list and half received the other.

Simply because the *S*s in the community sample might agree with the students' free associations was in itself no guarantee that the words were in fact the popularly-held stereotypes and self-images. An additional control was needed to demonstrate that the public would spontaneously think of these images. Thus, a sample of 30 Mexican American community residents was presented with a free association form similar to the one the students had completed; and the *S*s in this sample were given the same instructions as the students were given. Because it took the average resident over two hours to complete the two-page form (it took the students only 30 minutes), these forms were difficult to obtain, and the desired number, which was 50, was not attained.

Results

Tables I and II present the students' free associations which were most frequently agreed upon by the members of the community sample (excluding the 30 community residents who were asked to give free associations). In all cases the words shown in the tables are exactly as the students listed them. A series of 2 X 2 chi squares were run comparing the number of NBMA versus the number of FBMA who agreed or disagreed with each of the words; and these values, with their respective levels of confidence, are also found in the two tables. It should be noted that since there were 100 each of native-born and foreign-born subjects in this part of the sample, the frequencies presented may also be regarded as percentages.

Table I presents the stereotypes of the Anglo-American most frequently agreed upon by the two groups of *S*s. NBMA depicted the Anglo as (a) education-minded; (b) materialistic; (c) tall, thin, and light-complexioned; (d) scientific; (e) active in their own community; (f) prejudiced; (g) snobbish; (h) having little family loyalty; (i) hypocritical; (j) tense, anxious, and neurotic; (k) conformists; and (l) puritanical.

Of the twelve images, eight may be considered negative traits, while four ("education-minded," "tall, thin, and light-complexioned," "scientific," and "active in their own community") may be regarded as either positive or neutral. The last of these four, the word "active in their own community," may be interpreted, however, to portray the Anglo

TABLE 1
Stereotypes of the Anglo Held by NBMA and FBMA

Words most frequently agreed upon by NBMA	NBMA responses:		FBMA responses:		Chi	
	Agree	Disagree	Agree	Disagree	Square	p =
Education-minded	100	0	82	18	19.78	< .001
Materialistic	100	0	76	24	27.28	< .001
Tall, thin, & light-complexioned	96	4	90	10	2.76	< .10
Scientific	94	6	70	30	19.51	< .001
Active in their own community	90	10	68	32	14.59	< .001
Prejudiced	90	10	52	48	35.07	< .001
Snobbish	88	12	62	38	18.03	< .001
Little family loyalty	86	14	50	50	29.78	< .001
Hypocritical	84	16	56	44	18.67	< .001
Tense, anxious, & neurotic	82	18	68	32	5.23	< .05
Conformists	80	20	42	58	30.35	< .001
Puritanical	78	22	64	36	4.76	< .05

Words most frequently agreed upon by FBMA	FBMA responses:		NBMA responses:		Chi	
	Agree	Disagree	Agree	Disagree	Square	p =
Progressive	100	0	70	30	35.29	< .001
Democratic	100	0	64	36	44.66	< .001
Proud	98	2	74	26	23.92	< .001
Friendly	96	4	58	42	40.77	< .001
Proper and respectable	94	6	72	28	17.15	< .001
Tall, thin, & light-complexioned	90	10	96	4	2.76	< .10
Hard-working	90	10	64	36	19.09	< .001
Clean and neat	86	14	60	40	17.15	< .001
Education-minded	82	18	100	0	19.78	< .001
Religious	80	20	42	58	30.35	< .001
Individualistic	76	24	38	62	29.46	< .001
Materialistic	76	24	100	0	27.28	< .001

as selfish with regard to his community interests.

Except for the stereotype "tall, thin, and light-complexioned," the NBMA accepted the stereotypes significantly more often than did the FBMA. Furthermore, an insignificant number of FBMA agreed with the stereotypes "prejudiced," "little family loyalty," "hypocritical," and "conformists."

FBMA depicted the Anglo as (a) progressive; (b) democratic; (c) proud; (d) friendly; (e) proper and respectable; (f) tall, thin, and light-complexioned; (g) hard-working; (h) clean and neat; (i) education-minded; (j) religious; (k) individualistic; and (l) materialistic.

Ten of the stereotypes may be considered to be positive, while only "materialistic" is negative, and "tall, thin, and light-complexioned" is

TABLE 2

Self-images Held by NBMA and FBMA

Words most frequently agreed upon by NBMA	NBMA responses: Agree	Disagree	FBMA responses: Agree	Disagree	Chi Square	p =
Emotional	100	0	68	32	38.10	<.001
Unscientific	94	6	66	34	24.50	<.001
Authoritarian	92	8	72	28	13.55	<.001
Materialistic	92	8	70	30	15.72	<.001
Old-fashioned	88	12	58	42	22.83	<.001
Poor & of a low social class	86	14	70	30	7.46	<.01
Uneducated or poorly-educated	84	16	64	36	10.40	<.01
Short, fat, & dark	84	16	84	16	0.00	<.99
Little care for education	82	18	46	54	30.49	<.001
Mistrusted	78	22	46	54	21.73	<.001
Proud	78	22	100	0	24.72	<.001
Lazy, indifferent, & unambitious	78	22	28	72	50.18	<.001

Words most frequently agreed upon by FBMA	FBMA responses: Agree	Disagree	NBMA responses: Agree	Disagree	Chi Square	p =
Proud	100	0	78	22	24.72	<.001
Religious	100	0	70	30	35.29	<.001
Strong family ties	100	0	4	96	184.62	<.001
Athletic	98	2	62	38	40.50	<.001
Gregarious	96	4	72	28	21.43	<.001
Friendly	96	4	70	30	23.95	<.001
Happy	94	6	68	32	21.96	<.001
Field workers	90	10	58	42	26.61	<.001
Racially tolerant	88	12	66	34	13.66	<.001
Short, fat, & dark	84	16	84	16	0.00	<.99
Practical	80	20	56	44	13.24	<.001
Well-adjusted	76	24	68	32	1.59	<.30

neutral. Except for the stereotype "tall, thin, and light-complexioned," where no significant difference existed between the two groups of Ss, and the stereotype "materialistic," which was held significantly more often by NBMA, FBMA agreed with the stereotypes significantly more often than did NBMA. Furthermore, an insignificant number of NBMA accepted the stereotypes "friendly" and "religious," and significantly more of them disagreed than agreed that Anglos were "individualistic."

Table II presents the self-images most frequently held by the two groups of Ss. NBMA characterized themselves as (a) emotional; (b) unscientific; (c) authoritarian; (d) materialistic; (e) old-fashioned; (f) poor and of a low social class; (g) uneducated or poorly-educated; (h) short, fat, and dark; (i) having little care for education; (j) mistrusted; (k) proud; and (l) lazy, indifferent, and unambitious.

Eleven of the twelve self-images may be considered as negative, while only "proud" can be regarded to be positive. Except for two images ("short, fat, and dark" and "proud"), NBMA accepted the self-images significantly more often than did FBMA. Furthermore, an insignificant number of FBMA agreed with the self-images "old-fashioned," "little care for education," and "mistrusted," and significantly more of them disagreed than agreed that Mexican Americans were "lazy, indifferent, and unambitious."

The FBMA characterized themselves as (a) proud; (b) religious; (c) having strong family ties; (d) athletic; (e) gregarious; (f) friendly; (g) happy; (h) field workers; (i) racially tolerant; (j) short, fat, and dark; (k) practical; and (l) well adjusted.

Of these twelve self-images, ten may be considered to be positive, while only "short, fat, and dark" and "field workers" may be regarded as negative. The latter, however, may be only an indication of a former status, as many FBMA worked on the farm back home. Except for the images "short, fat, and dark" and "well-adjusted," where no significant difference existed between the two groups of Ss, significantly more FBMA than NBMA accepted the self-images. Furthermore, an insignificant number of NBMA agreed that they were either "field workers" or "practical," and a significant number of them disagreed that they had "strong family ties" (as a matter of fact, on this self-image a near-polar dichotomy existed between the two groups of Ss).

There were many other attitude comparisons made, but these, because of their low frequency of agreement, could not be presented in Tables I and II. The most significant of these indicated that more NBMA than FBMA pictured themselves as "dumb or dull" (p .001), "dirty and sloppy" (p .001), "promiscuous and immoral" (p .01), and "unsure" (p .01), and more FBMA than NBMA portrayed the Anglo as "quick-witted" (p .02) and "athletic and strong" (p .05). Furthermore, while the majority of both groups disagreed with the statement, significantly more NBMA than FMBA would "prefer their sons or daughters to marry Anglos" (p .001). On the companion to this statement, whether they would "prefer their sons or daughters to marry Mexican Americans," significantly more agreement was found for FBMA than NBMA (p .001). The majority, of both groups, however, agreed more often than not with the statement.

Community Free Associations

The 30 residents of the Mexican American community who were asked to give their free-associated stereotypes and self-images listed every word presented in Tables I and II. Furthermore, the same polarity of viewpoints was demonstrated, as the stereotypes and self-images held by FBMA were more positive and optimistic than those held by the NBMA. The Anglo was seen by the NBMA as "sloppy" (60 per cent), "boastful" (50 per cent), and "untrustworthy" (50 per cent), while he was seen by the FBMA as "well-mannered" (50 per cent), "humanitarian" (40 per cent), and "just as good as a Mexican American" (30 per cent). The NBMA viewed himself as "shy" (70 per cent), "fanatical" (40 per cent), and "pessimistic" (30 per cent), while the FBMA saw himself as "intelligent" (60 per cent), "humorous" (30 per cent), and "ambitious" (30 per cent).

Discussion

In light of the stereotypes and self-images presented in the two tables, as well as those images which could not be presented because of their lower frequencies, it must be concluded that the experimental hypothesis is tenable. In addition, as a result of the community free associations, it must be affirmed that these images are in fact the popular stereotypes and self-images held by the general Mexican-American public.

Because NBMA hold more negative attitudes about Anglos and about themselves than do FBMA, it is improper to speak of these aggregates collectively. A possible explanation for the differences between NBMA and FBMA may be found in the theories of social relativism and reference groups (including those by Stouffer, *et al.*, Merton and Kitt, and others),[11] which clearly demonstrate that an actor's frame of reference determines his evaluation of his present socioeconomic condition and his attitudes toward those in his social situation. The NBMA may have employed the Anglo as a reference group, comparing the Anglo's socioeconomic condition with his own and noting his relative disadvantage to the Anglo. Contrariwise, the FBMA may have employed his peer group in Mexico (from where he recently came) as a reference group, comparing his peer group's socioeconomic condition with his present one and noting his relative advantage over that peer group. Statements by the *S*s tend to corroborate these assumptions. A majority of the NBMA stated that they dislike Anglos because "they have everything," while the FBMA held that as compared with life in Mexico, conditions were much improved in their new home. Furthermore, most FBMAs did not view the ghetto as a final place of residence, but rather, as a "stopping off point on their way to a better life."

The optimism or pessimism resulting from the differential comparisons in turn may have influenced the nature of the stereotypes and self-images employed by the two groups. The NBMAs perhaps developed their strongly negative stereotypes of the Anglo, which generally picture him as grasping and dishonest, in order to explain his relatively superior position. Similarly, the fact that the NBMA generally described themselves as lazy and uneducated may have served to justify their own relatively inferior position within the society.[12] Simmons arrived at the same interpretation when he held that Mexicans often view themselves as inferior to the Anglo because of the latter's monopoly of the rewards and accomplishments within the society. However, the apparent self-hatred does not seem to be counterbalanced by the Mexican's "intensive racial pride," as Simmons maintains.[13] "Racial pride" seems to be more the characteristic of the FBMA. Furthermore, the Anglo stereotypes tend to explain, as Simmons notes, the Anglo's dominant status, as they depict him as something of a tyrant. The FBMAs, on the other hand, may have developed their strongly positive stereotypes in order to justify their recent move from their home in Mexico to the United States. If they view the Anglo as friendly and democratic, their decision to leave Mexico may have been easier to make. Similarly, they may have formed positive self-images again to justify their leaving Mexico. Conditions were uniformly worse in Mexico, so, by depicting themselves as practical, they may have justified their venture. An alternative explanation for the positive self-images would be that the FBMA, having done something to improve his socioeconomic condition, had a higher aspiration level than the NBMA, and hence would see things more optimistically.

At the present time these contentions are somewhat speculative. There are always alternative explanations. However, the present contentions appear to fit the data and also have the advantage of integrating stereotype and self-image formation with research on social relativism, reference group theory, and the general sociology of knowledge. Perhaps interviews in greater depth will ferret our more evidence to support the contentions, but this must be left up to some future investigation.

Epilogue

During the riots in the nation's ghettos in 1967, a random sample of 500 *S*s from Los Angeles County was drawn and stratified in a 5x2x2 factorial design by ethnicity (Jewish, Negro, Mexican American, Japanese, and White Protestant), sex, and education (college vs. non-college). All *S*s were between the ages of 18 and 24 years, or approximately the age range of college undergraduates. Among the questions asked of the *S*s were their stereotypes, self-images, and a series of items on civil rights activism and social protest.

As had been found previously, the Native-Born Mexican Americans (NBMA) and the Foreign-Born Mexican Americans (FBMA) differed in their stereotypes and self-images. The NBMAs had negative stereotypes of the Anglo (as well as of other ethnic groups) and negative self-images. The FBMAs had positive stereotypes of the Anglo and of the other target groups, and positive self-images.

The researcher then sought to determine whether the two categories of Mexican Americans also differed in their recognition, endorsement, and willingness to engage in social protests -- especially violent protests such as riots. Had the sentiments of the NBMA begun to constitute a rhetoric of revolt?

As a collectivity, Mexican Americans were not prone to rioting. To the question, "Do you favor riots as a means of social protest?", only 3 per cent of the Mexican Americans (as compared with 3 per cent of the Japanese, 4 per cent of the Jews, 5 per cent of the White Protestants, and 37 per cent of the Negroes) answered affirmatively. Further, when asked, "Do you think that riots are an effective means of social protest?", the Mexican American was the least likely group to agree. Only 22 per cent of the Mexican Americans agreed, while 24 per cent of the Jews, 28 per cent of the White Protestants, 34 per cent of the Japanese, and 68 per cent of the Negroes agreed that riots were effective.

However, when we compared the FBMAs and NBMAs on the latter question (too few Mexican Americans favored riots to make a significant difference, although all of the affirmative answers were from

NBMAs), significantly more NBMAs than FBMAs felt that riots were effective. Table 1 presents that finding.

TABLE 1

Question: "Do you think that riots are an effective means of social protest?"

	YES	NO	
FBMA	1	49	50
NBMA	21	29	50
	22	78	100

$$X^2 = 23.31 \qquad (df = 1; p < .001)$$

While only 2 per cent of the BMAs felt that riots were effective, 42 per cent of the NBMAs agreed to their effectiveness. The percentage of agreement by the NBMAs was second only to that of the Negro sample, whose stereotypes of White Protestants and whose self-images were only slightly more negative and bitter.

We may infer from these findings that the NBMA, like his Negro ghetto counterpart, has responded to White Protestant prejudice and discrimination in greater recognition, if not endorsement and implementation, of one of the more effective channels of protest presently available to oppressed minorities: the riot.

It is true, however, that a recognition of the effectiveness of riots is not synonymous with an endorsement of rioting. However, recognition that an action may be instrumental in achieving a goal may be the first step in the implementation of that action. The transition from recognition to implementation as yet for the NBMA is an empirical question.

The FBMA, on the other hand, is considerably different. His positive stereotypes and self-images may serve as a vocabulary of motives for non-violence, in fact, for non-protest. He compares his present condition not with the relatively prosperious Anglo, but with his *barrio* counterpart in Mexico. He sees little reason to protest the very life he believes will validate his American Dream. He might well retard the forces of revolution in the ghetto, unless his dream is also shattered.

FOOTNOTES

1. Ruth D. Tuck, *Not with the Fist* (New York: Harcourt, Brace, 1946).
2. Eugene S. Richards, "Attitudes of College Students in the Southwest Toward Ethnic Groups in the United States," *Sociology and Social Research,* 35 (September-October, 1950), 22-30.
3. Edward McDonagh and Eugene S. Richards, *Ethnic Relations in the United States* (New York: Appleton, 1953), Chapter VIII.
4. John H. Burma, *Spanish-speaking Groups in the United States* (Duke University Press, 1954).
5. Ozzie G. Simmons, "The Mutual Images and Expectations of Anglo-Americans and Mexican-Americans," *Daedalus,* 90, No. 2, (Spring, 1961), 286-99.
6. The present investigation employed Gordon Allport's functional definition of a stereotype, which held that a stereotype is "an exaggerated belief associated with a category. Its function is to justify (rationalize) our conduct in relation to that category." (Allport, *The Nature of Prejudice.* Cambridge: Addison-Wesley, 1954, 191.) Some stereotypes found in the present and in previous research contain a kernel of truth, while others are totally false. In general, stereotypes tend to apply to behavior of some members of a certain group (especially if the stereotype has been validated by the process described by Merton as the "Self-fulfilling Prophecy"), but no stereotype applies to all members of a group. For a detailed account of the controversies that persist regarding the essential and nonessential characteristics of stereotypes, see J.A. Fishman, "An Examination of the Process and Function of Social Stereotyping," *Journal of Social Psychology,* 1956, 43, 27-64.
7. Simmons, p. 288.
8. The majority of the students defined themselves as coming from lower class homes, with a parent's annual income of less than 3000 dollars. Ninety-six per cent of the students were born in the United States, of which 73 per cent had lived in Los Angeles County all of their lives, and four per cent were born in Mexico. Houses in the community sample were valued at well under 10,000 dollars, some of which had no electricity or indoor plumbing. Fifty per cent of the community residents were born in the United States, of which 89 per cent had lived in the same neighborhood all of their lives, and 50 per cent were born in Mexico. Approximately 13 per cent of the community residents were high school graduates, and 58 per cent were unskilled laborers.
9. In order to maintain the randomness of the sample every effort was made to obtain the opinions of the *S*s. If a person was not at home, the investigator returned several times until the *S* either reported his attitudes or refused to participate. If however, after four attempts to obtain the information from the *S* he was still not at home, he was counted as a refusal. The refusal rate, which was six per cent (60 per cent of which were due to absences and 40 per cent to actual refusals), was well below the critical level, and thus the community sample could still be considered random.

10. An Anglo was defined as "a person living in the United States who was born in Northern Europe (the British Isles, the Scandinavian countries, Germany, and France), or whose ancestors came from Northern Europe, no matter how many years ago." This definition was considerably more restricted than those given in previous studies, where an Anglo was defined as a "non-Mexican." The definition presented to the students needed to be more specific in order for the *S*s to picture the proper group. A Mexican American was defined as also being "a person living in the United States, but who was either born in Mexico, or whose ancestors came from Mexico, no matter how many years ago."

11. See especially Stouffer, *et al., The American Soldier,* V.I. (Princeton, New Jersey: Princeton University Press, 1949), and Robert K. Merton and Alice S. Kitt, in Merton and Lazarsfeld, *Continuities in Social Research.* (New York: The Free Press of Glencoe, 1950), 84-85.

12. Simmons, p. 294.

13. *Ibid.*

DIFFERENTIAL SOCIALIZATION OF LATIN AND ANGLO-AMERICAN YOUTH: AN EXPLORATORY STUDY OF THE SELF CONCEPT*

BUFORD FARRIS AND RICHARD A. BRYMER

This paper will be concerned with a particular aspect of socialization, namely the changes in self-concept that occur as a person moves through and participates in various social systems. Socialization itself might be defined as the process whereby an individual comes to participate in more and more social systems. This would be particularly true for the child, who begins life in a relatively restricted social group -- his home -- and gradually moves to wider and wider social circles. At any one point in time participation in these various "wider circles" depends to some degree upon the self-concept developed at an earlier period in an earlier group. That is, the self-concept is developed in a particular social context, and when the individual moves on the different social contexts, he carries his 'group experience' along with him in the form of his self-concept. And if the self-concept is too much at odds with the requirements of the group in which he is presently involved, participation -- or at least the kind of participation the particular group sees as ideal -- may be difficult.

Our conceptualization of the self-concept stems from the symbolic interactionist perspective. Essentially, the self-concept is the way in which a person sees himself; that set of characteristics, etc., that he attributes to himself. We would note that these attributes are inherently social in the sense that they name social objects, and that by adopting these "labels," the person comes to view himself in a social manner. In addition, these labels also stand for particular ways of behaving, so that by labeling himself in a particular manner the person is also controlling, or at least structuring his own behavior.

Consider for example, the process whereby an infant comes to apply to himself the label "boy" or "girl." His parents and siblings "know" what he is before the infant does. They assume that he is say, a boy, and being a boy, they have a set of relatively stable expectations for

*Unpublished paper presented at the Texas Academy of Science, 1965.

him. These expectations are in turn articulated with the way in which others are prepared to act toward the infant boy. By attaching these behaviors and expectations to the label "boy," and applying it to the infant usually with the admonitions "You are a little boy." "Boys do such and such.", the little boy slowly learns who he is. In effect, he has developed a "looking glass-self," i.e., he seems himself as others see him. He can then articulate his behavior with the behavior of others. He begins to approach other groups with this particular label. In these groups he guides his behavior in terms of this previously learned label. Dependent upon the meaning others have for the term "boy," and their particular identification of him as either a "boy" or what not, articulated interaction will occur. If there is a great deal of discrepancy between the two meanings, interaction will be relatively difficult and continued membership in the group will necessitate some sort of compromise. This compromise usually means modification of meanings of the label "boy," or the acquisition of new labels. In any case, socialization may be viewed as the process of going through a series of social groups, with continuing modification of old labels and acquisition of new ones. Each group influences the 'self-concept' its members carry into their initial participation in the next group. It would appear to be possible to study the effect of socialization upon a person by looking at his self-concept at various points in time with these definitions and perspectives. Furthermore, it would appear to be possible to detail the different experiences through which a group has gone by looking at the self-concepts of its members collectively.

In this paper, we will apply these concepts and definitions to the Latin-American cultural grouping. Persons in this grouping usually live in relatively segregated areas and are able to retain a larger proportion of their cultural ways as well as a separate language. On the other hand, they must participate to some degree in the Anglo world, if for no other reason than to go to school, work, etc. What then, is the effect on the Latin-American child, as he moves between these two different worlds, as compared to the Anglo child, who moves in only one world. Which aspects of their socialization are similar, and which are different? Since the drop out rate is quite high (at least in the break between junior high and high school) what kinds of Latin Americans are "successful" in negotiating in the Anglo world; or successful at least in the sense of getting into high school?

In an effort to answer these and other questions about the differential socialization of Latin and Anglo-American children, we administered a 'self-concept' instrument to school classes at three levels -- fourth grade, eighth grade and eleventh grade — in two elementary schools, two junior high schools and in one high school. The classes were set up so that there was approximately an equal distribution of Anglo and Latin children. In terms of success, we can say that the elementary schools should be most representative, with the high schools being the least representative. Somewhere in between, many more Latins than Anglos drop out of school, and thereby become defined as "unsuccessful" in Anglo terms. Therefore, we have essentially three different types of samples. The "undefined" at the elementary level, the "being defined" at the junior high level, and the "defined" at the senior high school level.

Our operationalization of self-concept is also relatively simple. It consists simply of asking the person to write as many possible answers as he can to the question "Who am I?" Traditionally this procedure has been referred to as the TST -- or Twenty Statements Test -- although it is not a test and one does not have to ask for 20 statements. This is a very open-ended procedure, and assures one that he is not forcing the respondent into any *a priori* categories to any large degree. In as simple a manner as possible then we. ask the respondent to go about the business of attributing things to himself.

The most crucial part of the TST is the structure of the coding categories. Usually, one looks for a "mention" of a particular form, and then compares percent of persons in a group "mentioning" this form with the percent failing to "mention" it. Generally, we were most concerned with a particular set of social groupings, common to both Anglos and Latins, and whether or not they were mentioned. Briefly, we looked for references to school, family, peer groups, sex and age groups, religious groups and ethnic statements. Other commonly occurring categories were also used, such as name, physical description, ambitions, interests and likes or dislikes, abilities and activities. Finally, we attended to the number of different social roles which the respondent attributed to himself, the number of different social groups which he mentioned and lastly, the number of statements containing various forms of the verb "to be." These latter statements were designated as "being" statements, as opposed to "having," "liking," "wanting," etc. It is thought that those persons who used "being" statements would have a more extensive anchorage in social phenomena than those who used other types of statements.

The data from the TST responses will in this paper be considered against the background of data we are collecting through the Youth Project at Wesley Community Centers. The centers have been involved with boys usually defined as "gang" members for more than five years. For the last year and a half, we have been evaluating this involvement and have observed a fairly large group of boys and their families. We are also involved at the present time in detail depth interviews of 100 "gang" and "non-gang" Mexican-American families. Some of the preliminary data from these interviews and observations are used in this paper.

Table 1 gives the total N in each group. Percentages listed in each table were computed upon these bases. All of the schools were from the same school district, located in San Antonio, Texas. Generally, the area is a lower to lower middle class, with sprinklings of middle class persons located throughout. One must take into account that the lower the school level, the more homogenous the area is likely to be, and consequently, the more homogenous the sample from that school is likely to be. Also, one should remember that the majority of the Latin elementary and junior high samples came from areas which are quite a bit lower-socio-economically speaking -- than the Anglo areas.

TABLE 1   *Number of Respondents in each Group. Bases upon which percentages in all tables were computed.*

	Elementary	Junior High	Senior High	Totals
Anglo	25	23	34	82
Latin	29	38	24	91
Totals	54	61	58	173

Table 2 lists the average number of statements made in each group. Actually, it would be more accurate to define these as "units of thought," rather than statements, since these units were not always complete sentences, and frequently contained only a few words. As might be expected, there is an increase in average number of statements over the socialization period, with the Anglo sample increasing more rapidly than the Latin sample. As one encounters and participates in more and more groups, one's "vocabulary of self" appears to expand, i.e., the social categories in which one can place one's self expands. From this table, it would appear that Anglos assign themselves to more social categories than do Latins. One must keep this in mind when inspecting later tables, since often Anglos appear to be represented in more categories than do Latins.

TABLE 2   *Average Number of Total Statements made on the TST.*

	Elementary	Junior High	Senior High
Anglo	7.0	13.0	15.0
Latin	8.0	10.4	12.4

This interpretation would appear to hold up in Tables 3, 4, and 5. It seems that generally Latins and Anglos appear to be approximately equal in terms of their participation at the elementary school level. As time goes on however, a divergence develops, so that by the high school school level, Anglos perceive themselves as articulated with more social groups, and acting in more social roles than do Latins. In effect, the Latin "subjective social world" is smaller than that of the Anglo by the time high school age is reached. This differential may make it somewhat difficult for the Latin to participate in the apparently complex social world of the Anglo, at least initially. We feel that it is necessary at this point to emphasize that these categorizations were made in terms of the Anglo world, if for no other reason than Anglos coded them. It is definitely possible that these Anglos -- the two authors -- may not be aware of the complexities and meanings in the Latin subjective world. In effect then, our comparison is not concerned with the adequacy or inadequacy of the Latin self-concept, but more a comparison of self-concepts as units in and of themselves.

Perhaps an additional note is also needed for Table 5. When we say "am" or "being" statements, we should note that many of these statements contained references not to social roles, as much as to "social types." By types we would mean a social category which is not necessarily found in any integrated system of role relations in a group, but which exists more in the social ideology or mythology of a culture.

TABLE 3   *Average Number of Social Roles referred to on TST.*

	Elementary	Junior High	Senior High
Anglo	.9	2.4	5.2
Latin	1.1	1.5	2.4

TABLE 4   *Average Number of Social Groups referred to on TST.*

	Elementary	Junior High	Senior High
Anglo	2.0	3.6	5.7
Latin	1.9	2.8	4.0

TABLE 5   *Average Number of "am" or "being" statements.*

	Elementary	Junior High	Senior High
Anglo	3.0	5.2	10.5
Latin	2.9	5.5	6.1

For example, a "student" is a role, which exists in a school system and has definitely specified relations to "teachers," another role. A type would be, for example "Don Juan." We all know what kind of person a "Don Juan" type is, but the type doesn't have any set of stable relationships to other roles. Attributing a type to one's self is, however, a mode of anchorage in a social system, in that the type is socially recognized and can be acted upon.

Tables 6 through 10 indicate the percentages of various kinds of statements that have reference to the school system, or to the student role. In terms of total statements about the school, there is no significant difference between Anglos and Latins. Both appear to be equally concerned with the school system. We must remember though, that the drop out rate is much higher for the Latins than for the Anglos, so that we have slightly different populations at the high school level. When we look further, however, especially in Tables 8 and 10, we can observe some probable significant differences. A larger percentage of high school Latins are concerned with academic factors than are Anglos; and a larger percentage of Anglos are concerned with informal aspects of school than are Latins. By academic aspects, we have reference to statement about subjects, courses, grades, etc. By informal extra-curricular aspects, we have reference to statements about friendships in school, dances, etc. As a matter of fact, we can see a decrease in Anglos concern with academic aspects from junior to senior high, whereas there is very large increase in academic concern among the Latins. And approximately the reverse of this exists for the informal extra-curricular aspects. The Anglo percentages increase rapidly between junior and senior high, whereas the Latin percentages decrease slightly. In terms of the statements about extra-curricular formal aspects, like football, clubs and other school sponsored groups, there is very little difference between Anglo and Latin, with both groups showing an increase as socialization continues.

TABLE 6   *Percentage of Persons making any type of school statement*

	Elementary	Junior High	Senior High
Anglo	52%	69%	84%
Latin	52%	62%	80%

TABLE 7   *Percentage of persons making statements about school in General*

	Elementary	Junior High	Senior High
Anglo	48%	56%	81%
Latin	52%	60%	68%

TABLE 8   *Percentage of persons making statements about informal extra-curricular activities*

	Elementary	Junior High	Senior High
Anglo	0	9%	44%
Latin	0	18%	12%

TABLE 9   *Percentage of persons making statements about formal extra-curricular activities*

	Elementary	Junior High	Senior High
Anglo	0	9%	29%
Latin	0	16%	24%

TABLE 10   *Percentage of persons making statements about academic aspects of school*

	Elementary	Junior High	Senior High
Anglo	20%	39%	26%
Latin	21%	21%	56%

We would interpret the above figures as indicating that those Latins who do go on to high school tend to be almost exclusively concerned with general and academic aspects of school, whereas the Anglos are apparently concerned with the overall aspects of school. Or at least they might be said to favor education in its broadest sense. When we also consider the fact that Anglos make more statements than Latins, the difference becomes sharper. That is, of the comparatively fewer statements that the high school Latins make, there is a very high degree of concern with school. This interpretation would also note that those Latins who do not have a high degree of concern for academic aspects of school may be the ones who drop out. This is supported by noticing that the junior high-high school transfer is accompanied by a big drop out rate, and the big "jump" in academic concern among the Latins appears to come at this same juncture. Apparently, the only Latins left are those with academic concerns.

When we look at Tables 11 through 13, we gain additional insight into this interpretation. In Table 11, indexing percentage of persons who made statements about peer and opposite sex relationships *outside* of school, we find Anglos running generally much higher at the junior high and senior high level than the Latins. The big change for the Anglos is the shift from elementary to junior high school. Latins also increase their peer group interests in junior high, but by the time they reach high school, this interest has subsided somewhat.

TABLE 11 *Percentage of persons making a statement concerning peer relationships, peer groups, or relationships with the opposite sex.*

	Elementary	Junior High	Senior High
Anglo	8%	77%	76%
Latin	21%	57%	40%

TABLE 12 *Percentage of persons making a statement concerning peer relationships or peer groups.*

	Elementary	Junior High	Senior High
Anglo	8%	73%	55%
Latin	21%	52%	36%

TABLE 13 *Percentage of persons making a statement that is specifically concerned with relationships with the opposite sex.*

	Elementary	Junior High	Senior High
Anglo	0	26%	35%
Latin	7%	23%	12%

If we break this set down into its components of peer relationships versus opposite sex relationships, another pair of interesting relationships emerges. For Anglos, peer relationships alone increase radically from elementary school to junior high school, and then subside somewhat during high school, although the percentages are still very high. This high school decrease in mention of peer group alone is offset, however, by an increase in concern with opposite sex relationships. For the Latin group, an increase in both peer and opposite sex relationships is noted from elementary to junior high, and a decrease in the transfer to high school from junior high. This would seem to lend support to our interpretation based upon the school percentages. It would also let us make the interpretation that Latin-American high schoolers are only minimally concerned with opposite sex relationships. What this may mean is that those who dropped out were the ones who had the peer and opposite sex concern in junior high. Certainly our tentative data from depth interviews with families of gang members and our observations of gang boys (most of whom are drop outs) themselves would support this. In these gang groups there is a great concern with the peer group and many early marriages. Those who remain in high school may be those who are able to defer gratification of marriage and peer contact for the academic life. Or it may be that they *never were* dependent upon peer and opposite sex contact and in effect were somewhat deviant within the "typical lower class Latin" context.

Table 14 also affords us evidence for this interpretation in that the Anglos maintain a relatively high and consistent concern with age status, with percentages at all levels remaining around 45%-55%, and the peak concern occurring in junior high school again. Latins on the other hand, remain around 20-25% in the elementary and junior high school periods and then increase to 56% in high school. We would note two factors in our interpretation here. First, age status conveys not only that one is "above" certain others i.e., "kids," but that for these teenage years, one is not yet an adult; one is somewhere in between, and as such adult responsibilities and behaviors are not perceived as expected. Secondly, our depth interview data indicate the lower class parents have a great deal of difficulty in discussing adolescence. It seems as if they have no ready conceptual categories for 'adolescence,' and really, no perception of behaviors as appropriate for adolescence. It is as if there were only two stages: childhood and adulthood, and around the age of 13-15, they indicate that their "children" are to a large degree beyond their control. Observations of the boys "in action" confirms this. They are really out on their own.

TABLE 14 *Percentage of persons making a statement concerning their age status or age role.*

	Elementary	Junior High	Senior High
Anglo	48%	56%	44%
Latin	24%	21%	56%

Again, this may indicate that those Latin persons who remain in school accept the notions of adolescence, and may see it as a period of training, whereas those who drop out see themselves as adults. This in fact may be the reason that they drop out. Many of the drop outs are behind in school in the first place and many refuse to go back because of pride.

In summary then, it appears that there are relatively distinct differences between Latins who "make it" in the school system, Anglos, and by implication those Latins who don't "make it." If these differences are valid, and we note their articulation with other data we have available, there are essentially two types of explanation that we can make: one, that from the elementary ages, there are two types of Latins — the alienated Latin and the integrated Latin — and the integrated Latin drops out at junior high school graduation because of outside pressures of the peer group and opposite sex relationships, as well as a low academic interest; secondly, we might argue that all Latins are essentially the same when they enter the elementary school level, but that over the years, certain of them get involved with the school system and literally, "out Anglo the Anglos," i.e., develop an over abundance of characteristics that ideally should get them through the school system. To this latter explanation we might also add that it may take this "overabundance" for the Latin to develop stable involvement in the school system because of discriminatory practices and selective perception on the part of the school. This may especially be the case with the peer group factor. We have noticed that the nature and activities of the gang peer groups (drop outs) are not designed to elicit acceptance and positive response from the school system personnel. The peer groups of "squares" on the other hand may elicit such approval and acceptance, in that they pursue less action-oriented and destructive behavior, and more "social" behavior such as dancing, dating, going to football games, taking on service projects, etc. Also we would note that square peer groups tend to be much smaller and therefore much less visible and less productive of the "gang" definition.

Actually, both types of explanation are probably at work. From our depth interviews and observations of gang and square Latin boys and their families, it would seem that there may be several types present at the elementary school age or at least several types of families from which they come: the lower class mobiles, the lower class unstable and economically deprived families, and the stable working class families. It may be that the lower class mobiles are the ones who have the "ideal school student" set of characteristics at elementary ages, and are the ones who are going on into high school; the lower class unstable persons may be the persons who drop out at junior high graduation (or earlier as we have found) due to outside pressures; and the stable working class persons may be the ones for whom *both* explanations are necessary. In any case, this particular sub-set of data appear to suggest such a phenomena.

Tables 15-25 also indicate some differences between Latins and Anglos, but as yet we have no strong explanatory context in which to place them. We offer them for your discussion, criticism and suggestions. Many indicate similar changes occurring in both Latins and Anglos (tables 15, 19, 22, 23) whereas other indicate that one group changes, whereas the other group remain constant. Perhaps the most interesting and surprising is Table 21, which indicates a very low percentage of Latins making statements concerning ethnicity. Actually it is only the Anglo high school seniors for whom ethnicity has any saliency.

TABLE 15 *Percentage of persons making statement of their sex role, either independently or as a qualifier to another statement.*

	Elementary	Junior High	Senior High
Anglo	72%	64%	59%
Latin	79%	75%	56%

TABLE 16 *Percentage of persons making an independent statement of concerning their sex.*

	Elementary	Junior High	Senior High
Anglo	40%	34%	41%
Latin	69%	52%	24%

TABLE 17 *Percentage of persons making positive, negative, or neutral statement concerning their physical properties.*

	Elementary	Junior High	Senior High
Anglo	56%	26%	24%
Latin	24%	18%	28%

TABLE 18 *Percentage of persons making a sex role statement as a qualifier to some other statement.*

	Elementary	Junior High	Senior High
Anglo	52%	47%	29%
Latin	48%	44%	48%

TABLE 19 *Percentage of persons making statement concerning religion, or church membership.*

	Elementary	Junior High	Senior High
Anglo	8%	17%	58%
Latin	14%	16%	40%

TABLE 20 *Percentage of persons making a statement concerning their family.*

	Elementary	Junior High	Senior High
Anglo	20%	69%	29%
Latin	41%	47%	36%

TABLE 21 *Percentage of persons making a statement concerning ethnicity, race, or nationality background.*

	Elementary	Junior High	Senior High
Anglo	0	4%	35%
Latin	0	10%	4%

TABLE 22 *Percentage of persons giving a statement about ambitions*

	Elementary	Junior High	Senior High
Anglo	0	30%	32%
Latin	0	13%	32%

TABLE 23 *Percentage of persons giving their name as a statement*

	Elementary	Junior High	Senior High
Anglo	76%	22%	23%
Latin	55%	21%	32%

TABLE 24 *Percentage of persons giving an interest, or a like or dislike as a statement*

	Elementary	Junior High	Senior High
Anglo	40%	39%	29%
Latin	34%	29%	32%

TABLE 25 *Percentage of persons giving an ability or activity as a statement*

	Elementary	Junior High	Senior High
Anglo	40%	34%	20%
Latin	21%	10%	20%

MEXICANS IN THE UNITED STATES

*A Problem in Social Differentiation**

LEONARD BROOM and ESHREF SHEVKY

Sharp differences in the level of economic organization of two countries in relation with one another are necessary conditions for substantial population movements between them. In the case of Mexico and the United States, although these conditions have been present for some time, the migration did not take place until recently. This delay was due to two sets of facts. On the one hand, the structure of Mexican society was not conducive to large population movements until the railroad system was developed to link Mexico with the world market, about the end of the nineteenth century. On the other hand, the demands of the American economy, at various stages of development, were largely satisfied by the historic pattern of European immigration. The developing demand for labor in the American Southwest coincided with the availability of Mexican migrants, who arrived in largest numbers between 1909 and 1929. At this point in history the crest of Mexican migration seems to have passed, and we are entering a period of critical importance for the adjustment of Mexicans in American society.

The twentieth century Mexican immigrants found already established in the United States an indigenous Spanish-speaking population of long standing. This group, localized in the Southwest, was a legacy of the land accession of the nineteenth century. The Mexican-American population is differentiated on the basis of this fact, and we must postulate that the position of the old residents will differ from that of the recent immigrants. We must provide for differentiating the old (i.e., Spanish colonial) and the new Mexican-American population, and the main points of analysis which we shall state below offer the basis for such differentiation.

Apart from the gross distinction indicated here and those variations related to regional characteristics such as the pattern of institutional-

*Sociology and Social Research, January-February 1952, pages 150-158.

ized segregation in Texas, the task of differentiation requires intensive locality and aspectual investigations. A rounded interpretation is at this time frustrated by the sharp limitations in detail of knowledge about the Mexican-American population in Southern California, its locality of highest concentration and differentiation.

We phrase the following discussion under four main headings: (1) economic function and mobility, (2) acculturation and urbanization, (3) status and assimilation, and (4) modes of isolation and integration.

Economic function and mobility. The bulk of the Mexican migration to the United States originated in the Mesa Central and was heavily weighted with laborers from village and town environments who had some familiarity with a technology more advanced than did the peasantry of the lowland agricultural areas. The other important source of migration was the more recently developed area bordering Texas, which provided a supply of seasonal as well as permanent migrants. As viewed from Mexico this was a secondary movement. New studies of Mexican society indicate a social and cultural heterogeneity within localities in addition to the well-documented differences among culture areas. The determination of differentials in status and function, especially in reference to relations with the land, is relevant to phenomena underlying population movements and important in interpreting the adjustment of the migrants.

Irrespective of the origin and prior occupational history of the immigrants, they entered the American labor market as common laborers in mass employment situations. Characteristically, this employment — whether agricultural, e.g., in the sugar beet fields, or industrial, e.g., in construction operations or in railroad maintenance — was periodic and migratory.

The problem is to determine the extent to which the population has left migratory labor, become occupationally differentiated, improved its position with respect to stability of employment, and achieved vertical mobility. A first basis for comparing the indigenous and immigrant populations of Mexican Americans lies in the answers to these questions. More broadly, the problem is one of establishing the position held by the populations in the industrial system and the hierarchy of occupations, their rate of movement, and a basis for predicting their future statuses. An essential condition for handling these questions is the development of histories of industrial experience in key areas of Mexican-American employment. These include furniture, electrical trades, and garment manufacture, in which Mexican

Americans are found throughout the hierarchy of skills and which are currently expanding fields of employment for them. Developments in the white-collar category are important for reasons of symbolic value and relative stability, and therefore have a greater significance than the number of workers involved. Job histories obtained in the course of locality studies will establish the relationship between occupation and other social characteristics of enclave populations.

Acculturation and urbanization. A number of factors have converged to retard the acculturation of Mexicans in the United States. The pattern of mass employment in which Mexicans worked in homogeneous gangs tended to insulate them from contacts with other ethnic groups. Although this was by no means peculiar to Mexicans, it is unlikely that gang employment was experienced by any other population in so many occupations and for so long.

Their position as casual laborers, linked with instability of employment and frequent migration, resulted in residential and institutional isolation. Both in rural and urban areas the ethnic enclaves were marginal neighborhoods detached from the life and economy of the large community, although dependent upon it for jobs and services.

Under these circumstances the language barrier which initially was an obstacle to relations between the group and American society became a persistent symbol and instrument of isolation. The language barrier effectively isolated a large part of the first generation and was an important factor in reducing the rate of naturalization. The second generation, very often confronted with learning English upon entering school, still suffers from retardation. To place this in context and avoid any deterministic implication it is well to note that the smaller Japanese population manifest no such retardation despite the far greater linguistic gap. The difference between Japanese and Mexican educational practices and valuations were the proximate causes of this difference in experience. Where no legal segregation existed the size of the Mexican population made possible administrative segregation. Retardation, in turn, imposed an educational ceiling on the group with the vicious circle consequences: limited schooling retarded acculturation, set arbitrary job ceilings, constricted job opportunities, and the group became symbolized by its stereotype.

In all populations where the immigrant group is predominant among adults, the strata of acculturation are age structured. The cleavage in the case of Mexicans in Southern California has gone so far that the second generation has become isolated from the parental group but has not secured access to the larger society. The formation of gangs of Mexican youth is an obvious manifestation of this condition. Through these gangs a critical period of the life span of the individual is ethnically delimited. Because of the cleavage from the parental generation and the age determination of youthful associations, the second generation enter adulthood with a dearth of appropriate models. Not all of the second generation, of course, become gang organized, and this fact is a further basis for differentiation in so far as it conditions relationships with the parental generation and such institutional forms as the school.

A necessary approach to this segment of the topic lies in the differentiation of the population on a typological continuum of acculturation. The continuum should be designed on operational principles which would permit cultural variation to be related to other scales based on population characteristics. To establish the relationship between acculturation and urbanization we propose to use a scale of urbanization which has already been constructed.

Status and assimilation. At first glance the constricted status of the Mexican-American group impresses the observer. Within the urban status system they occupy an apparently undifferentiated position, socially excluded, economically depressed, and politically powerless. Unlike other important American ethnic groups a middle class providing service functions is virtually nonexistent. Those individuals who have advanced substantially, either economically or in educational status, have tended to lose their identity with the group and have moved away from the ethnic enclaves which are entirely lower class. This movement is facilitated by the alternative definitions of "Spanish," "Colonial," "Californian," and the like, which do not carry the stigmatizing connotation of Mexican. The availability of alternative definitions provides a ready rationalization both for vertically mobile individuals and the host population and undoubtedly acts to reduce stress in transitional adjustment. In a higher status context the Spanish name carries even a prestige value and this is in contrast to the assimilating Jew, who often is confronted with the problem of name changing. Granting the economic and cultural prerequisites, color is the only arbitrary qualification to a ready change in Mexican self-definition. Vertical mobility and loss of identification as Mexicans should theoretically be easier for those who approximate the "Castilian type." It also remains to be discovered to what extent the factor of color is selective in affecting the permanence of settlement in the United States and the secondary movement of Mexicans in this country.

Some of the conditions present which might lead to development of further status differentiation of the Mexican Americans as such are ethnic nationalism as expressed in the concept *raza,* Mexican patriotism, culturally modified Catholicism, and a persistent interest in the ancestral culture, this last finding reinforcement in the friendly attitudes toward Latin America shared with the general population. The convergence of these and other factors could conceivably result in the assimilated and vertically mobile elements remaining within the ethnic group.

If then the status distribution of Mexican Americans so identified is very narrow, the problem of internally differentiating the relatively homogeneous population presents technical difficulties. These might be solved by performing a more meticulous assessment of occupational function, job stability, specific material possessions, and community functions than is done in broad schemes of status analysis. The validation of such objective criteria may well proceed through the operational verification of status judgments and sentiments.

Modes of isolation and integration. Unlike the classic form of the Black Belt and European immigrant settlements, Mexican-American urban neighborhoods are not large, continuous concentrations. The initially diffused utilization of this segment of the labor force, in Southern California at any rate, gave rise to a number of relatively small homogeneous nuclei, marginal to but dependent upon urban centers and those subcenters performing industrial functions. Many of the disparate settlements were engulfed in the growth of the city, but were hardly modified by their change in relative position. Los Angeles, with the largest industrial concentration in this region, attracted the largest population of Mexican origin. Peripheral communities of seasonal agricultural workers are being changed by the processes of urbanization into marginal neighborhoods of urban workers. This change and the tendency toward a greater urban concentration and localization have manifold sociological consequences which are the preconditions for further differentiation of the population and for their mobilization for political action on a scale heretofore impossible.

Three main patterns of development are possible in the future: (1) the continued isolation of atomistic enclaves; (2) the emergence of an integrated ethnic community; (3) reduction in the isolation of the Mexican-American population, their incorporation in the larger society, and the progressive liquidation of the ethnic enclaves.

The effectiveness of any program designed to ameliorate the status of the group may be assessed by the way it influences the trend of development in one of the indicated directions. At least the more overt kinds of institutional manipulation may be readily evaluated in these terms. Here we interpolate our opinion that a progressive reduction in the isolation of Mexican Americans should be the central objective of social action.

Under present conditions of isolation the service facilities of the group are rudimentary. For the most part, they are supplied by self-employed persons who operate marginal commercial enterprises functionally isolated from the mass economy. The chief service area catering to the Mexican-American population is located in the deteriorated urban center of Los Angeles. All important Mexican-owned enterprises are found here and, with all the risks involved, this is the entry point for independent commercial activity. The professional and semiprofessional personnel are also concentrated here, but the number and diversity of services rendered are even less adequate than is the case in Negro and Japanese-American neighborhoods.

Correlative with isolation and weakness are deficiencies of available capital and technical and professional skills. These conditions impede the integration and effective organization of the group. There is a dearth of personnel with sufficient resources or technical skills competent to cope with the bureaucracy of business enterprise or government. Strong leadership is unavailable either for periods of group crisis or for enduring community organization.

We specify four important criteria for the assessment of future trends in this sphere: (1) the accumulation of capital available to the ethnic group; (2) the training of a corps of skilled personnel in the professions, semiprofessions, and commerce; (3) the operation and control of the Spanish language press and other mediums of ethnic communication; (4) the emergence of leadership capable of coping with government on its several levels, including the achievement of public office.

The indigenous forms of organization are not now adequate to integrate a large part of the population or establish relations with the larger community. But early in the history of Mexican immigration mutual aid societies performed important functions within the group. Taylor refers to them as follows:

> *Sociedades* and the *mutualistas* are local societies, or lodges of the mutual benefit type customarily set up by Mexicans in the United States. They are supported by small monthly dues and pay modest sick benefits to members. These societies represent the *only continuous organized life among the Mexicans in which the initiative comes wholly from the Mexicans themselves* . . .
>
> The societies provide a forum for discussion and a means of organizing the social life of the community. In this respect their importance transcends the benefits which they extend to their members in case of illness.*

Despite the early significance of the mutual aid societies and the persistence of some of them over a period of years, they do not appear now to have any important place. Without exception, large immigrant populations in the United States developed this type of organization as an early and transitional form. In some cases the functions became incorporated in an institutional system within the ethnic group. Thus far, at least, this does not seem to have taken place among the Mexican Americans despite the fact that the group has remained isolated and in large part culturally distinct.

Like the mutual aid societies the first trade unions with Mexican leadership were a transitional form. Although their original leadership participated in the series of agricultural strikes of the 1930's, no effective organization persisted. Incorporation of Mexicans in any numbers into the American labor movement awaited the development of stable industrial unionism in areas of Mexican employment. No other secular organization appears at this time to be capable of affecting so decisively the pattern of Mexican isolation. Depending on the composition of the "locals," unionization may have important bearing on the rate of acculturation, the character of interaction between Mexicans and other groups, and their participation in civic and political activities.

The church is the principal agency of cultural conservatism for Mexicans in the United States and reinforces the separateness of the group. This is true, whether one has in mind the parish organization of the Catholic Church or the Protestant missions with their functionally sectarian attributes. Competition between the church and the mission reveals and accentuates cleavages in the Mexican population and is an obstacle to consensus. When Mexicans become participants in Protes-

tant denominational or nonethnic Catholic organizations the phenomenon is an aspect of vertical mobility and does not affect the isolation of
the group.

Summary

We have attempted to specify an analytic empirical approach to the
study of a most important ethnic group which by virtue of it size,
regional concentration, social position, and dynamic character merits
detailed and comprehensive study. Although directed at one population, our formulation is intended to yield findings amenable to
comparative treatment with other status and ethnic groups.

In the light of the foregoing, we indicate a series of research tasks
which may comprise a coherent program.

1. The first set of tasks centers on the problem of differentiating the
population with regard to its source and migration history. Here we.
consider the geographic origins of the population and prior occupational and status characteristics, with special reference to the degree of
industrialization and urbanization in Mexico and acculturation to
Hispanic norms. Related to all of these are the nature and consequences of internal migrations both in Mexico and in the United States.

2. The second focus of research involves the differentiation of the
population in respect to its present socioeconomic status, urbanization,
and acculturation to American norms. We need objective indices of
these characteristics so contrived that they appropriate to the range of
variation found in this population.

3. The third is a synthetic task: to determine the ways in which the
established differentials operate to produce varying modes of cultural
and institutional isolation or functional integration, and we postulate
three types: (1) the continued isolation of atomistic enclaves; (2) the
emergence of an integrated ethnic community; and (3) reduction in the
isolation of the Mexican-American population, their incorporation in
the larger society, and the progressive liquidation of the ethnic
enclaves.

SPANISH AMERICANS AND PUERTO RICANS

SPANISH AMERICANS AND PUERTO RICANS

There are in the United States a number of Spanish-speaking groups who cannot properly be called Mexican Americans. These include immigrants from South America, from Central America, and from Spain; all of these are present, but in very small numbers. Since the advent of Castro, tens of thousands of Cubans have fled Cuba to join a sizeable number of previous voluntary immigrants. None of these groups will be discussed in this book. Two other groups, however, are of considerable importance in the United States, the Puerto Ricans, and the Spanish Americans (Hispanos) of New Mexico and Colorado.

The heritage of the Spanish Americans and Mexican Americans is somewhat different. The ancestors of most Spanish Americans arrived in the American Southwest while Mexico was still a Spanish colony. There they mixed in varying degrees with the Pueblo Indians of the area, and lived for generations as farmers, cattle ranchers, and sheep herders, largely isolated from either more modern Mexican or Anglo cultural influence. They have thought of themselves more as Spanish than Mexican and have preferred to be called Spanish. When the author first became acquainted with the area, in the 1920's and 1930's, much of it was still very isolated from Anglo culture. As late as the 1940's there were many sixth to tenth generation adults who spoke no English. To the middle class, Mexico is an interesting place to visit, as a tourist.

To most Anglos, these people were "Mexicans," and they have been treated as such and discriminated against as such in most inter-group relations. Moreover, the problems and prospects of this group are so much like and so entwined with those of Mexican Americans that it is proper in a book of this type to include this sub-society. Ralph A. Luebben, an anthropologist who has studied this group and subculture for many years, presents a brief Hispano ethnography in "Spanish Americans of the Upper Rio Grande Drainage." Although the title sounds technical, it is only meant to convey the fact that the people described are those native to northeastern New Mexico and Southern Colorado. Other colonial Spanish settled in Texas and in Southern California, but Dr. Luebben's work purposely does not include them.

Luebben summarized the history of Northern New Mexico as a Spanish colony, as an outpost of Mexico, and as a "captured" portion of the United States. From 1540 to 1970 the land has been the crux of this area's prosperity and poverty; a high proportion of its problems, including those of 1970, are related to the land. The *Alianza,* which he describes, is an agrarian, nationalistic, charismatic movement. The economic conditions so vital to any area are strongly affected by the change from a rural-farming to an urban-industrial way of life. The area is highly politically oriented, and has been for many generations, but even the traditional Hispano political strongholds are coming under Anglo dominance. Finally, Dr. Luebben describes in detail and chronologically the continuing problem of the Hispanos in achieving a consensus on a clear self-identification.

The grandiose schemes of Reies Tijerina and others to take over old Spanish land grants throughout the Southwest recently has received great publicity. Since 1966 these people, organized as the *Alianza Federal de Mercedes* (Federal Alliance of Land Grants), engaged in a series of acts which have brought them newspaper, television, and magazine attention in considerable quantity. The *Alianza* is highly nationalistic, and it wishes to be given all the land once granted to the Spanish Colonists and now mostly in the hands of "outsiders" or "conservative" Spanish Americans, (i.e., that majority which does not support the *Alianza*). As part of his broad description, Dr. Luebben explains in general the posture of the *Alianza* and its actions. A historian, Joseph L. Love, in "La Raza: Mexican Americans in Rebellion," traces in considerable detail the growth of *La Alianza* and reports many of the specific actions of its leaders and supporters. The author, like Love, Luebben and others familiar with this area, finds it unusual that Tijerina is not himself a Hispano, and that he is directing the movement in a highly nationalistic, nativistic fashion which seeks to appeal to all Mexican Americans, and even to Blacks as well. Strong representations are made concerning brotherhood, "cultural unity," and the "historic way of life of people of Spanish heritage," but as of 1970 there has been no widespread Mexican American support for the movement.

In a newspaper article by Rueben Salazar (*Los Angeles Times,* August 25, 1969), not included as a selection, is an account of a very different type of attempt to ameliorate the poverty problems of the Spanish Americans. This is a cooperative effort of foundations, the federal government, private financial institutions, and a group of both Anglo and Spanish American leaders spearheaded by the Home Education Livelihood Program (HELP). Many Hispanos are small cattle ranchers. They traditionally sell their steers at about 350 pounds, receiving approximately $100. Under the new plan, HELP is setting up six feedlots, with an approximately four million dollar outlay, which will eliminate middle man profits. The Hispano rancher will turn his steers over to the nearest HELP feedlot which will fatten them to approximately 1000 pounds, sell them for about $300 and return the profit to the cattle grower. The feedlots are expected to pump as much as three million dollars a year into this chronically poverty-stricken area. Since 1958, HELP has been engaged primarily in sponsoring various types of adult education in the area. Poverty experts agree that poverty cannot be fully cured by money; that the whole entrenched subculture of poverty must be attacked. This is entirely correct, but money produced by one's own efforts is a significant anti-poverty weapon. For the large number of Hispanos who would prefer to be small ranchers if they could make a living at it, the feedlot program may be a major step out of poverty.

It would require another sizeable book to do justice to the history, present conditions, and future of the one million plus mainland Puerto Ricans in America. They, too, could and should be described economically, politically, educationally, socially, and in at least as many aspects and with at least as many selections as are here devoted to Mexican Americans. It is beyond the goals of this book to do so, but it seems highly useful to present at least one brief summary of the situation of the mainland Puerto Ricans, for comparative reasons if no others. In a recent article, "El Puertorriqueno: No More, No Less," Armando Rendon presents the most complete, brief, up-to-date report available on Puerto Ricans. In particular Rendon describes the urbanization in Manhattan of immigrant Puerto Ricans, the *barrios* in which they live, their housing, and their desire to have local community control of the schools and housing projects and other institutions which serve them. He explains their economic problems, their political aspirations, their organizations, and their leaders, and describes sympathetically their struggle to retain a historical and cultural identity.

SPANISH-AMERICANS OF THE UPPER RIO GRANDE DRAINAGE*

RALPH A. LUEBBEN

For more than four hundred years, Spanish-speaking people lived along the Upper Rio Grande and its tributaries and left an indelible mark on the physical and cultural landscape of that area. Distinctive place names, handicrafts, foods, architectural designs, social customs, and everyday usage of a foreign language reflects a heritage which stands in sharp contrast to that of normative American society. In this short essay, only a few facets of contemporary Spanish-American culture, namely land, economic opportunity, and identification will be explored.

The Upper Rio Grande drainage extends north from Belen, in central New Mexico, into southern Colorado. To the east, the Sangre de Cristo Mountains form a massive physical barrier; while on the west, Spanish-American occupation has been restricted in the past century by the creation of Navaho and Apache Indian reservations. Indigenous Pueblo Indians and more recently intruding Anglos have further limited Spanish-American utlization of this area.

After Coronado claimed this territory as a part of New Spain in 1540, colonization in the vicinity of present-day Albuquerque, Santa Fe, and Espanola was laboriously slow; furthermore, explorers failed to find either the Seven Cities of Cibola or the prophesied limitless wealth. Throughout the Colonial Period (A.D., 1540-1821), the Upper Rio Grande drainage remained primarily a Catholic mission area, a military outpost, and a base for exploration. Despite the vast distance and hazardous journey, Spaniards maintained at least sporadic ties with their fatherland via New Spain (Mexico). They introduced many Old World traits into the area, but they also readily borrowed adaptive techniques and material culture from Pueblo Indians. Because of the precarious power balance between the Pueblos and Spanish colonists, a state of co-existence existed for centuries.

*Unpublished manuscript, 1969.

When the Upper Rio Grande drainage was incorporated into the New Republic of Mexico in 1821, economic, political, and religious relationships acquired new orientations. The Mexicans severed all connections between this region and Old Spain, expelled all persons born in Spain, and deliberately secularized the Catholic Church. A few settlers arrived from Mexico and occupied new land grants; other Mexicans brought goods and traded with the local people; but spatial and cultural isolation generally persisted under Mexican rule. Spanish-Americans perpetuated surviving cultural traits, became increasingly economically self-reliant, and filled cultural voids with new local inventions, especially in religion and politics.

Acquisition of this territory by the United States in 1846 led to increased Anglo infiltration, contact, and eventually political and economic domination. While some Spanish-Americans attempted to remain apart from American culture, many were increasingly drawn into the new network of relationships.

Land

For the Spanish-American of the Upper Rio Grande drainage, land has both economic and great sentimental value. While it has been coveted because of its productivity, land has also generated many problems. First, the original land grants made by King Ferdinand I (*i.e.,* Carlos V) to colonists have been shrouded in controversy and confusion because of areal overlapping, lack of adequate boundary definition, and loss of titles and official registrations.

Eventually, land scarcity also became a crucial issue. The first Spanish villages were situated between present-day Albuquerque and Espanola; however, during the Seventeenth and Eighteenth Centuries, tightly nucleated settlements were founded as far north as the headwaters of the Rio Grande, along its permanent tributaries, and in the vicinity of Belen.[1] During the American Period, new communities and a new village form appeared. From the moment of contact, Spanish-Americans had competed with indigenous Pueblo Indians for good, tillable soil and irrigation water. Then as the population increased and its needs exceeded the existing agricultural potential, some Spanish-Americans were forced out of the long occupied areas into the well-watered, fertile inter-mountain valleys and, eventually, into even more remote and increasingly marginal areas. Line villages developed along the watercourses and roadways, but the vast desert or rugged mountain hinterland was never settled permanently. Thus, only small, usable segments of the total landscape were intensively populated and exploited.

Another kind of land problem results from a combination of a continuing high birth rate and local inheritance practices. Following death of a Spanish-American family head, land was traditionally divided among the numerous sons, although the oldest was sometimes specially favored. After several generations, continued fractionation of family holdings resulted in scattered, miniature fields, which could not be realistically or conveniently tilled because of size and/or location; yet people still clung tenaciously to the plots for sentimental reasons.

The rapidly increasing population was further confronted by a shrinking land base. Contributing factors included extensive overgrazing and unscientific land cultivation, which led to destruction of the land cover and soil wasting. Secondly, more than half (over 3½ million acres of private and communal property) of the original land grant acreage, including some of the best irrigated plots along the Rio Grande, has passed into the hands of outsiders. Such land loss is attributed to a number of causes: deceit and coercion on the part of unscrupulous Anglos or other land-grabbing opportunists, Spanish-American ignorance of legal procedures for land registration and for safeguarding property, discriminatory administration of laws, and eviction for failure to pay land taxes or to meet conservancy assessments. Thirdly, unclaimed land, which had been freely exploited by local inhabitants for grazing and wood-cutting, was eventually given to railroads or set aside as national and state forest preserves. Now, only if certain conditions are met, may Spanish-Americans use this forest land; but fees, limitations on the number of animals, shorter grazing seasons, and outside competition have restricted usage by them. So the exploitable world of many Spanish-Americans has continued to contract.

According to Reies Tijerina, the founder of the *Alianza Federal de Mercedes* (Federal Alliance of Land Grants), contemporary Spanish-American ailments can be directly attributed, first, to the loss of land which supposedly had been granted to colonists and their heirs in perpetuity and, second, to the failure of state and federal governments to guarantee the ancient rights of Spanish-American landholders (*e.g.,* taxation of their land was forbidden) as prescribed under the Mexican-United States Treaty of Guadalupe Hidalgo, signed in 1848. To resolve the land dilemma, Tijerina founded the *Alianza* in 1963. Its motto is "justice is our Creed, and the land is our heritage."

In order to resolve the land dilemma, the *Alianza* hopes to acquire control over all land situated in the Upper Rio Grande drainage which had been granted to Spanish colonists but which has since passed into the hands of outsiders. If return of the land is not feasible, compensation commensurate with the present value of the land and the profits earned in the interim by alien exploiters is to be made to the *Alianza.*[2] All land and money recovered would theoretically be held in trust; but members, land grant heirs, and sympathizers could be allotted plots of ground and share in the eventual division of funds. On the contrary, reactionary Spanish-Americans and "intruders" could expect eviction or harsh treatment.

A second major goal of the *Alianza* is to perpetuate and revive earlier Spanish-American culture. In this scheme, Spanish would be the basic language, and lower grade school classes would be taught in Spanish. Tijerina further urges curbs on, or preferably elimination of, Anglo culture in the *Alianza's* domain.

While the scope of their demands is great and questionably realistic, the *Alianza* would probably settle for extra state and federal subsidies, which would accelerate educational, welfare, health, and other services to Spanish-Americans, and for easier access to state and federal lands. So far, the *Alianza* has unsuccessfully lobbied with officials in Washington and Santa Fe and tried legal maneuvering.

On several occasions, the *Alianza* attracted attention to its cause and the problems of some Spanish-Americans. In 1966, amid much publicity, members and sympathizers marched from Albuquerque to Santa Fe and laid their case before state officials. Subsequently in October of the same year, Tijerina and several hundred Spanish-Americans seized a portion of the Carson National Forest, proclaimed the founding of a new independent theocratic city-state, the Pueblo Republica de San Joaquin del Rio de Chama, and attempted to evict "foreign" residents from this old Spanish land grant. Authorities soon routed the squatters and charged Tijerina and four followers with assault and expropriation of government property. In February, 1969, the United States 10th Circuit Court of Appeals, Denver, Colorado, upheld an earlier conviction; but an appeal has now been referred to the United States Supreme Court. Another incident took place in remote Coyote, New Mexico. Just before an *Alianza* rally and strategy meeting was to take place on June 3, 1967, the attorney for New Mexico's First Judicial District arrested and jailed eleven *Alianza* members and confiscated the membership list. Tijerina reacted by immediately disbanding the organization; however, two days later, fifteen armed men attacked the Rio Arriba County Court House at Tierra Amarilla with the intention of freeing the detained *Alianza* members and serving the district attorney with a citizen's arrest. During the melee which followed, two policemen were wounded, and two persons were kidnapped and held as hostages. After a gigantic manhunt, which included part of the New Mexico National Guard, Tijerina and several followers were apprehended, charged with kidnapping, tried, and subsequently acquitted. When the jailer at Tierra Amarilla was murdered in December, 1967, the *Alianza* was again suspected of perpetrating the crime.

Official state action during the above emergency further fueled the *Alianza's* claim of discrimination against Spanish-Americans. Charges that homes were entered without warrants, suspects were jailed without being informed of specific charges, and individuals, including women and children, were detained for two days without adequate food, clothing, and sanitary facilities were filed against the state by a newly formed Citizens Association for Human Rights.[3]

How successful the *Alianza* will ultimately be in uniting Spanish-Americans, in pressing for economic retribution, or in achieving social reform remains to be seen. Increasingly aggressive actions, unrealistic demands, questionable validity of claims, fears of ulterior motives on the part of the leadership coupled with a desire for retention of the *status quo* on the part of many upwardly mobile and affluent Spanish-Americans have generated resistance to or a lack of sympathy and enthusiasm for the organization and its present leadership.

Among Spanish-Americans, the *Alianza* is the first documented militant organization. It has all the attributes of a messianic, millenial movement, which has been triggered by relative deprivation. Tijerina, a migrant agricultural worker and fundamentalist Protestant preacher, came as a messiah to rectify and redress the wrongs perpetrated on poverty stricken Spanish-Americans. His actions and doctrine are sanctioned by divine revelation; thus God has selected Tijerina to bring about the millenium: land grants would be reclaimed, Spanish life would be revived, and Anglos, as well as their culture, would disappear. For at least some under-privileged, landless, elderly, less literate Spanish-Americans, Tijerina is a symbol of protest and hope.

Economic Opportunity

Much of the land originally granted to colonists by the king of Spain was agriculturally marginal and, at best, suited for herding. Even if the ground was tillable, water was the other crucial but highly variable element in agricultural success in the Upper Rio Grande drainage. Spanish-Americans cultivated small plots of wheat, maize, beans, chile, and vegetables; grew fruit trees; and herded sheep, goats, and cattle. By the beginning of the Mexican period, sheep had become the basis for wealth and status; and about 1900, sheep raising reached an apex and then began declining in economic importance. In some favorable localities, farming and herding are still important today. In others, such activities have not been sufficiently productive adequately to support the increasing Spanish-American population since the United States took possession of the area from Mexico; therefore other economic alternatives had to be found. Craft industries, like the weaving of Chimayo blankets, have never played a major economic role and could hardly be expanded to resolve the existing economic dilemma; similarly, local forests, coal, and mineral resources had been utilized only to a small degree by Spanish-Americans, who used hand techniques. However invasion of the drainage by Anglos in the middle 1800's brought new capital, new techniques for utilization of natural resources, and a new economic perspective. As the rail network began to link the Southwest together in the late 1870's and early 1880's, opportunities for wage work began to supplement and then to replace the Spanish-American farm as the economic mainstay. Track laying, other related railroading activities, like coal mining and commerce, ranching, and seasonal agricultural harvesting attracted male workers away from family farm and native village. For another half century, New Mexico remained a frontier area which produced raw materials but few industrial products. Slow Spanish-American integration into the modern world was disrupted by the depression of 1929; wage work nearly disappeared. Foreclosures and tax sales further reduced the land base and in some localities precipitated a mass exodus of youthful Spanish-Americans (*e.g.,* from the Embudo watershed). The sagging, fledgling New Mexican economy was soon bolstered by large doses of federal work programs and aid. Such welfare efforts offered seemingly temporary relief; but by the late 1930's, some persons became wholly dependent upon and have never relinquished these government subsidies. In some depressed areas of northern New Mexico, welfare payments continue to play a major economic role, and without them, entire villages would be depopulated. For many people, dependency has become a way of life.

The nation's expanding economic needs during World War II created new and numerous alternatives for employment. Large cattle and sheep ranches needed hands, though often on a seasonal basis; and defense industries situated outside the state attracted Spanish-Americans to Los Angeles, California; to Phoenix and Tucson, Arizona; to Pueblo and Denver, Colorado; and to Bingham, Utah. Induction into the armed forces of a large number of men also meant opportunity for experience and the acquisition of skills. Within New Mexico, establishment of industries related to atomic energy resulted in rapid economic development and subsequently urban growth between Belen and Espanola, the old Spanish Colonial heartland. Some Spanish-Americans resided near enough to work locations (*e.g.,* Los Alamos) so commuting was feasible; while others left rural for urban areas (*e.g.,* Albuquerque) in order to take advantage of employment opportunities. Consequently, the Upper Rio Grande drainage became quite urbanized, and fewer people depended directly on land for their livelihood.

Following the war period, the economy of the area has been sustained by continuing defense projects, government employment, tourism, manufacturing, forestry, mining, as well as the more traditional herding and farming. In the hinterland, development of natural gas, uranium, and other resources has resulted in further economic gains.

Not all of the residents, however, have shared in the economic opportunities and rewards. Over the years, per capita personal incomes from the northern, predominantly rural, Spanish-American countrties, (*e.g.,* Mora and Taos Counties) have been and continue to be the lowest in the state. They are about half that of the average income for residents of New Mexico (see Table 1). While all other counties have shown increased personal gains, 1966 income averages for Taos County dropped 14.1% below the 1965 figure. Rural counties within this Spanish-American block have been outstripped by the urbanized, industrial ones, namely Bernalillo County which includes Albuquerque, and Santa Fe County. Yet, in the latter, per capita personal income is still below the state's average, and economic growth for both fits a similar pattern.[4]

TABLE 1

*Per Capita Personal Income in Dollars for Selected Counties
and the State of New Mexico* [1]

Political Unit [2]	Income by Year				
	1940	1950	1959	1965	1966
Mora County	168	458	821	837	962
Taos County	172	457	858	1404	1206
San Miguel County	275	704	1128	1471	1678
Santa Fe County	437	1047	1673	1988	2122
Bernalillo County	482	1477	2323	2689	2771
State of New Mexico	375	1177	1917	2235	2385 [3]

[1] Regional Economics Information System, Office of Business Economics, September 19, 1968.

[2] Current data is not available for several counties, like Rio Arriba and Sandoval, because more than 10% of the total work force commutes to nearby work opportunities either in Albuquerque, Santa Fe, or Los Alamos.

[3] Ten Southeastern states claimed lesser per capita personal incomes than New Mexico in 1966.

For many Spanish-Americans, personal adjustment to the new economic world has not been easy. Before they can participate fully and compete successfully with Anglos and other English-speaking minority members, Spanish-Americans must speak English well, acquire usable skills, and understand something about Anglo-urban culture patterns. Ability to speak English varies considerably. In isolated rural or low-income urban areas Spanish is often retained as a basic, native language, and little value is placed on learning English. If it is spoken, the Spanish-American does so with great difficulty. Until 1930 many schools in the Upper Rio Grande drainage used Spanish as the medium of instruction; but more recently, the trend has favored English. Article XII, Section 8, of the New Mexican Constitution still specifies that teachers must be proficient in both English and Spanish; however, today few instructors meet this bilingual requirement. Because English is learned as a second language, the federal government financed a special remedial program (Title III, ESEA) in 1966 to assist in overcoming this cross-cultural handicap. Lack of English proficiency is a major reason for academic failure and discouragement. If this difficulty is coupled with poor health stemming from malnutrition, weak motivation, and confrontation by an alien culture, the student develops feelings of academic futility and cultural inferiority; consequently many children fall behind their Anglo peers and "drop out" of school. In rural New Mexico, this rate is several times that of Anglos; so ultimately about fifty percent of the Spanish-American students complete high school requirements. In urban areas, particularly Albuquerque, graduation is more frequent; but it is directly correlated with the student's degree of acculturation and position in the economic scale. A low level of academic achievement can also be at least partially explained in terms of inadequate school appropriations, poor physical facilities and equipment, low teacher quality, and political manipulation.

In many cases, a bad educational experience is a prelude to later problems encountered by Spanish-Americans. Because he often enters the work arena with the handicap of a minimal formal education, a minimal set of usable skills, a minimal ability to speak English, and a minimal familiarity with Anglo culture, he is relegated to an occupation with low earning power and low economic status. Such poor economic integration manifests itself in a poor standard of living, in lower class membership, and often in various forms of social disorganization. Underprivileged Spanish-Americans often complain about Anglo exploitation and discrimination and blame them on racial and/ or cultural prejudices.

Past relationships between Spanish-Americans and Anglos have frequently been colored by mutual distrust; moreover, prejudice and discrimination have operated in both directions and reached a tension peak during the late 1930's and early 1940's. Prior to that time, for example, few Spanish-Americans participated in Anglo-type secondary organizations like the American Legion. When they did, parallel Spanish-American and Anglo posts often existed side by side because of existing prejudices and discrimination. As these barriers diminished and Spanish-Americans became increasingly a part of the American scene, participation in voluntary Anglo secondary groups, like fraternal orders and service clubs, has increased, but at a slow rate. Participation is usually correlated with improving economic status and with the degree of acculturation to the American urban culture. In contrast to the above, the *Alianza Federal de Mercedes* appeals to the underprivileged residents of the Upper Rio Grande area and hopes to improve their living conditions. Prejudice and discrimination are foci of attention for the G.I. Forum and the recently organized Citizens Association for Human Rights. Some improvements in interpersonal relationships are apparent. By 1959, the United States Commission on Civil Rights pointed out that the presence and extent of segregation of Spanish-Americans in New Mexico was difficult to identify and evaluate; moreover Anglo discrimination had diminished and "one is led to believe that there is now no compulsion in whatever segregation may exist (Report of the U.S. Commission on Civil Rights: 1959: 254)." In many situations, self-segregation still is very evident (*e.g.,* many schools). Even though some overt signs of improved cross-cultural relationships exist, integration of Spanish-Americans and Anglos is far from complete; and some covert tensions persist, especially among the lower class Spanish-Americans, who tend to be somewhat antagonistic to Anglos and to more acculturated Spanish-Americans.

Social acceptance of upwardly mobile Spanish-Americans by Anglos has markedly increased. Although a Spanish-American middle class appeared after annexation of the area by the United States, growth has been slow until recently. Upwardly mobile Spanish-Americans are usually more fluent in English; moreover a growing number of them in Upper Rio Grande drainage no longer speak Spanish fluently or at all. As they ascend the economic ladder, Spanish-Americans tend to acquire middle class values (*e.g.,* the desirability of education) which are similar to their Anglo-American counterparts, and to reject those (*e.g.,* delinquency and sexual laxity) of lower income Spanish-Americans. Movement by Spanish-Americans into predominantly middle class Anglo urban neighborhoods is an indicator of acceptance, and today, a Spanish surname and cultural background may even have middle class prestige value, rather than being a social deterrent.

Since World War II, Spanish-Americans have seen the need for education and the development of new skills. Prior to that time, few of them, aside from children of the wealthy, attended college. Today a larger number seek degrees, yet Spanish-Americans still represent only a small percentage of the total university enrollment in New Mexico. Highlands University, the College of Santa Fe, and Northern New Mexico State School continue to attract local students, who most often major in Spanish language or are eventually certified as teachers. Meanwhile, a few register in programs of pharmacy, nursing, and law at the University of New Mexico or New Mexico State University. In the past, the latter was often the entree to local political wealth and prestige, but in other professions, Spanish-Americans are under-represented. Medicine, dentistry, engineering, and banking have had little appeal, and/or professional preparation was not feasible because of the monetary support necessary for such training. Today, Albuquerque and Santa Fe have the largest number of Spanish-American professionals. Many from the latter community are members of the upper class.

Upper class membership is correlated with wealth. By the end of the Mexican Period, great wealth differences already existed. Sheep and large tracts of land were the basis for economic success; and in turn, they brought political control. Today, if Spanish-Americans can acquire an education, accumulate the requisite wealth, and exhibit appropriate status symbols, they may be accepted by members of the upper class; however, with a Spanish-American background, this may still be more difficult than for a comparable Anglo.

One of the major areas of Spanish-American frustration lies in their inability to exercise effective political power beyond the local level. Because control has passed to Anglos, many Spanish-Americans distrust the contemporary system. *Alianza* members, for exmaple, blame the state and federal governments for the plight of the *conquistadores'* descendents and consider United States Senator Joseph Montoya a *Tio Tomas* (*i.e.,* Uncle Tom) who has "sold out" his low income Spanish-American constituents. The latter also resent the federal government's concern over Indian dilemmas, while Spanish-American problems, including high rates of tuberculosis, high infant mortality, poverty, and illiteracy go unattended. Until recently, this low income aggregate has not been organized or capable of exerting any power; however it has rallied behind the *Alianza* and touted Tijerina for governor. Only a technicality disqualified him from appearing on the ballot.

At the local political level, kinship and patronage have been most important in politics. A large number of actual and affinal relatives initially assures election at the ballot box. For supporting the candidate, the voter expects certain favors; thus familial attitudes toward mutual assistance and reciprocity carry over into the political arena. Often other criteria, among them competence, tend to be of lesser consideration. So long as local politicians control relief funds, appoint various minor officials, and pass out various "plums," politics will remain an attractive vocation and a stepping stone to wealth and power. The record of New Mexican political behavior is documented with cases of political abuse. As Spanish-Americans become urbanized, middle class citizens, they begin to demonstrate greater interest in the larger political arena. At the state and national level, Spanish-Americans have traditionally supported Democratic candidates; however in the 1968 presidential election, they bolted that party. In order to gain their support, both national parties have typically nominated a Spanish-American candidate for lieutenant governor of New Mexico.

In addition to having become a political minority, Spanish-Americans are now a numerical minority in New Mexico. While that state continues to have the highest percentage of population claiming Spanish ancestry, the percentage has drastically declined since 1846. As recently as 1940, they still claimed a majority, but by 1960, only 28.3% (269,122 out of 951,023) of the population had Spanish surnames (U.S. Bureau of Census: 1963: 8). This demographic trend is effected by both the exodus of Spanish-Americans from and by the influx of Anglos into the state. Even in the six northern rural New Mexican counties considered to be the stronghold of Spanish-American culture, five have declined in population and only Santa Fe County has gained. So the Upper Rio Grande drainage has become increasingly dominated by Anglos, and more urban.

Identification

Traditionally, Spanish-Americans identified with their family, their native village, *la raza,* the Roman Catholic Church, and certain sodalities. In the family, the bilaterally oriented kindred, which includes all close relatives on both father's and mother's sides, is the core of personal relationships; yet a patri-bias is readily detectable. In part, this last condition is a product of male land inheritance and virilocal residence. The latter localizes male family members and permits development of an extended family which is the responsible property holding group and basic economic unit. Within the virilocal extended family, the father stands as the dominant figure, final authority, protector of the family, and satisfier of material needs. A woman's status is that of wife, mother, housekeeper, and a subordinate to men. Children are much desired, but the eldest son is most favored. Kindred members constantly assist one another, celebrate crises, rites and holidays of the church, and are responsible for the upbringing of their children; also the kindred is a primary agent of social control, moral support, and advice. Significant family values include morality, hard work, and reciprocal obligations with other kinsmen.

In the Upper Rio Grande drainage, *compadrazgo,* god parenthood, further reinforces existing family relationships because godparents are typically selected from within the kindred, rather than from outside, and thus extending the network of relationships beyond the family. When both family and ritual are so linked, intensive social interaction and mutual assistance between *compadrazgo* participants follows. Thus, godparents compliment the biological parents in the social, economic, and religious life of a person.

Next to the kindred, the rural village or urban neighborhood is a focal point of the Spanish-American individual. He strongly identifies with his native village which in many cases is a kin group because of descent and affinal relationships existing among the residents. Until recently, many villages were largely endogamous, so an individual frequently married a person who was a cousin of some degree. Moreover marriages were often arranged more for the convenience of the families and for economic advantage than for the individuals. Even if a man resides outside his village, he still prefers a marriage partner who was born in his home community. Within the village, obligations are by no means limited to the family. Communal labor is essential in the constructing and maintaining of irrigation ditches, house building, and live stock grazing; further mutual assistance cushions personal and community crises. Other village participation is found in religious activity, celebrations, and maintenance of law and order.

As the expanding American economic sphere and urban influences begins to engulf Spanish-Americans, differing personal accommodations are made. Some retain the earlier family structuring and functioning to a large degree. With passing time, others establish neolocal families and perpetuate few of the old customs. Today, most Spanish-Americans lie somewhere between these two polar extremes.

The virilocal extended family mostly occurs when a person continues to reside in the community of his birth, but even out-migration does not necessarily destroy old familial and community relationships or attitudes. In fact, urban adjustment is often facilitated and cushioned by relatives or villages who are already established in the new setting; hence migrants from the same village tend to congregate in an urban neighborhood. Consequently interaction and reciprocity patterns, values, and customs not only survive, but they retain a high degree of viability and importance. In many ways, life in a Rio Grande urban area is quite similar to that in rural regions because housing, conveniences, and general setting is much the same. From an ecological viewpoint, low income urban neighborhoods in which Spanish-Americans typically reside tend to be much more rural physically than corresponding ones in most other American cities. Furthermore, the first generation of displaced persons retains an active interest in and intense loyalty to both kindred and the village of their birth; the migrant returns frequently to assist elderly relatives, to fulfill various religious and social obligations, and to relax on weekends or vacations. Many of the absentee families continue to hold plots of land, which usually lie fallow, and maintain a house, which is only used occasionally. Kinsmen who stay behind and cultivate the soil, herd sheep, and live the hard life often receive cash supplements from their relatives.

While some continuity may be claimed, migration immediately effects certain facets of family life. In the new setting, social control and socializing functions of the virilocal extended family, kindred, and village are much weakened or no longer exist. While male dominance seemingly continues, a more egalitarian relationships develops between the spouses; general parental authority declines; and a "generation gap" may develop between parents and children within the nuclear family. Village models are no longer appropriate to the new urban scene, or are often countered by juvenile peer pressure, and by competing foreign institutions. Secondary associations begin to play more important roles in peoples' lives. *Sociedad Espanola de Beneficienta Mutica* and similar organizations compliment or replace the family and community in rendering general assistance in time of need. Others, like credit unions, health cooperatives, and labor unions serve very specific purposes.

In a new unrestricted setting, a complete break with the past is possible. For the first time, individuals may exercise freedom in choosing residence, occupation, marriage partner, and recreation facilities. The latter often turn away from the traditionally sanctioned family, community, and church forms and toward commercial motion pictures, dancing, and drinking. When marriage was considered a family affair and women were carefully protected, opportunistic liaison was precluded. Prior to World War II, most outside occupations (*e.g.*, herding, railroad track work), which attracted Spanish-American males, were not conducive to establishing permanent cross-sexual contacts; moreover, men preferred a spouse from their native community or at least a partner who spoke Spanish; therefore Anglo or other women were not viewed as desirable marriage candidates. So long as such preferences and contact situations existed, cross-cultural marriages were few. When the urban migration began in the early 1940's, new contacts with a variety of people became possible; so during the last decade, increased cross-cultural marriage, typically involving an Anglo man and a Spanish-American woman, has occurred, although no great frequency is indicated. For many urban families, previously unknown forms of social disorganization, like divorce, broken homes, desertion, juvenile delinquency, crime, and drug addiction are manifested. In the Rio Grande drainage, Aid to Dependent Children and other forms of public assistance are largely concentrated among Spanish-Americans in the lower economic stratum.

Beyond the kin group and community, *la raza,* the race, is another symbol of cohesion and identification. Despite the seemingly physical connotation, *la raza* does not refer to racial characteristics. Any notion of racial purity must be discarded because present-day Spanish-Americans are a polygot aggregate with genes from Spanish colonists, Puebloan, Mexican, and other Indians, and Anglos. *La raza* does imply some degree of Spanish ancestry and serves as a mystical bond which sets Spanish-Americans apart from all other people, and politicians and messiahs, like Tijerina, often appeal to this vaguely defined concept when seeking support and approval. The Spanish language and surnames are also adjuncts to *la raza* and additional symbols of unity.

Lastly, the Catholic Church has been and is a strong influence in these peoples' lives. A very high percentage of Spanish-Americans are still baptized Catholic; however as adults, many tend to be inactive or participate only nominally in religious activities. Although in the more isolated villages, an occasional mass sung by a visiting priest is still eagerly anticipated and well attended. In urban areas, overt activity is more sporadic, especially on the part of males. Another dilemma of the church is in the current shortage of Spanish-speaking priests. This condition has led to integration of Spanish and Anglo parishes. Over its long history in the American Southwest, the church condemned, but never succeeded in eradicating certain kinds of beliefs which were considered religiously unorthodox: magic, the evil eye, and witches.

When Catholicism was brought to the Upper Rio Grande drainage by the conquistadores and padres, *cofradias,* voluntary lay brotherhoods sponsored by the Catholic Church, were imported at the same time. They were dedicated to satisfying religious and mutual aid goals. When the clerics and officially sponsored *cofradias* were removed from the scene by the Mexicans, the void was filled by *Los Hermanos Penitentes,* the Penitent Brotherhood. This locally invented secret, benevolent fraternity assumed the responsibility for religious, charitable, and social functions and kept alive the Catholic faith and tradition. The Penitentes are probably best known for their reenactment of Christ's crucifixion, and for doing penance by flagellation and other kinds of self-torture; so the main goal of mutual assistance is often overlooked. Today, the needs once met by this organization are satisfied in other ways, and internal organizational strains, waning political power and prestige, and declining membership are reported. Since only a handful of older members are now active in some communities, consolidation of local chapters has taken place. In some communities, antagonisms, which have long existed between Penitentes and non-members at a covert level, have suddenly burst into the open. A few years ago the Penitentes were formally welcomed back into and recognized by the Catholic Church; and more recently it has attempted to restructure the brotherhood into a hierarchical organization so more church control can be exerted over the normally independent chapters. Thus *Los Hermanos Penitentes* chapters would lose their unique flavor and more closely approximate an approved *cofradia.*

Although Spanish-Americans are supposedly bound together psychologically by *la raza,* the church, and a common culture, these do not prevent factionalism and differentiation. They are suspicious of any non-relative, even if the other person is a Spanish-American. Within the villages, homogeneity and agreement do not necessarily exist with regard to Penitente activities, community improvement, political affiliation, wealth, and religious belief. Villagers take strong positions in supporting their views. Some of the threats to local solidarity may come from outside, rather than being a by-product of internal confrontation. Recently, pentacostal missionaries have attempted to convert villagers to their beliefs. How successful the missionaries have been in wooing Spanish-Americans away from Catholicism is not generally known; however in some villages, conversion rates are quite high. At a time when the solidarity of the Spanish-American community is threatened by many internal and alien manifestations, consensus does not exist among the constituents.

Prior to the arrival of the Spanish, the Upper Rio Grande drainage was the homeland for a number of different Indian tribes. *Conquistadores,* padres, and peasants contributed Spanish culture traits to the already existing pluralistic system. Later, the Mexicans and Anglos confronted the area residents with still other alien cultures. Today, Spanish-American culture in the Upper Rio Grande drainage survives as a viable, but changing entity. While many traits and complexes are shared with people of Latin America, the New Mexican culture is a distinctive manifestation. It differs from both other Spanish subcultures of the United States and adjacent Mexico and the normative American culture. How long this unique tradition can be perpetuated in the land of *poco tiempo* can not be predicted at this time, but Spanish-Americans have left an indelible mark on the physical and cultural landscape of the Upper Rio Grande drainage.

FOOTNOTES

1. Settlement outside the Rio Grande drainage did not take place until the Nineteenth Century and is associated with the development of the livestock industry, particularly large sheep herding operations.

2. Descendents of American Indians, whose land was claimed by Spanish colonists, are awaiting the federal and state's responses to these claims. They ask who empowered the king of Spain to grant charters giving Indian land to the Spanish.

3. The Citizens Association for Human Rights, founded by Father Robert Garcia, a Roman Catholic priest, is in no way officially connected with the *Alianza.*

4. Average income for Bernalillo County is fourth and for Sante Fe County eighteenth on a scale for twenty-seven New Mexican Counties.

5. Rising Spanish-American influence in education was marked by the election of Arturo G. Ortega as the Board of Regent's president of the University of New Mexico on March 10, 1968.

6. A recently published research monograph by Nancie L. Gonzales presents an extensive analysis of *The Spanish-Americans of New Mexico: A Distinctive Heritage.*

LA RAZA: MEXICAN AMERICANS IN REBELLION*

JOSEPH L. LOVE

In early June, 1967, a group of Spanish-speaking Americans who call themselves the *Alianza Federal de Mercedes* (Federal Alliance of Land Grants) and claim that they are the legal and rightful owners of millions of acres of land in Central and Northern New Mexico, revolted against the governments of the United States of America, the State of New Mexico and Rio Arriba (Up River) County, formally proclaiming the Republic of Rio Chama in that area.

On June 5 an armed band of forty or more *Aliancistas* attacked the Tierra Amarilla courthouse, released 11 of their members being held prisoner, and wounded a deputy sheriff and the jailer. They held the sheriff down on the floor with a rifle butt on his neck, searched for the District Attorney (who wasn't there) and for an hour and a half controlled the village (population 500). They took several hostages (later released when the getaway car stuck in the mud).

Despite some of the melodramatic and occasionally comic opera aspects of the affair, both the members of the *Alianza* and the local and state authorities take it very seriously. This is not the first time the Aliancistas have violated federal and state law, attempting to appropriate government property (in October, 1966, for instance, their militants tried to take over Kit Carson National Forest, and to expel the rangers found there as trespassers); nor is it the only time their activities have resulted in violence. In this case the state government reacted frantically, sending in armored tanks, 300 National Guardsmen and 200 state police. They rounded up dozens of Spanish-speaking persons, including many women and children, and held them in a detention camp, surrounded with guns and soldiers, for 48 hours. The raiders got away, but in several days all of them — including their fiery leader, former Pentecostal preacher Reies López Tijerina — were captured.

It has become common to associate these actions of the Alianza with other riots or revolts by poor, dark-skinned and disaffected Americans

— with Watts, Newark and Detroit. Tijerina himself helps reinforce this impression by occasionally meeting with, and using the rhetoric of, some leaders of the black urban revolt. The fact is, however, that the Alianza movement is really a unique example in the United States of a "primitive revolt" as defined by Eric Hobsbawm, a kind almost always associated with developing nations, rather than advanced industrialized countries — and which includes such diverse phenomena as peasant anarchism, banditry, and millenarianism (the belief that divine justice and retribution is on the side of the rebels and that the millenium is at hand). The attack on the courthouse, in fact, had more in common with the millenarian Sioux Ghost Dance cult of 1889-91 than with Watts.

As the Aliancistas see it, they are not violating any legitimate law. The territory around Rio Arriba belongs to them. They demand the return of lands — primarily common lands — taken from *Hispano* communities, most of which were founded in the Spanish colonial era. Their authority is the famous *Recopilación de leyes de los Reinos de Indias (Compilation of Laws of the Kingdoms of the Indies,* generally shortened to *The Laws of the Indies)* by which the Crown of Castile governed its New World possessions. They claim that according to these laws common lands were inalienable — could not be taken away. Since most of such lands were in existence when the Treaty of Guadalupe Hidalgo was signed in 1848 — and since in that treaty the United States government pledged itself to respect property rights established under Mexican rule — the Alianza insists that those land grants remain valid. The members speak primarily of common lands, rather than individual heirs, and define the towns in question as "closed corporations, with membership restricted to the descendants and heirs of the founding fathers and mothers" — that is, themselves.

The Alianza's interpretations of law and history are, of course, selective, and tend to ignore inconvenient facts and other interpretations. It claims that *The Laws of the Indies* were not abrogated when "Mexico invaded and occupied New Mexico," nor when the United States did the same in 1946. The Aliancistas are the early settlers, the legitimate heirs.

The Maximum Leader

The Alianza and its actions cannot really be understood without knowledge of its background and its leader. First, the people from whom it draws its members and its strength — the Mexican-American minority in the US — and specifically New Mexico; second, the rapid economic changes throughout the area since World War II that have so greatly affected their lives; and last but surely not least the dynamism, determination and charisma of Reies Tijerina, without whom the movement would probably never have arisen.

In the 1960 census Mexican-Americans, though they made up only 2.3 percent of the population of the United States, constituted 12 percent of the population of Texas, New Mexico, Arizona, Colorado and California—almost three and a half million persons.

Generally they are a submerged minority that have only lately begun to articulate their demands. They formed "Viva Kennedy" committees in 1960; since then three Mexican-American Congressmen have gone to the House, and New Mexico's Joseph Montoya sits in the Senate. The end of the *bracero* program in 1964 opened the way to a successful unionization drive among agricultural workers; and the celebrated "Huelga" strike in Delano, California in 1965 was a symptom of and stimulus to the new awakening. The federal and state poverty programs, and the example of the Negro revolt, have also undoubtedly had their effects.

New Mexico is a distinctive area of Latin culture. It was the last state in the Southwest to be overwhelmed by Anglo-American civilization, and is the only one with two official languages. The Mexican-American population has been traditionally located along the Rio Grande and its tributaries, and extends into southern Colorado.

Until recent years, the Mexican Americans of New Mexico have been isolated from other members of *la raza* (the Mexican-American "race"). Texas and California have more than 80 percent of the Mexican-American population of the Southwest, yet most of these crossed over from Mexico after 1900, or descended from persons who did. But, the New Mexican *Hispanos* (the local name) have resided there for many generations, and some strains go back to the seventeenth century (Santa Fe was founded in 1609). Moreover, large numbers of English-speaking Americans only began to compete seriously for rural property in the 1880's, and appropriation continued into the 1920's.

In the 1960 census New Mexico had a higher percentage of "native born of native parents" than any other Southwestern state (87.4 percent). The mobility of Hispano males between 1955 and 1960 (defined in terms of changing residence) was lower in New Mexico than elsewhere. In 1960 New Mexico had the highest percentage of rural non-farm inhabitants with Spanish surnames.

In absolute numbers New Mexico's Anglo population was for many years roughly in balance with the Hispano. It is now surging ahead as a result of the economic boom which began with the atomic testing program of World War II. In no other Southwestern state was the disparity between the growth of Anglo and Latin populations greater from 1950 to 1960 than in New Mexico, where the former increased by 59.1 percent and the latter by a mere 8.1 percent. Yet in spite of this, New Mexico in 1960 still had a greater proportion of Mexican-Americans than any other state: about two-sevenths of its inhabitants had Spanish surnames, compared to one-seventh of Texans, and one-eleventh of Californians.

The job situation for the Hispanos of New Mexico has also worsened more rapidly than in other states. In 1950 male Mexican-Americans had a greater percentage of jobless in California, Colorado, and Arizona than in New Mexico; but ten years later the Hispanos of New Mexico had the dubious distinction of leading the list.

As some observers have noted, in certain ways New Mexico resembles Quebec: Both are centers of Latin culture founded in the seventeenth century, and both are subject to an increasing degree of Anglo domination. And like the Quebeckers, the New Mexicans have their fringe-group separatists — the *Alianza Federal de Mercedes.*

The Alianza was born in 1963, partly to combat the alienation and isolation of the Hispanos, but specifically to reclaim lands taken from the Spanish-speaking population since 1848. In colonial New Mexico (1598-1821), Spanish officials made land grants of indeterminate size to both individuals and to communities as commons, and the latter were respected through the era of Mexican rule (1821-1848). When Anglo-Americans began to enter New Mexico in significant numbers in the 1880's, they found it possible to wrest lands from the native inhabitants through the legal and financial devices of land taxes, mortgages, and litigation over disputed titles. By 1930, through legal and extralegal means, the Anglos had taken over most of the farming and ranching land in the state, and the state and federal governments appropriated much of the common lands that had previously belonged to the incorporated towns and villages. The Spanish-speaking population ultimately lost 1.7 million acres of community lands and two million acres in private holdings. The Hispanos sporadically reacted to this process by forming secret societies and vigilante groups; but at most this constituted harassment rather than effective resistance.

The Alianza now demands the return of these lands.

Yet in all probability, the Alianza would not exist but for the efforts of a single man, a leader who devotes his life to his cause, and inspires his followers to do likewise. Reies López Tijerina is a man of rare charisma who is most in his element when haranguing a large crowd. Of average height, he seems to have great physical strength as he grasps a microphone with one sinewy arm and gesticulates artfully and furiously with the other. He sometimes shouts violently as he asks rhetorical questions of his audience in Spanish — the language he uses by preference — and gets "Sí!" and "No!" bellowed back in appropriate cadences. The author witnessed a Tijerina performance last fall on the steps of the state capitol in Austin, Texas, where the Alianza leader told a group of Mexican-American Labor Day marchers he supported their demand for a state minimum wage of $1.25 an hour, but did so "with shame." Why should Mexican-Americans in Texas ask so little of the Anglos, whose government had repeatedly broken the Treaty of Guadalupe Hidalgo?

Reies Tijerina uses a demagogic style before a crowd, but he holds the tenets of his faith with unshakeable conviction: "It's something in me that must come out," Tijerina proclaims. His followers regard him with awe. He is "Caudillo" (leader) of the Alianza, but disclaims any desire to be dictator. He points out that a Supreme Council has ultimate control — though he, clearly, makes the decisions. It seems obvious that no one could step into his shoes, nor has anyone been groomed to do so. In any event Tijerina has no doubt that his followers require strong and able leadership. He justifies this by arguing that the Hispanos are a "young" race. They were "born," he explains, by virtue of a royal decree in 1514 allowing Spaniards to marry Indians; the term "Hispano" or "Spanish American" therefore can generally be equated with "mestizo." This young race is still learning, painfully, how to defend itself and requires strong direction. It is not an ancient and clever people like the Jews, he says.

Recognizing the diverse historical experiences of Texas, New Mexico, and California, the Caudillo realizes that his constituency for the foreseeable future will be limited to New Mexico. He does believe, however, that the land grants to Mexican-Americans in California can still be identified and claimed like those of New Mexico.

It is no coincidence that Tijerina's style and language recall Pentecostal protestantism. He has been a minister in the Assembly of God, and was an itinerant revival preacher for many years to Mexican-Americans throughout the Southwest.

But, unlike the vast majority of his followers, he was not born in New Mexico but in Texas ("A prophet is not without honor save in his own country"). One of seven children of a migrant farm family, once so desperate that they were reduced to eating field rats, he picked crops and preached in Illinois and Michigan as well as in Texas and Arizona. He did not settle in New Mexico until 1960; and, with his five brothers, formed the Alianza three years later.

The quasi-religious fervor of Tijerina has strongly shaped the aspirations and style of the Alianza. However, there is greater emphasis on Old Testament justice than New Testament love. *Justicia* is a word frequently on the Caudillo's lips.

The Alianza now claims to have 30,000 dues-paying members paying at least $2.00 per month. A scholar guesses that 10,000 may be closer to the true figure. It seems clear that Tijerina's computation includes sympathizers or at least persons who have only occasionally contributed funds.

As with some sectors of the American Negro movement, the Alianza's programs began with an emphasis on litigation; and when that failed, frustration and a disposition toward violence emerged.

In April 1966 the "President and Founder" of the Alianza journeyed to Spain in order to gather materials on the registraiton of New Mexican land grants in the colonial era; from such documents he hoped to generate a strong legal case to present in federal courts.

In July Tijerina presented a petition to the Governor of New Mexico, Jack Campbell, and stated, "We do not demand anything. We just want a full investigation of the issue." Yet Governor Campbell would do little more than receive Tijerina and hear him out.

In January 1967, the Caudillo, one of his brothers, and a self-styled legal expert in the Alianza named Gerry Noll made a trip to Washington, D.C., where they "limited" their claims to 500,000 acres in the Kit Carson National Forest and to an area around the city of Albuquerque. He only obtained a brief hearing with a State Department attorney and a sympathetic interview with New Mexico's Senator Montoya.

In 1966 the Alianza had already begun to give up hope of legal redress. The Supreme Council of the Alianza "passed a resolution of non-confidence in the Courts of the State of New Mexico and of the United States of America" because of "corruption" and "low standards of knowledge of law."

Aliancistas Proclaim Independent Republic

On October 22, 1966 the Aliancistas proclaimed the existence of the Republic of San Joaquín del Río de Chama (in Rio Arriba County) with Tijerina as "city attorney" (*procurador*) of the community; they simultaneously attempted to take over Kit Carson Forest, which covers most of the county. They arrested U.S. Forest Rangers for trespassing, decided to print hunting and fishing licenses, and commandeered government vehicles. The rebels were quickly dispersed by local authorities, and Tijerina and four lieutenants were charged on counts of assault, converting government property to private use, and conspiracy.

Demonstrations and protest meetings continued.' On January 15, 1967 the Alianza declared it would seek redress in the United Nations if the U.S. Congress failed to act. On April 17 several hundred Aliancistas paraded before the State House in Santa Fe, and Reies Tijerina, out on bond, delivered an ominous message: "We will . . . issue to the public and the federal government and the world the last human legal notice exposing the truth. . . . The government is being warned and advised if anybody is found trespassing on these land grants they will be arrested and punished. . . . "

At the beginning of June the District Attorney of Santa Fe, Alfonso Sánchez, expressed concern about the "communist philosophy" of the Alianza and alleged that Aliancistas were amassing "machine guns, M-1 rifles, and 15,000 rounds" of ammunition. Eleven members of the Alianza were promptly arrested and jailed in Tierra Amarilla, an Alianza stronghold and the seat of Rio Arriba County.

The reaction was swift and violent: On June 5, as noted, the Aliancistas launched their revolt and attacked the Tierra Amarilla courthouse. This time, when caught, the Caudillo and his principal aides were charged with kidnapping, three counts of conspiracy to commit murder, and bombing a public building (the courthouse). Despite the gravity of the charges, Tijerina and some of his men were released on bond after six weeks in prison. The failure of the attack by no means dampened the spirits of the Aliancistas.

In the months following, Tijerina traveled throughout the Southwest to gain backing. He found it, both in radical organizations of Mexican-Americans and Negroes, and in some Mexican-American associations with more traditional reformist leadership.

On October 15, Tijerina was in Los Angeles, linking his cause to the peace movement at an anti-war rally. Labeling the United States' involvement in Vietnam "the most criminal in the history of mankind," he contacted radical Negro and Mexican-American groups in the Los Angeles area. One week later, at a convention of the Alianza de Mercedes on October 21, Tijerina announced that a "Treaty of Peace, Harmony, and Mutual Assistance" had been contracted between his organization and SNCC, CORE, and the Black Panthers. The Caudillo also obtained statements of support from the Crusade for Justice, a Mexican-American organization of slumdwellers in Denver, and from MAPA, an important Mexican-American political action group in California.

While gathering support from non-Anglo groups outside New Mexico in the here and now, Tijerina and his deputies have not discouraged the movement's latent tendencies toward millenarianism and belief in special divine favor back home on the Upper Rio Grande. During the raid at Tierra Amarilla, several Aliancistas witnessed the appearance of a double rainbow, a sure sign of God's grace. According to others, the Caudillo is the prophet of Montezuma who will miraculously return in the imminent future to punish the Anglos for their appropriation of Hispano lands.

Another legend has it that a leader will come "from the east" and expel the foreigners who took the Mexican-Americans' lands. (Tijerina fits, since Texas is east of New Mexico.)

In the "*Corrido de Rio Arriba*," which appeared shortly after the June raid, the balladeer told his audience that when bullets started flying "*Las mujeres y los niños/iban corriendo y llorando,*

Y en este instante pensamos/Que el mundo se iba acabando."

("Women and children/Ran about in tears

And at that moment we thought/The world was coming to an end.")

Although the "free city-states" which Tijerina hopes to erect are of this world, they clearly represent a sort of secular paradise, a recaptured golden age; somewhat along the lines prescribed in *The Laws of the Indies*. The inhabitants will be able to do any work they please, explains the Caudillo; but most will be herdsmen using the common lands (*ejidos*) of the pueblos. Tijerina himself will simply become City Attorney of the Republic of Chama.

If "la raza" is specially favored and will come into its millenium, why is it suffering so now? This is explained as the result of a "fall from grace" which occurred after the Anglo-American invasion of New Mexico in 1846 and the collusion of certain Hispanos with the alien conquerors. An allegorical mural at Alianza headquarters tells the story: A sacred temple in the center of the mural represents paradise entwined by a serpent, which also clutches three figures symbolizing the oppressed races — the Negro, the Indian, and the Hispano. The snake personifies the "Santa Fe Ring" — the Anglo and upper-class Hispano politicians who appropriated the poor Hispanos' lands in the 1880's and later. Figures on the right side, representing the People, begin to emerge from the Darkness and a reptile-devouring secretary bird, personifying Justice, arrives to attack the snake. At the top of the canvas is a rainbow (a symbol of God's blessing) and the phrase "Justicia." Just below this emblem is the City of Justice, which will once more be reconstituted on earth.

Yet there is a sinister element in the apocalypse which must precede the millenium: Anglos must be driven out. And Hispanos will be judged by whether they aided, stood aside from, or hindered the cause. Those who hindered will be treated harshly.

Gerry Noll, the Caudillo's lieutenant, has proclaimed as part of the Alianza creed:

> . . . KNOW YE that We have exclusive and supreme jurisdiction within [New Mexico] over all persons and property situated therein.. . .
>
> We cannot afford to permit the present status quo to be maintained without actually destroying Our independence and autonomy. Consequently, We must take measures calculated to curtail the activities of any aggressors with the utmost dispatch . . . We shall enter troops into these territories to restore Our authority . . . woe to him who obeys the orders of the aggressor, for he shall be punished without mercy.. . .
>
> THEREFORE, KNOW YE that We shall commence to liberate Our kingdoms, realms, and dominions . . . We shall not take any prisoners of war, but shall take only war criminals and traitors and try [them] by a military tribunal and execute them.

At Tijerina's direction, the October 1967 convention of the Alianza unanimously set forth a weird dynastic claim: Gerry Noll was henceforth transformed into "Don Barne Quinto Cesar, King-Emperor of the Indies," the legitimate descendant of Ferdinand VII of Spain.

Dying Is Part of a King's Day's Work

In November Tijerina, "Don Barne," and several other Aliancistas stood trial for the charges stemming from the invasion of Kit Carson Forest in 1966. During the trial it was revealed that Noll's real name was Gerald Wayne Barnes, convicted of bank robbery in 1945, grand larceny in 1949, forgery in 1953, and third-degree assault in 1963. Found guilty, Noll and Tijerina were sentenced to three and two years respectively. At the trial Don Barne declared, "I am willing to die for my country and for my people. This is part of my job as king and all in a day's work." When sentenced in mid-December he retorted to the court, "It is I who make the laws — not the United States of America."

While waiting trail on the multiple charges of the June '67 raid and appealing against the decision in the first case, Tijerina and his co-defendants were once more released on bond. On January 3, 1968, again in Tierra Amarilla, Deputy Sheriff Eulogio Salazar was kidnapped and beaten to death. Governor David Cargo, Campbell's successor, immediately revoked the bonds. Protests rapidly poured into the Governor's office from SNCC, MAPA, and other organizations, and a short time later Tijerina was out on bail again.

Since that time legal problems have necessarily absorbed most of Tijerina's energies, as he appealed the verdict of the first trial and prepared for the more serious set of charges (including kidnapping) stemming from the Tierra Amarilla affair. But the Caudillo found time to break into national headlines again in May and June when he led his followers at the Poor People's March on Washington. Alleging that the Negro leaders of the march refused to grant Mexican-Americans an adequate place in the sun, Tijerina cancelled Alianza participation in Resurrection City. Instead, he made use of his appearance in Washington to lecture State Department officials on the meaning of the Guadalupe Hidalgo Treaty — namely, the legitimacy of the Spanish land grants.

Tijerina had hoped to run for governor in the November 1968 elections, but the New Mexico Supreme Court disallowed his candidacy in October because of his conviction the previous year. Meanwhile the second (Tierra Amarilla) trial took place, during which Tijerina dramatically dismissed his lawyers and conducted his own defense. In mid-December his self-confidence was justified by his acquittal of kidnapping and two lesser counts. Other charges against him and nine other defendants had yet to come before the courts at the end of 1968.

But the real historical and sociological meaning of the Alianza cannot be solely understood in terms of its current embroilments or recent history in New Mexico. Most of the literature on the movement, so far, has dealt with the spectacular, bizarre, or violent elements involved; but the roots of primitive revolt go far back.

Since the enclosure movement began in Europe in the twelfth century, there have been scores of peasant revolts. Many sought the restoration of common lands taken by nobles and gentry.

In medieval Spain, many villages owned herds and land in common, and a number of these arrangements survived as late as the Spanish Civil War. These towns had once enjoyed special legal sanctions called fueros, by which they could themselves decide whether or not to enforce royal decrees and pay taxes.

One historian has written that "The village communities spontaneously developed an extensive system of municipal services, to the point of their sometimes reaching an advanced stage of communism." A scheme was proposed in 1631 to "nationalize all pasturage and establish each peasant with sufficient head of sheep and cattle to support him." In 1633 the Crown tried to implement this project by regulating tenancy and fixing rents in perpetuity, making leases irrevocable and hereditary, and setting up regulation commissions. Though the plan failed, the demands of shepherds for adequate grazing land were part of the Hispanic tradition to which Tijerina appeals and went to Spain to study.

One student of Mexican-American culture, anthropologist Narcie González, writes that " . . . even now [1967] sheepherding remains an ideal way of life for the Hispano. . . . Virtually all contemporary accounts by social scientists comment upon the people's stated preference for this occupation. . . . " This preference explains why in Tijerina's Utopia the common lands are so higly valued. The Chama region, where the Tierra Amarilla revolt broke out, was principally a sheep-grazing area until after the Second World War.

What has occurred in New Mexico has been a breakdown of the traditional society, the ripping of the fabric of Hispano culture. In 1950, 41 percent of the Spanish-surname population in the state lived in urban areas; but by 1960, 61 percent did. Many of those moving to the cities (especially to Albuquerque) were ill prepared for their new way of life. In 1956 one investigator found that 834 out of 981 women in Albuquerque who received Aid to Dependent Children had Spanish surnames.

While the number of Anglo-Americans rapidly increased in New Mexico after World War II, the Mexican-American population was almost static, the high birth rate being offset by emigration to California. Consequently by 1960 the Anglo population in the state constituted almost two-thirds of the whole.

The legal structures of a modern capitalist society had by the late 1930's wrecked the traditional land-tenure patterns of the Upper Rio Grande. In 1940 Dr. George Sanchez reported that in Taos County "65 percent of the private lands represent land grants which have been subdivided or otherwise lost to the communities and families to which they were originally assigned. Of the original nine *mercedes* in Taos County, four were community grants and five were lands granted to individuals. . . . This cornerstone of Taos' economy has been destroyed by taxation and by uncontrolled exploitation." Furthermore, "Commercial livestock operators have acquired [the Hispano's] land grants and compete with him for grazing leases and permits on public lands. Exorbitant fees, taxes, and forced sales have crowded him out of his former grazing domain."

For a time the full impact of these changes were softened by the booming war and atomic energy economy in New Mexico, and by the fact that the National Forest Service seems to have acted as a surrogate patrón for the Hispano shepherd. Until drought in the 1960's forced a cutback, the Hispano could still obtain the use of federal lands for pasturing his livestock.

Rio Arriba County was one of the areas least affected by the state's economic growth. In 1960 it had the highest percentage of rural non-farm population of all New Mexico's counties (91.3 percent). It ranked high in native-born inhabitants, and low in the percentage of migrants. It had the third lowest median education and the fifth lowest median family income. In Rio Arriba and the other northern counties where the Spanish-speaking population predominates, the average per capita income in 1967 was less than $1,000, compared to the state average of $2,310 and the national average of $2,940. Furthermore, according to Governor Cargo, "11,000 of 23,000 residents of Rio Arriba County are on welfare rolls." The 1960 census showed that county with the state's highest rate of unemployment — 15.1 percent — almost three times the state average.

Government Controls Grazing Lands

But it is not only unemployment that makes the residents of Rio Arriba dependent on federal and state largesse — 72.1 percent of all land still available for grazing is owned by the U.S. government in Kit Carson Forest. And what the government grants, it can, and sometimes does, also refuse.

The disintegration of the traditional Hispano community seems well underway, and Tijerina articulates widely-shared feelings that his people do not want to assimilate into Anglo culture. He also rejects relief as demoralizing to its recipients, stating again and again, "We will no longer take powdered milk in exchange for justice." Recent increases in welfare assistance may actually have aggravated the situation by raising the Hispanos' hopes for greater improvement.

Reaction to social disintegration can take many forms, and the Hispanic religious tradition — plus Tijerina's own background as a Pentecostal preacher — have helped channel it into millenarianism. In the 1930's a religious group called the Allelujahs, an Hispano version of the Holy Rollers, became popular, and before it faded out as many as half the people of some northern New Mexico communities had joined, taking part in religious services in which "Passages from the Revelation of St. John are favorite texts [according to a 1937 report] and lead to frenzies of religious ecstasy." The Allelujah experience has helped prepare the ground. So perhaps have the *Penitentes,* a lay brotherhood of Hispano mystics and self-flagellants that traces its origins back to the colonial era.

When the Alianza failed to obtain redress through the courts, the hope for and belief in extra-legal and supernatural means of relief — natural enough in the presence of the charismatic and fiery Tijerina — became exacerbated. When the National Forest Service recently cut back the use of grazing lands because of drought, the Hispanos were the hardest hit — and Tijerina was at hand to transform frustration into action. The frequency of millenarianism when belief in and identify with the dominant society are lost has been well documented in sociological literature. The Alianza constitutes an almost classic case.

Yet there is a "modern" dimension to the Alianza, and this is a direct outgrowth of its appearance in an industrial society with rapid transcontinental communications and ever-vigilant news media. The Alianza fits the. requirements of a "primitive rebellion" or "revitaliza-- tion movement," but its links with urban radical and reformist groups outside New Mexico show its potential for evolving into something more modern. Thus there are two distinct dimensions of the movement — the "primitive," rural, grassroots constituency on the tributaries of the upper Rio Grande; and the "modern," urban, nationally-connected leadership in Albuquerque. The "visible" media-oriented sector is modern, but the "invisible" millenarian sector is not.

Tijerina's primary concern is still regaining lost community lands, as his action at the Poor People's March showed. The hunger for community lands — the *ejidos* — remains the basis for the "real" movement, despite manifestos of solidarity with the Black Panthers and denunciations of the war in Vietnam.

The ignorance of government officials of the basic nature of the movement is almost monumental. They tend to explain the Alianza away by easy, modern, clichés. Some find in the references to common lands the spore of modern communism.

At the November 1967 trial, the prosecuting attorney declared, "This is not a social problem we're trying. This is a criminal problem." Even some sympathetic observers have used singularly inappropriate terms. Tom Wicker of the *New York Times* and Congressman Joseph Resnick, chairman of the House Agriculture Subcommittee on Rural Development, have both referred to Rio Arriba County as a "rural Watts."

But Rio Arriba has little in common with Watts. The majority of Aliancistas, the rural grassroots, are not industrial proletarians but primitive rebels — peasants reacting and striking back in millenarian fashion against the modernization that is tearing their society apart.

EL PUERTORRIQUEÑO:
NO MORE, NO LESS

ARMANDO RENDON

"I'm not black; I'm not white; I'm not in-between. I'm Puerto Rican."

Few other words strike more powerfully to the core of the peculiar situation of the mainland puertorriqueño. The words of the "Newyorican," can tell America many things about the political and philosophical aberrations stemming from its color blindspot.

The Newyorican was saying that race and color don't matter, that personal identity does — at least for him. On the basis of being puertorriqueño, no more, no less, there is developing slowly, sometimes dramatically, a special vision among Puerto Ricans of what they stand for on the U.S. mainland.

Caught in the middle of the white and black extremes of society, the Puerto Rican strives to maintain his personal equilibrium based on cultural or ethnic identity which accepts the diversity of skin color or other features among his own people. He is aware of other factors of class and wealth which create formidable barriers within the group. But he must insist on his own personality, on his peculiar identity, which he considers not only unique but essential to his existence.

The Puerto Rican, it must be realized from the outset, does not derive from a single-purpose, one-minded community either in terms of motivation or methods. There is a true community of thought as to objectives, better jobs, quality education, a better life in general. There is more than one kind of puertorriqueño, though, in relation to birthplace and social orientation: some are born and reared on the mainland, some have come here within recent years; others come fresh from the island daily; one generation abhors the other; some Puerto Ricans become "dropouts" having cut ties with their past; others return to "el barrio" which is as much a state of mind as it is a few dozen square blocks called Spanish Harlem.

In many ways, the Puerto Rican is an up-to-the-minute version of the many past waves of immigrants to America. But he is not really an immigrant; rather he is a migrant, fully an American citizen, who relocates, seeking a better job and better life opportunities in the States. Most Puerto Ricans have come to the mainland within the past 15 years. More than half are under 21 years of age. Of the more than one million on the mainland, a great number have already served in the armed forces — many have died serving their country. For years, puertorriqueños have handpicked the fruit and vegetable crops in the farm areas of the eastern seaboard.

Yet Americans still make the same judgments and reach the same conclusions that were made in the late 19th and early 20th centuries. Any newcomer is considered a threat to the job market, to housing, to civil order. The slum dweller is blamed for the conditions in which he is forced to live, where he may well be the fifth generation tenant.

Much of the Puerto Ricans' problems stem, then, from the fact that they have literally been last in line for the jobs, the school desks, the tenements. But there is also an apparently self-perpetuating cycle of distrust and rejection by Americans of anyone who is foreign-sounding, or foreign-looking. By and large, it seems evident that Americans tend to depreciate the value of culturally different groups in their midst. This fact has been painfully demonstrated in regard to racially different groups, particularly the black man. Yet, it is only within recent years, because of the growing militancy of American Indians, Mexican Americans, and Puerto Ricans, that the white American majority has been made aware of groups other than blacks who are projecting a particular personality and view of life into the Nation's consciousness.

It is also part of the total social conflict that white Americans generally resent and cannot understand anyone not wanting to be or talk like the majority. One of the most articulate spokesmen among Puerto Ricans is New York-born Joseph Monserrat, director of the Commonwealth of Puerto Rico office in Manhattan. Puerto Ricans, he observes, are a continuation of the struggle each new group has had to wage to achieve freedom. Most immigrants have become carbon copies of something they're not, he says, because Americans already here have tended to negate anything foreign — to be foreign has meant to be less. In this sense, the Puerto Rican is an irritant because, as it is becoming more and more evident, he wants to be accepted and respected for what he is, not for what others may want him to be. When all the rhetoric is cleared away, this is essentially what his struggle is all about.

In early September, about 2,000 Puerto Rican people demonstrated before City Hall in New York City demanding that a manpower program of the Puerto Rican Community Development Project he maintained at the proposed funding level of $815,000. The Manpower Commission had been contemplating a cut of $215,000 but as a result of the puertorriqueño showing, the PRCDP program was given a respite. The project director, Mrs. Amalia Betanzos, and its board chairman, Rev. Ruben Dario Colon, and other board members met with Cyril Tyson, director of the Manpower Commission, who assured the group that the program funding would be reconsidered. However, only a few days later, the Commission announced that a $155,000 cutback had been ordered.

In no small way, such a demonstration illustrates the practical aspects of a growing activism and militancy among Puerto Rican individuals and organizations. Among the placard carriers were State Senator Robert Garcia and Assemblyman Armando Montano of South Bronx, the Puerto Rican community's sole representatives in the State legislature. Puerto Ricans themselves give ample reasons for their mounting concern and personal involvement. Many suggest that little is being done to offset the kind of street confrontation with city hall which took place in September; that, in fact, more overt acts of frustration and dissatisfaction can be expected. In at least four Puerto Rican neighborhoods last summer, tense encounters with police took place.

Puerto Ricans are acutely aware that on every count — housing, education, employment, income, welfare — the puertorriqueño ranks last in comparison to other groups comparable or larger in size in New York City. Scattered about the five New York boroughs are 841,000 Puerto Ricans, or *boricuas* (a term of self-identification that recalls very early Indian roots on the island of Puerto Rico). The figure increases daily. New York City's Puerto Rican population, in fact, is twice that of San Juan, the largest city in Puerto Rico. Commonwealth office estimates indicate a net migration annually for the past two years of about 30,000.

Despite the size of the Puerto Rican population of New York City as well as of other colonies found in cities along the east coast, in the midwest, and on the west coast, not a great deal is known about educational achievement, employment patterns, mobility trends, nor of the peculiar dynamics of the migration flow to and from the island.

Only recently have statistics begun to develop about this minority portion of one of the largest cities in the world.

In some cases, Puerto Ricans are made invisible by bureaucratic terminology. The residency makeup in public housing projects for example, is classified into "white," "Negro," "Asian," and "other." This "other" is mainly but apparently not entirely Puerto Rican. It may include a number of other national groupings, particularly South American immigrants, a semantical shortcut which only adds to the complexity of problems generally related to Spanish-speaking groups. In effect, persons of Spanish descent are lumped together under a rather vague and depersonalizing title. The extent of the difficulties caused by such generalizing may be difficult to assess but one can imagine that anyone reading or hearing a statistic about "other" with no explanation would tend to discount it as unimportant and never realize that "other" distinguished a large group of people having their own special problems and needs.

Some data are available which lend credence to the arguments and demands of Puerto Rican leaders. A recent study by Leonard S. Krogan and Morey J. Wantman of City University of New York reported that Puerto Rican family income was lowest among the three major groups in the city: $3,949 compared to $4,754 for nonwhites and $7,635 for whites. Puerto Ricans had made a gain of only $49 in the past two years in contrast to white gains of more than $900. Other studies by the Puerto Rican Forum, a young issue-oriented organization, indicate that Puerto Ricans on relief had risen in percentages more rapidly than any other group, from 29.5 percent in 1959 to 33 percent last year — a figure which is all out of proportion to the percentage of Puerto Rican population in New York — about 10 percent. But the percentage of Puerto Ricans on welfare rolls may now be even higher according to statements from officials in the city Department of Social Services, who suggest that as many as 40 percent of Newyoricans receive some public aid.

Employment trends among Puerto Ricans showed a decrease from 17 to 12 percent in white-collar fields while women's employment increased from 18.7 to 24.9 percent between 1960 and 1965. Unemployment rates in three densely puertorriqueño districts, East Harlem, South Bronx, and South Brooklyn, reached 12 percent, three times the national rate. Puerto Ricans made up 22.1 percent of the city's public school population, 244,458 out of 1,109,664. Academically, they fared badly: little more than 1 percent of Puerto Rican high school graduates in the last two years have received academic diplomas, about 8 percent received vocational certificates, but the rest, 90 percent, were given only general diplomas, which merely attest in effect to a student's class attendance. The Puerto Rican Forum estimated that half of Puerto Ricans in the city over 25 years of age have less than an eighth grade education and those reaching ninth grade read at a fifth grade level.

But even these figures and statistics cannot begin to tell the story of "el barrio." "There is only one 'el barrio,' " a young boricua explained as he leaned against a car parked not far from the subway entrance at Lexington Avenue and 103rd Street. Coming out of the subway into the streets of "el barrio" after being in downtown Manhattan is like stepping into another world. A senses-offending squalor is first apparent after the tall, glass and steel cityscape, a contrast suddenly sprawling before the eyes of squat three and four story tenements littering the streets. It is hard to judge which is more disturbing — the suddenness of the climb up the subway stairs or the abruptness of East 96th Street which runs like an invisible Berlin Wall between affluent Manhattanites and East Harlem puertorriqueños and Harlem blacks.

This might be the initial impression of "el barrio" or of most of the other slum neighborhoods in which thousands of human beings are compressed. Beyond that first jar, however, one can begin to sense the living that is going on there, to feel that very little goes on in those streets with which everyone is not familiar or involved. Life during the summer, of course, is conducted as much on the streets as possible. Poorly ventilated apartments are extremely close; the smell of the sweat and refuse of generations is stifling. Most of the dwellings are privately owned (few by Puerto Ricans themselves), and in final stages of dilapidation; most of the buildings, which house many times the occupants they were meant to house, were built before the First World War.

A middle-aged Puerto Rican, greatly interested in his community, told the story, perhaps only a story but vivid in its recounting, of a visit he had made recently to an apartment of three rooms in which eight people lived. The father, out of work, had just finished a plate of *cuchifritos,* a Puerto Rican dish, and was placing his plate in the sink. Distracted by the conversation he grabbed at what he thought was a piece of meat he had missed, recoiled with a curse when the thing he was about to put in his mouth turned out to be the slum's ever-present uninvited guest, a mouse, trapped to death in the yellowed porcelain basin.

Living conditions constitute the most easily measurable factor of the wide range of problems racing the slum dweller. The person can see the extent of the deprivation; touch and smell the inhumanity of it. Spanish Harlem, South Bronx, Brownsville in Brooklyn, other densely puertorriqueño areas are byproducts just as other slum ghettos in New York or any other city in America, of governmental neglect, landlord absentism, poverty, ignorance, in short, of public rejection of the poor and disregard for their true needs.

In 1962, representatives from a number of Puerto Rican organizations formed the Puerto Rican Citizens Committee on Housing to investigate the effects of housing and city planning in the Latin community. Their report cited a "conscious effort to remove the Puerto Rican from the so-called prime real estate in Manhattan," that urban renewal programs had "uprooted and destroyed established Puerto Rican communities," and called for a voice in the housing and planning agencies of the city.

The particular area studied by the committee was West Side Manhattan, a ghetto romanticized in the Broadway musical, *West Side Story,* above 79th Street to 125th Street. According to residents and community workers in the area, things haven't changed much since the citizens' group study. In fact the decision of the Housing and Development Administration to construct two middle-income projects as part of the West Side Urban Renewal Area (87th-97th between Central Park West and Amsterdam Avenue) has been vigorously disputed by community groups and leaders who consider it a threat to some 6,000 present tenants who might not be adequately relocated and regard it as an act of economic discrimination: monthly rents in the 325 apartments to be built will run between $48.61 and $50.64 per room.

One aspect of the kinds of housing problems which plague the poor is evident in the West Side Manhattan region, a heavily puertorriqueño populated neighborhood. On the outside, dilapidation is not obvious. Reconstruction and renovation of row brick homes is a common sight; multi-story apartments rub elbows with three story apartment houses; there's a new school at 84th Street near Columbus Avenue; other redevelopment projects are planned. Yet, just as the 1961 study indicated, the Puerto Rican, the black, the poor white, are being slowly squeezed out. The overriding issue for minority groups such as the

Puerto Ricans is the maintenance of community life which requires low-income housing, adequate relocation during construction phases, and adequate space and facilities for small to large families. For city officials, there is the dilemma of providing enough low-income housing while integrating the city at least economically by building middle-income housing and, as a byproduct, achieving racial and ethnic integration.

The solutions to such a complex issue will not come easily. In el barrio, the concept of private, minority group control of low-income housing is being tested by the East Harlem Redevelopment Corp., in a project codenamed "Pilot Block." The objective of Pilot Block, which evolved from the groundwork of the East Harlem Redevelopment Council, itself the offspring of a tenants' council, is to place the ownership and management of housing in the hands of former tenants. The block selected for the project, 122nd-123rd Streets between 2nd and 3rd Avenues, consists of several family residences, a handful of single occupant rooming houses, and, the source of greatest local resistance to the project, according to Pilot Block staff people, long established furniture and clothing stores.

There has been one major obstacle in the more than a year and a half negotiations in which Pilot Block promoters have been engaged: the city has not condemned the site for clearance and transferral to the East Harlem citizens' group. During the past six months, there have been at least two major confrontations with "city hall," a demonstration in front of Gracie Mansion, the Mayor's residence, and a presentation before a city housing commission meeting of six demands made by the Tenants Council. The project was approved by the Department of Housing and Urban Development more than 20 months ago but still awaits city action on condemnation.

A much-repeated theme among recognized Puerto Rican spokesmen and young activists was evident in the comments of the tenants' council and Pilot Block staff such as Rene Rodriguez, Tony Santos, and Bobby Azevedo. They conceived of their work as stemming essentially from the need for social change. "The Pilot Block means political power; it means that the politicians would have to give up some of their control over people," one of them said. Tenants — and first chance would be given to those people already living on the pilot location — would elect their own representatives to the management board of the four-building complex of high-rise apartments, medical, educational, and recreational facilities to be provided on the site. "It is also a social thing," another said, referring to the obstacles barring the progress of Pilot Block. "People on the outside don't want to give us middle class, material things."

Local community control is not an issue solely in the area of housing. Long-standing disputes between local school officials and community leaders erupted on the scheduled first day of school in a major teachers' strike which closed down all but one district, the Ocean Hill-Brownsville School District, an area about two-thirds black and one-third Puerto Rican. The district is an experimental one, testing the decentralization concept under Ford Foundation funding. The district's governing board demanded that it have the right to choose its teachers without interference from the central Board of Education. (It was earlier this year that the first Puerto Rican, Hector I. Vasquez, head of the Puerto Rican Forum, was named to the Board of Education.)

An important facet of this issue is the fact that although the eventual capitulation to the city school board by the local governing board seemed inevitable, the coalition of black and Puerto Rican parents managed to keep the school doors open. In so doing, the parents proved something to the city and to themselves. The struggle in the cities has always been between those who have power and those who don't. Blacks and Puerto Ricans clearly demonstrated that alliances have a greater impact on a recalcitrant opposition, whether it is a city administration or a 40-thousand member teachers' union.

Fundamental to the stance adopted by the Ocean Hill-Brownsville area residents toward the entreaties and pressures from the central school board and the teachers' union is a widely divergent understanding of equal education opportunity with its dualities of integration and segregation. The down in the ghetto or barrio view of integration is that it means breakup of established communities, another parallel to the housing issue. The Puerto Rican community, again reverting back to a strong sense of cultural and historical precedent, does not conceive of segregation as a problem in the same way that civil right leaders and educators have viewed it. Segregation is not something to be eradicated solely because it means allocation of teachers and students to schools on a racial basis — an all-Puerto Rican school may differ widely in the skin color of its student body, and thus be "racially integrated." When segregation entails educational deprivation based primarily on the location of the school — in the barrio or ghetto — or on the racist or anti-poor attitudes of some official, that is to be fought. Ocean Hill-Brownsville demonstrates this principle clearly. Whereas the black community rejected and withstood the pressures of city officials and teachers on the basis of black pride, Puerto Ricans stood firm on the basis of cultural pride. Faced with a confused tangle of principles stemming from the unionizing efforts of teachers and from school officialdom, the black and Puerto Rican parents of Ocean Hill-Brownsville decided to rely on themselves and their concept of what was right for their children and their community. As a result, they gained a great deal of ground on the principle of local control over local schools and programs.

To a great degree, the confrontation between the Puerto Rican Community Development Project supporters and the city administration presents another aspect of the problems facing the Puerto Rican because he is the last minority to enter New York. Mrs. Betanzos, PRCDP director, frames the issue in this way:

"The blacks want us to be black and the whites want us to be white because they both want to use us. In terms of issues, I would have to side with the blacks — but I'm a Puerto Rican and no one has the right to tell me or want me to be black or white.

"In the poverty program, black organizations have not wanted Puerto Rican groups funded. This is unfortunate because they have been using the same arguments that the whites have," she contends. "They say that the Puerto Ricans cannot run their own programs." She points out that the scattering of the Puerto Rican population has led several groups to seek anti-poverty funding on an at-large basis, that is, taking in an entire borough or even all five boroughs. This conflicts with the concept of geographic representation inherent in the makeup of the poverty program governing board, which consists of representatives of 26 geographic areas.

Mrs. Betanzos, a native New Yorker, notes that under this system Puerto Ricans control only one area, the Hunts Point district in South Bronx, while the black community, which is much more "homogeneous" in the various geographic regions, virtually controls the poverty board. "The Puerto Ricans must have citywide programs," insists the Project director, who is also chairman of the National Association for Puerto Rican Civil Rights. At present, the Project and three other groups, ASPIRA, an education-oriented program, the Puerto Rican Forum, a young activist business development group of professionals, and the Puerto Rican Family Institute, concerned with family social services, operate citywide programs.

A Puerto Rican who can observe the difficulties of the puertorriqueño community from two angles, as a member of the community and as a city official, is Manny Diaz, deputy commissioner in charge of the Manpower and Career Development Agency. His agency coordinates Neighborhood Youth Corps, Concentrated Employment Programs, and other manpower and training contracts with community groups.

Generalizing on the employment problems among Puerto Ricans, Diaz approached the subject from the perspective of the need for more Puerto Rican-owned businesses. "There are probably 2,000 small businesses owned by Puerto Ricans, mostly bodegas (grocery stores) or service type businesses. The Puerto Rican needs to turn to developing goods-producing companies." This new dimension, which would have a great effect on job opportunities, "is moving rapidly," he believes, "and will outstrip the Negro's efforts in 10 years." Still, he added, the present picture of jobs for Puerto Ricans is critical: about 14 percent of those 21-24 years old are unemployed, of those 25 to 30, 9 percent — two to three times the national rate.

A study of three areas, Harlem, East Harlem, and Bedford-Stuyvesant in Brooklyn, released in late September by the regional office of the Bureau of Labor Statistics, disclosed that: Puerto Ricans were unemployed or underemployed (working less than full time or earning no more than the minimum wage) at a rate higher than the overall rate in two of the three areas — 36.0 percent to 33.1 percent in East Harlem and 29.7 percent to 27.6 percent in Bedford-Stuyvesant. The data indicate that one out of every three Puerto Ricans has a serious job problem and that Puerto Ricans in general fare worse than Negroes in the job market.

Employment was just one of many areas which Diaz cited as critical to the general wellbeing of the Puerto Rican community. "Puerto Ricans are far behind in voting, 20 percent behind the blacks in voter registration, worse off in terms of housing and in education," he said. "The Puerto Rican should relate himself to issues; he has to look for alliances, work with anybody else. If the school system is failing, both black kids and Puerto Rican kids are losing out; if we don't have

perverse environment. "The most significant aspect of our struggle," he believes, "is also one of our biggest problems: whether we will be able to make the contribution which we can make by being and remaining Puerto Rican. There is a great gap between third and fourth generation groups and ours which hardly has a second generation. We have upward mobility but the rate and spread depends on what is happening now, and what is happening doesn't promise much for the great number of the people."

A former director of the PRCDP, Jose Morales, brought up a significant new factor in the political thinking of puertorriqueños. A great many Puerto Ricans, he believes, have withdrawn from "politics" because of the assassination of Robert F. Kennedy. They have given up on political involvement, he says, but the full effect may only appear following the November elections.

Morales views the present status of Puerto Ricans in terms of organizational progress: "There is a widespread concern that we're not moving as fast as the blacks, but I think it's a matter of Puerto Ricans still moving at a different phase of the cycle of development. We should next develop citywide organizations taking in the five boroughs."

Direct confrontation and organizational skill are the two sides of a double edged sword being honed by young activists such as Jack Agueros, currently working for a private firm concerned with business development and chairman of a new group called Puerto Rican Institute for Democratic Eduation. Last June 30, Agueros began a five-day fast in his office when he was deputy commissioner of the city Community Development Agency. He sought a number of specific changes by his fast, that a Puerto Rican be named to the Board of Education, that city colleges and universities alter their policies toward minority students, and, his major objective, that Puerto Ricans be included at the decision-making levels throughout the city administration.

"I want a better economic situation for the Puerto Rican," he says, "I want for him to come out of an invisible category, to be considered and consulted with in city, State and Federal programs. The answer to our problems is political — when we can sit on the policy-making bodies, everything else will fall into place."

Agueros continues, "I'm disturbed that many my age removed themselves from the barrio, but some have returned through the poverty program. I am concerned with creating a mentality in the

Puerto Rican community that a voice in government is owed them and due now, so why doesn't the power structure give us that voice?" A self-proclaimed militant, Agueros also noted a withdrawal syndrome following the Kennedy assassination and that no candidate seemed in view who could arouse enthusiasm among the puertorriqueños, at least for a while.

Political withdrawal, growing group identity, overwhelming social problems, new organizations and coalitions, devastating physical needs — a complex and perplexing picture of el barrio. And what of the threat of violence in this picture? No one denied that violence could occur. When asked about the prospect of barrio violence, most persons suggested that the points most in question were the time and place of street disorders. The subject usually evoked cautiously phrased responses.

Mrs. Betanzos remarked that Puerto Ricans "have tried to resolve problems in a law-abiding way, but they're getting the impression that the only way they will be resolved will be by militant, non-law abiding action."

Monserrat of the Commonwealth office foresees a greater trend toward aggressive action as Puerto Ricans "develop methods within the reality of our present status to keep from being swallowed up." A case in point, he cited, was a confrontation a few days earlier (in mid-July) between barrio residents and Tactical Police Force units which was touched off by a gang incident. The appearance of TPF united the opposed groups and other local people against the police: several officers were injured, many barrio residents arrested. A quickly-formed council of Puerto Rican leaders persuaded police officials to withdraw the TPF; relative calm ensued. Stressing the role of police as a key element in preventing disorder, the Commonwealth official observed, "Most police and governmental agencies have not become sophisticated in handling riots and disorders. Police in general," he said, "do not defend the civil rights but property rights — they're not geared to the maintenance of civil rights and civil liberties."

Few if any Puerto Ricans talk of riot as inevitable or desirable. Among the youth, there was always talk of working out answers some way, of aggressively strengthening the sense of unity by building on the fact of being puertorriqueño. A young community organizer hopes to institute television and radio programs aimed at developing cultural and group awareness among boricua youth. Or, a few young Puerto

Ricans block traffic at a bridge entrance to get funds for a poverty program, and succeed. The trend is to reject "the racist bag." Besides, one young puertorriqueño said, "There's always the temptation to cut out of the barrio but luckily someone will ask you, are you Spanish — with that sickly smile — they won't let you forget."

It seemed obvious that Puerto Rican activists were optimistic in seeking solutions through political, democratic methods and that all other alternatives to violence simply have not been eliminated. Also, goals are generally short-range so they seem more attainable. No one plans more than 15 years ahead, a young community leader in his mid-20s commented, because "that's all anyone can see ahead."

Finally, the Newyorican has less of a history or experience either of oppression, or, even less, of violent action. In fact, he has a vastly different life style in which violence and disorder for its own sake, are out of tune. If violence erupts in the barrio, it will be in reaction, one can be sure, to tremendous pressure, in effect, of surrender to the larger elements of our society.

Still, the future is bleak. With a touch of cynicism, a barrio community leader remarked: "I figure by 35 I'll either have made it on my own terms, or I'll have sold out to the highest bidder, or I'll be dead."

The Puerto Rican people are also struggling to "make it" on their own terms. They are striving to resist the pressures of the dominant elements of the society which threaten to suppress or disperse them. For they realize that only by being and remaining Puerto Ricans can they truly enhance the quality of life in the Nation. Indeed, if they and their way of life were to be disintegrated, the loss in the end would be America's.